Beyond Hostile Islands

World War II: The Global, Human, and Ethical Dimension
G. Kurt Piehler, *series editor*

"In this engagingly-written book, McKay has convincingly bridged the fields of literary studies and memory studies to offer a nuanced and thought-provoking account of the Pacific War in anglophone literature. The New Zealand/Pacific Islands perspective adds a fresh comparative angle to the more familiar issues within US-Japan literary representations. The impressive range of (hi)stories discussed covers the well-known (Bridge on the River Kwai) to the all-but-forgotten (Japanese internment in New Zealand)."

—**Philip Seaton**, Tokyo University of Foreign Studies, author of *Japan's Contested War Memories: The 'Memory Rifts' in Historical Consciousness of World War II*

"A meditative and incisive reading of literature about WWII, *Beyond Hostile Islands* is a book of brilliant comparisons: of US and Aotearoa-New Zealand literatures and of the bellicose topics of combat, internment, propaganda, and nuclear munitions. McKay's reading of what was known as 'The Pacific War' takes a hard look at the ambivalences of war and its aftermath, providing a much-needed addition to anglophone literary and cultural criticism and a new conversation about contemporary American and New Zealand island literatures."

—**Rebecca Weaver-Hightower**, Virginia Tech University, author of *Empire Islands: Castaways, Cannibals, and Fantasies of Conquest in Post/Colonial Island Narratives*

"Although it derives from 'peacemaking' (*pācificus*) etymologically, the term 'the Pacific' cannot fail to provoke the memory of war ironically. What McKay reveals in this book is not so much the political causes as the literary effects of the war, effects that foregrounded the power of nations by means of racialized stereotypes in narrative form."

—**Takayuki Tatsumi**, Keio Academy of New York, author of *Full Metal Apache: Transactions Between Cyberpunk Japan and Avant-Pop America*

"*Beyond Hostile Islands* is an insightful and rewarding investigation of Pacific War literature, particularly that which confronted the economic rise of Japan in the 1980s and that which turned away from the atomic bombings of 1945. By comparing representations of the war across two different canons, the United States' and New Zealand's, McKay is able to bring a strong light to bear on this under-examined area of literary history."

—**Ian M. Richards**, Osaka Metropolitan University, author of *To Bed at Noon: The Life and Art of Maurice Duggan*

"From combat novels to the corporate thriller, *Beyond Hostile Islands* examines the literary history of the Pacific War, while interrogating stereotypical renditions of the Japanese. The Pacific theatre is/was intrinsically archipelagic, and McKay—aware of an uneasy US-NZ juxtaposition—warns us that source material from island cultures/authors may unsettle, but also align with, continental world views. *Beyond Hostile Islands* is binary-bashing: It upsets culturalist, colonialist and imperialist narratives, exposing a messier humanity, and thus uncovers commonality amidst the dissimilar."

—**Godfrey Baldacchino**, University of Malta,
Founding editor, *Island Studies Journal*; Former President,
International Small Island Studies Association (ISISA)

"This book goes beyond more obvious avenues of enquiry to discuss how war stories may (or may not) be shaped by geographical 'islandness' or the political and cultural heritage of (interacting) anglophone countries. The discussion of how representations of the Japanese shifted away from wartime combatants to quirky salarymen is especially illuminating."

—**Vandana Saxena**, University of Malaya,
author of *Memory and Nation-Building:
World War II in Malaysian Literature*

Beyond Hostile Islands

The Pacific War in American and New Zealand Fiction Writing

Daniel McKay
Foreword by **Patrick Porter**

Fordham University Press | New York 2024

Copyright © 2024 Fordham University Press

All rights reserved. No part of this publication may be reproduced, stored in a retrieval system, or transmitted in any form or by any means—electronic, mechanical, photocopy, recording, or any other—except for brief quotations in printed reviews, without the prior permission of the publisher.

Fordham University Press has no responsibility for the persistence or accuracy of URLs for external or third-party Internet websites referred to in this publication and does not guarantee that any content on such websites is, or will remain, accurate or appropriate.

Fordham University Press also publishes its books in a variety of electronic formats. Some content that appears in print may not be available in electronic books.

Visit us online at www.fordhampress.com.

Library of Congress Cataloging-in-Publication Data available online at https://catalog.loc.gov.

Printed in the United States of America
26 25 24   5 4 3 2 1
First edition

Contents

Foreword by Patrick Porter — vii

Introduction — 1

1 **Revelations and Comedy: The Combat Novel** — 25

2 **Camera Men: Postwar Japan-Bashing** — 55

3 **Captive Memories: Internment North and South** — 81

4 **The Poetics of Apology: FEPOW Narratives** — 106

5 **Scientists and Hibakusha: Project Novels** — 132

Coda — 163

Acknowledgments — 173
Notes — 177
Bibliography — 217
Index — 243

Foreword by Patrick Porter

It is an honor to write the foreword to Daniel McKay's rich, painstakingly careful work, *Beyond Hostile Islands*. Not least because it offers the chance to engage in a dialogue often promised but rarely delivered in academia, a dialogue across disciplinary frontiers. McKay writes primarily as a student of literature, but his attention to political context makes this equally a work invaluable for students of history and politics. Let me sketch out some ways it resonates for me.

One feature of modern war is the unprecedented scale, variety, and creativity of the literature it has spawned. While armed conflict and storytelling are obviously prehistoric practices, only relatively recently in history have societies produced large quantities of written accounts by participants, across every military rank, that millions of people could access and read. A convergence of developments—modern mass education, literacy, large readerships with disposable income, and, more recently still, the paperback revolution—brought the published war memoir, novel, or poem to public attention. For the first time, war's horrors could be made known to a vast readership beyond those who had first-hand experience of it. "The horror of war" as a widely agreed reality, in large measure, is an image of a modern, literate marketplace. This in turn has raised problems and disagreements among scholars about such sources. How far can we rely on them, given they are, of necessity, never written at the exact time of combat? To what extent, as often retrospective accounts, are they self-censored performances that tell us more about memory and identity than "what it was like"? Apropos the present book, how did survivors of battles in the Pacific Theater come to terms with a war that had been characterized by intense, mutual racial hatred, atrocity, and counter-atrocity, and which began and ended so differently to the war in Europe, not with a declaration of war and a conventional defeat, but with a shock assault and atomic strikes? Could the "war without mercy," in John Dower's famous words, also be a "good" war?

Beyond Hostile Islands is a seminal step forward in a neglected task, namely a consideration of how war literature coped with, reinvented, sidestepped, or confronted the peculiarities of the Pacific struggle. As well as the racial hatred, there was disease (at times deadlier and more disabling to units than combat). There was the geography of distance and water, so that the fighting moved from standoff strikes, to amphibious landings, to the harsh intimacy of blasting or bayonetting dug-in defenders out of fortified positions. There was the mutually reinforcing suspicion of the other side's motives and mentality. The notorious fanaticism of Japan's defenders was principally generated by the Tojo regime, which propagated a popularized credo of honor/shame, encouraged an attitude towards surrendering enemies as worthy of enslavement, and told its people that Americans would do horrific things to them if they surrendered. In turn, Imperial Japanese forces' refusal to surrender even against hopeless odds, their ruthless tactics such as the booby-trapping of corpses, and their mistreatment of captives all served to reinforce an image of fanaticism and to emphasize the imperative for force-protection, if necessary with forms of behavior that were themselves merciless. As McKay demonstrates, while the war in Europe was hardly clean, there was a carefully curated notion that it was ultimately waged, not to eliminate a racialized enemy, but to liberate "good" Germans from Nazism. The war against Japan, by contrast, fed off a more visceral, popular desire for annihilation, even if that did not always determine Washington's policy.

For anglophone readerships at least, the consumption of the "war experience" as a literary event is one primarily based on a European or Mediterranean memory, with its focal points ranging from the Western Front in the Great War, 1914-1918, to the Second World War campaigns from North Africa and Sicily to Normandy. For American readerships, too, Europe remains the epicenter and the main scene of the "good war" and the "Greatest Generation." There isn't a uniform "Western" memory, of course. For instance, Britons had a memory of predatory threats getting uncomfortably close in 1940, whereas mainland Americans perceived direct dangers as flowing from the more distant assaults at Pearl Harbor and the Philippines. As for life in the Antipodes, McKay skillfully shows that New Zealanders went to war from a distinctive vantage point—the danger was not quite as distantly "over there," even though the distances were still great, and the Māori population, of course, 'came to' the Pacific theater with an awareness that it was more than a strange exotic battlefront. (To McKay's credit, unlike so many authors he does not fall prey to counter-stereotyping, in which Indigenous New Zealanders become separate, primordial others.) Still, across the board, there remained a sense that the war in the Pacific, all told, was a stranger affair, more existentially distant to the thought-worlds of fellow citizens. It was more unfamiliar to the mental maps of citizens who still often had a primarily European orientation. Given the mercilessness of the combat and the greater prevalence of disease, it was harder to incorporate into stock-standard narrative conventions about war as a process of moral struggle, redemption, and the preservation of humanity under fire. McKay navigates the different ways authors retold the story of such a conflict, amplifying the idea that the countries who waged the war see themselves as Oceanic as well as continental in their history and outlook, and that islanders need not be insular.

Patrick Porter is Professor of International Security and Strategy at the University of Birmingham and author of *Military Orientalism: Eastern War Through Western Eyes*.

Beyond Hostile Islands

Introduction

> Compassion must be elicited constantly in warfare. Our natural tendency is to think of the enemy as an animal inferior to us. This serves to help warriors accomplish very ugly tasks, but it brings on unnecessary suffering if not constantly checked.
> —Karl Marlantes, *What It Is Like to Go to War*

> In 1932, [Baron Takeichi] Nishi took Uranus to the Olympics in Los Angeles, and again his charm and vitality conquered all, even the intense anti-Oriental feeling of the West Coast. On the afternoon of August 14, the Baron and Uranus won the gold medal for Japan in the Prix des Nations, the individual jump event. As the newspapermen crowded around him, the Baron said very simply, "We won it," meaning himself and the horse, himself and Japan.
> —Richard F. Newcomb, *Iwo Jima*

"They're animals." No matter the formulation or the moment, this accusatory conflation is a recurrent refrain in the vocabulary of war, as observable in anecdotes as it is in mass-produced texts.[1] Most readers of this book will recall a past or present-day conflict that proves the point, several of both if they put their minds to it.[2] So assuredly does the historical record bear out the trend that, for present purposes, one is hard put to say why any given example should take precedence over another. Certainly, those researchers who confine their studies to the post-Westphalian era ought to concede that the nation-state has done nothing to retard the trend. For present purposes, the main reason to focus on the modern era—and the Second World War especially—is that the nation state throws the phenomenon into high relief, mainly thanks to print media and, by the mid-twentieth century, cinema and radio broadcasts.[3] In the aftermath of Pearl Harbor, the United States, hitherto isolationist in posture, generated a steady stream of government-level propaganda that was of a piece with the productions of other belligerent powers.⁴ Surviving examples of anti-Japanese posters present a gallery of insect, rodent, and reptile analogies, along with boldface imperatives to *guard against Jap, trap the Jap, blast the Jap, slap a Jap*, and, in general, objectify the enemy as Japanese (the linguistic erasure preceding the bodily).⁵ This fever pitch of vitriol stands in marked contrast to the more conventional objectification of the German enemy in wartime propaganda, which clearly distinguished between the Nazi leadership and 'good Germans,' a model that tended to hold true throughout the British Dominions as well.⁶ Notably, state-owned radio stations in New Zealand continued to broadcast German music during the war and the ruling Labour Party publicly announced that the enemy was Nazism rather than German people as a whole.⁷ Such carefulness trickled down into battlefield behavior and thence into literary works such as New Zealand author Gordon Slatter's 1959 novel *A Gun in My Hand*, the protagonist of which recalls his wartime service in the following terms: "He hated the war but he didn't hate the enemy because that was for civilians. He respected the front-line German because he was a damned good scrapper but he killed him because it was kill or be killed."⁸

American soldiers had felt the truth of this just as keenly, but whereas most did only their professional duty by killing Germans, a majority actively looked forward to killing Japanese.⁹ Whether these impulses first announced themselves outside the combat zone or within it, in either case those who returned did not do so unchanged. Texan author Larry McMurtry, best remembered for his depictions of the Old West, wrote his first novel, *Horseman, Pass By* (1961), primarily as a study of the yawning gap between the wholesome values of a prewar ranching generation and a younger generation of get-rich-quick oil prospectors. Among the latter is Hud, a young man whose horrendous behavior—drunkenness, swearing, womanizing, and casual rape—would be almost inexplicable, were it not for the fact that he is a combat veteran of the Pacific War.¹⁰ Using a pistol, he executes his injured stepfather as unhesitatingly as he approves the liquidation of his stepfather's cattle herd after an outbreak of foot and mouth disease.

The present study is not devoted to exploring what made the Pacific War distinctive in military terms, for on that question there exist any number of print resources. Book-length enquiries into how the war influenced anglophone war literature, on the other hand, have been all but non-existent up to this point (Elena P. Polo's study of American and Filipino literature, *The Negating Fire vs. The Affirming Flame* [2000], is the only other work of this kind). That being said, filling this void in the scholarly record necessarily means that the war's distinctiveness—not just for military personnel, but also for civilians and those future generations who had no direct experience of the war years—remains a pertinent issue, as does the selection of literary traditions that can underpin a study. Where the first of these is concerned, it is worth noting that although Americans experienced the Pacific War as they had every armed conflict since the Civil War—that is, as an affair that took place overseas, leaving their contiguous territory untouched by the conflagration—this strategic continuity belied signal differences. For one thing, the attack on Pearl Harbor, Guam (Guåhan), and the subsequent war in the Aleutian Islands made the war feel closer to home, even if, in practice, an invasion of the North American continent was never a likelihood. Just as importantly, the war's environmental and historical reference points required an entirely new lexicon, so different were they from what had gone before.[11] Other sovereign nations, notably the United Kingdom, confronted far more proximate and, at times, potentially overpowering threats during the Second World War. Yet for the British as well, the Pacific and Southeast Asian theaters of operations were destined to occupy a detached category in the historical and literary imagination. Eurocentrism is one term under which to pigeonhole these cultural formations, although a delayed response to the urgency of national self-preservation ought to factor just as strongly. Either way, British combat veterans would ruefully reflect on the strangeness of their wartime posting in ways that, allowing for shifts in dialect, were nowise different from the thoughts of the average GI. Thus, English-Scottish author George MacDonald Fraser on serving in the Burma Campaign:

> What I had been trained for was to be an obedient cog in the great highly-disciplined machine that was launched into Europe on D-Day. That would at least have been in civilised countryside, among familiar faces and recognisable environment, close to home and the main war effort, in a campaign whose essentials had been foreseen by my instructors. The perils and discomforts would have been no less, probably, but they would not have been unexpected. It is disconcerting to find yourself soldiering in an exotic Oriental country which is medieval in outlook, against a barbarian enemy given to burying prisoners up to the neck or hanging them by the heels for bayonet practice, among a friendly population who would rather turn dacoit than not, where you could get your dinner off a tree, be eaten alive by mosquitos and leeches, buy hand-made cheroots from the most beautiful girls in the world (with granny watching, puffing her bidi and rolling the tobacco leaf on her scrawny thigh), wake in the morning to find your carelessly neglected mess-tin occupied by a spider the size of a soup-plate, watch your skin go white and puffy in ceaseless rain the like of which no Westerner can imagine for sheer noise and volume, gape in wonder at huge gilded pagodas silent in the wilderness,

and find yourself taken aback at the sight of a domestic water-tap, because you haven't seen such a thing for months.[12]

List-form retrospectives on the unpleasantries of jungle warfare are a hallmark in the canon of Pacific War literature. Survival in this environment was so precarious that unit cohesion would quickly collapse if the enemy gained the upper hand, a dispiriting scenario that English playwright Willis Hall made much of in his 1959 play *The Long and the Short and the Tall*. American writers also acknowledged the natural world as an important factor but tended to be more interested in the mindset brought back to the United States by those who had survived it. On this matter, the premise of Norman Mailer's *The Naked and the Dead* (1948) is as simple as it is controversial: the American Century, once it comes about, will be a Fascist Century.[13]

To read Mailer's novel is to conclude that the Pacific War was less important in itself than as a means for Americans to become what they became, a tautology that Mailer invites his readers to internalize as a primer for the left-wing activism he espoused. Not every author took the same approach. Whether as veterans or nonveterans, anglophone literary writers repeatedly returned to the episodes of the war years and, in particular, to the anti-Japanese ideology with which it began, which, as a matter of course, means that those scholars who turn their attention to the literatures of the Pacific War must heed the ideological dimension. *Beyond Hostile Islands* shoulders that task as the first of a series, for if one examines writings from the early 1960s to the present day, as I do in the chapters that follow, the imprint of racial discourse, conspicuous by its careful excisions at least as much as its barefaced inclusion, is impossible to ignore. Taking the measure of American fiction writing through well-known novels such as James Jones' *The Thin Red Line* (1962), Michael Crichton's *Rising Sun* (1992), Ruth Ozeki's *My Year of Meats* (1998), David Guterson's *Snow Falling on Cedars* (1994), and Jim Lehrer's *The Special Prisoner* (2000), I enquire into how these works sustained, retired, or resurrected the racially-charged ideologies of the war years. What concessions, I ask, did these authors make to those ideologies in their narratives? How did subsequent historical moments—Cold War geopolitics, the rise of 'Japan Inc.,' and the commemorations of 1995—provide the occasion to revisit the war's signature episodes? Finally, could a sense of geographical separateness, New Zealand's most prominently, develop a war literature canon in ways that were less disposed to the tropes and ideologies commonly found in American writing? Among these questions, the lattermost signals a comparative structure inherent in this project's methodology, one that rejects any framework that imagines the Pacific War as a closed-off, dualistic conflict after the fashion of the Mexican-, Spanish-, or Philippine-American Wars—the Pacific War, in its nomenclature, is rightly criticized for implicitly omitting military actions on the Asian mainland, but insofar as the name does not reduce the conflict to an argument between two nations it avoids at least one conceptual pitfall.

Having mentioned things one ought to avoid, I confess a certain amount of unease with the notion that the American military strategy of 'island hopping' toward the Japanese mainland makes the intellectual shortcutting (away) of other anglophone historical and cultural traditions a legitimate undertaking (a conceit that reprises longstanding tendencies in US-centered narratives set in the Pacific).[14] The process of bypassing certain islands and leaving them to 'wither on the vine,' as happened to New Ireland and other redoubts of Japanese power, proved its worth in military terms. As a strategy of literary research, however, the analogy implies that the canons of anglophone Pacific War literature have a single stem (American) on which the branches (Australian, British, Canadian, New Zealand, et al.) depend for their succor. The most immediate lesson of the current study is that, if any withering has occurred, it has not been because of a dearth of cultural stimuli within the respective literary traditions of participant nations. Among these stimuli, the rise of Māori writers and, more broadly, a recognition that Pacific Island characters are of signal importance to Pacific-based narratives is a noticeable element within New Zealand writing (I avoid the term 'Aotearoa-New Zealand' only because it would not have been familiar to the writers of mid-twentieth century source material). Admittedly, the legacy of a false bifurcation that sees Māori as a separate identity from Pacific Islanders has meant that a Pacific-oriented sensibility, as distinct from the mere presence of Pacific Islander characters, is only evident in the work of James George (whose work I read in Chapter 5).[15] Moreover, ethnic or Indigenous identity, while a possible indication of particular perspectives on a given issue, is no more of an absolute guarantee that such perspectives exist than, say, island inhabitation is of cultural exceptionalism (a point to which I shall return later). Warning readers against these conceits, Epeli Hauʻofa concluded his essay on "Anthropology and Pacific Islanders" by noting how West African anthropologists had tended to produce works that were not much different from anthropologists of non-African descent writing on the region.[16] Following this observation, I have refrained from underscoring Keri Hulme's indigeneity in Chapter 2, leaving it to the reader to determine how or whether at all it manifests in her writing. My own sense of things is that the literary works of a war that took its name from the ocean which Māori identify as their ancestral home will at some point invest themselves in notions of indigeneity and/or Pacific Island solidarity in ways that are distinct from the response typically found in American literature (the most striking exception to the rule, Robert Barclay's novel *Meḷaḷ* (2002), is addressed in the Coda found at the end of this book).

Whereas fears regarding the inconsequentiality of individual literary traditions are easily retired, the issue of whether individual genres of Pacific War writing are somehow stunted, be they American or otherwise, requires of the researcher a painful honesty. While the war had its fair share of striking historical junctures that have long inspired literary writers, close acquaintance with the specific genres associated with them reveals ingrained authorial predispositions, not the least of which is the non-integration of perspectives that lie 'off the beaten track.' Thus, stories of Allied Far East Prisoners of War (hereafter 'FEPOWs') go unmentioned in combat narratives (prisoners are seldom central to any given war story); FEPOW narratives, struggling for legitimacy in a field of memory freighted with misconceptions, have had little to say about the atomic bombings of Hiroshima and Nagasaki; and Japanese American internment narratives, underscoring minority experiences behind barbed wire, are seemingly unaware of camp systems on the other side of the Pacific Ocean (these were soldier camps and had no bearing on the 'main' story: the political battlefield of civil rights in the United States).

From the '60s through the '90s, the majority of Pacific War narratives shored up the genres they inhabited and, in a corollary that might or might not have been purposeful, turned a blind eye to politically nonconvergent topics such as righteous retribution (in times of war), war guilt and revenge (in the postwar era), and, in particular, the politics of apology (likewise postwar). If there is a signature feature of Pacific War literature that distinguishes it from the writings of other wars, it lies in the ways that creative writers have fallen into or baited this trap. The rule is not fixed, admittedly, but it holds true more often than not. In the chapters that follow, therefore, I have first provided literature overviews in order to map this phenomenon as it has occurred in discrete genre canons, before offering lengthier considerations of writers who have, with varying degrees of success, divested themselves of its straightjacketing polarities. In doing so, I take inspiration from literature scholar Erin Mercer's dedicated study of genre writing in New Zealand, which refrains from employing the term 'subgenre,' given that the term invokes differences of category that are hard to sustain on close examination.[17] Her enquiry into why certain modes of writing have been judged more appropriate than others is also pertinent, although it is an easier question to ask within the framework of a single national tradition. When one takes war as a central topic, the question is more along these lines: "Which identity groups and their politics have been judged more appropriate than others at particular times and which genres have best represented their positions?"

To return to the comparative dimensions of my project, the rewards of engaging with more than one literary or cultural tradition as a means to destabilize these apparently 'innate' genre boundaries will be readily apparent, although care must be taken to anticipate this process without presuming that it will occur at every turn. At times, I have been intrigued by the remarkable capacity of New Zealand writers to (re)conceptualize a particular historical episode of the war, while at other times, they have wrongfooted me by falling into narrative patterns altogether in keeping with American models. Of course, neither scenario occludes the other and, having noted that anglophone literary traditions in the Pacific are not dependent on literary or historical source material of an American provenance for their inspiration, one should not presume that this suggests a pervasive unawareness that such sources exist (on the contrary, given that literary works on wartime episodes have tended to emerge in the United States earlier and with greater marketing fanfare than near-equivalents in New Zealand, it would be remarkable if this were so). At this point, then, one must ask whether New Zealand culture as a whole—or perhaps, more intriguingly, in part—possesses any 'exceptional' attributes that provide a vantage point from which to view American cultural productions. Some literary theorists, such as Elizabeth McMahon, caution against overinvesting in *islandness* as a basis for exceptionalism, observing that such flights of fancy may betray the subjectivity of a fantasist more than they reveal the island cultures supposedly in question.[18] Such was the rueful self-confession, in another context, of Scottish author Gavin Francis: "I was in search of distant islands, in love with the idea that, on a patch of land, protected by a circumference of sea, the obligations of life would dissolve and a singular clarity of mind would descend. It proved more complicated than that."[19] A more accommodating school of thought comes from literature scholars Doreen D'Cruz and John C. Ross, who back away from absolutes and focus instead on trends and possibilities. Taking a leaf out of Margaret Atwood's suggestion that every country has a unifying symbol at its core (Canada's being 'Survival'), the scholars do not struggle to isolate New Zealand's, for, naturally, isolation is itself the symbol: "Through the shifting nature of the dislocations through which isolation is manifested, we demonstrate the mutation and adaptability of this idea in New Zealand fiction [. . .]"[20] For D'Cruz and Ross, whether the mythos is objectively true may matter less than whether literary writers themselves believe in it or invest in it to some extent.

If isolation exists as a trend in New Zealand literature and culture, can this provide the aforementioned vantage point through which to view US culture in turn? The possibility is complicated by the longstanding presence of American culture within New Zealand and as a feature *of* New Zealand. This dimension has been usefully explored by social historian Miles Fairburn, who complicates matters still further by arguing that New Zealand culture is, in fact, a combination of constituents found nowhere else (the other principal dimensions being Australian, British, and Māori).[21] An earlier study by media studies scholar Geoff Lealand likewise observed the presence of American culture in New Zealand, but added that when New Zealanders compared themselves with Australians they tended to take American culture as an index of difference: "Australians no longer seem to be our kin and seem more like second-hand Americans than trans-Tasman soul-mates."[22] The dissemination of American culture in New Zealand clearly heralds its place as one aspect among several that people 'take on' in a hybridized cultural makeup, and yet it also serves as something against which New Zealanders can 'push back' (a trend that is, perhaps, less the case when it comes to the Australian, British, and Māori components).

Balancing the 'take on' against the 'pushback' necessarily means that scholarship incorporating New Zealand literature must allow for a certain amount of inconsistency in the voices that come through. Where my study is concerned, this is a roundabout way of saying that New Zealand fiction writing occasionally bucks the narrative and ideological trends set by American exemplars, while at other times it toes the line in a process that I have come to think of as an 'ideological coproduction.' As I conceive it, this term refers to a practice in which the writers and artists of small countries acknowledge the cultural dominance of a larger power in a process that is accommodationist when it comes to shared ideologies (meaning, in the present instance, the depiction of Japanese servicemen and/or civilians in various scenarios) but dissimilar on particular points and in narrative details (which derive from the localism of the smaller country). In such instances where the coproduction occurs—which is to say most, but not all—New Zealand literature may appear as a parochial version of a larger discourse that is as ingrained in the small settler cultures of the anglophone Pacific as it is in the larger ones. This state of affairs remains familiar to any scholar of the Second World War, because the concept of total war applied not only to combat but also to the propaganda disseminated throughout society (something English author James Hilton knew well when he wistfully dreamed up the idea of a Tibetan lamasery as a sanctuary from such language in his 1933 novel *Lost Horizon*). That the ideologies of war in the Pacific were as inescapable as the war itself is therefore something of a given in what follows and constitutes the 'take on' components of an American or wider anglophone identity in New Zealand. If the possibility of 'pushback'—against the ideologies themselves or American vehicles for the same—remains present as a possibility more than demonstrability at certain turns, geographer Elaine Stratford cautions us against measuring island cultures purely by the yardstick of non-continentalism. In a spirited position on the salience of the archipelagic, she puts the matter succinctly:

> [t]hinking *from* islands and archipelagoes means not just standing on the shores or margins (or indeed in the littoral zone, or up to one's knees, or from below the waves) "speaking back" to others elsewhere. It means deploying what is implicit in the term "from"—movement, departure, forward motion, and accomplishment; this is speaking to and up and into, and it seems ontogenic to me.[23]

Occasionally, source material from island cultures may unsettle continental paradigms or ideologies derivative therefrom, and yet this need not always be the case. In a project such as this one, the trend ebbs and flows, sometimes questioning, more usually conjoining, at all times insisting on its presence in a way that confounds mistaken notions of island cultures as 'left behind.'

If the Pacific War had been a matter of stronger powers ganging up in an ABCD encirclement (Japan's menacing summary for America, Britain, China, and the Dutch East Indies), then focusing upon the Allied propaganda motifs that supercharged this endeavor would present an obvious avenue for enquiry. The ubiquity of propaganda posters that sought to dehumanize the Japanese meant that Admiral Halsey could put up a sign on the bow of the US Cruiser *Honolulu* reading: "Kill Japs. Kill Japs. Kill more Japs."[24] Public language of this sort was noteworthy only because it was blatant and, as part of a larger discursive whole, contributed to the decision to drop the atomic bombs.[25] One must keep such 'signs' and their 'signifiers' in mind lest the human costs of war become lost in the niceties of scholarly argumentation.[26] By the same token, however, it is possible to overstate the influence of cultural representation, obviating other complexities—of which there were many—in the American decision to drop the Bomb, to say nothing of the wartime atrocities perpetrated by the Japanese (a factor in itself). The paradigm of Critical Race Studies, in short, risks obscuring as much as it reveals if it slips into overdependence and, in an ironic turn, may betray itself as Eurocentric (the frequency and regularity with which the

Nazi Holocaust enters American college campus discussions of German culture is curious when one notes how subdued are discussions of the Bataan Death March, the Burma-Siam Railway, Unit 731, and the comfort women system when it comes to Japan).[27] It need hardly be said that perceived or actual one-sidedness of this sort is all but guaranteed to provoke a counter response, as took place during the planned exhibition of the *Enola Gay* at the Smithsonian Institution in 1995, when irate representatives of the American Legion and Air Force Association lobbied to have the exhibition content changed or pulled altogether (alleging that it dishonored American veterans by focusing too much on photographs of the atomic bomb victims). One veteran, who found himself living among expatriated Japanese professionals in a Pittsburgh housing complex, published an essay that, in a rhetorical reversal, showed more friendliness toward his Japanese neighbors than the historical revisionists who, in his eyes, had mischaracterized the United States: "There is also a group of little Japanese toddlers, and I'm on special hugging terms with a number of them. These families are, of course, a very bright and special group of people, and I am very glad they are here with us and willing to be part of America's evil intentions."[28] In an earlier scholarly context, the historian Bernard Lewis adopted a similar pose, warning of trends in humanities scholarship that took as assumed—and as the preeminent topic of consideration—a totalizing misrepresentation of non-Western peoples in American culture: "This responds well to the sentiments of those in the West, and especially in the United States, who condemn their country as the source of all evil in the world as arrogantly and absurdly as their forbears acclaimed it as the source of all good."[29] Heading off the assumptions that feed into the binaries Lewis describes does not require that one give up the paradigms of postcolonialism, but it does caution against overinvestment in the study of a single empire at the expense of multiple interacting empires across time and space. Literature scholar Laura Doyle advances precisely this corrective in her suggestion that, on at least a few occasions, 'postcolonialism' should be reconceptualized or retitled 'inter-imperialism.'[30] More publicly still, the married Japanese artists Iri Maruki and Toshi Maruki had made an identical point with the paintings that formed their *Atomic Bomb Panels* series (1950–1982), which illustrated the sufferings of atomic bomb survivors in the immediate aftermath of the bombings, before following up with panels that depicted the torture and murder of FEPOWs by those same survivors, as well as further panels depicting colonial subjects from Korea who, present in Hiroshima at the time of the bombing, likewise perished in the blast.[31]

Having accepted that critical paradigms derived from postcolonialism must attend to the ways in which the Pacific War was, in essence, a conflict between imperial systems, I am aware that this even-handed approach is by no means welcome to all and sundry. Of a certainty, it is far easier—preferable, even, given the gravitational pull of moral dichotomies—to wag one's finger in a single direction only. To short-circuit this linear thinking takes an act of genuine nonconformity, of a sort evinced by Japanese American novelist Mako Yoshikawa who, in a biographical piece, recalled a dawning moment of clarity in which this balancing of imperatives impressed itself upon her:

> Watching movies as a teenager, I felt ashamed and confused when I saw Japanese soldiers portrayed as sadists and killers: while I identified with the American soldiers they were torturing, I knew that to everyone sitting around me in the theater, I was one of the Japanese. Yet in spite of my shame and confusion, those overblown, offensive images sank in, as did more credible information about the brutality of the Japanese Army.[32]

Pervasive anti-Japanese imagery, inarguably evident in American cultural productions of the war years, would resurface during the era of Japan's 'bubble economy,' shifting from depictions of island combat to multinational business corporations and their 'takeovers.'[33] At the height of this phenomenon, which grew from the late 1970s through the early-to-mid 1990s, those Americans who had not lived through the war years were given a glimpse of what it had been like to inhabit a discourse of racially-charged geopolitical rhetoric.[34] Thus, literary writer David Mura, on journeying to Japan and discussing the war and its cultural legacies with an equally astute critic of Japan's socio-political landscape:

> Matsuo was like a terrier gnawing the pants leg of the postman. He wouldn't give up until he had drawn blood. But as he spoke about the violence of the Japanese soldiers, as he described their invasions of Asia in the first half of the century, the executions in Manchuria, the rape of Nanking, I began to feel as if he was carrying things a bit too far.
> "Japan is peaceful now," he said, "but it's always there, that violence."
> I told him he sounded like an American racist. The Japanese couldn't be trusted, were sneaky, inscrutable. A recent article in *The New York Times Magazine* had described the rebirth of Japanese nationalism and had focused on groups on the far right. I felt that the article completely obscured the marginality of such groups and the apolitical nature of most present-day Japanese. Such distortions helped many Americans legitimize their resentment toward Japan's economic resurgence.

> Though I didn't say so to Matsuo, I suspect that the main reason I found his argument troubling was that I felt much more comfortable with America-bashing than Japan-bashing.³⁵

Mura and Yoshikawa's respective considerations of Japan's actions during the war years is illustrative of an identity politics—in this case, those of Japanese Americans, although the term applies equally to combat veterans and former FEPOWs—that invests in specific genre boundaries of storytelling, which, in turn, draw upon historically 'discrete' episodes of the war (research into British FEPOW stories carried out by Yoshikawa's mother, plus Matsuo's telling of his uncle's military service in Manchuria, mean that for Mura and Yoshikawa these 'other' stories do not remain discrete for long). In another context, the South African author Laurens van der Post, himself a survivor of Japanese-run camps on the island of Java, would incur the vocal displeasure of surviving FEPOWs who did not allow, as he had done, that the war had brought feelings of victimhood to both sides and that forgiveness was a worthwhile practice.³⁶ For each of the aforementioned writers, 'buying into' a hitherto unexplored narrative from the war years, with specific moral vectors and an attendant genre canon, treads perilously close to 'selling out' nominal socio-political allegiances.

As should now be apparent, my book takes the legacy of racialized propaganda depictions of the Japanese as a core topic in the study of Pacific War literature, even as it stops short of assuming that White anglophone authors are inescapably drawn to its racialized tropes and topoi (or that Māori writers are somehow immune to them). My intellectual debt to Edward Said's 1978 treatise *Orientalism* is evident in every chapter of this project, but I have refrained from following Said's lead in selecting only the most Eurocentric/ethnocentric source material to support my observations.³⁷ As Stuart Hall notes, representational practices seek to 'fix' the meaning of the Other in the mind of the Self and yet the meaning of a given image of the Other 'floats' and resists such fixity.³⁸ British writers W. H. Auden and Christopher Isherwood had occasion to learn this for themselves, experientially as much as intellectually, when in 1938 they visited the Mayor of Canton, Tsang Yan-fu, and were struck by his unhateful opinion of the Japanese invaders:

> We both liked Mr. Tsang. If this was typical of China's attitude toward the Japanese, it was certainly an example to the West—with its dreary hymns of hate, and screams of 'Baby-killer,' 'Hun,' 'sub-human fiends.' This scornful, good-natured amusement was, we agreed, exactly the note which a cultured, pacific country should strike in its propaganda against a brutal, upstart enemy.

Mr. Tsang's kind of humour, if properly exploited, should win China many friends abroad.[39]

What Auden and Isherwood realized, if they did not already know it, was that structuring a world view around a principal cultural identity of the Self as 'Western' against an Other as 'Asian' was too simple. Differences in nationality and behavioral standards—in this case, between the mainland Chinese and the Japanese—would already have sufficed to complicate such a sweeping dichotomy in peacetime (much as differences in gender, race, and class have a similar destabilizing effect in other texts and moments).[40] But the two travelers go further still and compare Mr. Tsang's style of bellicosity with that of their own countrymen in ways that upend traditional assumptions regarding the inherent shortcomings of the Other.[41] Simply put, East Asian customs, outlooks, and institutions could as well provide the Westerner with the chance to engage in self-criticism as self-aggrandizement, particularly in times of war (itself a destabilizing influence).[42] The cultural methodology of Edward Said, on the other hand, suggests that the mind of the Western author or traveler cannot unbend itself from its preconceptions, for the interplay of the Orientalists' West and the Orientalists' Orient subsumes differences between individual people or between specific national cultures. In this arrangement, the Other possesses only one 'essential' identity—that of the 'Oriental' or 'Asiatic'—and the different opinions that 'Westerners' might arrive at in regard to China and Japan, or that Chinese and Japanese might have of each 'other,' do not suffice to disturb the dialectical opposition.[43]

As the propaganda posters of the Second World War make clear, the preeminent Other in the human imagination is, strictly speaking, not human at all and therefore neither 'Western' nor 'Eastern' in any meaningful sense.[44] In times of war, this fact typically matters only to the extent that images of nonhuman animals—in particular, those that are judged verminous, poisonous, and alarmingly multitudinous—can be leveraged in order to denigrate one's enemy by association. In peacetime, however, certain cultural productions may come to light in which the otherness ascribed to a past or future enemy is called into question by that same association. Such an occasion took place in 1932, when Baron Takeichi Nishi and his horse Uranus won the equestrian show jumping event at the Olympics in Los Angeles. In this instance, recalled in the epigraph, the identification of the ethnic Other not away from a nonhuman animal but rather alongside a nonhuman animal—a 'favored' species—elicited admiration sufficient to disturb preexistent forms of dehumanizing rhetoric, a practice that abolitionists had already utilized in the nineteenth century when they penned stories for children and young adults using domesticated animals to mediate the reader's sympathy for slaves.[45] One sees the same strategy employed by New Zealand novelist Susan Brocker in her young adult novel *Dreams of Warriors* (2010), which is set in rural New Zealand during the Second World War and illustrates a world on the brink: of immobility in the case of the protagonist Bella (her leg has withered from polio); of bankruptcy, in the case of her family's dairy farm; and of euthanasia, in the case of Bella's disturbed horse Gipsy. Brocker resolves these difficulties by lifting the figure of the 'horse whisperer' from British author Nicholas Evans' eponymous novel (1995), substituting for him a Japanese prisoner of war who then performs in the role. Rejecting heavy-handed methods of horse training, the Japanese POW instructs Bella to take account of Gipsy's deafness and traumatized mind, to communicate silently, and earn the mare's trust instead of presuming upon it.[46] In due course, these lessons prompt Bella to revise her knowledge of the Japanese enemy and thus the novel stands as an example of an intervention strategy against the dehumanizing motifs of the war years.[47]

In real-life encounters or the world of literary imagination, my acting assumption is that a degree of intellectual reciprocity is possible between Self and Other, sufficient to make apparently 'inert' notions of 'the Orient'—Japan, in the present instance—contestable and changeable in a process that Said's study, for all its insight, never granted.[48] Allowing for this possibility and arguing for its persistence are, however, different prospects and I concede that, in times of war, there are seldom enough good-humored Chinese mayors and captured enemy horse whisperers to go around. Likewise, if one looks to literature published in and set during the postwar years, it is not necessary to reach for well-known interracial romances like James A. Michener's *Sayonara* (1953) or George Campbell's *Cry for Happy* (1958) in order to convince oneself that the idea of Japan as an 'essentially feminine' and/or 'infantile' land of erotic pleasures was at least as strong in the American imagination as it had been in, say, Giacomo Puccini's.[49] Passing quips such as those at the start of John Updike's *Couples* (1968), in which White American veterans casually recall their appreciation of Japanese pornography and prostitutes, are, if anything, all the more compelling and suggest that the 'identity' of Japan has become inseparable from such images in the minds of these characters.[50] As a peacetime nation, Japan would 'offer' these pleasures; as a wartime nation, it had 'offered' prison guards, torturers, and banzai-yelling soldiers in a set piece routine critiqued in Japanese American playwright Philip K. Gotanda's *Yankee Dawg You Die* (1991). Thus, one of the Japanese American characters in Gotanda's play asks, while he attempts, against his will, to act the part of a sadistic prison guard, "Why can't you see me as I really am?"[51] To students of Said's model of Orientalism, this question is freighted with a meaning at once unanswerable and incontestable, for how can the White anglophone subject, the 'seeing man' in Mary Louise Pratt's ground-breaking study of nineteenth-century autoethnography, see a non-White ethnic minority or non-White national except through a taxonomy of representation internalized through self-authorizing cultural productions?[52] Such is the foregone conclusion arrived at by the protagonist of Viet Thanh Nguyen's novel *The Sympathizer* (2015) when he collaborates in the production of a Vietnam War movie and chides himself for misplaced idealism: "I naively believed that I could divert the Hollywood organism from its goal, the simultaneous lobotomization and pickpocketing of the world's audiences."[53]

If there is a caveat embedded in this lament, it lies in the presupposition that the world's audiences do have 'pockets,' not wholly empty of knowledge, which nominally fall outside the reach or purview of American cultural productions. While it is tempting to take this as assumed, it is now a matter of scholarly record that the historical episodes of Japanophobia in the anglophone world, along with the Sinophobia that preceded it, are as transnational in their roots as they are in their stems. What this means, in essence, is that discursive phenomena that arise in one anglophone culture have a habit of manifesting in others, particularly when these cultures are aware of their geographic ties to the Pacific region.[54] Keeping these interconnected trends in mind, alongside the virulent wartime propaganda that made Japanophobia altogether commonplace, the question arises as to how, or whether at all, these interconnections have survived through the contemporary era. Confining one's source material to those of the United States as a means to formulate an answer is less than satisfactory, methodologically speaking, and also inappropriate for a project, such as this, which draws upon novels that derive from an inter-imperial, trans-hemispheric conflict spread over a vast geographic area. References to Australian, British, Canadian, and South African source materials can therefore be found in this project at certain turns, but I have made particular use of sources from New Zealand, an island nation that, in geographic terms at least, lies further 'east' than Japan and has even been known to 'fall off' some maps altogether. Scholars of New Zealand culture frequently shake their heads at this state of affairs, but it was ever thus and not just in the world of cartography either. In James A. Michener's *Tales of the South Pacific* (1947), Flight Lieutenant Grant enters and leaves the text as a sort of airborne beachcomber whose stoic façade cracks under the pressure of defending his New Zealand homeland.⁵⁵ Later on, mindful that his previous work had left out a good deal, Michener wrote another story, "Until They Sail" (1951), which acknowledged different forms of race relations in New Zealand and the United States, something US Marines had discovered for themselves during an altercation over how to address the Māori whom they encountered on Manners Street, Wellington.⁵⁶ This historical episode, along with the attention granted it by Michener, is but one example of a contrast in cultural outlook that makes the notion of ideological equivalency between New Zealand and American perspectives on the war more of an hypothesis than a given.⁵⁷ Granted, in my study I conclude that the contrasts are more a matter of degree than of kind, but whereas the earliest American and New Zealand cultural productions of the 1960s and those that occurred during Japan's 'economic miracle' were uniform in their ideological trajectory, the same cannot be said for those published around the turn of the twentieth century.

To tease out these divergences, I have focused each chapter upon a specific genre, beginning with the combat novel before moving on to what some might consider a continuation of the form, the corporate thriller. I then examine the rise of internment novels that narrate the story of Japanese Americans or, in the case of New Zealand, Japanese sojourners initially domiciled on Tonga and Fiji at the outbreak of the war; novelizations of the Far East Prisoner of War (FEPOW) experience of captivity under the Imperial Japanese Army; and, finally, Manhattan Project novels, with particular attention paid to the figures of the scientist and the atomic bomb survivor. In a pairing strategy, I match the American novels already mentioned with New Zealand fiction writing in the form of Errol Brathwaite's *An Affair of Men* (1962), Keri Hulme's "Kaibutsu-san" (1985), Wendy Catran's *The Swap* (2004), Peter Wells' *Lucky Bastard* (2007), and James George's *Ocean Roads* (2006). Scholars and literati in New Zealand will be familiar with these names, and it is hoped that those further afield may likewise develop an interest in New Zealand war literature if they have not already done so. This suggestion, I'm aware, will be unobjectionable to the majority but, in practice, followed through by hardly anyone outside Australasia, for it flies in the face of longstanding trends in war studies scholarship and attendant reading practices, which privilege source material from 'big' continental powers at the expense of 'small'—read: 'marginal'—islands, islets, and archipelagos.⁵⁸ Not coincidentally, such perspectives are themselves a form of othering, one that reached a widespread consensus within the framework of scholarship on the 'Pacific Rim,' a term that visually alluded to the horizon of East Asia and inscribed the Pacific Ocean and its island cultures as mere way stations on a journey between West and East.⁵⁹ Taking steps to avoid this elision in my own scholarship, while simultaneously granting that the rollback strategies adopted by the United States involved precisely those perspectives, has meant that I have had to strike a balance between foregrounding American sources (at the risk of seeming to privilege them) or, in a countertrend, doing the same with New Zealand sources (losing sight, temporarily at least, of how the United States was inarguably the larger actor in the fight against the Empire of Japan). Wrestling with the merits and demerits of placing New Zealand literature in conversation with (non)equivalent traditions in the United States, William J. Schafer put the matter resignedly but evocatively: "Comparisons may be odious, but anyone reading a map needs a compass rose and a scale to understand the cardinal directions and the distances implied."[60] Striking a more optimistic note, literature scholar Rajeev S. Patke embraces comparativism with studied abandon in his quest to isolate how literary island communities have addressed circumstances analogous to one another: "The aim is to suggest a kind of stereoscopy, which discovers commonality amid much that is dissimilar."[61]

Whether one's metaphor of choice be a compass or a stereoscope, the forever unequal balance between the volume of American and New Zealand source material requires explanation beyond self-evident disparities of population size, density, and financial resources. As with other artistic forms, war literature reflects these dimensions to one degree or another, yet its development is likewise traceable to wartime decisions taken at the political level. These began for New Zealand in 1939 when the Labour government under Michael Joseph Savage declared war against Nazi Germany and sent the 2nd New Zealand Division for deployment in Britain and North Africa, a commitment that prioritized the integrity of the British Empire on which New Zealand depended for its economic prosperity.[62] When war came to the Pacific, New Zealand forces were caught in the dilemma of how to fight in two theaters of war when their manpower resources were already overstretched. In recognition of the seriousness of the threat posed by the Empire of Japan, the 3rd New Zealand Division was formed for garrison and, latterly, combat deployment, serving alongside US forces in Guadalcanal and playing a significant role in capturing the islands of Vella Lavella, Treasury Island, and Green Island.[63] However, the competing demands placed on New Zealand, which continued to involve fighting in the Mediterranean, as well as working essential industries, ultimately led to 3rd NZ's disbandment in 1944.[64]

Given the commonplace desire throughout the anglophone world to emphasize contributions to combat roles along with the sacrifices those entailed, the preferred settings for New Zealand writings on the Second World War have remained Europe and North Africa. In this way, the Allies' strategic decision to 'do Europe first' has had the knock-on effect of peripheralizing literary works set in the Pacific, despite the fact that the authors previously mentioned have all written as citizens of a Pacific Island nation. In Australia, an island nation somewhat easier to find on the map, the situation is similar in essence but complicated by memories of the Bombing of Darwin and fierce fighting on the Kokoda Trail, as well as an ever-present uneasiness that Australia's greater geographical proximity to the Asian region translated into greater vulnerability (the Curtin government went as far as to draw up plans intended to deny military and civilian resources to the occupying Japanese forces).[65] These episodes, and their attendant literatures, might present more obvious bases for comparison with near-equivalents from the United States than New Zealand's do, but it is precisely the sense of greater geographical and experiential remove that makes New Zealand source material of interest. As a trope of settler colonial culture, 'distance' has generally carried self-doubting or otherwise negative valences across New Zealand arts and letters, even those in which Britain wasn't necessarily considered 'home' (as it often was, even during the war years).[66] During the Pacific War, however, fears of prospective invasion, manifest, for example, in the precautions taken by the protagonist of Frank Sargeson's 1945 short story "The Hole that Jack Dug," belie New Zealand's relative good fortune as a country that was never bombed and never invaded (the 1942 loss of Singapore, a military base of the British Empire to which New Zealanders had looked for protection, is the closest approximation). As stated earlier, it is possible to presume too much upon the *islandness* that underwrites these distinctions and one must keep the admonitions of Island Studies scholars in mind, ably offered by Elizabeth McMahon and Bénédicte André: "Literature rehearses the continuous interplay of these two contradictory elements of the colonial island gaze: the illusion that the island can be grasped whole, and the illusion that the island is always in the distance, which is the space of desire."[67]

New Zealand's greater remove from the military operations of the Pacific War is no figment of a colonialist imagination, but if a scholarly project that discounts this fact risks becoming ahistorical, then a project that conjoins historical difference with geographical distance (even without quotation marks) risks treading awfully close to the illusions McMahon and André identify. Recognizing that this presents something of an impasse, I am beholden to sociologist Godfrey Baldacchino for suggesting that Island Studies can and should be playful in its ideas rather than stolidly committed to a single paradigm. As he puts it, "islands, both real and earthy as much as concocted, or even those occupying the fuzzy space in between, stand out as sites of novelty, of coy experimentation, of deliberate or coincidental pathbreaking events."[68] Similarly, Alice Te Punga Somerville conceded in her study of Māori as a Pacific Island identity that, notwithstanding the wide and deep connections Māori have with the Pacific Ocean and its inhabitants, Māori need not be involved in all Pacific-related matters (accordingly, they are not in every single one of my chapters).[69] If this sounds a tad noncommittal, particularly for a project focused on war literature, it echoes the real-life experimentation of wartime events rather well. Tracing the folkways of the First Marine Division, historian George McMillan recalled the run-up to war as especially experimental, methodologically speaking: "The story is well known of how the Marine Corps persisted between World Wars I and II, amid almost contemptuous indifference from other branches of the American armed forces, in its pursuit of a technique for landing against a defended beach."[70] The North Island of New Zealand had plenty of beaches, and US Marines would die on those same beaches practicing their amphibious maneuvers in last-stage preparations before closing with the Japanese in the Solomon Islands. New Zealand's simultaneous proximity to and distance from what would become the Solomon Islands campaign was selected as the most appropriate staging ground for the Marine Corps and yet, of course, New Zealand was a place and a society in itself, as Americans would find when they went on leave (among the best-known publications, Leon Uris' 1953 novel *Battle Cry* teased out the cultural differences between the two groups).

The vastness of a war that spanned and took its name from an ocean means that the chapters that follow cannot hope to be comprehensive in their examination of genres and historical episodes, although they are by no means idiosyncratic for all that. Chapter 1 throws readers into the maelstrom of the Guadalcanal campaign (James Jones' *The Thin Red Line*) and New Britain campaign (Errol Brathwaite's *An Affair of Men*) by examining literary portrayals that focused exclusively upon the American or the Japanese side in attempts to isolate the 'essential' cultural characteristics that each brought to the battlefield. In pursuit of this literary objective, Jones and Brathwaite are deceptively unconcerned with the highly specific island locales in which their characters 'find themselves' because their primary intent is to take the island as a form of social laboratory, following a literary tradition traceable at least as far back as the twelfth century.[71] For Jones, this involves putting the men of Charlie Company through a series of *en masse* front-line assaults, in the course of which a number of revelatory thoughts penetrate through the malaise of combat disorientation to reveal the American soldier as fully capable of on-the-job learning. Likewise character-driven, the narrative of Brathwaite's novel focuses in painstaking detail upon Captain Itoh of the Imperial Marines, a man who single-mindedly pursues Allied airmen through the jungle but, for all his commitment, remains incapable of revising his worldview to encompass pacifist positions on war. Situating these two texts side-by-side, one notices that each author tells one half of a story that, in discursive terms, reaches completion through the other source. The emergent coproduction allows for revelatory experiences for the Allies—as we shall see, Jones depends on them to generate narrative momentum—but closes off investigations of enemy subjectivity except at the formulaic level.

The combat novel of the 1960s recalled the war in ways that made Japanese servicemen appear so far removed from the self-aware, improvisational Allied soldier as to seem a separate species. As an analogue, Itoh's behavior was always threatening and pedantic to the nth degree. Nor did his civilian incarnation in the literature of the postwar years complicate this impression in any fundamental way. From the '50s through the early '70s, Japanese civilian men devolved into quirky, sometimes comical, more often uncomprehending background entities, less interested in backstabbing than photographing. Their presence in anglophone writing went unremarked by literature scholars, although the subsequent era—responding to Japan's high-growth 'economic miracle'—could not be brushed off so easily. This was the period in which Itoh was reborn as a smooth-tongued, white-collared salaryman intent on buying up foreign industries just as his imperial forerunners had been on sabotaging or destroying them. Among the many commentators who took note of his presence, American poet Robert Bly, leader of the Men's Movement, would summarize the power disparity between Japan and the United States in evocative terms:

> The Americans are very weak in the warrior now, the American men. The Japanese men were strong in the warrior during the Second World War and they somehow transferred that into their briefcases and into their VCRs, and so we don't have warriors to stand up against them even in the business world.[72]

The warrior analogy, mythopoetic in Bly's idiom, took on qualities of sinister purposefulness in the hands of thriller writers such as Michael Crichton. *Rising Sun* played upon American fears by imagining that Japanese corporate executives were planning a 'takeover' of the United States, an idea that Māori writer Keri Hulme also indulged in her depiction of a Japanese tourist in New Zealand. These 'plot-driven' works, and sundry others such as New

Zealand author Vivienne Plumb's short story "The Wife Who Spoke Japanese in her Sleep" (1993), reveal the literary output of this period as being, in essence, a shadowy afterimage of the combat novel and thus Chapter 2 serves as a companion piece to the first. Yet the period in question also came at the tail end of the Asian American Movement, which, among other things, sought to foreground minority perspectives on wars fought by the United States in and/or against East and Southeast Asian countries. Japanese American author Ruth Ozeki, best-known today for her 2013 Booker Prize-shortlisted novel *A Tale for the Time Being*, drew attention to 'Japan-bashing' in her first novel *My Year of Meats* (1998), by incorporating the signature tropes of that phenomenon into her narrative before subjecting them to a process of gradual dismantlement.

Chapters 3 through 5 differ from the prior two, shifting away from the literary representation of military or economic combat toward wartime and commemorative events that also concerned non-combatants, beginning in Chapter 3 with the internment of Japanese American civilians hitherto domiciled on the fictional island of San Piedro (David Guterson's *Snow Falling on Cedars*), and of Japanese civilians who had been living on the real islands of Fiji and Tonga (Wendy Catran's *The Swap*). At the current time of writing, the canon of writing on Japanese American internment, fictional, nonfictional, or scholarly, is established to the point where public awareness of internment, in the United States at least, may be raised through any number of readily available publications. The absence of any monographs or book chapters on internment as it took place in New Zealand, on the other hand, reveals a paucity of scholarly attention that could be mistaken for rank indifference—until, that is, the particulars of the wartime situation in the South Pacific and its demographic consequences become apparent. To underscore these dimensions, this chapter differs from the others by providing a history of this little-known episode before turning to how Guterson and Catran complicate the mutually non-integrated narratives of ethnic Japanese internees and Pacific War veterans. The narratives of both novels put the veteran and the former internee in conversation with one another, reaching not for moral resolution or the primacy of one over the other so much as a recognition that each side's position contains a civic and/or humanistic imperative to speak and be heard. These speech acts do not come easily to the characters, all of whom inhabit a silence that falls outside the logocentric norms of nonveteran and nonethnic Japanese society. To explore this theme, I pair theater studies scholar Emily Roxworthy's analysis of how trauma silenced Japanese Americans with literature critic King-Kok Cheung's study of silence as a literary strategy.

If silence is common to the cultural norms of specific communities or in response to traumatic events, it can also arise from a sense that national memories of war have occluded certain stories while privileging others. Even before the war was over, General Slim had warned the British Fourteenth Army, which had fought the Japanese in Burma between 1944 and 1945, that they would be the 'forgotten army' following demobilization. The war in Europe, Russia, and North Africa was already preeminent in the British public imagination and there was nothing to be done about it. His prediction proved true and might have gone double for those FEPOWs who had fallen into captivity after barely three months of fighting at the outset of the war.[73] In due course, however, something strange happened: the Fourteenth Army faded into memory, but the British FEPOW experience entered a mythic form, offering enormously popular tales of 'stoic resilience' through novels and their adaptation for the big screen.[74] The critical and commercial success of these productions meant that the British experience of captivity would dominate the wider anglophone imagination and, for that reason, Chapter 4 begins with a cultural history of the FEPOW genre from the 1950s to the present day. This serves as necessary background to two relatively recent sources, set in wartime Japan as well as the United States (Jim Lehrer's *The Special Prisoner*) and in occupied Japan and twenty-first century New Zealand (Peter Wells' *Lucky Bastard*). Having joined a well-established, but largely British, canon of FEPOW fiction writing, the American and New Zealand contributions de-emphasize the importance of 'original' captivity narratives and focus instead upon the field of memory in which FEPOW narratives are increasingly marginalized or problematized. For Lehrer, this means focusing upon the politics of apology and, in particular, the controversies surrounding the 1995 commemorations; whereas, in Wells' case, a growing New Zealand enthusiasm for oral histories decenters the knowledge landscape away from national and imperial histories to focus on individual stories. In neither instance do the characters gain any satisfaction from their investigations, for they inhabit a socio-political milieu in which reactions to stories of Japanese prison guards abusing their White captives trend toward indifference or outright dismissal.

The canon of FEPOW novels has developed in sophistication by acknowledging Japanese atrocities as the genre's nominal *sine qua non* while avoiding moral one-upmanship as the be-all and end-all of every story, a project that continues in recent writing from Australia and Malaysia.[75] Balanced imperatives of this sort, I would argue, must at some point become the norm in every genre of Pacific War literature—arguably in all war genres—if they are to avoid appearing moribund. Yet this is far easier to advance as an ideal than it is to achieve as an outcome and there are some canons of war writing, of which Manhattan Project novels are a candidate example, that would serve as a case in point were it not for revitalizing contributions that originate in other anglophone literary traditions. As befits a wartime episode that punctuated the end of the war with great finality, my last chapter is given over to the ways in which the atomic bombings of Hiroshima and Nagasaki fell like a thunderclap on the anglophone public consciousness and thereafter underwent a steady occlusion in the face of 'preferred' narratives. In the United States, the country most readily associated with the Bomb and its production, it was preferable to dwell upon the atrocities of an Axis power—in particular, the Nazi Holocaust—than to allow that one's own side might have perpetrated a needless act of annihilation.[76] Manhattan Project novels tended to focus on the scientific and industrial dimensions of the Bomb and thereby made this process of occlusion a good deal easier. Yet the Bomb's production never existed as a purely scientific and industrial endeavor—'pure,' that is, both in the moral and intellectual sense—wholly separate from its prospective application in war.[77] Over time, therefore, the authorial project of bifurcating the Manhattan Project story from the destruction of Hiroshima became steadily harder to sustain. In the South Pacific, the rise of antinuclear politics in New Zealand would likewise have the effect of focusing the national attention upon a 'preferred' narrative at the expense of raising awkward questions of complicity in the use of the Bomb. Chapter 5 therefore concludes my study by focusing upon two works that juxtapose the character subjectivities of the atomic bomb scientist and the atomic bomb survivor, intertwining their postwar lives in Canada (Dennis Bock's *The Ash Garden*) and New Zealand (James George's *Ocean Roads*).

By the end of this book, it should be clear that efforts to move beyond the analogously hostile islands of 'discrete' genre canons have not only furnished arresting forms of Pacific War literature, but now point the way toward an approach that tomorrow's fiction writers ought to embrace more fully (history writing, of course, is another matter and the question of whether or not the same imperatives are at play in that domain is one that I gesture toward but have refrained from pronouncing upon). Should the trend reach maturity and gain the sustained attention it deserves, the emergent texts may yet contribute to an evenhanded acknowledgment of Second World War storytelling traditions beyond Europe. For the time being, though, it is not conceding much to say that most literary depictions of the Southeast Asian and Pacific theaters of war remain just as 'forgotten' relative to Europe as did General Slim's British Fourteenth Army. That this reflects readerly and, perhaps, scholarly preferences more than it does the merits or demerits of the texts themselves will become apparent in the pages that follow. By inference, readers will grasp that I am not much taken with an approach that sweeps aside the issue of why one region of a war should gain more attention than another. Instead, I enquire into the ways in which this attention deficit came about and go on to ask how literary writers may have taken account of it in their narratives. My strongest contention is that answers to these and equally pertinent questions reveal themselves more easily through comparisons across literary traditions than would be the case in a single tradition. Given the scale of the American military commitment to the Pacific theater, the inclusion of literature from that quarter will likely remain a fixture in any such study (notwithstanding that certain genres show more diverse origins, FEPOW narratives being a case in point). If New Zealand material, by contrast, appears rather peripheral alongside the American canon, then the positionality written into such judgments will make the following observations all the more salient.

1 Revelations and Comedy: The Combat Novel

War is a lot of things and it's useless to pretend that exciting isn't one of them. It's insanely exciting. The machinery of war and the sound it makes and the urgency of its use and the consequences of almost everything about it are the most exciting things anyone engaged in war will ever know. Soldiers discuss that fact with each other and eventually with their chaplains and their shrinks and maybe even their spouses, but the public will never hear about it. It's just not something that many people want acknowledged.
—Sebastian Junger, *War*

I can't think of any good American fiction that is not anti-war.
—Joseph Heller, "Conversations with Joseph Heller"

That a soldier's experience of war offers anything other than moral, psychological, or physical degradation is not a common observation in writerly circles. After a certain amount of rhetorical throat clearing, the pleasurable dimensions of war generally arise parenthetically (after 'the fact' of its rupturing processes). According to Vietnam War veteran William Broyles, Jr., the reason for this evasiveness has to do with the social conditions of civilian life, which render war's pleasures unspeakable: "Nothing in the way we are raised admits the possibility of loving war. It is at best a necessary evil, a patriotic duty to be discharged and then put behind us."[1] On occasion, narrative interludes in film and print media break the mold and provide clues that servicemen, in the field at least, might not always share this point of view. Thus, Staff Sergeant Sykes, a character in the 2005 film *Jarhead*, takes Lance Corporal Swofford into his confidence during an awestruck moment in front of the towering Kuwaiti oil fires of 1991: "I mean, who else gets a chance to see shit like this?" In the dead of night and far from human habitation, their mutual affirmation is mellow to the point of insouciance and, to the skeptical eye, ultimately dependent on the absence of hostile forces. One wonders, to put it bluntly, whether either of them would feel as they do were they looking down the barrels of enemy riflemen. That, presumably, would be different shit, and yet not enough to dissuade civilians from seeking a similar sense of unit cohesion. In his memoir, soldier-priest Sam Childers is characteristically upfront about the allure of cooperative behavior that he experienced during the Second Sudanese Civil War: "One of the reasons I like war is that you don't find many people arguing on the battlefield. [. . .] You can go to a war zone and pretty much work in peace. Everybody there is humble and looking out for the common good because their lives depend on it."[2]

Peace, tranquility, and communal living might not sound like the typical conditions of a war zone and hardly compensate for the awfulness of combat. At least, one would presume not. Again, though, the responses of civilians who voluntarily go to war confound expectations—their own, more often than not—by not always or necessarily lapsing into numbed horror. Take war correspondent Sebastian Junger for example, a man whose exposure to combat in post-9/11 Afghanistan was not less than Swafford's during the Gulf War of 1990–1991, and whose recollection follows the moment in which his Humvee hits an Improvised Explosive Device or "IED." In the firefight that ensues the author did not lose his mind. On the contrary, he perceived his situation with a piercing clarity, which, as he goes on to explain, was both profound in itself, and also anticipated the post-combat realization that battlefields alone provide such sensations: "Don't underestimate the power of that revelation. Don't underestimate the things young men will wager in order to play that game one more time."[3]

Nothing that Junger states at this juncture is distinct from twentieth-century precedents, be they literary or experiential. Although his book sits alongside a series of Iraq War literary works that take traumatized veterans as a core narrative focal point, passages like those above caution readers against assuming that trauma is inevitable.[4] The pleasures of war and the horrors of war have long since jostled for attention as themes within the literary works they inhabit, just as they do within the scholarship and pedagogy that draw upon them, although, in practice, the horrors of war receive a good deal more emphasis from both quarters. To paraphrase Joseph Heller, I can't think of any good English-language war writing that can't be *read* as anti-war and which hasn't been categorized as such in a majority of critical and historical works that draw upon it.[5] These reading practices constitute the most ethically informed and intellectually astute models in a majority of instances, so long as one bears in mind that not every anti-war writer is intrinsically thus at every turn.

Be that as it may, the supposition that anti-war sentiments occupy a place on a spectrum of responses to war, instead of comprising the whole of the spectrum to varying degrees, remains a disturbing one. The reasons are familiar: whether one takes the poetry of the Great War, the prose of the Vietnam War, or the online blogs of more recent military ventures as a reference point, anglophone culture is suffused with instances of indifference to human suffering, particularly as regards the first two cases. Indeed, the moral lessons of the Great War and the Vietnam War have become retrospectively intertwined, as Vietnam War veteran Ron Kovic noted in his autobiography *Born on the Fourth of July* (1976), and as the New Zealand conscientious objector Archibald Baxter pointedly underscored in the Foreword to the 1968 edition of his book *We Will Not Cease* (1939).[6] As an addendum, one must also acknowledge that there are those who sidestep moral issues altogether and, rather than condemning war, adopt a celebratory mode after the fashion of, say, Studs Terkel's 1984 book *The Good War*. Typically, this involves taking the Second World War, particularly military campaigns such as the Battle of Okinawa or the liberation of Nazi concentration camps, as a chance for vainglorious posturing—a practice that literature scholar Marianna Torgovnick eye-rollingly describes as 'guy talk.'[7]

Fortunately, when it comes to literary writing one seldom encounters a work that wholeheartedly falls into the guy talk category (Broyles, Childers, and Junger could hardly be described that way). As literature scholar Samuel Hynes asserts, war may be enjoyable at certain times but war lovers do not, as a general rule, make good writers.[8] That being said, one must take care when reading the literatures of the Second World War to keep in mind that, in the interwar years, there was no one slogan or perspective on war that encapsulated the opinion of literary people in the United States or New Zealand—and, by extension, no dominant 'mode' of war writing. In the latter country, those veterans who decried war found their sentiments eclipsed by self-congratulatory literature, public memorials, and official histories celebrating New Zealand's contribution. Imperial loyalty kept many New Zealanders from fully participating in an anti-war culture that was expressed far more vocally by their British counterparts.[9] As for the United States, a latecomer to the Great War, questions over the war's 'inherent' meaning recede and blend into debates between isolationists and interventionists, both of whom made full use of the war as a reference point to advance their respective positions.[10] These twin contexts offer correctives to the critical orthodoxy, still with us today, that those who came of age during the Great War saw themselves as bearing witness to the destruction of Western civilization and thereafter marched in lockstep with Britain's anti-war literati. The so-called 'Lost Generation,' which included Ernest Hemingway, John Dos Passos, e. e. cummings, William Faulkner, F. Scott Fitzgerald et al. was, of course, aware of this perspective and integrated it into their writings at certain points. Between these writers and the likes of Siegfried Sassoon, C. S. Lewis, J. R. R. Tolkien, and Robert Graves, however, lay a significant distinction in life experience, for whereas these British writers had all gone to war as enlisted servicemen destined for combat, none of the Americans could claim likewise. Fitzgerald, Hemingway, and Faulkner were all turned down for full military service or command, a humiliation that they went to considerable lengths to ameliorate or cover over in their writings and private lives (Hemingway, like Dos Passos, served in the ambulance corps on the Italian Front, a form of participation that he viewed as an embarrassing substitute). As literature scholar Keith Gandal has compellingly argued, these American authors "were not literally lost in the war, or figuratively as a result of it; they "lost out" in the meritocratic competition to be significant players in the "Big Game."[11]

Today the dominant memory of the Western Front is one of fixed lines for which infantrymen on both sides were killed or wounded in a series of pitched battles that, at most, brought pyrrhic victories. How anyone could have regretted 'losing out' when the costs of participation were readily apparent is difficult to fathom. Still, it is possible to get close by recollecting that, when the Americans arrived in significant numbers during the Summer of 1918, the Western Front was becoming more mobile. Inhabiting this impossibly different reality, the doughboys' impression of war differed in crucial respects from that of the other Allies and, for them if no one else, a degree of romanticism was still just about possible (tempered by a hushed acknowledgment that others saw things rather differently).[12] Had any man in the American Expeditionary Forces gone on to become a writer of some ability, then the literary history of the Great War might look rather different than it does now or at least more varied. Instead, whether they agreed with the anti-war position in full, in part, or not at all, Americans during the interwar years were left with the unavoidable impression that the most significant anglophone perspectives on the war had come from Britain.

Fighting in the Pacific

The Second World War, and its Pacific theater in particular, would be a different matter. Those literary writers who came to the topic did so with a self-confidence that was born of the knowledge that they were American veterans aspiring to be authors (rather than vice-versa). One feels no surprise, given this difference, that combat emerges as a major narrative component in all the major novels, often incorporating protracted considerations regarding the nature of the American military as an institution, a strong theme in Norman Mailer's *The Naked and the Dead* (1948) and James Jones' *From Here to Eternity* (1951). (Mailer in particular was prepared to explore—or unwittingly discovered within himself—dark areas of the unconscious that did not always show American soldiers in a flattering light, his premise being that the mechanization of war was reshaping minds, leaving automata where there were once human beings).[13] Other writers focused on the grueling challenges of training exercises, such as the long route marches inflicted on US Marines in New Zealand, graphically portrayed in Leon Uris' *Battle Cry* (1953); or the terminal shock that awaits a married couple who have yet to learn of their son's death, delicately ventured in Anton Myrer's *The Big War* (1957). In all these cases, combat narratives invariably observed that the war had involved not one but two enemies: the Japanese, supposedly the principal opponents; and the jungle environment, on a less deadly but more consistent basis. This was something new that neither the Great War writers, nor those Second World War writers who had served in Europe, had encountered or described. In an experimental novella that sought to capture a soldier's thoughts during one hour of battle, Peter Bowman itemized the jungle's discomforts as follows:

Leeches make getting next to your skin their one ambition,
and enter openings in your clothes—the fly, the collar,
and even the holes for laces in your jungle shoes.
They are perfectly at home anywhere, including up your rectum,
and when they bite they secrete a kind of juice
that lets them suck blood without fear of its clotting.

No doubt the fabulous little sweat-bee is around here, too,
ready to foregather in mass meetings on any exposed parts
of your body and drink your perspiration so that they
may produce a form of inedible honey from your sweat.

There are large and hairy spiders with eight-inch leg spreads
that are relatively harmless, and there are little, unnoticeable spiders
that will strike without warning and hurt you like hell.

Under leaves, logs and stones are scorpions and land crabs
and centipedes dancing jigtime on their long rows of legs.

And hovering expectantly above them are chiggers and cone-nosed bugs
and an unlimited selection of airborne midges and flying bedbugs.
Ants are everywhere. Large, small, medium—red, black and white.
Some bite and some sting and some bite and sting.
The biting ones overwhelm their victims by attacking in swarms
while the stinging ones confine their maneuvers to sporadic infiltrations
and pour their formic acid into openings in the skin.

And then there is the universally uninvited parasite, the louse.
It is small, grey, wingless, with claws on its legs.
Once it deposits itself in the seams of your clothing
it will be almost impossible for you to remove it
and you will go right on getting lousier and lousier.

All the insects seem to sting with a Japanese accent.[14]

When authors like Bowman came to public attention, their military service would remain a consistent reference point alongside whatever literary merits they were deemed to possess. As time went by, however, this aspect became a mixed blessing insofar as some scholars would cite military service as an impediment that many authors had struggled to outgrow. Among those who judged this to be the case was the critic John W. Aldridge, who dismissed Mailer as a polemicist moonlighting as a fiction writer and Jones as an incorrigibly backward-looking author unable to move beyond the war years as a cultural moment.[15] When Jones passed away in 1977, an obituary likewise described him as "a self-willed anachronism out of step with his literary generation."[16]

A politer way of putting this is to say that Pacific War writers belonged to the literary period known as late Modernism.[17] As a corollary, one is almost tempted to conclude that a significant reason for the Lost Generation's stylistic innovativeness lay in the fact that they had escaped any collective identification as combat veterans, an ironic deduction given how sensitive they were to their past (in)experience in that quarter. Certainly, there is a degree of scholarly consensus that the Great War novelists were qualitatively more impressive than anything that emerged in the immediate aftermath of the Second World War.[18] As for the postmodernists, emblematized by Joseph Heller's *Catch-22* (1961), Kurt Vonnegut's *Slaughterhouse-Five* (1969), and Thomas Pynchon's *Gravity's Rainbow* (1973), Heller and Vonnegut both saw service in Europe while Pynchon, born just before the war began for the United States, enlisted in the US Navy during the 1950s. For present purposes, however, these details are less significant than the decision each of them made to set their war novels in Europe rather than the Pacific. Among the many conjectural reasons for this, besides the powerful impression that his time as a POW had made upon Vonnegut (on the receiving end of Allied bombs) and life as a bombardier had made upon Heller (delivering them), one finds three overarching differences between the two theaters. First, there were the large civilian populations, urban centers, and cultural landmarks through which American soldiers moved, all of which could serve as topics in their own right (beyond Australasia, the Pacific had few equivalents except the colonial cities of Manila and Singapore); then there were the attendant scenes of bombed-out urban landscapes, which usually occasioned at least some remarks from soldiers and authors, most of whom had family ancestry that originated in Europe (jungle habitat, by contrast, elicited nothing except disgust); and finally there was an awareness that the precedents established by the Lost Generation constituted a literary history that was intimately concerned with European affairs (the literary history of the Pacific, on the other hand, was tied to the South Seas genre, a colonialist legacy toward which American authors felt ambivalent).[19]

If American war writers were constrained by these challenges, of equal importance was the ideological dimension that had accompanied war in the Pacific and, in particular, the perspectives servicemen and authors entertained toward the Japanese enemy. Unfavorable opinions of the Japanese decisively formed at the tail-end of 1937, when news of the Nanjing Massacre first broke in the pages of the *Chicago Daily News* and *The New York Times*.[20] Immediately thereafter, commentators seeking to explain Japanese military behavior confined themselves to the briefest forays, a state of affairs that said little for the imagination of the journalist, but also hinted at a somewhat less than forthcoming response on the part of Japanese interviewees. The tenor was captured by Clark Lee, of the Associated Press: "In China acts of brutality by Japanese soldiers were commonplace, and when protests were made the Japanese officers always replied that they were unable to control their troops."[21] Properly speaking, Lee's explanation was, in fact, a non-explanation or, just as probable, the reinscription of the Japanese officers' non-explanation, neither of which were calculated to sustain an open discussion. Had Pearl Harbor not taken place, one may only speculate as to what deeper and lengthier pieces may have emerged, either in nonfiction or fiction form. Once Pearl Harbor did take place, such explanations as Lee's became embedded in the context of the story that mattered to Americans most, that being their own war against Japan. The origins of Japanese militarism thereafter mattered less than how it might be distinct from German

Nazism (the Cold War would result in a further diminishment of interest in China's wartime role, as evidenced by the fact that hardly any major anglophone novelists turned to the topic during that period).[22]

In an assessment of stories published in *Collier's* and *The Saturday Evening Post*, a 1941 article observed that "There were no pro-Nazi stories [published in the United States], although in many it was made clear that individual Germans may be gallant, courageous and efficient" (Nazism was generally portrayed as an illness affecting the German people, who were seen as its victims).[23] Japanese characters were never granted such qualifications in a major publication—not, at least, until Jeff Shaara's novel *The Final Storm* (2011). In films, the situation would be only partly ameliorated with the bi-national production *Tora! Tora! Tora!* (1970), which granted complexity to the Japanese in its depiction of the bombing of Pearl Harbor but frustrated some critics who deemed the finished result 'undramatic.' Ironically, this apparent shortcoming derived from the film's relative success in depicting the perspective of both sides. As anthropologist Geoffrey M. White observed, the film's decentered perspective meant that it had no unified subject position—an innovation for some, but quirkiness for those who were unused to such things.[24] Clint Eastwood's films *Flags of Our Fathers* (2006) and *Letters from Iwo Jima* (2006) solved this problem by splitting the two national perspectives between two separate productions. Cultural historian Leo Braudy summarized the result as follows:

> Each depends on a crucial aspect of modern war, which also has an eerie resonance in any visual art—the essential invisibility of one side to the other. [. . .] While both films use virtuoso special effects to present the horrific battle for Iwo Jima and each focuses on an array of combatants, the central revelation is that neither side really knows much of the human nature of the other.[25]

Whereas Eastwood underscored this truth in his films, literary works of the twentieth century had shown just how entrenched the habit was when it came to anglophone depictions of the Japanese. One only has to contrast their effacement with American depictions of the German enemy during the Great War, or the even more startling sympathies of fiction writers such as Irwin Shaw toward the German soldiers of the Second World War, and the neglectful stance toward Japanese characters appears altogether unusual.[26] So willing, indeed, were writers and artists to humanize the German enemy that the unhostile public attitude was a matter of persistent concern to President Roosevelt (as late as 1963, James Michener's novel *Caravans* would depict an American Jew and a German Nazi forging bonds of friendship in Afghanistan).²⁷

Something of the light-heartedness with which the erstwhile German enemy could be viewed survives in the form of British comedic productions for the small screen such as *The Army Game* (1957–1961), *Dad's Army* (1968–1977), *It Ain't Half Hot Mum* (1974–1981), and *'Allo 'Allo!* (1982–1992); and *The Phil Silvers Show* (1955–1959), *No Time for Sergeants* (1964–1965), and *Hogan's Heroes* (1965–1971) in the United States. Settings in occupied territories or in German-run prisoner of war camps allowed for diverse portrayals of enemy subjectivity, including the suggestion that not every German, whether in uniform or in 'civvies,' was a Nazi or a militarist. At no point, however, did a comedy emerge that encompassed situations or peoples based in East or Southeast Asia (partly because the production costs would have been higher and also because Southeast Asia had become associated in the public imagination with wars against Communism).²⁸ The most significant reason was that life in Japanese-run POW camps was known to have involved extremes of human suffering better suited to—although never fully explored in—dramatic miniseries such as *A Town Like Alice* (1981) and *Tenko* (1981–1984). Only once was an exception made. In 1958, Frank Tashlin's film comedy *Geisha Boy* starred Sessue Hayakawa in a brief cameo role that reprised his casting as Colonel Saito in *The Bridge on the River Kwai* (1957), a film that had understated the suffering of Allied soldiers in Japanese run camps.²⁹

If the war in the Pacific was seldom treated humorously this was not because island combat was barren of humor but because humor worked differently there than elsewhere. In an introduction to a journal issue on the topic of humor in war, Valerie Holman and Debra Kelly have drawn attention to the unpredictability of comedic practices, both in the messages conveyed and their reception: "At no time is it so important to be seen to belong, and to be able to situate the opposition, as in time of war. While distinctive types of humour characterize or describe different nations, political parties and social classes, humour of all kinds is highly complex and even contradictory in its effects."³⁰ Censors in Britain and Nazi Germany learned the truth of this when they both tried—unsuccessfully and for quite different reasons—to discourage witty remarks about the cowardice and general ineffectiveness of the Italian military under combat conditions.³¹ In the United States, on the other hand, the contradictions and tensions built into wartime humor were not immediately apparent. In 1941, the main task facing humorists was to make the prospect of military service, particularly the shock of basic training, look less daunting. To that end, film production studios released a number of titles that took a lighthearted view of military service, starring old favorites like Jimmy Durante, Bob Hope, and Laurel & Hardy, as well as new talent such as Abbott & Costello.[32] But whereas the ostensible purpose of this humor was to release tension, an opposite result was just as likely. In his 1975 memoir, James Jones recalled how it felt to inhabit this cultural moment:

> Humor was the civilian soldier's catharsis and saving grace. In 1941, before Pearl Harbor, a man named Marion Hargrove wrote a shallow, humorous book called *See Here, Private Hargrove*, about this peculiar process of induction into the draft, and achieved fame and riches and a cushy job writing for some army paper. His book worked because humor, even shallow humor, was bearable to the folks back home, more acceptable than tragedy while they were worrying about their sons' lives. Later Hargrove went to work for *Yank*. Meanwhile, the sons themselves dreamed in their sleep nightly, and frequently daydreamed consciously, of killing their "sadistic" sergeants in cold blood. Dreamed of murder, as it was hoped they would. Another step in the Evolution of a Soldier.
>
> It was as if a massive conspiracy had been put together, everybody conniving at it in secret accord, home-front civilian and serviceman alike, in a nation which had eschewed war as insanity, to keep the semblance of sanity through a semblance of humor and good will. Humor and good will, if pursued diligently enough, might keep back out of sight all the dark side of humanity which was now being let out, must be let out. Must be stimulated and used.[33]

Narratives of 'acceptable incompetence' by volunteers and draftees (the US term for a conscript) would outlast the war and become signature features in literary and filmic works on both sides of the Atlantic and even, to some extent, in Japan.[34] As Jones reminds us, however, during the war such humor served a camouflage function, enabling the American public to maintain the illusion of a cultured and considered response to war and, it must be added, easing the exaggerated fears of invasion that were commonplace in the wake of Pearl Harbor.[35]

This illusion was particularly glaring to the men in uniform, whose drill instructors emphasized that the war in the Pacific would not be like the war in Europe and that, by extension, American servicemen should not follow too closely the rules of war when engaging the enemy.[36] Even before they shipped overseas, therefore, attitudes were shaped and behaviors encouraged. Of course, not everyone fully succumbed to the 'dark side of humanity' and the change was not immediately evident even among those who did. A crude form of humor continued to provide some protection, as one veteran of the Guadalcanal Campaign later recalled: "The worse things got, the more sarcastic everyone got, instead of showing sympathy or emotions. I realize now—I didn't then, exactly—that humor fights horror."[37] Yet for every man who used humor this way, there were plenty more who indulged their violent dispositions at every opportunity and still more for whom combat forged a new self-awareness, one that defied summary categorization because it drew from them features of their unconscious or brought with it a heightened sensitivity to the surrounding environment that, to recall Sebastian Junger's term, was nothing less than revelatory. Add to these dimensions the sheer messiness of combat, in which a man might evince one characteristic in a given moment and a different one the next, and the idea of pigeonholing combat, or narratives of combat, solely under the 'anti-war' category looks dichotomized, to say the least. Far clearer, by contrast, is the way in which the Japanese enemy was presumed to be incapable of the combat revelations that Americans would see themselves as undergoing. For writers, it was easier to believe that the Japanese all thought alike, an assumption Peter Bowman followed in his conflation of enemy combatants with insect 'invaders.' If they were all the same, they could be treated the same in literary writing as they had been in wartime.

Charlie Company: Revelations of Combat

James Jones was no sentimentalist where the US Army was concerned, nor was he predisposed to glorify combat for its own sake. *From Here to Eternity* had introduced readers to the Old Army of the prewar years, an overtly nepotistic regime in which advancement was based not on merit but on currying favor with one's immediate superiors. Such an army cannot long survive exposure to combat, in which a premium is placed on leadership qualities, and in 1962 a sequel of sorts, *The Thin Red Line*, proved the point.[38] By this time, a number of literary works had already drawn attention to the difference between prewar 'regular' soldiers and those who entered the services after Pearl Harbor. In the opening to Leon Uris' novel *Battle Cry*, for example, the narrator recalls the shock he received when civilians turned up for basic training: "They told us to make Marines out of them. They were kids who should have been home doing whatever the hell eighteen-year-old kids do. God knows we never thought we could do the job with them ... God knows they fooled us."[39] Owing to its smaller size and keenness to maintain a separate military tradition, the Marine Corps would survive the influx of wartime draftees with its culture relatively intact, allowing Uris to wax nostalgic for this initial moment of uncertainty. The same could not be said for the Army, in which the influence of civilian culture was felt at every level.[40] One of the earliest casualties of war in Jones' narrative is the good relations between officers and enlisted men, with officers learning an especially harsh lesson once they notice how unloved they are.[41] Having landed on Guadalcanal, the men of Charlie Company are ordered to march through the jungle, the climate of which proves so debilitating that Fife, the company clerk, explodes in a fit of rage at Stein, the Captain: "Stein could not be sure he had not lost face with his company by deciding to ignore Fife. This tormented him and inside his helmet his ears burned. [...] At the side of the road in the thick leaves, almost in Stein's ear, some mad tropic bird screamed at them irritably, then whistled shrilly as though it had seen a woman."[42]

During the war, newspaper editorials had gone to some lengths to depict the resentment that GIs felt toward their superiors as largely good-natured in tone, but subsequent novelists such as Norman Mailer, as well as press coverage during the Korean War, made that resentment look more sinister.[43] By the early 1960s, these cultural trends had prepared the American public for less-than-flattering depictions of their military leaders, which allowed Jones to follow through by portraying almost every officer as wholly ineffectual.[44] In due course, Stein's lieutenants throw their lives away in frontal assaults that accomplish nothing, while Stein retreats into a bewilderment that recalls how he felt upon being told that his college ROTC training would mean being fast-tracked into active duty.[45] To Jones' contemporaries and fellow US Army veterans especially, these representations had a truth value that inspired their own commentary, a noteworthy example of which came from Norman Mailer who took a dig at the Army with his own trademark pugnacity: "*The Thin Red Line* ... is so broad and true a portrait of combat that it could be used as a textbook at the Infantry School if the Army is any less chicken than it used to be."[46] But if veterans were satisfied, early scholarly reviews tended to dismiss Jones' work on grounds that his rough-hewn syntax and grammatical howlers were too blatant to ignore.[47] To the trained eye, these shortcomings are as evident today as they were then and, of course, unalterable. For language purists, the challenge involves overlooking them to address other aspects so as to make clear that the novel still has value. Later studies tacitly adopted this approach and in 1998 the historian M. Paul Holsinger listed it among "the most world-renowned fictional re-creations of the military side of the conflict" in his survey of Second World War fiction.[48] More recently, scholars have examined Jones' novel through the prism of adaptation studies, sexuality studies, and masculinity studies, although if Mailer was correct in surmising that combat depictions lie at the heart of the narrative then a dedicated examination of this theme is a curious omission.[49]

Guadalcanal is where the combat takes place, a setting that might appear incidental to anyone who is unfamiliar with the battles of the Pacific War, although that may be because the brutality of the battles that followed have tended to overshadow it in public memory. As Paul Fussell reminds us, "The Japanese 'defense' of islands like Tarawa, Saipan, or Iwo Jima could hardly be called 'combat' at all in the traditional sense. It was suicide stubbornly protracted, and for the Americans, the experience argued the uselessness of agility and cunning when sheer overwhelming force was available. More than the Japanese and Americans died on those islands. Cleverness died too, and fine distinctions."[50] There is a reason why Fussell does not include Guadalcanal on his list, for in mid-to-late 1942 the war against Japan was in its early stages and, as both sides took the measure of the other, individual deaths still had a certain meaning.[51] Later on, as one campaign led to another and Japanese tactics transitioned from banzai charges to defense-in-depth, American deaths and casualties would reach such heights that Guadalcanal looked almost favorable by comparison. Alongside this, there was also an element of excitement that many felt at entering an 'exotic' setting (better imagined than inhabited, as the men of Charlie Company find out), as well as the trepidation of closing with an enemy whose tally of victories had made him appear almost unbeatable as an opponent (hence the 'Guadalcanal' inscription that the 1st Marine Division would carry on their insignia thereafter). As Jones states in the Special Note that precedes his narrative, "what Guadalcanal stood for to Americans in 1942–43 was a very special thing." The relief of victory was felt by civilians as much as servicemen, but combat veterans had encountered a plurality of 'special things' before the island's name was on everyone's lips, many of which were unknown to noncombatants or otherwise incomprehensible to them (wartime journalism such as Richard Tregaskis' 1943 publication *Guadalcanal Diary* touched on some of these, but only in a passing way).[52] *The Thin Red Line* could not bridge the experiential gap, but it alerted readers to the fact of its existence and, crucially, to the tortuous attempts that soldiers made to arrive at a fixed meaning for the situations they came upon and the changes their mentalities went through.

Literature scholar John Limon has suggested that Jones did not sufficiently describe his characters' interior lives.[53] Measured against war writing, past and present, they are thinly drawn in places and yet to focus upon qualities of characterization is to go down the same path as the language purists and detract attention from the author's principal purpose. Whether one examines them collectively or individually, none of the characters in *The Thin Red Line* are as important as the experiences they undergo and, more particularly, the process of psychological disintegration that combat entails. Again, geography matters here because the men who took part in the island invasion quickly discovered that, beyond the beaches and the coconut plantations, Guadalcanal had only two terrains: the jungle and the battlefield, with considerable overlap between them. Although retreat was theoretically possible, the Americans and Japanese were well aware that this would be difficult without a naval evacuation (a recourse to which the Japanese eventually resorted). Unlike the Allied invasion of Italy, say, in which rest and relaxation took place in any number of places behind the front lines, Guadalcanal afforded no such opportunities (nor was there an established 'line,' as such). Combat or the lead-up to combat was all that the men could expect and thus combat, along with topics that consciously veer from or draw inspiration from it, would necessarily figure as the dominant theme in any literary work based upon that campaign. As Jones well knew, this meant that the interiority of any given character would be responsive to multiple and contending stimuli, many of which would interrupt 'linear' thought processes or otherwise knock them out altogether. In short, the behavior of the mind under combat conditions was of paramount concern.

Strictly speaking, the first moment in which this discontinuity manifests, both in narrative terms and within the psychology of individual characters, comes before Charlie Company have had their first casualty and are tentatively crossing the threshold that separates a coconut grove from the jungle and, by extension, life as infantrymen to life as fighting infantrymen. For those who venture forth, the difficulty of this feat is made all the greater by the proverbial impenetrability of the jungle: "It really was a wall; a wall of leaves; meaty green leaves jostling and elbowing each other, with hardly a minute opening anywhere between them."[54] The men cannot take in this jungle as a topic for objective consideration, for they realize that to enter the jungle is to be taken in by it in ways that call one's agency and preconceptions into question. After coming upon a bloodstained shirt, what they feel is not anticlimactic so much as post-climactic, given that the battleground upon which they stand and the article they examine belong to a moment that preceded their arrival, and which is therefore closed-off to them experientially. Their initial idea of entering the jungle in order to deepen their familiarity with the land around them, and gain bragging rights among their fellow soldiers, gives way to the acknowledgment that they remain wholly uninitiated:

> A curious sense of unreality had come over all of them with the discovery of the shirt. The dripping, gloomy, airless jungle with its vaulted cathedral-like ceiling far above did not serve to lessen it. Fighting and killing, and being struck by death-delivering bullets which keyholed through you, were facts. They existed, certainly. But it was too much for them to assimilate, and left them with a dreamlike nightmare feeling which they couldn't shake off.[55]

As the men try to reassure themselves, the inadequacy of heroism and masculinity as cultural standards becomes plain. In itself, this literary feature is not uncommon in war literature and, as literature scholar Alberto Casadei persuasively argues, the sight of dead bodies is a trope that tends to evoke it: "There is nothing noble or solemn in the rotten corpse of the humble soldier—its materiality cannot be avoided, especially in the most degraded and dreadful traits (the dirtiness of the feet, the wide-open eyes)."[56] Battlefield Gothic, to give this aspect its proper name, requires an unflinching quality in the writer, although that very quality, pushed too far, might also betray the weakness of a writer who is desperate to avoid cliché. Jones spares his characters nothing, not even an assault on the olfactory system that accompanies the disinterment of a Japanese corpse, which sends them reeling in nausea.[57] Given that this entry-into-the-jungle scene occurs at a relatively early part of the narrative, and to only a handful of characters, it is probable that Jones took the opportunity to dispense with the ideal of heroism and the more time-worn antiheroic motifs in a nominal fashion, accepting the inevitability of falling into a few genre conventions as a necessary trade-off. Thereafter, the reactions that men evince under actual combat conditions becomes the primary topic.

Among the first of these is the realization that personal armament—firearms, knives, bayonets, and pilfered weaponry of any kind—serve as accoutrements that increase a man's standing among his fellows, but more in the realm of imagination than application. Before engaging the enemy for the first time, Charlie Company witness two soldiers from another company who are physically overpowered by the Japanese and dragged into captivity in plain view of their comrades. To Doll, who has gone to some trouble to steal a pistol, the sight is especially unnerving: "He meant to keep one round in [the pistol] at all times for his own head. But those guys there, they wouldn't have had time to use a pistol if they had it. If he was using his rifle or bayonet, how could he keep his pistol ready to hand? He couldn't. Doll decided he would have to give this problem more thought, serious thought."[58] Had Jones chosen to dwell upon Doll's serious thoughts, as John

Limon possibly wished he had, the narrative would then have taken on features familiar to writers at least as far back as the Civil War, during which many soldiers had likewise realized that the weapons they brought to the battlefield were unsuitable and, in a process known as 'simmering down,' better discarded altogether.[59] But events on Guadalcanal were not conducive to contemplation, and in Jones' narrative news of the bayoneting, decapitation, and mutilation of the two prisoners is swiftly followed by the spectacle of failed assaults upon Japanese-held defensive positions, along with the unwelcome news that Charlie Company will assault a more heavily defended position yet.

Once the assault begins, the narrative divides its attention between descriptions of the bloodbath that ensues and those who bear witness to it. In the 1960s, Americans had grown used to the sight of soldiers dying on the silver screen, but in Jones' narrative several dying men have a chance to describe their sensations to whomever is around them or, failing that, privately come to terms with their impending demise.[60] Thus Lieutenant Blane, upon being hit by rifle fire: "He lay on his back and, dreamily and quite numb, stared at the high, beautiful, pure white cumuli which sailed like stately ships across the sunny, cool blue tropic sky. It hurt him a little when he breathed. He was dimly aware that he might possibly die as he became unconscious."[61] Blane's realization is an example of what historian Yuval Noah Harari terms a 'materialist' revelation. In a 2008 monograph, Harari resituates revelations away from their religious background, envisaging them, rather, as the outcome of a pathway to knowledge over which an individual has little or no control. Revelations tend to be thrust upon people by force and the twentieth century was the era in which Americans and Europeans consistently imagined the battlefield as a site where these happenings were more common (although the idea is traceable as far back as the eighteenth century).[62] In his taxonomy, Harari identifies two schools of thought, put forward by veterans, as to what happens to the mind under combat conditions. The first, idealists, assert that essential truths become apparent once the cultural accumulations of everyday civilian life are stripped away, while the second, materialists, see no truths whatsoever beyond the materiality of the human bodies we inhabit. (Once the body acts or is acted upon, no 'purer mind' is liberated).[63] The conclusions of these different schools of thought are different, yet their acting assumptions are identical: "Combatants argue that the experience of war is completely independent of all previous cultural constructions. They agree that the tame experiences of peace are culturally constructed, but not so the wild experiences of war. War experiences reveal the truth precisely by blowing apart all cultural constructions."⁶⁴

Had Jones written in a didactic mode or narrated the experiences of only a few select characters, his novel might have veered toward explicit partisanship over this point. As they come across, however, the men of Charlie Company do not 'line up' one way or the other but manifest a striking range of responses, some of which are categorizable under one of Harari's terms, while others are chaotic—but not incoherent—amalgams of both. One frequently cited passage that contains both strains occurs when Bead, a rear-echelon fighter, departs from the rest of the company to relieve himself and is then surprised by a Japanese infantryman who attacks him. Fighting hand-to-hand, Bead manages to kill his opponent in a state of mind akin to an out-of-body experience (he performs actions, such as screaming, without being fully aware of them). To the passing of time he becomes hypersensitive and, upon returning to camp, he is overcome with unbidden recollections such as the punishment his mother meted out after she caught him masturbating as a child.⁶⁵ Features such as these veer toward an idealist revelation, but Bead's final thought on the matter is decidedly down-to-earth: "he realized now, quite suddenly, that he could survive the killing of many men. Because already the immediacy of the act itself, only minutes ago so very sharp, was fading."⁶⁶ Bead's battle with the Japanese soldier is a significant episode in the narrative, partly because it is loosely based upon the author's own experience on Guadalcanal, but also because it heralds a succession of deaths, almost none of which are gallant, graceful, or edifying.⁶⁷

As events proceed and the men of Charlie Company are killed in rapid succession, the narrative focuses upon individual characters and their thinking only at certain junctures, moments that are remarkable by virtue of their apparent disengagement from the battle raging around. Harari describes the idealist experience of combat in the following terms: "The flow of time changes, slows down, or stops altogether. Unfamiliar sensations appear, and familiar sensations mutate. Awareness becomes completely absorbed in the present moment, and combatants feel more alive than ever before."⁶⁸ Jones' own understanding of this type of experience finds its way into several sections, such as the moment when Bell, a somewhat older soldier, is pinned down by enemy fire and stares unwittingly into the glasses of a dead American:

> They had not fallen off. But something about their angle, at least from where Bell lay, magnified the open eyes until they filled the entire lenses. Bell could

not help staring fixedly at them, and they stared back with a vastly wise and tolerant amusement. The more Bell stared at them the more he felt them to be holes into the center of the universe and that he might fall through them to go drifting down through starry space amongst galaxies and spiral nebulae and island universes.[69]

None of the revelations are objectives in themselves, whether for characters or the author. They simply surface between moments, and, as the toneless quality of Bell's experience makes plain, they are not always or necessarily unpleasant. Once the tide of battle turns and Charlie Company have the advantage, there are even moments in which killing becomes a consistent and sought-after pleasure, as when Doll, having shot his first Japanese, feels his mind letting go of the culturally-conditioned prohibition against taking life; or when Bell volunteers for another mission, despite the obvious dangers, because of a desire almost sexual in nature; or when Queen runs amok in a spontaneous killing spree that proves his courage, but also turns out to be delightful in itself.[70]

None of these moments invalidate Jones' stance as an anti-war writer, but by their multifariousness they greatly complicate it. In like turn, the author's critique of the US Army as an institution, widely acknowledged since his first publication in 1951, certainly places him among contemporaries like Norman Mailer who asked probing questions about how the militarization of American culture might reshape civil society.[71] Literature scholar and US Army veteran Edmond L. Volpe recalled how infantry training had swallowed him up into a 'massive organization' and felt gladdened by Jones and Mailer's depictions of what this meant to the men involved.[72] But while this was a compelling truth, it was not quite the whole truth. Whereas the Army rode roughshod over individual interests and trampled on personal objections, it was also a sanctuary for working men who had been unable to escape the lingering effects of the Great Depression.[73] Understandably, therefore, Jones' feelings toward the Army were more ambivalent than they are sometimes made out to be, and the same complexity manifests in his literary renditions of combat. In fact, these aspects may interrelate, as historian John Bodnar has suggested, by pointing out that the Pacific War offered opportunities for American men to enjoy inflicting violence because, no matter how they felt about the Japanese enemy, their long-lasting frustrations at the effort to forge a life back home had at last found a sanctioned outlet.[74] As Jones' narrative draws to a close, however, it becomes apparent that Charlie Company's experience of combat has left the men forever changed. Ruinously stimulated or hopelessly disillusioned, the combat revelations they experienced can never be undone. As a long-term implication, this post-combat psychology would be a principal concern in Jones' posthumously published sequel *Whistle* (1978), but the author provides a hint of what is to come when some of the men go fishing with hand grenades and one of them prematurely explodes. Although apparently tragic, the event is taken matter-of-factly and as another chance for excitement: "When he finally woke up, Culp grinned groggily. 'I never felt a thing!' he said proudly. 'Didn't hurt at all!' His hand was already in a big wire frame that looked like a huge glove. Next day he was flown out to New Zealand."[75]

Captain Itoh: The Reluctant Beachcomber

Had *Whistle* been set in wartime New Zealand instead of Tennessee, then Jones not only would have portrayed life in a veterans hospital but also, quite probably, the peculiarities of social culture in a country to which many Americans had been posted for overseas service. With the exception of Leon Uris and James Michener, however, American authors largely ignored this topic, as did New Zealand's own war writers for whom the story of the 'friendly invasion' remained a touchy subject in the immediate postwar years. Far better to tell reassuring stories of soldiering, flying, or sailing and ignore the home front altogether. In practice, this also meant stories that were set in Europe and North Africa, reflecting New Zealand's earlier entry into the war and its commitment to supporting Britain's imperial defense system. Military contributions to the Pacific theater, always of secondary importance, would become secondary in official histories and literary writings also. Among those veterans who thought differently, only one would achieve any prominence as a fiction writer. After enlisting in the Army in 1942, Errol Brathwaite had transferred to the Air Force and was then posted to New Britain, an island off the coast of Papua New Guinea. His first novel, *Fear in the Night* (1959), followed the plight of a downed Allied aircrew evading a search party of Japanese sent after them in the jungle. Although not explicitly stated, his next work, *An Affair of Men* (1961), entailed an identical scenario from the perspective of the pursuing Japanese. The publication of the story coincided with the centenary of the *Otago Daily Times*, which held a literary competition and awarded the prize to Brathwaite's novel. Since then, humanities scholars have neglected both works, an understandable outcome where the first publication is concerned but regrettable in the case of the prize-winning piece. Setting aside questions of stylistic merit, the content of the latter not only fills a void in Japanese characterization left in the works of writers like James Jones, but also affords the opportunity to expose the form and purpose of 'enemy image' representations. This latter issue is of paramount importance, but it is also worth pointing out that the novel generates many of its most compelling representations through the use of irony, absurdity, and satire—in short, through a comedic turn that is, by now, relatively familiar to scholars of twentieth-century war literature, but almost unknown in a novel of the Pacific War. If Brathwaite's novel deserves to be recalled in current scholarship, therefore, one might measure its value both as a window into the representation of a specific ethnic-national group and as a window into the attempt, common to writers and artists who make war their topic, to adopt a comedic idiom as a means through which to express the social collisions and psychological deracination of war.[76]

The Japanese that appear in Brathwaite's novel are hardline military professionals whose commitment to a warrior code settles them comfortably within a lineage of anglophone portrayals—and a national self-image cultivated by Japanese authorities—rooted in the aftermath of the Russo-Japanese War and consolidated during the Second World War.[77] The resultant mode of narration reinstates the warrior stereotype but also counterbalances it with a sardonic touch that comes through on several occasions, as in Brathwaite's portrayal of a Sergeant's antisocial contemplations:

> Sergeant Hiryo was relatively unmoved by the fate of the corporal and his men. This was war, and patrols were ambushed and wiped out every day, somewhere. Death in action had been so commonplace for so long that he had long since denied himself the pleasure of forming deliberate friendships. Sometimes friendship happened unasked, and then death brought pain, which was not easily deadened, though it was possible to dull it for a time with saki [sic] or any other available intoxicant. This could only be resorted to during off-duty resting periods, and since the final killing of pain required many such libations, sorrow stayed with a man for a long time. Sorrow, or loneliness, there was little difference.[78]

Stylistically, this step-by-step 'how to' guide bears some resemblance to a military report inasmuch as it leaves nothing unsaid and becomes steadily more tone dead as it goes on. Or rather, it almost does. In fact, the final two sentences have nudged the sergeant's thoughts over the narrow boundary that separates thoroughness from superfluity, although at no point is the maudlin tone in any way compromised. By means of this (un)balancing act, the author tips his readers the wink: this is low bathos, coming to us from a military mind that has grown so used to treating situations in terms of cause and effect that it cannot sense its own absurdity. In moments of quiet brooding like Sergeant Hiryo's, Brathwaite reveals his talents in pedantic language and steady build-ups. Wielded in unison, this skill set allows him considerable control over the precise moment in which the realization of humor 'detonates' in the reader's mind.

The first way in which Japanese are objectified in Brathwaite's writing is, therefore, not dissimilar from parodies of German Nazis. In either case, it is not militarism in the abstract but rather a particularly military people who comprise the object of derision. Needless to say, such portrayals never contain any suggestion that some Allied nationals might be similarly predisposed toward regimentation, though, to be fair, Brathwaite's novel contains no Allied characters at all. Instead, the story is framed almost entirely around the circumstances of Captain Itoh and his attempts to persuade or force the inhabitants of Sipuri, a village in the New Britain hinterland, to work for the Japanese. When Itoh encounters the educated headman, Sedu, this process becomes drawn-out through a series of discussions that sees Sedu's Christian pacifism checking Itoh's arguments at every turn. The scenarios thrown up by their confrontations are of paramount importance in the representation of enemy subjectivity and repay scholarly attention. But first, where pedantic language is concerned, it is worth remarking upon Brathwaite's capacity to render social contact between Indigenous Pacific Islanders and Japanese subjects in buffoonish terms, as when Itoh commissions the local guide Torasi:

> He raised his voice and ordered the sergeant to call Corporal Terasaki, who stood near enough to hear the entire conversation anyway. The corporal did not stir, however, until Sergeant Hiryo had relayed the captain's order. It was a trivial thing now, but it wouldn't do for a marine to acquire the habit of short-circuiting chains of command. It could lose battles. The apparent ridiculousness of this method of communication between officer and adjacent N.C.O., therefore, did not strike the Japanese. To Torasi, however, who was an intelligent young man with a keen sense of humour, it was immoderately amusing, and he laughed delightedly. Sergeant Hiryo whirled about, crashing a fist into the black face, sending Torasi reeling back, hurt and bewildered.
> "You do not laugh at Nippon," Captain Itoh said furiously.[79]

Brathwaite's capacity to play off a premodern, non-military island culture against a Japanese warrior code, and thereby achieve an increased or redoubled comic effect at the expense of both, is a technique to which he has recourse on several occasions. The recurrent image of broad Black smiles—especially frequent in descriptions of Sedu—are one example of this, for they are intended as amusing in themselves but also as a social context that throws Japanese pedantry into high relief. The image of a Black smile, free of mockery but intolerably undisciplined, also raises the issue of how racism is situated within characterizations as well textual narrations. The following passage, lifted from one of Itoh's interrogations of Sedu, illustrates Brathwaite's capacity to make racism a feature of individual characters:

> "Suppose," the captain said musingly, "I ordered my men to kill every child in this village, now."
> "I understood you to say that you loved children."
> "That has nothing to do with it. It might, for reasons best known to myself, be expedient to kill them. Wouldn't you resist?"
> "I'm afraid I would," Sedu said.
> "I understood that to be against your principles."
> "I am far from being a perfect Christian," Sedu said.
> "And supposing I ordered them to kill every second man?"
> "I would protest, of course, and some of them would certainly offer a fight."
> "And if I ordered a beating for you, personally?"
> "I think, in any of those cases, I would feel extremely sorry for you."
> "For me!"
> "Yes. It's a sad thing to see a man add to his own load, Captain. I'm sorry for you now, but I certainly don't hate you. You are still my brother."
> "I'm afraid," Captain Itoh said, "that I can't say the same about you. In fact, I almost resent the suggestion that I am a brother to you. It isn't a personal reflection, Sedu, but our cultures and outlooks are worlds apart. Anything I have done has been for my country and my Emperor. Thank you. That's all I want to know."[80]

Once again there is a steady build-up in the form of a precisely controlled dialogue that terminates after a moment of perceived impudence, and again it is the terminus that provides the real insight into Japanese character traits.

That Itoh is a racist there can be no doubt, although his opinions are more explicit on other occasions, and were his position one of absolute domination then racism would merely comprise another facet in the ideological armature of an oppressor. But Sedu's doctrine and education tempt Itoh to cross swords with him at the level of dialogue and reduced to this, Itoh's expression of power is reduced to the power of expression. In such a scenario, racism does little to reinforce one's argument and may, in fact, suggest the absence of argument. One possible function of racism is thus to facilitate a greater objectification of Itoh as a racist, possibly allowing

White New Zealand readers to displace their own complicity in European colonialism onto the Japanese version. However, this conclusion cannot be too casually drawn, for there is no way of gauging whether Brathwaite's readers felt any such guilt—or desire to displace such feelings—at the time of publication. A likelier possibility is that the spectacle of racism serves a double function insofar as Brathwaite could thereby lull his readers into tacitly endorsing Itoh's observations whilst also objectifying him for making them. In short, Brathwaite's use of racist language enabled his readers to be luxuriously hypocritical, either caring little or suspecting themselves of nothing because the brazenness of Itoh's opinions is so obviously comical. A further example of the way in which comedy is overlaid upon racism involves Itoh's definition of civilization as coterminous with professionalism, a definition for which Black people—as non-professionals—can provide no positive example. As well as being a missionary, however, Sedu is also a medical doctor and Itoh cannot help but acknowledge him as such. But instead of rethinking his definitions, Itoh's discovery makes him adhere to his original hypothesis more strongly: thus Sedu, as a doctor, should not only prefer the built environment (as every civilized man should), he must also be non-Black.[81] These non-sequiturs are gently refuted by Sedu, whose own definition of civilization is one in which nonviolence, informed by Christian doctrine, holds as a universal principle.

The interplay of pedantic and racist language quickens the pace of Brathwaite's narrative but does not drive it. To generate the sort of situations from which they might convincingly derive, the plotline is organized around the unusual scenario—unusual, one might say, as far as White anglophone readers were concerned—of a community of Indigenous Pacific Islanders whose conversion to Christianity has proceeded without European intervention and whose foreign visitor, as a follower of Shintoism, is an animist. Prior to the novel's publication, the majority of anglophone cultural productions followed longstanding precedents in their depictions of Indigenous Black communities, whether on the African continent or in the Caribbean and the Pacific. Most often, the literary or filmic narratives resorted to cannibalism as a leitmotif, which in turn served as a pretext to and legitimization of European colonialism and as justification for converting Indigenous societies to Christianity.[82] In the 1930s, a number of American and British feature films had responded to the Great Depression and the resultant crisis in White masculinity by reinstating these perspectives. Nineteenth- and turn-of-the-century literary characters like Allan Quatermain and Tarzan appeared on screen against a backdrop of savage hordes, cowering porters, and beating war drums as sturdy role models who might, by their example, restore confidence to White American and British men.[83] Although no jungle films were produced in New Zealand, the Depression's effects had been similarly dire, giving rise to classic novels like John Mulgan's *Man Alone* (1939) and, retrospectively, Jack McClenaghan's *Travelling Man* (1976). By the time Brathwaite's novel appeared, however, the socio-economic situation could not have been more distinct. White masculinity in the 1950s and 1960s was occasionally troubled by social and vocational regimentation (the gift of the war years) but not joblessness. On the other hand, memories of jungle warfare against the Japanese were still vivid and, with the decolonization of European empires in process, the time was ripe to introduce a new characterization of the Black savage, not only 'noble' but potentially more 'civilized' than his nemesis. One way in which to read Brathwaite's novel is therefore to see colonialist binaries of civilization and savagery reversed in the figures of Sedu and Itoh, a shift that becomes more opportune when one recalls that stories of Japanese cannibalism were not unknown by the early 1960s. The Australian War Crimes tribunal, for example, had turned up several accounts of Japanese cannibalism that took place during the war; and Shohei Ooka's *Fires on the Plain* (1951), a novel that contained some disturbing depictions of cannibalism among the Japanese army in the Philippines, had appeared in English translation in 1957 and a film adaptation in 1959.

Tales of Japanese cannibalism that circulated prior to the publication of Brathwaite's novel may conceivably have provided a stimulus to his literary imagination, although it is just as probable that the residual tropes of 1930s jungle films were sufficient on their own. To be sure, the author's ability to reconstruct set pieces in the colonial tradition comes through strongly on a number of occasions, as, for example, when the drums at Sipuri prevent Itoh from falling asleep:

> Nervousness returned with the quiet chantings and flickering firelight and the drums, talking from near and far until the throbbing answers seemed to be coming from every direction, from every dark mountain and jungle-shrouded valley.
>
> Several times he was tempted to go to Sedu and withdraw his permission for the drum-talk, because the night was full also of quiet paddings and creepings, which could have been the little brown toads from the bush coming near to the light, or the gentle self-caressing of tree branches stirred by the night breeze, but which were impossible to identify positively because of the super-imposed, incessant mutter and throb of the drums.[84]

Itoh's fear of cannibalism is part and parcel of a general dislike for the jungle environment around him, an environment that he takes pains to keep separate from his person. As a literary trope, of course, antipathy toward the jungle habitat matched the real-life struggle on both the Allied and Japanese sides to keep jungle sores, malaria, poisonous insects, dehydration, and moldy equipment from becoming overpowering. Itoh's fastidiousness—his keen ear for jungle sounds, his watchfulness where the hanging of mosquito netting is concerned, his tap-tapping of boots for spiders—is a survival trait that would have been familiar to jungle veterans of the Pacific War (as well as those of the Malayan Emergency that had concluded one year prior to publication). His fear of cannibalism, on the other hand, derives almost solely from literary and filmic traditions.

Itoh's anxieties intrude into his back-and-forth conversations with Sedu and lead him to misjudge the customs and practices of his host. To pedantic language and racist beliefs, one may therefore add irrational fear as a constituent feature of Itoh's character, and when these traits act in concert, as they often do, the impression is one of mutual reinforcement. But even so, Itoh's 'representative' aspect would probably not have come across so strongly had Brathwaite not used context, and another literary history associated with that context, as a means to 'frame' his character. From the moment he first appears, marching through the jungle, Itoh's interior musings take up a considerable amount of the narrative. This trend holds throughout, and for good reason: Itoh is isolated, first as the only officer of the search party; then as an ethnic East Asian outnumbered by Indigenous Pacific Islanders; and, finally, by his location at Sipuri. Each form of isolation gives Itoh reason to keep his own counsel, but the last is especially significant because it involves a spatial, rather than communal, separation that exposes a gap in Itoh's training: he is unprepared to be a 'castaway' or 'beachcomber' far removed from comradeship and the prosecution of the war; and also, somewhat absurdly, entirely incapable of appreciating the potential advantages such a situation might bring. In his study of humor in wartime, literature scholar John Parkin has argued that incongruity—the sense, that is, that the practices and habits of everyday life have been disturbed—underpins a number of comedies, and that because wartime brings about a good deal of disruption, humor comprises a significant and underappreciated response:

> In war, normal behaviour patterns are disrupted, social organization comes under threat and may even collapse and people temporarily adopt different

roles and identities and confront situations for which they are unprepared and whose outcome is impossible to predict.[85]

Among the more famous satirical war novels, Joseph Heller's *Catch-22* (1961) goes a long way toward illustrating the incongruity of war and, importantly for present purposes, the lure of a guaranteed safe haven. Throughout the novel, the protagonist Yossarian yearns for a respite from the war in Europe and is ecstatically jubilant when Orr, another character, demonstrates by his own example that refuge can be sought and found.

To readers at the time of publication, a safe haven located somewhere in an ocean of small islands and atolls, among which the habitable ones had either changed hands or been subject to consideration as potential strategic outposts, was a possibility that evoked a certain wistfulness. Admittedly, the war had ushered in a new wave of 'popular' cartography, detailed study of which might have made the safe haven hypothesis appear rather unlikely.[86] But in the United States and Australasia, a body of postwar fiction writing dispensed with such skepticism, having as it did a great deal more to do with fantasies of an 'exotic' Pacific than any branch of scholarly enquiry (they were anticipated in this by World War II servicemen, who had entertained fantasies of exotic islands long before they shipped overseas).[87] Addressing the question of whether industrial warfare made clichés of an exotic Pacific more difficult to perpetuate, Judith A. Bennett has emphasized the power of lineage:

> For most of the Pacific War, the battleground was unfamiliar. Unfamiliarity left spaces for speculation. Beginning with the eighteenth-century European explorers' accounts of 'discovery' of the Pacific Islands, an exogeneous parade of commercial, evangelical, and intellectual entrepreneurs peddled their versions of islanders, causes, and schemes, whether as critiques of their own societies or for investment, conversion, and colonization. Because of such selective representations, to many outsiders these faraway islands had become a hotbed for their dreams, fantasies, and fears.[88]

In a roll call of names and titles given over to dreaming and fantasizing the Pacific War, James A. Michener's *Tales of the South Pacific* (1947) must feature strongly, possibly alongside the Australian Charles Shaw's *Heaven Knows, Mr. Allison* (1952), and the New Zealander Olaf Ruhen's *Scan the Dark Coast* (1969), each of which featured protagonists in highly specialized and/or isolated roles.[89] The 'signature' feature of such works is that they attempt to convince their readers that the war had been only minimally unpleasant, and that war might not have registered strongly among some island communities.⁹⁰ When the inevitable happened and Hollywood began to churn out its own versions of these fantasies, some film treatments even borrowed a trope from the jungle movies of the 1930s, specifically that of the White heroine in need of saving or 'taming,' to suggest that the Pacific War had, at various times and places, involved more Eros than Thanatos.⁹¹ Ruefully conscious of his contribution to such representations, Michener would later offer the following disclaimer: "I was always mindful of the fact that while I was exploring the joyous wonders of Polynesia many of my friends were landing on quite different islands: Tarawa, Saipan, Okinawa. I never forgot the difference."⁹²

One notes how careful Michener was to specify his own awareness of 'the difference' rather than asserting that this sensitivity manifested in his fiction writing. As he well knew, his Pulitzer Prize winning novel, the Rodgers and Hammerstein musical, and the 1958 film version, had all spurned depictions of combat in favor of the lone man image or what literary scholar Jolisa Margaret Gracewood alliterates as a 'castaway in khaki.'⁹³ In Brathwaite's portrayal of Captain Itoh, the features of wartime castaway narratives—namely, refuge and sensual delights—comprised stock tropes that the author found especially useful. Taking the fantasy version of life in the Pacific as a point of contrast, Brathwaite constructed Itoh's psychology as that of a reluctant beachcomber: he who finds himself in an enviable and long-lasting refuge but whose thoughts run to war. All else is carefully chipped away, beginning with the sex drive, presumably a distraction to any castaway, but, for Itoh, a mere afterthought to the climax of his death in battle. While resting at Sipuri, for example, a momentary daydream of his wife blurs into the fantasy of Japanese women receiving his cremated ashes, an egomaniacal scenario the novel does nothing to confront, for it fits too readily into the stock explanations of enemy psychology.⁹⁴ Bordering on anhedonia, the deflected eroticism provides the first glimpse of someone for whom violence is a desirable end in itself, rather than a last resort or even just one option among several.

If isolation reveals Itoh to be sexually repressed, journeying—or, rather, the inability to complete a journey—brings forth an equivalent response, this time manifesting in more explicit violence. On several occasions, Itoh attempts to leave Sipuri, only to find that he has unwittingly gone full circle as a result of human error or defective equipment—or, as Sedu prefers it, divine intervention.⁹⁵ Such episodes bring Itoh to a pique of fury, ultimately revealing him to be a tool of violence rather than its master.⁹⁶ By keeping his character at a single location against his will, Brathwaite comes close to employing yet another scenario familiar to the war generation: that of

Shangri-La, a supernatural refuge from war that is possessed of 'magical' or otherwise inexplicable properties of benefit to its inhabitants.[97] An additional way of reading Brathwaite's novel, therefore, involves taking this formula and then observing the mismatch between place and the newcomer who might—should he wish—reside there. Both Shangri-La and Sipuri are self-enclosed and withdrawn, hugging a select few in a protective embrace, and yet Itoh desires no such protection. Indeed, the absurdity of his predicament is in no small part linked to his refusal to take hold of the lifeline Sipuri represents. The prospect of kindred spirits, united in self-preservation and mutual regard, does not slip away, but Itoh's psychology distorts the tone of the narrative, taking it, once again, toward bathos. By transforming refuge into entrapment, Brathwaite transforms Itoh from a professional military man into a recalcitrant oddball. Should the reader likewise observe him as such, there would then be but a small step between pondering what one might do in Itoh's place and speaking of a quixotic Japanese 'difference.'

American novels of the Pacific War sometimes include depictions of Japanese psychology—through the underbrush, as it were—and yet they are few and far between. In Brathwaite's novel, there is no need to seek out the Japanese character: he stands present and accounted for from beginning to end. To take a dedicated literary representation of the Japanese serviceman such as Brathwaite's is, therefore, methodologically expedient. It also repays the researcher's efforts by providing insights into the ways in which distinctive literary and filmic trends converged within (upon) Brathwaite's characters, meaning, most obviously, jungle narratives and, in particular, castaway narratives. The purpose of the latter is to place the Japanese subject under a textual microscope, cordoned off from his fellows, the better to identify (reify) his essential particulars. Certainly, there is something scientific about the way that Brathwaite systematically removes Itoh's companions, through ambush, headhunting, and suicide, to expose the corresponding effects this has upon the captain, *homo sapiens japonensis*. One might draw comparisons with the way in which social removal plays out in *Heart of Darkness* (1902), although Conrad's novel shocked readers by exposing the interiority of a European subject, whereas Brathwaite's text, by contrast, is not meant to shock at all. On the contrary, the story's main purpose is to confirm all the suspicions that readers were presumed to have entertained in respect to Japanese behaviors. Admittedly, the Captain's Machiavellian analyses of motives and situations serve to camouflage these developments somewhat, although at no point do they remove him as the object under consideration, and ultimately his contemplations only take him further toward the point of violent hysteria that is the alleged terminus of all Japanese psychology.

Eventually and inexorably this violence turns inward, as in the following scene:

> Sedu was all he had claimed to be, no more and no less, and had been all the time. He had no strength, yet he had beaten Captain Itoh, and thereby disgraced Nippon. Honour was almost irreparably tarnished. Almost. Yet something of honour might still be salvaged. There was a way. He was sitting up, now, and he turned his head and gazed at the table, and at that which lay upon it.[98]

At this point, the contest between the worldviews of two characters is replaced by a contest between two stereotypes: the cannibalistic savage and the suicidal Japanese. The narrative cannot accommodate both (and also cannot shed itself of both) and thus one of these stereotypes, with the tropes that go along with it—the drums, the fire, the pot, the dances; or the room, the mat, the sword, the bared chest—must prevail. When Sedu chastises Itoh for his lack of "decent instincts," Sedu's position as 'the cannibalistic savage,' already at odds with his character, stands revealed as wholly incompatible with his textual role as well.[99] What this appears to mean is that Itoh, saved from the pot, must then commit 'hara-kiri,' foreclosing his life, the novel, and the reader's perception of enemy psychology in one fell swoop.

Press Rewind: (Re)Mastering the Enemy

Brathwaite and Jones published their works in the early 1960s, after which World War II combat novels set in the Pacific would become more of a rarity. Subsequent attempts to revive the canon never matched the success that these two authors achieved, partly because the following three decades saw the emergence of a cognate branch of fiction involving narratives that were of the Pacific War in an ideological sense, even if they were no longer set in the Solomon Islands or New Britain. The majority of these would recapitulate the idea of Japan's essential cultural 'difference,' harnessing it to frightening scenarios of a possible 'takeover' of Western countries at the economic or corporate level. These literary works were not all of a piece, as the frequency and severity of the discourses they disseminated depended on factors that were simultaneously shared by anglophone cultures and yet, as the next chapter will reveal, specific to each in their particulars. In more innocuous cases, a double-edged humor served to release tension and poke fun at the discourse of Japanophobia rather than recirculating it in a didactic form. Such was the case in English humorist Sue Townsend's novel *The Queen and I* (1992), which pushed the premise of a Republican Britain into the realm of the burlesque. Much of the story centers upon the Royal Family who, following the Queen's abdication and eviction from Buckingham Palace, find themselves rehoused on a council estate. The new era does not bring financial prosperity to Britain, however, and after the national economy is bankrupted by profligate welfare policies, Japan finances a bailout (as part of the deal, Britain's Royal Family is forcibly intermarried with the Imperial Family).[100]

Comedic narratives such as Townsend's were made possible by Britain's location in the North Atlantic, a geographic remove that brought a studied nonchalance to East Asian power in the years of Japan's 'economic miracle.' Writers from countries with Pacific borders were less cool-headed. The expatriated New Zealander Ian Richards, resident in Japan during the years in question, drafted an unpublished manuscript, *Kuromaku* (2005), using the thriller genre to imagine a series of acrimonious confrontations between a British man and leaders of the Japanese corporate world. In this instance, a British protagonist may have been a more convincing choice than a New Zealander, because writers of the thriller genre drew heavily on current affairs and New Zealand possessed no domestic industries of interest to the Japanese. The genre was embraced earlier and more enthusiastically by American authors, for whom the prospect of smarter, faster, more efficient workers and machinery outcompeting American industries warranted dedicated attention.[101] Oftentimes, American thriller writers would return to the notion of Japanese people as inherently fanatical and then conjoined this character trait to a supposed vengeful streak that manifested in conspiracies to reverse the defeat of 1945 or otherwise topple the United States from its superpower status.[102] Thus, the combat of the Pacific War was displaced onto an analogous plain and, as we shall see, American and New Zealand authors would attain an unwitting ideological complementarity much as their predecessors had.

2 Camera Men: Postwar Japan-Bashing

Years ago, at the height of the crisis in which Japanese imports were devouring our domestic market like sharks at the belly of a whale, I had vowed never to buy a Japanese car. But my wife's sewing circle insisted that the only solution to our driveway problem was an all-wheel-drive Subaru. Every patriotic bone in my body screaming, I was dragged into the orbit of the rising sun. Our Subaru skimmed up the driveway just as my wife's consultants had said it would, but otherwise it was as glamorous as a breadbox. The propaganda about Japanese cars proved true: they rarely needed repair. We replaced our third Audi with a Japanese version of (as the dealers delicately put it) "near-luxury," an Infiniti; we have propped up the staggering Japanese economy and added several former Detroit assemblers to the welfare rolls. My fifty-year ride on rubber tires has become a guilt trip.
—John Updike, "My life in cars"

Now the long-feared Asiatic colossus takes its turn as the world leader, and we—the white race—have become the yellow man's burden. Let us hope that he will treat us more kindly than we treated him.
—Gore Vidal, "The Day the American Empire Ran Out of Gas"

The 1940s through the early 1960s witnessed the high tide of the Pacific War combat novel, a genre that had clear-cut ideological and narrative parameters. Not the least of these involved drawing a clear line between Allied and Axis characters vis-à-vis their individuality and personal qualities. In the best-known literary works, Americans were usually the main characters and sometimes the only characters at all. Thus 'the line' was drawn invisibly, leaving questions of Japanese subjectivity a moot point. In 1961, as we have seen, New Zealand author Errol Brathwaite flipped this narrative investment on its head and demonstrated that it was possible to write a novel that dwelled upon the interiority of an enemy combatant whilst denying that character a capacity for psychological development at every turn. As an end in itself, and as a means to naturalize this locked-in characterization, Brathwaite adopted a comedic mode that reinscribed the difference between Allied and Japanese subjectivities at an implicit level. Whether a Japanese character was exiled to the margins of a narrative or ostensibly occupied the centerground, the psychological adaptability of Allied characters would always demonstrate innate capacities that were beyond him.

This literary period coincided with the re-industrialization of Japan, a process that, in turn, took place in the still larger context of Cold War geopolitics. American scholars and public commentators anxiously took on an instructive pose toward erstwhile enemies, the hope being for a redoubled commitment to a capitalist system of global trade. Their expectations seldom ran high. Anthropologist Ruth Benedict, for example, qualified her optimism in the following terms: "Japan, if she does not include militarization in her budget, can, if she will, provide for her own prosperity before many years, and she could make herself indispensable in the commerce of the East."[1] The salient point here was that Americans hoped that Japanese industrialists would market their products abroad—but only in the sphere of Japan's former colonial possessions.[2] Some thirty years later, the short-sightedness of this perspective was clear to one and all, for by then, Japan was well on the way to achieving the status of economic giant (circa late 1970s to 1994). Throughout the anglophone world, news coverage and cultural productions fixated on this development and dusted off old binaries of the war years through a rhetorical sleight of hand that substituted finance and economics for military conquest. In the United States especially, the 1980s would become an apprehensive decade for business and labor union communities who felt, rightly or wrongly, that the strength of Japanese corporations, measured both in purchasing power and product quality, would raise unemployment levels and outcompete domestic industries.[3] Sometimes a comedic 'spin' made light of these anxieties, as in the case of film director Ron Howard's 1986 feature *Gung Ho*, in which a series of madcap cultural collisions take place between white-collar managers and blue-collar workers at a Japanese-owned Pennsylvanian car factory. Here and elsewhere, however, a self-reflexive touchiness was now discernible, given that tales of American industries 'falling prey' to Japanese acquisitions needed no recourse to fictional exemplars for their veracity.

Sony's 1989 purchase of Columbia Pictures Entertainment for $3.4 billion was a real-life case in point, while the increasing popularity of Japanese motor vehicles, such as the Honda Accord, spoke to the equally real crisis that had taken hold of Detroit's auto manufacturers.[4] Writers of paperback thrillers, such as Steven Schlossstein, Clive Cussler, and Tom Clancy, noted with alarm the rising market share of Japanese products in the United States.[5] Their didactic narratives served as rallying cries that invested in the image of Americans sleepwalking toward a cliff edge (coded as the industrial, financial, political, and moral bankruptcy of the United States).[6] Buoyed by a steady presence on bestseller lists, these works propagated a hysterical response that was difficult to ignore. Nonetheless, a more considered opinion about Japan's rise was present in the nonfiction retrospectives of writers such as John Updike, Gore Vidal, and James Michener, each of whom grounded their observations in an historical or biographical context rather than current affairs. In his 1992 memoir, *The World is My Home*, Michener, for example, ruefully owned up to the presumptions that had blunted his insights during the 1940s:

> I am ashamed to confess that I witnessed an economic miracle in Japan but failed at the time to appreciate its significance. When I landed there after the war, taxicabs were Rube Goldberg affairs at which we Americans laughed: crude, beat-up bundles of junk carrying a load of charcoal in the back and a small round stove in which to burn it so that the gases would propel the taxi. Later there were the famous sixty-yen cabs (basic fare sixteen cents), which were no bigger than a child's pram. Made by Toyota, they were called Toyopets and were both dangerous and ridiculous.
>
> But as soon as practicable after the war Toyota produced a car—mostly tin, it seemed—that did provide space and run smoothly, but had someone told me then: "Jim, in a few years these Toyotas are going to drive Detroit right into the ground," I would have had him certified as a nut. I failed to anticipate the economic miracle that the Japanese automobile industry was about to create. I had not fully realized that hard work, inventive genius and skilled management could produce reliable products that all the world would want to purchase.[7]

Michener's confessional tone was appropriate to one who had made a career out of writing well-informed narratives of foreign cultures, but by stepping carefully around the issue of the purpose and intentionality that lay behind Japan's industrial boom he avoided placing himself in opposition to those for whom 'Made in Japan' product labels served as menacing declarations of a de facto 'takeover.'[8] Besides the workaday issue of product origins, an existential question had arisen as to where the bedrock of US national identity lay, economically speaking, given that the nation's industries no longer appeared especially unique or even proficient.[9]

In New Zealand, by contrast, the situation could not have been more different, as the country possessed no hi-tech sector, car factories, or other heavy industries that were likely to inspire protectionist sentiments.[10] Given that American concerns were ostensibly grounded in the 'trade wars' surrounding such industries, it followed, on the face of it, that there was no basis for equivalent concerns in New Zealand. Yet the rising number of Japanese tourists and 'salarymen' in that country was the first time that most civilians had experienced their might-have-been-conquerors of the Second World War as approachable subjects and this in itself was cause for consternation.[11] Some artists, among them the short story writers Keri Hulme and Vivienne Plumb, responded with a gothic mode of representation, literalizing the threat of a 'takeover' in individual encounters. Under their pens, the Japanese tourist emerges as a protean subject that ebbs and flows, shifting between the visible and the invisible, and squeezing New Zealanders out of their very bodies in the process. As in the case of the combat novel genre, therefore, New Zealand fiction writing reflected a localism that took a different narrative turn from that of the United States, even as the ideologies that resided in both literary traditions intersected at crucial instances.

Had ethnic Japanese subjects resided in New Zealand in large enough numbers, then the conversation might have diverged still further, and yet, as we shall see in the next chapter, New Zealand's experience of Japanese immigration differed from that of the US in ways sufficient to make that outcome unlikely. As for Japanese Americans, dissenting voices from that quarter were evident but heavily nuanced. For the most part, commentary involved critiques of prevalent Japanophobic tropes (the robot, the cyborg, the 'samurai' salaryman, et al.) without delving too deeply into the ideologies from which they sprang, although science fiction writers occasionally touched on this matter.[12] Thus, the memoirist David Mura on how it felt to witness the changing media tropes:

> Before the television set, wearing my ever-present Cubs cap, I crouched near the sofa, saw the enemy surrounding me. I shouted to my men, hurled a grenade. I fired my gun. And the Japanese soldiers fell before me, one by one.
>
> Of course, by the eighties, I was aware, as everyone else was, of Japan's burgeoning power, its changing image—Toyota, Nissan, Sony, Toshiba, the economic, electronic, automotive miracle. Rather than savage barbarism the Japanese were now characterized by a frightening efficiency and a tireless energy. Japan was a monster of industrialization, of huge, world-hungry corporations. Unfair trade practices, the trade imbalance. Robot people.[13]

Critics of this discourse tended to follow Mura's lead, ticking off tropes one by one and dismissing the fears as overblown. Part of the reason for this roll call approach was that the fearmongering language used to describe Japan never coalesced into an iconic narrative capable of crossing medium, language, and national boundaries—as, say, the story of *Madame Butterfly* repeatedly had over the preceding hundred years (providing the basis for a counter-hegemonic narrative in David Henry Hwang's 1988 play *M. Butterfly*). In lieu of an urtext, the corporate thriller emerged as a genre that styled itself as consistently pertinent to Japan, in essence or in representation.[14] Among these works, Michael Crichton's 1992 novel *Rising Sun* was arguably the most prominent and became the only one of its kind to inspire a film adaptation (released the following year). Yet to Japanese Americans, the publication of Crichton's novel was no more remarkable than any of the other manifestations of Japanophobia. Indeed, instances of violence, such as the death of Vincent Chin in 1982 or the public smashing of a Toshiba radio set by US congressmen in 1987, tended to occasion more vocal remarks.[15] It is therefore unsurprising that one of the more noteworthy proponents of an opposing narrative, American-Canadian fiction writer Ruth Ozeki, wrote her 1998 novel *My Year of Meats* as an ecocritical narrative first and foremost and only latterly a critique of the fears projected onto expatriated Japanese nationals.

Whose Pleasure Periphery?
The phenomenon of 'Japan-bashing,' as Japanophobic discourses tended to be called in mainstream media, received its first critical examination during the 1990s, particularly in David Morley and Kevin Robins' coauthored study *Spaces of Identity* (1995), which appended the term to the newly-emergent cultural phenomenon known as techno-Orientalism (itself a distant derivative of the still-larger discourse that Edward Said had identified in his 1978 treatise *Orientalism*).[16] Said's study had focused upon the Near East, hypothesizing that Anglo-French imperialism invested in and was dependent upon knowledge industries (libraries, institutes, encyclopedias, etc.) so as to create a mutually reinforcing relationship between information and power that denied autonomy to subject races/peoples. Part of the imperial project, as Said saw it, involved representing the culture of 'the Oriental' as unchanging and premodern, the better to justify foreign rule.[17] A distant strain of the phenomenon Said identified would permeate turn-of-the-century American cultural productions that depicted East Asian societies as remote from the corruption of Western industrialism and urbanization.[18] Techno-Orientalism,

by contrast, did not sustain formal colonialism, nor has it depicted East Asian peoples as inhabiting a timeless/changeless culture overwhelmingly 'different' from the Westerner's own. On the contrary, the techno-Orientalist imaginary constructs East Asian societies as following the same developmental trajectory as the West. Sustaining this perspective was not at all difficult in the 1980s, as long as one focused on East Asia's commitment to capitalist principles and the gradual phasing in of democratic governance (while politely omitting mainland China and North Korea from consideration). The difficulties arose not in the matter of essentials, but rather the degrees of development involved. More specifically, high levels of industrialization, managerial competency, and technological literacy throughout the region problematized the notion of 'follower societies.' Acknowledging these trends, fiction writers and film directors in the US began to construct narratives that were, if not declarative in their thesis of a future centered on Tokyo, resoundingly suggestive in their aesthetics.[19]

These productions went hand-in-hand with media commentary and nonfiction publications, all of which disseminated anxieties that 'the West' was likely to become, if it had not already become, less developed than 'the East.' Scenarios of fast-slipping technological supremacy therefore underpinned techno-Orientalism, although the otherness of East Asian societies was not always or necessarily intensified thereby. When anglophone commentators looked at the Japanese 'economic miracle,' they saw themselves—more specifically, a version of themselves as they would wish to be—reflected back at them:

> Japan today is an intensely globalized society with skyhigh literacy, very low crime, excellent life expectancy, tremendous fashion sense, and a staggering amount of the electronic substance we used to call cash. After centuries of horrific vicissitudes and heartbreaking personal sacrifice, the Japanese are fat, rich, turbo-charged, and ready to party down. They are jazzing into the 21st-century global limelight in their velcro'd sneakers, their jeans stuffed with spare film-packs and gold-plated VISA cards.[20]

This was techno-Orientalism in its complimentary/complementary form, a discourse that, in the words of theorist Toshiya Ueno, enabled the West "to preserve its identity in its imagination of the future."[21] Sundry cultural productions of the era followed the same mode of representation, paying tribute to Japan's economic dynamism while simultaneously consuming it as a form of spectacle. In all cases, the 'up-to-date' technologies and urban landscapes of Tokyo and Osaka 'backdated' the cultural vantage point of the onlooker in alarming but simultaneously affirming ways.[22]

Alarmism and self-affirmation were never wholly separable as responses, and yet alarm was undeniably ascendant at times and, in its Japan-specific accusatory form, came to be known as 'Japan-bashing.' Once public discourse went down this path, the root cause fixated upon Japan's increased exports (particularly cars and consumer technology products) and high-profile corporate purchases of American companies and real estate (such as California's Pebble Beach Golf Course in 1990). Although overstated, this point of view was not wholly unfounded either. In the earliest period of the postwar Japanese 'miracle,' automotive exports had been greeted with indulgent condescension, as the 1964 American song title "Little Honda" reveals.[23] By the '80s, however, this diminutive perspective had long since faded into history and Japanese commentators had begun to take up condescending positions of their own. Prominent among these was Sony Chairman Akio Morita, who observed that, in supplying high-quality manufactured goods to the US, Japan was providing a service that Americans could no longer provide themselves.[24] Inflammatory generalizations like Morita's, by no means unique, inadvertently revealed the interpenetrative discourse of the 'trade wars,' each side carrying—but seldom taking—responsibility for the tensions.[25] So intransigent did these stances become, that variations on the arguments appeared inconsequential or were absent entirely. Aware that this was the case, foreign correspondents and expatriate educators made it their business to uncover the historical dimension that lay hidden beneath the language of tariffs and trade deficits. Japanese journalist Mitsuko Shimomura, for example, recalled her time in mid-1960s New York City as a 'peak moment' in US history, before the nation became bogged down in Vietnam, Watergate, and civil rights movements. In her judgment, the robustness of Japan's economy was partly explained by the absence of these quagmires.[26]

Curiously unexplored in these and other commentaries was an attendant phenomenon to the 'trade wars,' namely the increased visibility of the commentators themselves or, more generally, those expatriated Japanese who, as beneficiaries of Japan's economic prosperity, chose the US as a tourist destination or perhaps a business posting. In 1987, Japanese tour guide Yukio Nakayama published *Tourists' Bashing*, the title of which revealed the humorous tone of the text while also alluding to an offshoot of 'Japan-bashing' that took tourists as its object. There was need for such levity, for Japanese tourists were the subject of lengthy ruminations, especially among the war generation. Combat veteran and historian William Manchester, for example, visited Guam (Guåhan) and noted the indifference to battlefield sites and war memorials among Japanese tourists, an observation that was echoed among tourist-watchers in Hawai'i.[27] This rhetoric eventually found its way into veteran fighter pilot-turned-thriller writer Joe Weber's novel *Honorable Enemies* (1994), the opening of which begins with a Japanese cruise ship being machine-gunned by a helicopter off Waikiki Beach.[28] The intensity of such images may partly have derived from a colonialist sense of chagrin, insofar as the war generation had come to identify Hawai'i as 'their' pleasure periphery, not Japan's.[29]

As a term common to tourist studies, 'pleasure periphery' denotes a conception (usually urban) of places and peoples (usually rural) as both non-threatening and 'exotic,' attitudes that have enabled international tourists to objectify host cultures for their own consumption.[30] This model takes on additional complexity when tourist groups originate from more than one nationality, each of which may implicitly identify the host culture as 'theirs.' Such was the case when Japanese and American tourists crossed paths on Pacific Island resorts. To some extent, the racial antagonism that Americans brought to these encounters could be concealed within a genteel distaste for tourism generally, which has a discursive lineage every bit the equal of 'yellow peril' anxieties and which employs a similar language of fear or contempt. Making the point succinctly, cultural geographer Mike Crang states that "Mass tourists are frequently treated as a homogeneous mass, who are often metaphorically described like animals as hordes, herds or flocks, making them sound almost like a separate species."[31] Needless to say, those who invested in such binaries never considered themselves tourists, but rather as 'travelers' (an older term with a 'nobler' linguistic heritage). Comparative studies of anglophone literature also reveal that, during the same period, Australian writers were expressing antipathies of their own toward Japanese tourists and sojourners.[32] Common to these writers, and to those of the United States, was a cultural double-standard, which saw White male tourists/sojourners, present in Japan, as inhabiting a free-spirited pleasure world of sexual indulgence (even as Japanese men were reduced to workaholics); whereas those literary works that depicted Japanese male tourists/sojourners in the US, envisaged them as sexual predators (while White American men were out of work).[33]

Mr. Moto "does" New Zealand

The most alarmist American rhetoric restaged old arguments about Japanese expansionism, drawing upon the icon of Pearl Harbor to assert that the spate of corporate acquisitions amounted to another 'sneak attack,' albeit shifted onto the plane of economics.[34] Part and parcel with this was the racial profiling of the enemy in animal terms, suggesting that the deep-rooted artifice epitomized in Pearl Harbor was ineradicably and irrepressibly representative of the Japanese people as a whole.[35] That New Zealand armed forces had not been a victim of the original 'day of infamy' did not necessarily render the rhetoric inoperable. But to fully deploy the Pearl Harbor referent, one had to imagine New Zealand as an imminent or recurrent victim, and herein a nagging caveat remained: to wit, what targets did the country have to warrant such an attack? Up until 1973, the United Kingdom had guaranteed a market for New Zealand exports, these being dairy, agricultural, and forest products in the main, and although British accession to the EEC forced New Zealand to diversify its customer base, this did not translate into a shift from agribusiness to the high technology and/or entertainment industries so desirable to the Japanese. Farms remained the chief source of tradable goods, which effectively meant that New Zealand possessed few objects likely to attract Japanese attention, and likewise suggested that the introduction of competitively priced Japanese imports would not force New Zealand businesses into bankruptcy. As it turned out, there were noticeable benefits to the increasing economic ties with Japan, not the least of which were affordable and reliable second-hand cars, off-loaded from container ships, that swiftly consigned the previous generation to an overdue retirement. So popular did the new cars become that one New Zealand hard rock band changed its name from the Trinkets to the Datsuns, a relatively transparent sign of the recognition value attached to Japanese marques. But although the correlation between industrial history and cultural history undoubtedly stands, it does not suffice to explain away less neighborly New Zealand responses to the Japanese.

In Australia, as in the United States, novelists drew upon specific examples of business trends, leaving no doubt as to the author's stance in respect to them.[36] But one did not require a cache of ready-to-order leitmotifs to feed the engine of alarmism. New Zealand writers would prove that the fact of Japanese power was sufficient in itself, particularly when melancholy eyes looked back at the self-enclosed socioeconomic environment of pre-1973. Literature scholar Patrick Evans has identified, in this moment, a key turning point in New Zealand's approach to the world:

> Now, suddenly, the country was being defrosted, its citizens socially, psychologically and economically exposed to the air, abandoned by the mother country to an indifferent and newly challenging world in which its competitors were unfamiliar nations from outside the old colonial matrix.[37]

Rather unfortunately, this 'defrost cycle' coincided with the increased visibility of Japanese tourists and 'salarymen,' whose bulging wallets made them the bitter personification of a nation on a far surer economic footing. Responding to the presence of Japanese tourists, New Zealand writers eschewed corporations as sites of contestation and infestation, preferring instead the human-to-human relations of the body politic as a terrain in which the weaker (New Zealand) vessel falls into the hands of an all-consuming foreign agent.

Exemplary among these gothic 'possessions' is Keri Hulme's short story "Kaibutsu-San," the title of which ("Mr. Monster") suggests that the formal titles of everyday life are but a pose that conceal innate aggressions or regressions known to both predator and prey, yet only dominant under certain conditions. Described as someone who "bows like a pocket knife folding" (a diminutive reference to size but suggestive of cutting ability, concealment, and perhaps an outwardly respectable manner), the Japanese tourist occupies a steadily engulfing textual space as the story progresses.[38] Undergoing the opposite process are two Māori larrikins who become literally miniaturized by the end, but start out in a position of confidence, expecting to enrich themselves at the drunken tourist's expense with an easy game of cards. As the card game progresses, their plan bears fruit: the man steadily loses his money, all the while appearing too inebriated to comprehend his position, until only his briefcase remains as collateral. One might read into the exchange a microcosm of how international trade and business agreements play out when the Japanese are involved—that is, as a succession of incentives leading up to an impoverished adjournment—but Hulme is more concerned with the nature of her creation than with ties to current affairs. We see the monster's purpose at the end when he quickly wins the game, having goaded his hapless opponents into gambling everything they have, including their bodies and selves:

> "Keep the money," he says. His face is becoming leaner. "Keep your patches and gear." He has stopped sweating. "You can even keep the glasses." He points the handle of his bag at us. We are sitting stunned, mouths O, Mi's hands limp as though the life has gone from them. "I only want everything from you." Somehow his teeth are more pointed than before. There is a flash and click like someone took a photograph. Immediately I feel something essential, vital, drain out of my belly, and Mi feels it too because he screams and the cards spray out of his hands.
>
> [...]

The Teeth smiles suavely, one last time.

"So sorry," he says, and is back among the Friday night crowd and lost.[39]

In this passage, the Japanese tourist is reduced to the three principal icons of briefcase/camera/teeth, each one of which comprises a means to absorb or contain, thereby signaling that the roles of predator and prey have undergone a reversal.[40] But the meaning of these images stretches outside the narrative, triggering associative values and interlinking with historical nodal points.[41] That the camera, beloved of tourist groups especially, should act as trapdoor to a portable prison suggests a tourist gaze in operation, one that captures people's 'essence' and leaves a hollow shell in its wake. The sociologist John Urry intended 'the gaze' as a term that gets to the bottom of what forces, social, cultural, economic, or otherwise, impel societies to examine others and how this reflects upon society back home, but Hulme's text figures New Zealanders as objects, not practitioners of the gaze.[42] Thus, one cannot approach the text as a means to understand New Zealand society in any comprehensive sense, and the tourist gaze stands only for the acknowledgment that host societies undergo alterations at the behest of those who approach them as objects of consumption.

Hulme's story manifests an awareness of this trend and conjoins it to a set of images with a long bloodline, foremost among them being the portrayal of Japanese as vampires, a publicly-endorsed trope during the Pacific War, as evidenced in the 'Tokio Kid' series of American posters, each one of which featured a Japanese face sporting incisors and pointed ears. The tourist-vampire's highly ironic apology is also a throwback to the conniving, smooth-tongued, frequently bespectacled Japanese villain-figures of monochrome Hollywood cinema, and more specifically to the Mr. Moto series created by American author John P. Marquand.[43] What emerges, disinterred, as it were, from the vault of undead wartime stereotypes is therefore nothing less than a means to dehumanize the Japanese, and indeed the story could sit just as well in a 1940s context. Only a persistent strain of anti-tourist sentiment saves Hulme's work from a charge of anachronistic pastiche, if barely, since it covers the vitriol of her Japanophobia with a veneer of genteel distaste for tourist behavior as a whole, allowing readers to give her the benefit of the doubt, should they so wish.[44]

Somewhat less vindictive is Vivienne Plumb's 1993 short story "The Wife Who Spoke Japanese in her Sleep," which likewise involves a 'takeover bid,' albeit of an epidemiological rather than a technological turn. Here, the possession is voluntary and gradual rather than swift and coerced and examines the 'other within' (domestically and psychologically) rather than a soul-gathering confidence man without. Addressing the improbability of gothic themes situated within New Zealand houses, film researcher Misha Kavka asserts that the gothic can be brought home in any number of Kiwi visual and literary tropes where an undead history meets unsuccessful efforts at its repression: "Indeed, however short our past, it seems curiously prone to gothic metaphorization; however short our history, it seems particularly undead."[45] As with most allusions to dark histories in the *Gothic NZ* (2006) volume, Kavka is concerned with Māori-Pākehā relations in colonial times, but her observation as to the failure of Kiwi households to repress history does as well for the leftover relics of Pacific War propaganda and, in Plumb's case, the exhumation of an early trope of Cold War fiction, namely the covert alien parasite whose unstoppable reproduction stands analogously for assumptions underpinning the Red Scare in the United States. The 'body snatchers' of Jack Finney's 1955 novel infiltrated their new environs in gradual, measured steps, ensuring that those who underwent the compulsory metamorphosis resembled their original selves almost perfectly. Textually, this brainwashing process takes place with only minimal reference to supernatural powers, it being important to retain the human dimension as much as possible, so as to convince readers of the plausibility of the scenario. Life remains quiet and predictable, features that make clear how ill-prepared communities are to cope with the opening of an alien frontier in their own backyards.

Plumb's short story is a condensed version of the same state of affairs, coalescing around the figure of Honey, a bland and vacuous housewife who discovers that she harbors another self, that of a Japanese matriarch whose nocturnal skills take the form of prophetic conversations. Each self is content to remain in the Kiwi household, which becomes a context that measures the course of the changes and their effect upon Honey's husband, Howard:

> "Did I do it?" she asks.
> "Yes," says Howard. His voice is low. "They were very pleased. You were very successful. Miss Florica thinks you could help even more people."
> "I see," says Honey. "Tell her she can have thirty percent."
> She turns and goes back to the bedroom. Howard comes inside. He's surprised. Honey seems so different, so business-minded, it's not like her. He frowns at the lock, pulls the chain across and slips it into its tiny slot. Tomorrow he'll ring Miss Florica and make her an offer.[46]

Unlike the body snatchers, whose 'snatching' brings with it a declining work ethic, Honey becomes enhanced, supercharged one might say, by her takeover. She is more productive and certainly more interesting, but, like the body snatchers, the process flushes her out emotionally and renders human relationships purely functional. Howard is the casualty here, representing as he does the unsophisticated Kiwi 'bloke' who, bewildered but curious, lets events take their course. The forces that power Honey's changes are never revealed, but whether they involve pathology, reincarnation, or alien intervention matters less than the discord that arises when the alter ego assumes dominance. As with "Kaibutsu-San," cash flow serves as a digestive aid, facilitating the consumption of the New Zealand 'vessel' until it all but disappears from view, and again the ending takes on a grim aspect when Howard, no longer cost-effective, is buried beneath the foundations of a Japanese garden. Although the results are various, the Japanese component thereby overlays itself upon both characters, consigning them to the rubbish bin of history.

Messrs. Yunioshi & Sakamura

To read Hulme and Plumb is to take the measure of how widespread anti-tourist sentiments became in the anglophone world, although one notes that these sentiments did not take hold in the immediate postwar years. Indeed, overseas Japanese tourism was almost unknown until the Tokyo Olympics of 1964, prior to which Japanese citizens had faced travel restrictions imposed by the US Occupation and their own government (which sought to limit private expenditure abroad as much as possible, the better to speed domestic economic recovery). In the postwar period, Americans therefore had little contact with expatriated Japanese and only a contemptuous regard for the 'tinker' products of Japanese industry.[47] Correspondingly, one finds the Japanese presence within American cultural productions of the era to be of a passing, derisive sort. The pidgin-speaking photojournalist Mr. Yunioshi, a character from Truman Capote's 1958 novella *Breakfast at Tiffany's*, is a case-in-point. Early in Capote's narrative, readers get an abridged travelogue of this figure's journey through Sub-Saharan Africa:

> On Christmas day Mr. Yunioshi had passed with his camera through Tococul, a village in the tangles of nowhere and of no interest, merely a congregation of mud huts with monkeys in the yards and buzzards on the roofs. He'd decided to move on when he suddenly saw a Negro squatting in a doorway carving monkeys on a walking stick.[48]

The association of Africans with/as monkeys dominates the passage, and yet the curiosity and comedic value lies not so much in this age-old conflation, soon to be played upon more fully in Errol Brathwaite's novel, as in its juxtaposition to the stereotype of the Japanese as inseparably attached to their cameras. Mr. Yunioshi might or might not photograph the Black woodcarver, but the narrative has already 'framed' Mr. Yunioshi from an angle that reduces him in turn. At first glance, the fact that nothing else about this figure's person is acknowledged, much less described, might enable readers to imagine him any way they wish, yet the image of an always-present camera serves as a narrative quirk that adjourns the process before it has had a chance to begin. Not only do readers end up knowing nothing about Mr. Yunioshi, but the stereotype of camera-toting Japanese that Capote's narrative endorses implicates the reader's imagination in his textual erasure. Simply put, the camera image disestablishes Mr. Yunioshi's characterization by calling the notion of autonomous, camera-free behavior into question.

In the era separating the end of the Second World War from the rise of 'Japan Inc.,' expatriated Japanese featured in American cultural productions, where they featured at all, much as Mr. Yunioshi did. Not only were they harmlessly and ridiculously gadget-loving, but they were also harmless and ridiculous largely *because* they were gadget-loving. Naturally, all of this changed once 'Japan-bashing' took hold of media discourse, at which point the presence of expatriated Japanese, with or without their cameras, became a good deal more than risible. The clearest example of Mr. Yunioshi's metamorphosis comes across in the figure of Eddie Sakamura, a character in Michael Crichton's novel. Ostensibly, the narrative of *Rising Sun* centers upon an investigation into the murder of a young White woman, Cheryl Austin, whose body is found in a Japanese corporate high-rise, newly erected in Los Angeles. On the scene are Peter Smith and John Connor, police detectives who struggle to solve the crime over the course of two days. Variously a suspect, an informant, and long-time acquaintance of John Connor, Sakamura is also an expatriate whose status as such is established early in the narrative when Connor confiscates his passport as surety of cooperative behavior.[49] What has led Sakamura to reside in the US is never clear, for Crichton's novel is not an immigrant narrative and the transpacific story is left out altogether. Nor does Sakamura's mind dwell upon the omission, for his primary concern is not that he will lose his passport but that he will lose his driver's license after breaking too many traffic rules.[50] So the first conclusion one might draw, strange though it may be, is that urban mobility matters more to this man than does national identity. However, Crichton invests too little in Sakamura for this character to be considered a Japanese

Beatnik of the 1990s. His love of cars is not symptomatic of a psychological malaise or anomic value system, but rather a generalized perception in US media discourse that Japanese industrial products were outpacing those of the United States (by performance standards and in sales figures). One must therefore read his presence in the text, not in terms of character development, but as a focal point for images of expatriated Japanese current at the time of publication. As a female character summarizes it, "He loves it here. Why not? He's got everything. He buys a new Ferrari every time he bangs up the old one. He's got more money than God."[51] Notwithstanding the reference to Ferrari (a possible acknowledgment that luxury Japanese marques such as Acura and Infiniti had not achieved equivalent market penetration), the message is one of extraordinary wealth and a reputation that precedes the man.

As a character trait, Sakamura's love of cars is unreadable except in terms of the polemics that inflected current affairs. The loss of thousands of American jobs on the automotive assembly lines meant that Japanese imports invariably featured in discussions as to the cause. Moreover, Americans entertained 'proprietorial' feelings toward their domestic car companies that rendered the associations more than economic. As one study observes, "By doing so well in making a product so near to the heart of modern American popular culture, the Japanese inadvertently pushed a collective emotional button."[52] The brazenness of Sakamura's love affair with the car constitutes a purposeful attempt, on Crichton's part, to tap into this emotional response from his readers. More than any other Japanese character in the narrative, Sakamura moves rapidly from place to place, until he apparently perishes in a high-speed car crash.[53] This moment is significant in another way also, for it follows a scene in which Smith breaks into his house to arrest Sakamura, only to be assaulted by two White women who have been keeping him company.[54] In Capote's novel, Mr. Yunioshi is an anhedonic whose attachment to his camera substitutes for sexual virility almost to the point of implied castration. Sakamura, on the other hand, is a self-professed *hipparidako* or 'popular guy.'[55] Far from robbing him of sexual virility, his love of technology augments it considerably, at least in the opinion of his female admirers. Indeed, the woman who first describes his flamboyant habits, previously quoted, bundles his 'fast' automotive history and 'fast' sexual history together as if the two are mutually inclusive. In short, he encapsulates the sexist self-image that White American men had entertained in regard to their own auto-mobility, the main problem being one of excess rather than total 'difference.'[56]

As an ongoing project in anglophone cultural representation, the remasculinization of the East Asian male subject might appear to have advanced somewhat in the figure of Eddie Sakamura, were it not for the fact that his sexual behavior is coded as perversion.[57] It is he who first alerts Smith and Connor to Cheryl Austin's fetishistic need for asphyxiation during sexual intercourse, a practice that he indulged before thinking better of it. In addition, his private residence is akin to a bordello and part of his unofficial position in the US involves supplying girls for visiting dignitaries.[58] These details are a continuation of narrative references to the mistreatment of White American women at the hands of Japanese expatriates, beginning with a salaryman's curt dismissal of Cheryl Austin as a "common prostitute" and carried along by Connor's description of private clubs as a "shadow world" catering to Japanese businessmen in major American cities.[59] The latter recalls an aspect of anglophone thriller novels set overseas, which see whole East Asian cities as dens of decaying morals.[60] Thus the implication may be that, in return for exporting consumer products to the US, Japanese men have turned American cities, and the people who reside there, into objects of consumption.[61]

Scholarly readings of Crichton's novel have paid considerable attention to the intersection of gender and race, particularly Cheryl Austin's role as symbol of a United States that has been murdered on the boardroom table of a Japanese corporation.[62] The latter image ties together prevalent fears of collapsing American industries with sexually predatory expatriate Japanese, undoubtedly the two most pressing concerns in Crichton's narrative. To these, though, one might add a third fear, less obvious and, thus far, unexamined: the possibility that advances in technology might enable the Japanese to mediate or (re)master American perceptions of the world around them. As with the contrast between Sakamura's happy-go-lucky driving habits and the unhappy state of American manufacturing, these concerns grew out of real-life industrial achievements across the Pacific. Tape recorders were first developed in Germany during the Second World War, and in 1965 Philips Electronics patented the cassette tape. By the 1980s the technology had become portable, although the most popular model was not a Philips or RadioShack device but the Sony Walkman.[63] Most Americans saw little harm in this, for their feelings toward the new product were not 'proprietorial.' Among the enthusiasts, William Gibson acknowledged that the Walkman had already changed his own experiences of everyday life for the better.[64] In *Rising Sun*, the best that may be said of these changes are that they are wearisome, although they are also quite menacing. The narrative opens, for example, with Smith's attempts to learn Japanese by following pre-recorded sentences on a tape.[65] By the early 1990s, the numbed wretchedness that these 'teach yourself' sessions tended to evoke had become a minor literary trope in its own right, satirized in Ishmael Reed's *Japanese by Spring* (1993). As in Reed's novel, bilingualism for Smith is neither an end in itself nor especially desirable on its own terms. Instead, functional fluency is something he simply must acquire if he wishes to keep his job as liaison in the Los Angeles Police Department's Special Services Division.

One of Crichton's speculative hypotheses is that Japanese visual technologies might change American perceptions much as audio technologies already had. By the time of publication, Japan's status as the world's most media-saturated society was widely acknowledged. The French documentary *Sans Soleil* (1983) alluded to this and in 1990 Carl Eugene Loeffler envisaged Japan as a giant 'video garden':

> In Japan, you can find public video displays wherever people gather—stores, transportation centers, and places of rest. Japanese public video takes on the same cultural meanings as the presence of water in gardens and parks: it is a kind of religion. People immerse themselves in it, and as with most religions, some people are fanatical, while others remain aloof.[66]

Gibson and Loeffler were struck by the power of medium, but more especially by Japan's role in expanding the reach of a given medium. However, these commentaries presupposed that the content of the medium was confined to Japan (Loeffler's assumption) or that users would be able to decide for themselves what they would experience (Gibson's assumption). Both premises became increasingly open to question in the aftermath of Japanese investments in Hollywood production companies. As one study noted, "Investing in Hollywood cinema more intensely than its own 'national' cinema, Japanese companies and producers blurred the definition of 'Japanese cinema' by making Hollywood cinema, in part, identifiable as Japanese [. . .]"[67]

Crichton's response to this media history was not overtly articulated, but the subtext to his narrative is that Japanese control over American media industries (emblematized in Nakamoto Corp.'s investment in hi-definition video) could indeed change the way that Americans perceive the world around them. That the Japanese might attempt this is clear from the moment in which Smith and Connor search Cheryl Austin's room and discover that, prior to their arrival, the contents have already been examined and placed back in their original positions.[68] The rearrangement is painstakingly accurate, and yet Japanese reliance upon analog photographic technology betrays the deception. As the police investigation proceeds, however, the Japanese discard analog technology for digital formats when they provide Smith and

Connor with security tapes recovered from the murder scene.[69] Once again, the content of this evidence appears to be true and accurate, until Smith takes the tapes to media laboratories for close analysis. As a last-minute recourse, this move provides Smith with a glimpse into the dire state of American research institutions, complete with a mini lecture on the influence of (Japanese) financial donors.[70] Thwarted at every turn by Japanese corporate leverage, the original content of the tapes is at last revealed and Smith gradually comes to understand how the Japanese had been planning for such a contingency from the moment the detectives first arrived at the crime scene:

> Theresa said, 'Did anybody cross the room? Anybody at all?'
> 'No,' I said. 'We had the yellow barrier up. Nobody was allowed on the other side of the tape. In fact—'
> And then I remembered. 'Wait a minute! There was somebody! That little guy with the camera,' I said. 'He was on the other side of the barrier, taking pictures.'
> 'That's right,' Connor said.
> 'What little guy?' she said.
> 'A Japanese guy. He was taking pictures. We asked Ishiguro about him. He said his name was, ah . . .'
> 'Mr. Tanaka,' Connor said.
> 'That's right, Mr. Tanaka. And you asked Ishiguro for the film from his camera.'
> I frowned. 'But we never got it.'
> 'No,' Connor said. 'And frankly, I never thought we would.'[71]

Although the narrative is not intertextual at this point, the image of the 'Japanese guy' is clearly a holdover from the prior era, even to the point that Mr. Tanaka's 'littleness' makes him an object of ridicule much as his literary ancestor in Capote's narrative had been. His after-presence serves as a reminder that, even as the global footprint of Japanese technology became ever larger, the dominant image associated with expatriate Japanese shifted away from the camera (Mr. Yunioshi) toward the car (Mr. Sakamura), the camera's menacing potential never disappeared entirely. Indeed, in some literary productions, such as "Kaibutsu-san," the image of the camera-toting Japanese had become menacing enough to connote an image of 'capture' all on its own.

Messrs. Suzuki & Oh

The Japanese American reaction to Crichton's brand of 'Japan-bashing' was one of general distaste, tempered by an uneven response to the rise of Japanese tourism and corporate investment in their own neighborhoods. Indeed, (counter)reactions to the latter preceded the engagement of Japanese American literary writers like David Mura and Ruth Ozeki by several years. Since the late 1960s, in fact, those Japanese tourists who chose to holiday in the US had tended to prefer Los Angeles as a destination, with first-time tourists dividing their time between Hollywood, Beverly Hills, Century City, and Olvera Street. The Japan Travel Bureau had offered overnight stays in these areas, but continued to accommodate the majority in the city's 'Little Tokyo' district (one of three such districts in the country).[72] Financially speaking, this arrangement served the needs of the tourist group and the host community alike, and yet the influx of tourist dollars belied a growing controversy that was already evident by the mid-1970s. The older generation of native-born Japanese Americans or "Nisei" resented the erosion of their cultural heritage, which was tied, in part, to the stories of their immigrant parents and, in the opinion of the Nisei, not one and the same with 'fixed' notions of Japanese culture that tended to be brought to the United States by tourists and corporate executives. These divisive issues were intensified by the redevelopment of Little Tokyo in the late 1970s, a process that was partially sponsored by Japanese corporations (which tended to choose Los Angeles as their US headquarters). Subsequently, the annual Nisei Week festival underwent a similar 'makeover,' epitomized in its new name ('Japanese Festival'), which shifted the cultural emphases away from local Japanese American culture toward an idea of Japanese—that is, Japan-derived—culture, with corresponding expectations as to how participants would publicly express their identification.[73]

These developments predated the publication of *Rising Sun* and show that the influence of Japanese overseas investment could be every bit as controversial for Japanese Americans as it sometimes was for White Americans. In fact, Crichton's narrative includes a Japanese American forensic pathologist, Tim Yoshimura, who tersely rebukes Smith and Connor for presuming that he is a Japanese national.[74] However, the history of Little Tokyo and its controversies are left out of Crichton's narrative entirely, a curious omission for a novel that focuses the reader's attention upon Japanese influence in Los Angeles.[75] More curious still is the response of Japanese American writers, who tended to address the topic of 'Japan-bashing' in a passing way as though the issues either did not concern them or were too sensitive to handle. The reasons for this are beyond the scope of the present study, although it is possible that memories of World War II-era internment left writers unwilling to weigh into the controversies.[76]

Asking whether Japanese American authors may have incorporated tropes of 'Japan-bashing' as constituent features of characters and situations requires an enquiry into why they may have done so. One answer comes to us by way of left-wing Asian American critics, writers, and anthologists active from the 1970s onwards, especially Frank Chin, Jeffrey Paul Chan, Lawson Fusao Inada, and Shawn Wong. Spearheaded by Frank Chin's categorizations of 'real' and 'fake' Asian American writers, these cultural nationalists looked askance at Asian American authors whose writings recycled, for any reason whatsoever, the stereotypes of ethnic Asians commonly found in White anglophone cultural productions. Those who did so were branded 'sellouts' or traffickers in 'racist love.'[77] Among the problems with this school of criticism was the way in which it envisaged hegemonic discourses as presenting writers with a zero-sum choice whereby stereotypes are either interpellated wholesale or contested outright. More recently, Sheng-mei Ma has adopted a less polarized position, suggesting that contestation might involve the evocation—perhaps the redeployment—of ethnic stereotypes as a necessary first step before their retirement, an idea that has also found favor with Jane Park, whose study of techno-Orientalism in Hollywood cinema is less concerned with playing 'spot the stereotype' than examining the narrative development of a given stereotype once it emerges.[78]

Ruth Ozeki's novel *My Year of Meats* (1998) is usually read through the prism of feminism or ecocriticism, although the narrative focus upon documentary filmmaking easily lends itself to examinations of ethnic stereotypes as they form, reform, and transform within the production process. The production in question is *My American Wife!* (hereafter '*MAW!*'), a weekly Japanese TV documentary, sponsored by the US lobby group BEEF-EX, featuring profiles of American housewives whose lives and meat recipes are held up as examples for Japanese housewives to follow. Scholars Emily Cheng and Jodi Kim have provided the most thorough examination of how US-Japan histories are critiqued in this storyline, specifically the gendering of Japan as a female consumer (traceable to US Occupation food distribution policies), and the ways in which the US meat export industry became a way in which Americans imagined the restoration of hegemony in their relations with Japan.[79] It should now be clear, however, that the polemics of the era, although mainly focused upon export products, also fixated upon the passage of human beings between Japan and the US, particularly the former to the latter. When Japanese nationals enter the US for the purposes of 'capturing' it photographically, as they do in Ozeki's narrative, a set of tropes and assumptions come into play that writers such as Crichton had already circulated in their most sinister form. As the most recent scholarship on *Rising Sun* makes clear, the greatest challenge confronting Smith, the narrator of the novel, is the Japanese capacity to use visual technology to disrupt the meanings attached to an original event by editing a 'master copy' to comply with their own preferred meanings.[80] In like turn, the Japanese American narrator of Ozeki's novel, Jane Takagi-Little, feels dismay after shooting the show's first episode because subsequent Japanese editing (over which she has no control) glamorizes an otherwise distressing confession of marital infidelity.[81] At first glance, therefore, the techno-Orientalist stereotype of manipulative Japanese video editing appears to feature in Ozeki's narrative wholly unchanged.

Furthermore, the values associated with camera-toting expatriate Japanese are especially evident at times. To shoot *MAW!* properly, the Japanese production company sends over two employees, the cameraman Suzuki and the soundman Oh, both of whom Jane describes using a number of stereotypes, beginning with Suzuki's eyes: "You could never tell if they were open or shut, or if he was watching you. "He has a great eye," I liked to say to Americans and then watch them glance dubiously at him and wonder, Where?"[82] This *double entendre* reduces Suzuki's face to a blind mask, substituting the 'great eye' of a video camera for human vision and thereby suggesting an all-encompassing scale as well as discernment. Thereafter, Suzuki and Oh encounter the US much as Mr. Yunioshi encountered Africa, meaning that their pleasures are primarily visual and that social relationships are either non-existent or heavily mediated. The same holds true for their immediate superior, Joichi Ueno, whose recreational pursuit in the US involves visiting striptease clubs and admiring the 'vigor' of White American women.[83] Suzuki and Oh observe American women as similar to the products lining supermarket shelves, their eyes lingering on specific 'items' and 'tracking' bodily movement. Taking these moments into account, scholarly readings of Ozeki's novel make much of the link between an all-pervasive American consumer culture and the sexism that intrudes into gender relations.[84] In truth, just as it is apparent that Ozeki's main purpose in the early sections of the novel is focused upon exploring such links, so it is equally apparent that the characters of her expatriate Japanese are diminished in the process, an aspect that Monica Chiu points out in observing how Jane never bothers to provide Suzuki and Oh's first names and addresses them as 'boys.'[85]

Chiu's critique remains the most censorious to date, mainly because she sees Ozeki's narrative as accepting of racial minorities and women only at the expense of othering and essentializing Japan.[86] Unlike Ma and Park, however, Chiu does not envisage cultural or ethnic stereotypes as undergoing development and, perhaps because of this, her critique is confined to the

MAW! sections of the novel and not the second documentary that Jane embarks upon. This second documentary is a clandestine affair that Jane pieces together from the editorial discards of *MAW!* after breaking from the show's original thematic focus to investigate the role of Diethylstilbestrol (DES) hormone injections in the farming industry. Crucially, Jane retains the services of Suzuki and Oh for this purpose, both of whom have already undergone a moral recuperation after shooting an episode on the Bukowsky family, whose daughter has emerged from near-total paralysis after being run over by a Walmart truck. In a 2009 interview Ozeki recalled how "The first part of the book is kind of a picaresque novel . . . and then about half way through the book, it changes. Something happens."[87] Among the happenings, I would suggest, is a renegotiation of the original *MAW!* concept and the gradual retirement of tropes associated with the camera-toting Japanese expatriate, narrative processes that commence with the Bukowsky episode and culminate in Jane's commitment to feminist documentary filmmaking.

The Bukowsky family constitute a challenge to Jane and her film crew, as the *MAW!* concept requires that a given family have ingredients ready for cooking and a willingness to share their life stories. Yet the Bukowsky parents have partially rehabilitated their daughter by asking that visitors bring a food gift and offer a few words to Christina in her near-catatonic condition. In short, the expectations of the family and the show are at odds with one another, although *MAW!* is less adaptable in practice and thus retains its place as the structural paradigm.[88] As Jane and her film crew become better acquainted with the Bukowsky family, however, the influence becomes social and mutual. The narrative provides early clues that this is likely to happen, for Christina's 'vegetable' mind is an antithesis to the normative 'meat is the message' concept and her single-eye vision, opening and closing for no apparent reason, is akin to a camera insofar as those who are 'exposed' to her never know whether their presence has been 'captured' or not, nor what their presence betokens to the mind within. Christina is thus the equal and opposite of Suzuki, and even though he comes to her at a time when her mobility is somewhat improved, her effect upon him is immediate. This comes across most obviously when a White, former flight attendant lewdly speculates as to whether Christina possesses sexual desires: "[Suzuki] let loose a torrent of Japanese expletives that I'd never before heard or even imagined. It was like being transported back in time, into the thick of a samurai drama, and this effect was only heightened when, having finished cursing him, Suzuki stepped back and slapped the flight attendant's face."[89] In the era of 'Japan-bashing,' samurai analogies were seldom intended as compliments and hardly ever associated with defending women.[90] In fact, the opposite tended to be the case, as one of the more aggressive anti-Japanese characters in Crichton's novel makes clear when he speculates that Cheryl Austin had been murdered by "a big samurai cocksman."[91] In the figure of Suzuki, however, readers encounter a character whose language and behavior are ennobling rather than sinister. Having recuperated Suzuki's masculinity, Ozeki then does the same for his sexual virility, which is neither in recession (as in Mr. Yunioshi's case) nor overbearing (as in Eddie Sakamura's case) but gently responsive. This aspect comes across when Suzuki and Oh awaken Christina's sexual consciousness (formerly held in abeyance by her condition) by 'pursuing' her at the same time as they 'propel' her, thereby illustrating the Japanese presence as curative rather than perverse.[92]

The Bukowsky episode is a significant turning point in the renegotiation of stereotypes, a process that climaxes during another episode when the film crew visit a farm and interview the Dunn family. At this point, Jane breaks with the *MAW!* concept by focusing the episode on an abattoir instead of a kitchen, as well as the bedroom in which the five-year-old Rose, sick from DES poisoning, sleeps unawares. The first of these scenes is necessarily an audial as much as a visual experience, and accordingly the sequence is 'picked up' most acutely by the soundman Oh. The latter's presence in the narrative goes unremarked in most scholarly readings of the novel, which neglect to acknowledge that the one characteristic Ozeki repeatedly emphasizes in respect to this man is his love of animals.[93] Thus, the sensory imagery of the killing scenes, already visceral in the literal sense, undergoes a narrative enhancement by association with the Japanese soundman who recoils from it.[94] The purposefulness of this narrative strategy reveals itself in the final scene, in which Suzuki matches Oh's audial sensitivity by recording a wholly visual spectacle: an aborted calf fetus lying on the 'kill floor.'[95] Structurally, therefore, Suzuki and Oh 'frame' the narrative as well as the filmic material that is their reason for being present, and they do so as investigative documentarians intent upon revealing truths rather than covering them over, a clear break with the expectations hitherto endorsed by writers like Crichton.

At least one scholar has detected a sexual undertone in the abattoir scene, which has a forbidden quality that titillates almost as much as it horrifies.[96] However, the stronger insinuations come through when the team enter Rose's bedroom, and it is here, too, that the imagery is intriguingly similar to Crichton's. Guided by Jane and Rose's mother, Suzuki films Rose's prematurely developed body, which her mother tiredly acknowledges as already signifying sexually: "It's not like it's her fault. And with a body like that, who's gonna be looking at her face, right?"⁹⁷ To this, the Japanese have no reply and yet their presence is not passive, for by recording the mother's testimony they become agents against women's exploitation. In narrative terms, the scene pivots upon the inauguration of a politically active consciousness among the documentarians, because Rose's mother is too drained of emotional strength to intervene personally (until they supply her with the video, that is). This consciousness is ushered in by Rose's body, which "shockingly intrudes into the mix of polemical rhetoric, factoids, multiple narrative sources and voices . . . and the hyperbolic, darkly comic—bordering on the cartoon-like—invented stories."⁹⁸ In these respects, the body's place in the narrative is altogether similar to that of another character, Michelle, Peter Smith's daughter in *Rising Sun*, whose significance is underscored in the final paragraph of his own video-recorded testimony:

> I walked into my daughter's room. I looked at her crib, and her covers with the elephants sewn on it. I thought of the way she slept, so trustingly, lying on her back, her arms thrown over her head. I thought of the way she trusted me to make her world for her now. And I thought of the world that she would grow into. And as I started to make her bed, I felt uneasy in my heart.⁹⁹

Crichton and Ozeki both position a White infant daughter as symbolic of the country's future, and each strike a pessimistic narrative pose (one daughter faces a world of toxic farming practices, carcinogenic meat, and medicalized female reproduction; the other confronts a world of corrupted American institutions, perpetual trade imbalance, and sexual practices akin to White slavery). These features reveal both novelists as essentially issue driven. As literature scholar Emily Russell correctly points out, in US politics the child is an 'apolitical' figure whose invocation cuts across ideological lines.¹⁰⁰

That Crichton and Ozeki use the child figure as a politically redolent signifier is suggestive either of intertextuality or a shared sense of dominating discourses, a conclusion that is further reinforced by the significance of the tape recordings to the plot development of both stories. In *Rising Sun*, Japanese corporate executives attempt to keep the tape recordings of Cheryl Austin's murder from Smith and Connor, while in Ozeki's novel, Jane's tapes almost fall into the hands of Joichi Ueno, who strictly adheres to his version of the original *MAW!* concept and has no patience with Jane's boundary-pushing approach.¹⁰¹ In both narratives, the denouement hinges upon the repossession of the tapes with their incriminating footage and the narrators of both stories watch the footage many times, to an almost obsessive degree.

Indeed, students who read Ozeki's novel frequently report that the narrative itself "has a cinematic quality or . . . the pacing of a multi-episode television show."[102] However, Ozeki's work inverts Michael Crichton's narrative inasmuch as the tapes' content is preserved by Oh and Suzuki, not altered.[103] In addition, the Japanese security tapes that record Cheryl Austin's death are visual-only media, meaning that the reader cannot imagine a multisensory response on the part of the Japanese who view her death. Instead, the latter proceed impassively and heartlessly, whereas in Ozeki's narrative, Oh and Suzuki respond emotively to their work, enabling the reader to recover them from the stereotypes they inhabited at the start of the novel.

Closing Scene: The Departure Lounge

"The passage from the modern to the postmodern is also the passage from Fordism to Sonyism; the passage of the locus of technocultural power from the manufacture of standardized, mass-produced goods to the manufacture of quality products designed to sit in a variety of specialized market niches."[104] This observation, offered by the Australian media theorist McKenzie Wark, encapsulates the sense of transition that pervaded socio-economic analyses in the United States during the late 1970s through 1994. Sensing that the trade winds of global finance had changed direction, writers like Gore Vidal offered stern guidance about the much-anticipated 'Pacific Century,' while Hollywood responded to the decline of 'rigid' Fordist production methods in Detroit by ushering in a new wave of thrillers and science fiction films that envisaged a future centered on Tokyo or Osaka (or a machine world in which humans are all but extinct).[105] 'Japan-bashing' was a cruder response, less creative and more didactic—in a word, more Fordist inasmuch as authors like Crichton responded to a perceived threat by mass-producing tropes in an assembly-line fashion.

A separate consideration of the national cultures of the United States and New Zealand permits one to observe the formation and progression of 'Japan bashing' in localized forms, although its contours and particulars show up more vividly through comparison. The 1980s was the decade in which 'Japan Panic' reached its zenith in both national cultures, 'possessing' and tormenting fiction writers with images of a conquest that was always on the brink of taking place (although this was more evident in American publications). After the bursting of Japan's economic bubble, the tropes and ideologies left over from Second World War propaganda underwent interment, leaving only the imagery of assembly-line 'robot' personnel and other technocentric vocabularies for reanimation.[106] To date, those Asian Americanists who have revisited this era have proceeded as far as to acknowledge, ruefully but honestly, that being enthusiastic consumers of at least some anglophone cultural productions that include ethnic minority Asian characters might render critical reading practices an intriguing experience.[107] In one article, Stephen Hong Sohn attempts to strike a balance between the need to grant ethnic minority writers the integrity of their depictions and the equally pressing need to acknowledge the imprint of Orientalism within their published narratives, whether the writer is aware of its presence or not (a variation on Sheng-mei Ma's idea of writers as fully self-aware in their confrontation with stereotypes). Erring on the side of (semi)autonomous writing practices, Sohn reconfigures Orientalism away from the pejorative mode of domination, as originally conceived by Said, toward a "value-neutral approach to Orientalist representations that affirms their various rhetorical stances."[108] In my reading of Ozeki's novel I have plied the same course, given that the first half of *My Year of Meats* reveals clear instances in which the author incorporated tropes commonly associated with expatriated Japanese in White American cultural productions of the era. Just as clear, however, are the instances in which Ozeki breaks the mold even after having constructed it. Although Oh and Suzuki do not emerge as developed characters at the end of this process, their transition from myopic, would-be womanizers to critically astute documentarians is the clearest instantiation of this process.

3 Captive Memories: Internment North and South

So powerfully did the whole grim aspect of Ahab affect me, and the livid brand which streaked it, that for the first few moments I hardly noticed that not a little of this overbearing grimness was owing to the barbaric white leg upon which he partly stood. It had previously come to me that this ivory leg had at sea been fashioned from the polished bone of the sperm whale's jaw. "Aye, he was dismasted off Japan," said the old Gay-Head Indian once; "but like his dismasted craft, he shipped another mast without coming home for it. He has a quiver of 'em."

—Herman Melville, *Moby-Dick*

The staged commemoration of wartime events often functions as a seismographic measure of the heft and clout of veterans' affairs organizations and other, sometimes antithetical, special interest groups—the American Legion, say, or Veterans for Peace, to pick two influential examples from the United States—whose respective mandates jostle one another for attention in committees, meetings, hearings, and private offices. As an oft-cited case in point, the furor that engulfed the Smithsonian National Air and Space Museum's planned exhibit of the *Enola Gay* (the B-29 Superfortress that dropped an atomic bomb over Hiroshima) in 1995 may be described as an almost theatrical performance of breast-beating tragic choruses, the effect of which is now a matter of public record (explored in Chapter 4). At around the same time a more literally theatrical, but no less contentious, affray took place in New Zealand, where one commemoration involved a production of Vincent O'Sullivan's *Shuriken* (1985), a play that deals sympathetically with the plight of Japanese prisoners who were spirited to New Zealand in the aftermath of the Guadalcanal Campaign.[1] As with the Smithsonian exhibition, surviving Allied veterans responded with skepticism as to the national self-criticism underpinning the production. The recalcitrance of Japanese officials when it came to public apologies for wartime atrocities rendered the play, as well as a proposed peace garden adjacent to the site of the original camp, signally inappropriate in the veterans' opinion. After strong opposition from the Returned and Services' Association, plans for the garden were shelved by the local council, although the play itself drew public acclaim in Hamilton and Tokyo, a fleeting but heart-warming salute to the war generation of the North and South Pacific.[2]

Knowingly or not, writers of historical fiction may find themselves heralded in like turn by the vested discourses of a politically active community, although the extent to which this happens—and, more importantly still, the writing process in which it is implicated—is seldom, if ever, a matter of public record. Book reviews and interviews notwithstanding, readers are left with the finished product, the politics of which, if they hold true to the discursive boundaries of a given genre, may appear wholly unremarkable. In what follows, I retain the comparative methodology of prior chapters to render conspicuous—without making aberrant—the political geography of the internment of Japanese civilians/minorities in New Zealand and the United States. To date, the grounds, if not the practice, of comparison have never been in doubt, given that internment was a Pacific-wide practice in the British dominions, as were the Asian (particularly Chinese) exclusion acts that foreshadowed internment, yet literary novels from and about Australia and New Zealand have been scarce, to say the least. Canadian novels, on the other hand, and those of Kerri Sakamoto and Joy Kogawa in particular, have facilitated insightful comparisons with the writings of American authors John Okada and Monica Sone, among others, although an unintended result of scholarly efforts has been the discursive construction of internment as a North American rather than broadly Anglo-Pacific concern.[3] Moreover, structural similarities between the Japanese American and Japanese Canadian novel mean that studies have been largely, though not entirely, founded on equivalent, rather than contrastive, historical and political exemplars. Literary scholars Fu-Jen Chen and Su-Lin Yu suggest as much in their study of internment fiction writings, tactfully concluding that the emphasis novelists place upon the political, legal, and military dimensions has given rise to a somewhat linear narrative form. According to Chen and Yu, the effect of this linearity has served to underscore the temporal and the sequential at the expense of the spatial landscapes in which internment took place.[4]

In this chapter, I extend the geographical radius of Chen and Yu's criticism to address the manner in which anglophone Japanese civilian/minority internment narratives reach for, or avoid, an awareness of their interrelationship with the stories of Pacific War combat veterans. By framing this investigation alongside the controversy that surrounded the 1995 performance of *Shuriken*, I hope it is now apparent that publications or performances about underrepresented (or otherwise captive) groups of people during the war years may serve the political and cultural interests of survivors and descendants, but may also act to displace the concomitant interests of veterans' groups and their cultural artifacts. Let me be clear, at this point, that I do not suggest that scholars must necessarily take sides or act as advocates of one group over the other, even though, in practice, that does tend to be the rule. My intention is rather to pay special attention to those literary fictions that seek to accommodate stories relating to more than one form of captivity (what I term a 'multimodal' approach) or to the combat veteran's story alongside that of the civilian/minority internee. Such fictions cannot sustain an overtly liberal or conservative political partisanship but must instead strike a balance, if not necessarily an accord, between the respective communities.[5]

Answering this need with a literary style that can address the recovered histories of veteran and former internee constitutes, in my opinion, the defining quality of my two sources, David Guterson's *Snow Falling on Cedars* (1994) and Wendy Catran's *The Swap* (2004). Admittedly, the congruence between these texts may be hard to perceive at first glance, although that is as likely attributable to the difference in their target readership and in the literary history behind the two novels. Guterson benefits from a lineage of literary efforts that seek to deepen the reader's knowledge of Japanese American internment, whereas Catran stands alone as the first author to draw attention to internment in New Zealand. Additionally, like a number of the earliest Japanese American publications, Catran writes for young adults, and so the fairest comparison would more properly match her work with, possibly, Florence Crannell Means' *The Moved-Outers* (1945).[6] But whereas early writings of the Japanese American experience were almost solely concerned with internment, Catran shows an awareness of how Pacific War veteran memories may come into conflict with memories of internment. (To be sure, writers like Yoshiko Uchida had known this also, but Uchida manifests her awareness in narratives that underemphasize the suffering of Japanese Americans, the better to avoid drawing the wrong sort of attention to her community. Catran, by contrast, does not impose any such restraints on her writing, mainly because there are no groups of former internees or their descendants living in New Zealand. Her writing therefore contains no power to advance any sociopolitical agenda in relation to the community she describes, addressing instead a readership that is wholly unaware of the histories or peoples in question.) This quality places Catran's writing in a different category from early Japanese American equivalents and so, too, does her willingness to use the figure of the Pacific War veteran as the bearer of a competitive discourse, often sullenly resistant but also commanding sympathy on his own terms.

Guterson and Catran put the internee and the veteran in conversation, although more often than not this encounter leads to withdrawn silences that function to underscore the political and individual divisions between the two parties. Such moments are hard to ignore, as the thrust and cadence of the prose tend to come up short with an abruptness that is startling. Since the origin of these 'breaks' is left deliberately unclear, a challenge facing both writers is to map out life stories in a way that does justice to the characters' damaged subjectivity. Above all, this involves taking readers toward a moment or 'place' in which they can observe the essential brokenness of the former internee and veteran, a journey that can plug some of the gaps in our understanding, though not all.[7] Clearly demarcated temporal distinctions like 'then' and 'now'—the hallmarks of a linear narrative—run counter to the nuances of this project. Instead, Guterson and Catran employ shifts in character perspective, juxtaposed moments in time, and deliberate confusions in the narrator's subjectivity, qualities that literary scholar Anne Whitehead has identified as characterizing 'trauma fiction,' a body of work that confronts the reader with nontraditional modes of narration while seeking to reestablish a meaningful connection with the past.[8] By this route, readers come to sense the weight of meaning dammed up behind the silences of the veteran and the former internee and to better appreciate the ways in which their silences attempt to cancel each other out. Even so, our sensitization is not, and can never be, 'complete,' for the characters themselves emerge from, and represent, distinctive literary traditions that are resistant to closure. In her seminal study, King-Kok Cheung describes how Asian American writers have used an 'articulate silence' as a way to communicate meaningfully or otherwise register the imposition of silence on them:

> The writers question the authority of language (especially language that passes for history) and speak to the resources as well as the hazards of silence. They articulate—question, report, expose—the silences imposed on themselves and their peoples, whether in the form of feminine and cultural decorum, external or self-censorship, or historical or political invisibility; at the same time they reveal, through their own manners of telling and through their characters, that silences—textual ellipses, nonverbal gestures, authorial hesitations (as against moral, historical, religious, or political authority)—can also be articulate.[9]

But if silences can be articulate, there are other forms that speak to the incapacity of the subject to communicate meaningfully, even when communication is frequently attempted and most desired. This is a condition Trevor Dodman has identified in his analysis of Ernest Hemingway's *A Farewell to Arms* (1929), where "narration functions as a prosthesis meant to stave off a sense of the self as a disarticulated scar."[10] While an articulate silence may communicate nonverbally in lucid and coherent ways, war veterans more often suffer under "enforced silences" that register "the disruptive workings of traumatic memories aggressively imposing themselves on the survivor."[11] These two forms of silence comprise wholly different practices and mental conditions: in one we see an individual who communicates well, if she or he chooses to, but through such verbal economy as to seem, to those unfamiliar with the practice, devoid of meaning, whereas the other case reveals a subject whose preference is to communicate verbally but whose self, shattered or partially maimed through exposure to combat or atrocity, cannot find expression adequate to impart meaning or provide relief.

In both novels, the veteran and the ethnic Japanese minority employ (as a standard communicative preference) or resort to (through no other choice) forms of silence that either speak to their individual conditions or comment on 'the other's' (perceived) identity. It is in the meeting ground, or lack thereof, between these silences that the novels generate political stances in respect to the reformulation of (inter)national histories. I shall shortly pay closer attention to this process in both novels, but first a brief explication on the facts surrounding New Zealand's internment of Japanese civilians is in order, not to affirm or contest the depictions that Catran provides, but to offer some basis for understanding why Catran writes out of an historical vacuum that thus far remains unchallenged. Thanks to historical and literary efforts spearheaded in the United States, a considerable body of scholarship exists on Japanese American internment and the internment of Japanese Canadians. On the other hand, internment in the rest of the Americas is relatively underexplored and what took place on the small islands of the South Pacific is all but unknown. The following summary is necessarily fragmentary, involving as it does a patchwork quilt of clues pieced together from published histories that, until now, have invariably been concerned with other matters. But the basics come through clearly enough.

Internment in New Zealand

When President Franklin Roosevelt signed executive order 9066, authorizing the internment of over 120,000 persons of Japanese ancestry, the evacuation took place within full view of the general public. Notices appeared, informing people of the decision, sympathetic neighbors rallied round to offer support, avaricious fortune hunters preyed on the vulnerable, photographic journalists took shots as trains carried people away, and, before the war was over, nonfiction writers staked out political stances with respect to the phenomenon. Among the latter, Alan Hynd asserted in *Betrayal from the East: The Inside Story of Japanese Spies in America* (1943), that a Japanese immigrant population had entrenched itself in the fabric of American society primarily as a means to cause mischief through industrial sabotage and guerrilla activity. Representing a contrarian discourse were writers such as Florence Crannell Means, who imagined their subjects as family units rather than sleeper cells and emphasized the families' helpless incredulity toward the War Relocation Authority. Even as the internment process was in effect, therefore, American civilians encountered cultural productions that invited them to take up a political position in respect to the phenomenon. In the South Pacific, on the other hand, the situation could hardly have been more different. There, it was entirely possible, indeed it was almost a universal rule, that one would never have heard about the treatment of Japanese beyond the ongoing saga of military campaigning. Now and then, there were references in the newspapers to the Japanese prisoners of war at Featherston, but nobody heard tell of another camp somewhere else. The studied indifference toward the compromised status of local human rights, which most civilians acknowledged as a necessary part of the war effort, goes some way toward explaining the lack of awareness.[12] More significant by far, however, was the manner and degree to which Japanese civilians experienced internment in New Zealand, a process that differed markedly from that of the United States.

Upon the outbreak of war, the chief difference between the two countries' situations was that, in New Zealand's case, the Japanese civilians in question were not domiciled on national territory, nor were they in possession of citizenship or residency rights. Instead, migration patterns had taken them to the islands of Fiji and Tonga, where they remained sojourners, occupying relatively humble jobs as shopkeepers and fishermen. Their status was called into question as a matter of course following Japan's attack on Pearl Harbor and Tonga's declaration of war twenty-four hours later.[13] Neither of the small northern islands had adequate numbers of personnel to intern the Japanese in their own territory, and although New Zealand might have provided a guard unit along with the Third Division that assisted in the defense of Fiji, New Zealand's army was already overstretched and the Japanese advance pressed home the issue of how, if at all, an attack on the islands could be repulsed.

The question grew in urgency, particularly in light of the New Zealand government's 1938 declaration that Fiji and Tonga would comprise its outer defense perimeter (Japan too would later place emphasis on the security provided through its island possessions). What happened to Fiji and Tonga was regarded as a harbinger to what could happen to New Zealand, and preparations were made accordingly, the first step being to remove segments of the population.[14] Residents of Japanese descent were immediately caught up in the arrangements, as were *papālangi* (White) and part-*papālangi* women and children, who were compulsorily evacuated on the Union Steam Ship Company's *Matua*.[15] By January 1942, those Japanese who had formerly been resident in Fiji and Tonga were all in New Zealand and divided between two locations: fourteen Japanese men from Tonga and a further thirty-one from Fiji were placed on Somes Island, a onetime quarantine facility in Wellington harbor that now served as a holding area for German Nazis and nationals, Italian fascists and nationals, Japanese civilians, and others marked as suspicious characters, including Jews.[16]

Women were held in less restrictive inland areas, but unlike with the men, the rule was to divide the nationalities, thereby ensuring that the Japanese women were not domiciled among groups of people whose culture or political creed reinforced or conflicted with their own. To this end, the Department of Internal Affairs rented a house at Pokeno for the eight Japanese women and nine children from Tonga. This house proved dispiriting indeed, requiring, among other things, the removal of rank, mosquito-harboring growth, the installation of new toilet facilities, the repapering of interior walls, the repairing of the roof, and the demolition of a rat-infested shed. All such defects were quickly remedied, however, and the Japanese women remained under the relatively benign administration of the police, a stark contrast to army supervision on Somes Island.

While improving the conditions of accommodation at Pokeno was a necessity in the short term, the long-term intention was to repatriate the Japanese in return for Allied POWs, an objective also pursued by the Americans with respect to some of their internees.[17] Negotiations between the Allied and Japanese governments was a protracted process, but on June 23, 1942 the possibility of repatriating the Japanese was established, and, accordingly, a questionnaire was issued to the male internees, the purpose of which was to determine their willingness to participate in an exchange of prisoners. All except three internees expressed their wish to participate and, on June 25, the Police Department confirmed that the women at Pokeno also wished to be exchanged.

By July 1943, arrangements were well under way for the transfer of most of the Japanese to Australia on board the vessel *Oranje*. They would then be transported to the neutral port of Goa for a linkup with the Allied POWs held by Japan. The journey had several legs to it, and there was some concern for the safety of the vessels involved, but, in the event, these anxieties proved moot, when, on August 2, 1943, a Liberator-type aircraft leaving Auckland and containing ten men (seven Japanese and three Thais), five women, and ten children crashed on takeoff. There were thirteen fatalities: some died in the crash itself, while others, in all probability, drowned in muddy waters before rescuers could arrive. The reasons behind the crash prompted an investigation, the results of which placed blame on mechanical failure. Meanwhile, Australia's repatriation process continued unabated and, two weeks later, *The City of Canterbury* set sail with 834 Japanese on board. For their part, those transferees who remained in New Zealand had to wait to attempt a second exchange until they and the urns of the deceased could be taken to Australia, this time on the *Wahine*. As New Zealand divested itself of its Japanese, a few remained behind, though these were truly exceptional. Among the latter, two of the original internees from Tonga, Mitsuichi Saito and Juhei Nakao, wished to return there but had to wait until the end of the war and for the assent of Tonga's queen, Sālote Tupou III. A further two Japanese nationals, resident in New Zealand at the outbreak of the war, Harold Kunioka and Kiyo Kameda, were interned for the duration and released at the end.[18]

With the exchanges complete, the story of New Zealand's role as an internment state during the Second World War was laid to rest for the remainder of the twentieth century, leaving today's historians and literary scholars with the twin challenges of coming to terms with a near-total void in the public consciousness and an absence of former internees whose testimonials might otherwise go some way toward infusing raw facts with a human dimension. In the United States, political activism on the part of former internees speeded the production, reception, and quality of cultural productions, but in New Zealand no such activism has taken place and those wishing to address the matter of internment must take heed of the masculine tradition of war service still current, as well as the comparatively better-known stories of Allied POWs.

The sensitive nature of the Japanese story and its potential to unsettle valorizing notions of wartime service, puts writers and artists in a position somewhat akin to those American writers in the immediate postwar period whose publications edged around the story of Japanese American internment without emphasizing the American government's role in the matter. Moreover, the case of the 1995 production of *Shuriken* illustrates how veteran sentiment and the Allied POW experience may, through their presence in national memories of the war, foreclose creative ventures that seem to impinge on their status. None of this bodes well for authors who seek to write of internment in New Zealand. However, given that New Zealand's internees were, from the outset, considered in terms of their potential for prisoner exchange, cultural productions addressing the events are compelled to view the internment experience, not as a singular event, but as part of a Pacific-wide series of imprisonments whose division into nationally specific histories belies their interconnectedness.

In Catran's writing, therefore, the manner in which different wartime narratives collide, converge, or cancel one another out becomes a matter of pressing significance, alongside the details of the internment itself. Hers, in short, is as much a historiographic as a historical novel. American productions, by contrast, have tended to treat internment as an incomparable matter of national significance rather than an inseparable episode of Pacific-wide activity. The effect has been a remarkable succession of works that explore and excoriate the deep-seated prejudice that led to the internment of persons of Japanese descent, of which Guterson's novel is among the more established.[19] These efforts, and the quality of the results, have unquestionably placed American literature far ahead of New Zealand's still-nascent attempts at self-criticism where Japanese civilian/minority internment is concerned, and, as we shall see, Guterson's language continuously arcs back toward the United States as the object of a search for the ideological origins of trauma.

The Veteran as Savior

The circulation and circularity of prejudicial notions—that is, their dispersal among diverse communities and the return of actors and agents to the places (and peoples) from which they first received their indoctrination—lie at the heart of Guterson's text. Internment is just one stage in this process, albeit a crucial one that is described in some detail. Intertwined with the internment narrative are the stories of the inhabitants of San Piedro Island, just off the coast of Washington State, a large number of whom fish for a living. One of these, Kabuo Miyamoto, is charged with the murder of fellow fisherman Carl Heine after the latter's body is found in a net. A trial ensues, covered by the local reporter, Ishmael Chambers, whose narrative persona is the most consistent touchstone throughout the novel and whose own history involves a childhood love affair with the accused's wife. Moments of courtroom cross-examination alternate with the memories of witnesses, drawing the reader's attention to inconsistencies between past events, their recollection in testimony, and their incorporation within a legal framework skewed toward the exploitation or rectification of anti-Japanese prejudice within audience and jury. Stereotypes and their capacity to foster (mis)assumptions comprise the currency of exchange in these moments.

As different social classes, ethnicities, ages, and dialects occupy the witness stand, the picture that emerges takes on an American resonance by its very plurality, yet the individuals are frequently at odds with one another, and the story they speak of, without vocalizing it necessarily, is one of suspicion and hostility, charting their inevitable course toward persecution. Measured and contemplative, the narrative pace obscures this process somewhat, suggesting ample latitude for characters to consider each other's situations dispassionately, and this slow pace serves another purpose as well in allowing readers to get a close look at the discriminatory practices that underpin people's motivations. To a large degree, the discriminations that take place on a day-by-day basis derive from standards of social inclusion and exclusion traceable to the wartime profiling of the Japanese, a process that conflated their racial and national characteristics. The capacity of the San Piedro residents to think outside this conflation is so limited that the outcome of the trial appears to be a foregone conclusion, and the narrative takes on a sense of convergence, such that one cannot consider individual characters without likewise measuring the extent to which each confronts or avoids their part in the process. Page by page, the weight of the past hangs over every character in the novel.

Intertwined with the private burdens of the individual is the struggle of the novel to overcome the canonical weight of its literary progenitor, *Moby-Dick* (1851).[20] In a moment of private musing, Ishmael Chambers recalls reading Melville's tome and judging his namesake tolerable, unlike the figure of Ahab, whom he finds distasteful.[21] The significance of *Moby-Dick* comes to readers mainly through Ishmael, whose sense of propriety makes him something of a social caretaker, someone who stands apart from the trial's polarizing cause and effects in contemplation rather than hostility. Such reflection, at least, remains both possible and ideal, although Ishmael's role and his built-in watchfulness are not as emotionally detached as they first appear, since his condition as a veteran renders him vulnerable to prejudices of his own. Indeed, war has twisted him into a composite that balances reason and friendship against anguished separateness, the principal characteristics of Melville's Ishmael and Ahab, respectively, and while the Ishmael of both texts maintains a position of power, as actual narrator or as a journalist,

Guterson's Ishmael shares with Ahab the grim authority of the amputee. This latter feature is especially significant, providing both characters a reason to seek retribution against the agent of their disfigurement, and for both, an opportunity arises and an ideal (profit from whaling, justice in the courts) becomes clouded by self-interest. On the matter of intertextuality, Anne Whitehead writes that "in returning to canonical texts, novelists evoke the Freudian notion of the repetition-compulsion, for their characters are subject to the 'plot' of another('s) story. Novelists can also revise canonical works, however, reading them against the grain and providing a new perspective on familiar texts."[22] For *Snow Falling on Cedars*, a national history of prejudice and a literary history of madness converge and reinforce one another, creating a quality of predestination that pushes the story forward, although the resolution of the former ultimately proves enough to counteract the damage of the latter.

This superstructure barely registers on the novel's character-driven surface, which is so finely drawn that the mechanisms of ideology and intertextuality appear wholly natural, quietly ensconced behind areas allotted for the expression of each character. Art Moran's contemplations on the *Susan Marie* and Horace Whaley's forensic flashbacks in the mortuary illustrate this aspect. These are moments when characters appear to step out from the text, not so much unfettered as aided by their human flaws, which they carry with them into their solitary meditations. The quality of Guterson's writing owes much to his uncompromising commitment to this soul-searching project, as well as to a deft-handed fairness where human weakness is concerned. A linear spectrum of virtue and vice is redundant alongside such a framework—there is only the full measure of characters as they appear to themselves and the half or near-empty estimates of them that others arrive at. Nor is this a one-way street particular to the double consciousness of the minority subject; rather, it describes the existential reality of all characters. Thus, Ishmael is not only acutely aware of his place as an outsider in the discourse community of the fishermen but also of the values his appearance signifies.[23] As in his case, sometimes characters are aware of what their appearances connote; whereas in others, such as Kabuo's, they misapprehend their effect on others.[24]

The origins of misreadings are various, partly ascribable to the cultural separatism of islanders, the pastoral rivalries of landowners, and the reactionary suspicions of German settlers. By far the greater cause, however, is the impact of the Pacific War on the public consciousness, which runs like a seismic rift through the text, splintering people in opposing directions to one another and to themselves. The silence of beleaguered identities emerges from within characters as a response to what the Pacific War has meant for them, as Horace realizes when he notes how the veteran Carl Heine was formerly jocular but became virtually mute after the war.[25] Elsewhere, Ishmael's mother responds to her son's request for guidance and advice by frankly admitting that his emotional numbness has placed him beyond comprehension, and when Hatsue takes the stand, her mind recollects how Kabuo's war service rendered him an unknown quantity. The novel is replete with such cases, and in each the Pacific War stands not so much alongside characters as between them, severing rather than binding social connections.

It is worth taking a close look at the estrangement of Ishmael and Hatsue, a process that provides a paradigm by which readers may approach the aforementioned characters too. Once the Pacific War breaks out, it impacts upon both characters, rending them apart from each other so that communication becomes limited to carefully inflected silences in which reproach and disdain figure strongly as meanings. Yet the Pacific War serves only to break an already strained relationship, under pressure from the silencing effect of adults, although it would be unfair to say that all silences are indicative of emotional damage, a lesson Ishmael learns when, as a child, he kisses Hatsue and realizes that her silence is typical of her and not tied to the event itself.[26] As it transpires in this case, Hatsue's silence most likely affirms a requited longing, yet it also looks back on her schooling in diffidence, a practice that is bound to her position as an ethnic minority and a woman: "Mrs. Shigemura was open and forthright with Hatsue about matters of a sexual nature. With all the seriousness of a fortune-teller she predicted that white men would desire Hatsue and seek to destroy her virginity [. . .] Stay away from white men, said Mrs. Shigemura, and marry a boy of your own kind whose heart is strong and good."[27] Hatsue's education in equanimity contains no ideological component until this point and need not be a vessel for racialized sentiments, as Hatsue herself realizes upon discovering that her outward composure provides a perfect façade for her inner imaginings, which are effectively directed toward the forbidden fruit Mrs. Shigemura holds out.

Thus, while a planned inoculation of Hatsue's mind is the aim, incubation is the result. Yet it remains a doubtful, halting, imperfect incubation riven with guilt at the contravention of familial expectations, and it entices Ishmael toward a point where Hatsue presents a promise of romantic fulfillment that she eventually reneges on, prompting in him an embittered turn toward anti-Japanese sentiment. Mrs. Shigemura's teachings are the starting point for this process, and her influence is indelible: it is internalized by Hatsue

Internment North and South | 93

and reemerges in her in the form of suspicion toward Ishmael's integrationist ideas. The two children do not, of course, comprehend their position in these terms, and they only glimpse their differences obliquely through discussions that reveal their commitment to holistic and divisible worldviews, a difference that contains obvious repercussions for their own relationship:

> "Oceans don't mix," said Hatsue. "They're different temperatures. They have different amounts of salt."
> "They mix underneath," said Ishmael. "It's all really just one ocean."
> [. . .]
> "The main thing is, water is water. Names on a map don't mean anything. Do you think if you were out there in a boat and you came to another ocean you'd see a sign or something? It—"
> "The color would change, I've heard that," said Hatsue. "The Atlantic Ocean is brown, sort of, and the Indian Ocean is blue."[28]

Hatsue's insistence on partition doubles as a statement of racial fixity and describes the limits of her own future, as she draws a prophylactic demarcation across her relationship with Ishmael after her mother learns of it. The language of loyalty to one's descent, whether racial or cultural or both, and the disjuncture that arises in harmonizing these codes with consensual practices in everyday life—between prescribed and proscribed behaviors according to issei, on the one hand, and the pull toward practices that follow individual choice, on the other—show Hatsue's dilemma in terms characteristic to the ethnic subject.[29] By placing family dictates ahead of personal choice, Hatsue does not fail to realize an American ideal, for she takes on this decision in an internment camp, the political solution to the selfsame issues writ large on a national scale—that is, whether to place emphasis on a conflation of White cultural and racial identity to the exclusion of specific ethnic groups or whether to recognize in the latter the realization of an ideal that makes American identity a matter of choice. In fact, the doctrine of racial exclusion, whether enforced by the government, as it is in Hatsue's case, or by a family, as it is in Ishmael's, is so similar in both cases that the text reflects each side back on the other.

The mutual reflexivity built into such moments is most obvious in the language Hatsue's mother, Fujiko, uses to rein in her daughter's errant impulses: "You must live in this world, of course you must, and this world is the world of the *hakujin*—you must learn to live in it, you must go to school. But don't allow living *among* the *hakujin* to become living *intertwined* with them. Your soul will decay."³⁰ Given that these words echo the practices of the state, Fujiko speaks with considerable authority. The language of prejudice has gone full circle by this point, entering the racialized subject and emerging, reworked, as an equal and opposite reaction. Indeed, although the story makes clear that the issei foster their own suspicions about White sexual predators, there are, in Fujiko's history of immigration, the moments in which she first experiences the "humiliating disdain" of Whites, suggesting that mainstream American society may, after all, be the origin of the prejudice that shuttles across generations and from minority subject to veteran.³¹ Whatever the case, by the time of internment, Fujiko and the state act almost in concert, not only echoing one another's language but speaking in each other's stead. Thus, the FBI agents who check over the Imada's house casually play at parenting, and Fujiko's prediction that the war will force her children to become more Japanese could well stand in for government sentiment.³² In the face of the harmonization of parental and internment discourse, Hatsue's resistance crumbles. Her only refuge is in silence, the practice of which is bound to her training as a Japanese woman. Fujiko thereby traps her daughter in a quandary: if Hatsue speaks out, she reveals an intemperance anathema to state and family; if she remains silent, she proves her Japanese-ness and must behave as a Japanese according to her mother's terms or live a life of contradictions. The silence that follows has multiple agents, being the product of her ethnic identity, as seen by the state, and her status as a female subject, as dictated by her mother. In common with other ethnic women, the sources of Hatsue's silence may share similar or even identical ideological components, and yet the doubling of their influence results in a compound effect.³³

The silencing of the internee by multiple, interpenetrating agents explains her effect on Ishmael, whom Hatsue effectively silences in turn when he tries to speak with her in the courthouse.³⁴ As noted, the veteran subjects are distinct in their deracinated behaviors, to the extent that they alienate those nearest to them by their unreachable malaise, so for Ishmael to move beyond his nominally disarticulated selfhood requires significant effort and must hold out the promise of betterment in psychological or emotional terms for him to attempt it. The prospect of such relief is tied to Hatsue's position as his former lover but also to her rejection of him while she is interned, and, since love and trauma are each defined primarily by the need to make a compromised subject whole, his return to her is unsurprising. Yet this effort cannot succeed. Ishmael is associated with a consensual, pre-internment subjectivity in which social possibilities, unchallenged by relocation, and romantic intrigue, undiscovered by Fujiko, are attainable.

Then there is the matter of the trial itself, an inherently public affair that recalls the internment, which, as Emily Roxworthy notes, objectified Japanese Americans within the public gaze at the same time it displaced them:

> By framing the evacuation and internment as *spectacles*, the United States positioned the American public as passive spectators to the unconstitutional treatment of their ethnic Japanese neighbors and, simultaneously, cast the public as heroic 'patriots' opposite Japanese Americans, who were cast in one of two thankless roles: expressionless automata or melodramatic villains.[35]

Although Ishmael is not involved in the trial's proceedings, just being a spectator is enough to make his overtures to Hatsue problematic, and, in fact, his own prejudices have already proven his capacity to conflate the Japanese military and former internees.[36] Hatsue's rejection of Ishmael is therefore an act of throwing prejudice back at the veteran, recycling it in the face of the evident reprisals taking place against her husband in the courtroom.

The outright disestablishment of his relationship with Hatsue leaves Ishmael no reason to hope for personal gain in the outcome of the trial, and so he adopts an attitude of indifference to it. Who Ishmael is, not what he can obtain, becomes the only issue at stake in determining the likelihood of actions on Kabuo's behalf. As the trial nears its close, the two attorneys take up positions encouraging reactionism (Alvin Hooks' approach) or contemplation (Nels Gudmundsson's message), and Ishmael's torn identity gravitates to each in turn. The lawyers' surnames reveal their textual and ideological positions, for Hooks seeks to conjoin or otherwise affix his interpretation of Kabuo's actions to memories of war and propaganda images of the Japanese. The surname 'Gudmundsson,' on the other hand, recalls lineage, wisdom, and fatherly guidance, evoking a paternalistic expectation of upright behavior. These siren calls vie within Ishmael, who voices the tortured condition of the whole community when, in mourning time's inability to heal wounds, he muses that "ten years was not really such a long time at all, and how was he to leave his passion behind when it went on living its own independent life, as tangible as the phantom limb he'd refused for so long to have denervated?"[37] The amputee's grievance, alongside the trial's headlong rush toward resolution, suggests the specter of an Ahab-esque imperative that must triumph over Ishmael's conscience.

To counteract the array of prejudicial sentiments in the San Piedro community and also the stricken sense of self-mortification that has made him a half Ishmael, half Ahab, Ishmael must recover his role as the eye through which the novel sees itself. In meeting this challenge, Ishmael learns to look past social veneers, including his own, and is aided in his efforts by a boyhood history that contains episodes, such as observing with Hatsue the world of marine life through a glass-bottomed box or mastering a box camera, which speak to his potential to 'see through' areas that others cannot, especially in regard to ocean worlds.[38] The talent returns to Ishmael in later life and on an altogether different scale when he visits a lighthouse and discovers records pertinent to the trial. These findings, as well as his realization of the importance of Carl Heine's lantern, are crucial, and although they do nothing to reintegrate Ishmael in any social sense, his commitment to comprehending how the individual is placed or displaced in society is reaffirmed and, through him, a narrative circle of character development reaches its completion, thereby ending the succession of persecutions in the community as well.

Having overthrown his compunctions and the prosecution of Kabuo in a single stroke, the specter of Ahab's drive toward communal destruction recedes from Ishmael and from the novel, leaving open the possibility of an alternative future for both. Only the matter of prejudice within the wider San Piedro community remains, and while the closure of the case against Kabuo appears to draw a line under this as well, whether this is actually so remains an open question. To be sure, the sense of resolution encompasses the wider community as well as Ishmael, but this may have less to do with the trial than the novel's use of a scapegoat on which to project the worst aspects of social prejudice. On this subject, the German scholar Heike Paul observes that the depiction of German Americans and, more especially, the figure of Carl Heine's mother, enacts a textual displacement of prejudice from White American society as a whole onto the ethnic German community, thereby absolving most (White) American readers of the need to take Guterson's writing as pertinent social criticism.[39] Paul's argument is compelling, but, even so, it supplies only half the answer to the means by which social prejudice apparently dissipates at the end. If the novel emphasizes the deep-seated antipathies of German Americans, it disburdens Ishmael of the same features and enables him to recover the role of Melville's Ishmael when he almost closes the novel as its narrator, seated in front of his typewriter, musing and possibly writing the final thoughts that serve as epilogue. The final account of what happened to Carl Heine comes to us through him, and we gradually understand how his fastidiousness, that maternal characteristic that deprived the Miyamotos of their land, deprived him of his life.[40] As a form of poetic justice, then, Carl's death balances the books, and yet it comes to us purely in this allusive form and thus does not exist outside

Ishmael's subjectivity. Readers are left to speculate on why Ishmael renders events as he does.

In my reading of *Snow Falling on Cedars*, I have illustrated how prejudice circulates among individuals in the novel and how silence can take many forms, including those that apparently implicate Japanese immigrants and minorities in the same cyclical discourse. The figure of the veteran stands as the most significant party to this process, at various times a source of, or solution to, the prejudices surrounding him. To this figure Guterson adds a compulsive drive toward self- and communal ruin that comes from *Moby-Dick*'s functioning as urtext. When Ishmael halts the progression of prejudice in its judicial manifestation and throws off the mantle of intertextual pre-determinism, then, he achieves a measure of peace for himself that carries over into his final role as quasi narrator. In short, the satisfying neatness of these developments for Ishmael stands in for a resolution for the whole San Piedro community. Readers may wonder about the more general reaction in San Piedro to Kabuo's acquittal and about people's opinion of Ishmael's editorial, but the novel does not take us that far. Instead, it rests easy in Ishmael's grasp, tidied up and rounded off in a manner that is geographically, morally, and psychologically self-contained and self-defined.

The Veteran as Protestor

Literary fictions that seek to disclose the Japanese American or Canadian internment experience have sometimes redoubled their commission by simultaneously probing and filling the vacancies in mainstream history writing and political discourse. The ways in which authors narrate internment, that is, originate not solely in the intrinsic worthiness of the story, but also from an extrinsic assessment of how it has been (mis)dealt with in past productions. As Gurleen Grewal puts it in her reading of *Obasan* (1981) and *Beloved* (1987), "When [conventional historiography] is the dominant group's version of an oppressed group's experience, it becomes imperative that the elisions, the repressions, and the silences be explored."[41]

If one approaches Wendy Catran's *The Swap* with the same set of assumptions, however, one must take into account the silence surrounding the story of internment in New Zealand, which amounts to a total void. Unlike Joy Kogawa, who wrote *Obasan* in the form of historiographic metafiction, Catran cannot place her writing in conversation with the published writings of government and the academy, as there have been none that have even touched on the Fijian/Tongan/New Zealand internment story. Naturally, one might retort, this only makes the project all the more worthwhile. To be fair, however, the ignorance of the New Zealand public is almost definitely not willful, having more to do with the suddenness with which the internees came to New Zealand and the equal suddenness of their departure. In the absence of surviving internees and their descendants living in New Zealand, it would be partly true to say that the story was forgotten (by the police, the army, and administrators), but truer still to say that it was never really known in the first place (by the general population). These matters are crucial to a reading of Catran, for they place her in the extraordinary position of being the first to publish on internment, even as they close off certain thematic areas that scholars have come to associate with internment in North America.

In particular, debates over immigration and exclusion acts, or assimilation and multiculturalism, are extraneous, and their absence forces a consideration of how a novel can challenge concepts of nation and society when the ethnic experience was so temporally transitory and geographically transitionary. This problem appears to have preoccupied Catran also, her solution being a family-centered story in which individual histories converge and compete for attention in formations wholly absent in other families but conceivable in every one. In other words, the author writes her story into the lives of characters who belong to a 'generic' Kiwi family. To reinforce the impression of the commonplace, Catran leaves the precise details of time and location to the imagination, beginning her chapters with headings like "Somewhere in the Pacific, Wartime" or "The Fifties, New Zealand." A few characters are also left nameless, being referred to only as "Uncle," "Mum," and "Dad." Deliberate vagueness of this sort is a recognized convention in many young adult novels, the effect being to bring events into high relief, almost as if they were happening to the people next door.

But there is another purpose here besides imagined proximity, or more properly in league with it, for, by prompting us to identify with a 'generic' family, Catran forces readers to recognize traits and thinking patterns that may be one's own—and not always of the most edifying sort, either. Committees for redress, community workshops, and conferences on political activism may not feature in her story, but readers do get a hard look at dining room quarrels, kitchen sink churlishness, and backyard moodiness. Within these moments, the foundations of the family are revealed as intimately dependent on the assumptions of the past, so that realignments in the latter disturb the structure of the former. Individual family members clash with one another, that is, because they represent vested historical interests, meaning that the past is not approached as an intellectual abstraction but carried within as an intensely personal, visceral reality that challenges the leveling, homogenized demands of family. What sets these tensions in motion is the departure of the parents' only son, Alan, to the Korean War. Readers do not learn what Alan experiences in this conflict, as his military service is viewed from the point of view of his younger sister, Maree, who judges it only in terms of "Alan before" and "Alan after," a comparison that reflects unfavorably on the returned version. Politically cynical and emotionally wasted, Alan himself implicitly agrees with the judgment, primarily because he has come to regard nationalism and militarism as a chance for states to extract a blood sacrifice of every passing generation.[42] Such sentiments put him at odds with the patriotism of Dad and Uncle, who are both veterans of the Second World War and proud of their service.[43] But Alan's attempt to break with the culture of the military answers the needs of his new wife, Keiko, whom he has met in Tokyo while defending her from the badinage of American GIs.[44] Keiko, in turn, carries with her the story of New Zealand internment, not her own but that of her adopted brother who survived the airplane crash before being repatriated, and it is really her presence, more than any subsequent event, that disturbs Uncle and Dad and, by extension, the emotional balance of the family. With these two sides occupying distinctive political and historical subjectivities, events do not have to unfold in order for the story to achieve momentum; instead, the characters look askance at one another while the only untouched innocent, Maree, tries to pick up the pieces of shattered family life.

In the following reading, I propose that the lateness of the first New Zealand publication on internment, arriving some sixty years after the evacuees departed, as well as the relative uniqueness of the facts of internment in comparison with North American equivalents, has allowed the author to construct a story that pays heed to how an internment narrative might interact with or come up against more 'established' bodies of knowledge. Such awareness, in particular, of the ways the internment and the Allied POW narrative counterbalance one another—or fail to—raises a set of questions that internment novels elsewhere rarely confront: can public interest sustain equal regard for the Allied POW and the internment experiences, or are political, social, and cultural movements inherently predisposed toward one at the expense of the other? If they are not so predisposed, what type of scale or measuring mechanism ensures that the balance of discursive power does not incline in prejudicial directions? If they are so predisposed, does the delivery of one signal the silencing of the other? Is moral geography tied to the spatial geography of the Pacific region, so that one assigns historical precedence to the memory of camps in a given area about which one knows a fair amount, but not to another about which one knows rather less? Can there only ever be one camp, one victim, one story?

Marching under the banner of 'correctives' and 'interventions,' nationally self-critical writers and scholars tend to satisfy themselves with productions that do indeed focus on one regional phenomenon, although, as in the case of John Okada's *No-No Boy* (1957), they readily acknowledge that multiple forms of victimhood may arise from that original moment.

Generally speaking, the response of groups and individuals who recall camp life (and camp deaths) at similar times, but in different regions, does not preoccupy nationally self-critical scholars and writers in the first instance. On the other hand, when one encounters a writer who adopts a 'multimodal' approach in the way that Catran does, one sees that although there are worthwhile questions to ask, the asking is easier than the answering. To read Catran is, in fact, to witness the birth of a well-researched impasse that takes the story of internment and inserts it into a field of contested knowledge in which it cannot function as more than an inert fixture. Literature scholars may observe this trend in novels of the Allied POW experience as well. Jim Lehrer's *The Special Prisoner* (2000), for example, likewise attempts to strike a balance in a match of 'dueling victimhoods,' and he, too, founders at the end—for what 'end' can there be when victimhood belongs equally to each side or, in any event, appears to?[45] One does not wish to be too hard on either of these writers, who are ultimately brought up short by their relative thinking and who, once they have thrashed out the reasons why others think in more absolute terms, come to the realization that they have created or 'encountered' a Gordian knot whose structure resists disentanglement. The value of their writing lies in describing the knot rather than undoing it, as well as ascribing moral and emotional imperatives to the knot's different historical strands.

To help readers get the point, Catran interweaves her strands in a structure of chapters that alternate between the 1940s narrative of Japanese internment and the Korean War veteran's hopes for a future with his Japanese war bride in mid-1950s New Zealand. In the narrative of the internment, the story focuses a good deal on those who stayed at Pokeno, perhaps because the situation of the Japanese men on Somes Island, thrown together with other nationalities and creeds, involved situations, and raised questions beyond the novel's capacity to address. Catran, in any case, prefers to approach internment from the point of view of those who are least equipped to endure it: the children who require schooling, the infants who are too young to comprehend, the women who are pregnant, and the wives who miss their husbands. Through these characters, readers come to understand the debilitating effect of forced separations as well as the irony built into a process that breaks up homes and then tucks women and children away in a country house. Perhaps another, more obvious reason for focusing on Pokeno rather than Somes is that the domestic setting facilitates comparisons with Keiko's travails as Alan's wife in the 1950s. Keiko's arrival into the Kiwi household heralds the possibility of binding ethnic-national groups together and bridging the divisions of the past, yet her presence elicits only an exclusionary silence and quickly reveals the limits of tolerance within the family, and in Uncle and Mum especially.[46] The notion of family, as Uncle and Mum conceive it, indicates ideals and expectations that cannot be contravened. In the case of women, gender roles dictate that they remain at home and not compete against men in the workplace.[47] In the case of veterans, the stress and temptations associated with overseas service typically grants them a degree of license, but in return for 'licentious' freedoms abroad and sexism in the workplace at home, they are enjoined to avoid marrying foreign women. Keiko does not seek work, yet she signifies a break in the expectations associated with veterans, and so she shuts herself away and is in turn ostracized by a wall of silence. Here, it is interesting to compare Keiko's situation with a moment in which the Pokeno women try to speak with their husbands during a visit to Somes Island:

"English," barked the guard.
"She's only—" began Lani.
"English!" said the guard, and scowled at them.
[. . .]
And then there was silence. Sakura wanted to scream. This was her father, whom she hadn't seen for so long. There was so much she wanted to say, tell him, ask him. The words wanted to pour out of her, in Tongan, in Japanese.[48]

Since Keiko is the only possible narrator of these events, the silencing of Japanese families throws her own condition into a new light. As the bearer of the story, her quiet demeanor may have less to do with an ability to accept the ostracism of Alan's family and more to do with an internalized constraint, the effect of the guards being to enforce silence in testifiers as well as visitors. Seen this way, the discipline used at the internment camp bears some similarity to the discursive violence committed at Nazi concentration camps, where a dehumanizing vocabulary was deployed to render victims invisible within language as well as in fact, which resulted in the memories of the survivors being 'covered over' and left them with the sense that, having spoken the language of their persecutors, they had been made to replicate the ideology that put them there in the first place, resulting in an indelible mark on the mind that calls the possibility of objective witnessing into question.⁴⁹ The silencing of the Japanese reverberates through the text, so that readers can never be certain whether it is indeed Keiko who narrates—that is, whether she has recovered a capacity to speak. What becomes clear is that the constraints placed on Keiko by Alan's family have the same purpose of enforced separation as that experienced on Somes Island. They are intended to break her marriage with Alan and speed the ejection of her from the family, the home, and the country.

The demands placed on Alan to reconsider his marriage, implicitly fall back on the exclusionary paradigms that reached their zenith during internment, and their effect within the family is to push Alan to the brink of breakdown, at which point Maree confronts Uncle and questions his resistance to Keiko. More than anyone else, Uncle has objected to Keiko, and his motivations remain concealed until the novel's end, at which point he provides Maree with a collection of material so that she can draw her own conclusions:

> She picked up Uncle's papers again. Read "Changi"—then turned to the photos. She gasped. Men, skeleton-thin, skulls in which sunken eyes glittered. They lay on the ground in rows, as if waiting to be buried, but it seemed to be their sleeping quarters. Then another photo. One man, grinning, startled, as if surprised he was still alive to face a camera. It had a caption under it, in Uncle's handwriting– My dear friend Jim; survived for seven months after the war. Maree stared in horror at the emaciated face, she couldn't remember seeing a Jim. No doubt her family, Uncle, had kept her and Alan away from him.⁵⁰

The discovery of a second history of captivity within the family disturbs the moral equilibrium of the novel, which had nudged readers toward the pronouncement of deep-seated prejudice within New Zealand society, and although Maree's revelation does not counteract this conclusion, it does reframe the problem to allow that taking a high moral tone toward Allied POWs may be tantamount to another act of silencing. At around this time too, Maree learns from Keiko the story of the Japanese in New Zealand—that which we, as readers, have already received, without knowing its source. But while Keiko's testimony provides a certain narrative neatness, it does not result in moral settlement. Her story and Uncle's are intertwined strands, given that the repatriation of the Japanese was arranged as a 'swap' for Allied POWs (but that does not mean that she and Uncle can 'swap' moral guilt and/or victimhood, for these conditions are not tradable articles). The result is an impasse in the face of two stories, each of which seeks to address and redress an attention deficit in a way that defies contravention, such is the authority with which they hold forth. On the matter of the politicized nature of testimony, trauma theorist Kalí Tal writes that "Bearing witness is an aggressive act. It is born out of a refusal to bow to outside pressure to revise or to repress experience, a decision to embrace conflict rather than conformity, to endure a lifetime of anger and pain rather than to submit to the seductive pull of revision and repression. Its goal is change."[51] As Tal's study makes clear, testimonials contain a degree of political intention outside their deployment as moral, psychological, or legal discourses, and Catran's narrative captures the deadlocked quandary that results from manifold attempts to dismantle 'the other's' position.

Guterson and Catran are both concerned with creating stories that reflect on the experiences of Japanese civilians/minorities in the United States and New Zealand during the Pacific War, but they also recognize the veteran's capacity to complicate this process. I began this chapter by remarking on how the objections raised by returned servicemen to the production of Vincent O'Sullivan's *Shuriken* in 1995 illustrate the discursive interconnectedness of stories appertaining to Japanese victimhood and Allied victimhood. Guterson and Catran take this fraught sociopolitical contestation and make it a constituent feature of their writing, encouraging readers to step back from partisanship and observe the historical position of the veteran without necessarily acceding to him. The reasons for Uncle's objections to Keiko are distasteful but understandable—forgivable, even, when one acknowledges his experience as an Allied POW—and we may accept their validity even as we receive Keiko's testimony of internment. For his part, Ishmael proves that the veteran may partially overcome the ideologies that he uses to vilify Japanese and Japanese Americans and may even come around to a more accepting point of view than the larger community around him.

Having said that, Guterson and Catran also represent different stages in the development of the internment narrative within their respective national cultures, and so one ought not to assume that these publications are coeval in a qualitative or contextual sense. Scholars need to remember, most of all, that nothing had been published about internment in New Zealand prior to Catran's novel. Thus, it is not surprising that Catran treads carefully around the topic, knowing that it represents new information to her readers, 'closeting' the story as a topic shared between two people, Maree and Keiko. In *Snow Falling on Cedars*, by contrast, the story of internment (and the prejudices surrounding it) emerges squarely in the public arena of a court of law with due confidence, for Guterson's book is a maturity of both style and subject matter.

Finally, one should recall that literary fictions dealing with internment in the United States have only ever framed the phenomenon in terms of national significance, in large part because of the communities of surviving ex-internees and their descendants, who remain fiercely vigilant regarding the story's place and function, politically, socially, culturally, and so on. In New Zealand, on the other hand, the story must necessarily fit into a wider network of interacting captivities. As a result, Catran's sympathies are too various, her ending too deliberately irresolute, to make this a novel purely concerned with civil liberties in a single national context, although it is that.[52] What remains are a set of problems and issues, filtered through the interiority of veteran and minority, and caught by a child for future consideration. As is so often the case with New Zealand literature, the awkwardness and hesitancy, consequent to an underdeveloped canon, contrast markedly with the richness and élan of other national literatures, but the promise of a new knowledge horizon likewise brings to light neglected areas and approaches in ways that may make critics and scholars reconsider notions of literary 'development.'

Archipelagic Narratives

Ishmael's war experience takes him away from his home on San Piedro Island to Marine Corps training on Parris Island; thence to the North Island of New Zealand for further training in amphibious maneuvers; and finally, to his baptism of fire on Tarawa atoll in the central Pacific Ocean. Catran's Japanese internees are spirited from Fiji and Tonga to New Zealand, before going on a multi-stop trip to Japan; or, in the case of Keiko, a voluntary migration from Japan to New Zealand takes place and the story of a previous island journey goes with her. For each novelist, island journeys—figurative, literal, or both at certain points—structure the narratives in ways that destabilize the notion of the Pacific War as a conflict between Japan and a 'continental' power. As such, the novels anticipate and contribute to the objectives of recent American Studies scholarship for which the deficit of island narratives in scholarly publications has become a trend deserving of greater exposure and disestablishment.[53] In common parlance, islands sometimes form chains (figured in metageographical terms as archipelagos) and these, in turn, provide a ready analogy for the chains of conjoined narratives—across land space and maritime space—that Guterson and Catran centralize in their respective works. The story of internment forms one such archipelago, involving as it does a forced migration from one place of settlement to another (or several). POW narratives form another archipelago, for much the same reason. Structurally speaking they have much in common and, in historical terms, they are deceptively interconnected—not only in terms of the 'swaps' that took place during the war years themselves, but also insofar as the Redress Movement, in which Japanese Americans sought an official apology and monetary compensation from the US government, inspired former POWs to seek similar justice from the Japanese government, their own governments, or from the private corporations that exploited their wartime labor.[54] Nonetheless, a multimodal approach that conjoins internment and POW narratives is a rarity in published works and, more often than not, Asian American authors have preferred to keep the Japanese American story largely 'continental' in nature (although Hawai'i features regularly in historical accounts as a contrastive example to what took place on the 'mainland').

In his 2009 internment novel *Hotel on the Corner of Bitter and Sweet*, for example, Chinese American author Jamie Ford develops the relationship between young Henry (his Chinese American protagonist) and Mrs. Beatty (a White canteen lady), in the course of which the latter reveals that her husband has become a POW—in Germany (a country that adhered to the rules of the Geneva Convention in respect to American and British POWs).[55] Had Ford directed this episode toward the Pacific-wide systems of captivity previously described, it is hard to imagine Mrs. Beatty's family story being passed over so briefly. In Japanese-run POW camps, the bodies of prisoners degraded to such an extent that human anatomy would become a recurrent topic in the nonfiction accounts of survivors. Diseases such as malaria, pellagra, and dysentery, as well as infections of ringworm, hookworm, and leeches, combined to turn the body of the captive into an alien vessel to its inhabitant; and those who succumbed to these hardships, to the beatings meted out by the guards or the tropical ulcers that ate away the flesh of open wounds, added their number to a death toll conservatively estimated at 30,000.[56] But if the violation of the POW's body became a literary topic in its own right, much as the violation of civil rights was central to internment narratives in the United States, the resultant sequestering of the narrative in its own discrete canon would become increasingly difficult as the twentieth century drew to a close. In the following chapter, we shall observe the political influences that came to bear on the canon and the responses of literary writers who structured their narratives in a 'multimodal' fashion.

4 The Poetics of Apology: FEPOW Narratives

I would have remained silent even now if it had not been for the fact that I see another kind of one-sidedness being introduced into the thinking of our time, as dangerous as the other one-sidedness that I feared in ourselves at the end of the war. This one-sidedness results from the fact that more and more people see the horror of Hiroshima and Nagasaki out of context. They tend to see it increasingly as an act of history in which we alone were the villains. I have been amazed to observe how in some extraordinary way my own Japanese friends do not seem to feel that they had done anything themselves to provoke us into inflicting Hiroshima and Nagasaki on them and how strangely incurious they are about their own part in the war.
—Laurens van der Post, *The Night of the New Moon*

What I heard and read was surprising to a European: the treatment of Western POWs was hardly remembered at all, even though *The Bridge on the River Kwai* had been a popular success in Japan. (I often wondered who the Japanese identified with, the Japanese commandant or Alec Guinness. Neither, said a Japanese friend: "We liked the American hero, William Holden.") Bataan, the sacking of Manila, the massacres in Singapore, these were barely mentioned. But the suffering of the Japanese, in China, Manchuria, the Philippines, and especially in Hiroshima and Nagasaki, was remembered vividly, as was the captivity of Japanese soldiers in Siberia after the war.
—Ian Buruma, *The Wages of Guilt*

What is it that so disturbs Laurens van der Post and Ian Buruma in these passages? Is it that a preferred model—*their* preferred model—of historical memory should be contested or, on a less personal level, is it the abstracted revelation that a national discourse, normalized through public and private media alike, should purposely neglect whole episodes in the history of a subject or people? Even if many Japanese continue to overlook specific episodes of the Second World War, can a foreign writer—especially a White, anglophone war veteran—frame Japanese subjectivity in cultural terms without erring toward essentialism? When all is (not always) said and (not always) done, would van der Post and Buruma prefer Japanese friends of a more compliant disposition? Of these questions, this last one at least can be answered in the negative. Sensitive to differences of opinion, van der Post and Buruma are not invested in Eurocentrism as much as in a line of inquiry that is structured as mutual self-implication in the service of healing. While neither writer lays claim to an unarguable understanding of world war in the Asia-Pacific theater, each of them takes, as assumed, a model of communication that, when unsuccessful, falls back into the writer's lap like a dud.

In the aftermath of these failed social experiments, Buruma's disappointment seems the more persuasive and also the more pronounced of the two, for he clearly expected to reap some benefit from a shared cultural referent: *The Bridge on the River Kwai* (1957) as captivity narrative. To his chagrin, however, this sign does not signify to Japanese subjects in the expected ways.[1] Rather than being drawn into a commentary on the captor-captive binary, Buruma's friend prefers to deploy an American icon, William Holden, as a means to make a dignified, if rather evasive, withdrawal. (Holden's character is, coincidentally or otherwise, the only one in the film to successfully escape imprisonment). This substitution leaves Buruma with an inchoate sense of Japanese war guilt as a moving target within everyday conversation, raising tensions despite, and possibly also because of, its dissolvent nimbleness. The alleged waywardness and evasiveness of the Japanese would migrate as a trope, about six years later, from Buruma's documentary mode of travel writing to the interfusion of journalism and geopolitics that is Jim Lehrer's novel *The Special Prisoner* (2000). One finds some predictability in this development, less because of Lehrer's own status as a journalist than because of the internal gravities of the literary genre within which he wrote—the Far East Prisoner of War (or 'FEPOW') novel, the history of which predates any of Buruma's musings and, for that matter, *The Bridge on the River Kwai*.

Much as journalism and geopolitics would reshape the FEPOW genre in the United States, New Zealand writing would undergo a change of its own during the 2000s when author Peter Wells borrowed premises and sources from the field of oral history to write *Lucky Bastard* (2007). Having achieved widespread recognition with American historian Studs Terkel's landmark 1984 compilation *The Good War*, the oral history revolution had quickly crossed the Pacific and manifested in David McGill's *P.O.W. The Untold*

Stories of New Zealanders as Prisoners of War (1987), as well as Megan Hutching's edited works *Inside Stories: New Zealand POW's Remember* (2002) and *Against the Rising Sun: New Zealanders Remember the Pacific War* (2006). Central to oral history was the observation that national histories, having structured much of modern war writing, were as much a hindrance as a resource and could, at times, obscure narratives that were better revealed through testimony. Having already ventured outside the library, or, more accurately, taken the world of veteran memory *as* a library, oral historians sidestepped the national narrative in favor of individual storytelling on an individual's terms, leaving nationality and nationalism on the veteran's doorstep, to be picked up, or not, according to preference. No longer was it necessary, if creative writers followed this route, to remain 'attached' to grand narratives of British and American endeavor. For a relatively small island community in the South Pacific, with a role in a war that had, throughout the latter half of the twentieth century, been consistently represented in Hollywood feature films as a Japan-US affair, oral histories were attractive. Yet the field of memory in which oral testimony would become situated was, if not necessarily as acrimonious as Lehrer's writing depicted, increasingly fickle and liable to dismissive rhetorical rejoinders. In the early twenty-first century, Lehrer and Wells would herald the FEPOW narrative as valuable on its own terms before subjecting this 'nominally accepted' narrative to increasing levels of contestation.

Revisiting the Far East Prisoner of War Novel

In the war's immediate aftermath, tales of captivity under the Axis powers were in rapid circulation throughout Britain, the United States, and the British colonies, but it was mainly in England that these stories found their way into artistic productions. More precisely, one may say that in England a preexistent cultural narrative proved especially malleable as a framing mechanism for captivity narratives. Unlikely though it may seem, given the age ranges involved, the tale of the public schoolboy—that is, the privileged but wretched inhabitant of a private boarding school—was dusted off and deployed as an analogy for life in a POW camp.[2] As the public intellectual Christopher Hitchens characterizes this narrative amalgamation in discussion of P. G. Wodehouse, who himself was interned during the war in Belgium and Poland:

> Innumerable English reminiscences of prison-camp life during the Second World War are devoted to making one point: It was all much easier to bear if you had the experience of an English boarding school under your belt.

Nicknames for obnoxious guards, complaints about the food, jokes based on the absence of females, the lampooning of stupid routines—it was an invitation to re-create the lost world of boyhood.[3]

As a discursive strategy, grafting a satirical or bathetic mode onto the POW narrative proved effective as a means to avoid penetrating too deeply into prison-camp psychology and the tedium that underpinned it. The strategy carried the added advantage of reducing the war in Europe to a cultural binary that made it possible to portray camp life as a 'playing field' on which military defeats of the early war years could be conveniently set aside. Once prisoners and camp guards had been equalized in these terms, English upper-class pluck and ingenuity would inevitably carry the day.[4]

Public school paradigms were not wholly inapplicable to POW narratives of the Asia-Pacific theater, but differences in cultural and material conditions that shaped the memories of surviving FEPOWs placed clear restrictions on how far this analogy could be pushed. It took some nerve for scriptwriters and raconteurs to portray prison life in Nazi Europe as a succession of knowing winks, jolly japes, and boyish fibs. It took still more nerve to envisage a ragged, starved, malarial prisoner in Japan's 'Co-Prosperity Sphere' being drawn into the same antics. To their credit, most anglophone authors knew better than to tarry with this narrative model, although the perils of misrepresentation did not diminish with its foreclosure. A less obvious, but more treacherous, pitfall for many writers opened with the reinstatement of Japanese 'character profiles' as they existed in accounts of frontline Allied combatants and war correspondents. By the war's end, the training and tactics of Japanese combatants—to say nothing of how these played out on the front line—were so much embedded in the Anglo-American public consciousness that drawing on them to fashion a composite Japanese character would have occasioned no controversy at all. Indeed, American anthropologists such as Ruth Benedict became household names by doing so. As a literary venture, however, this strategy would have won few plaudits for originality, increased the likelihood of reducing the genre to an appendage of colonialist fiction, and more to the point, made possible the intrusion of wartime propaganda—particularly the racialized varieties—into the text. American writers of the combat novel, such as James Jones, Norman Mailer, Leon Uris, and Anton Myrer, had circumvented this latter outcome by concentrating on the Allied side and leaving Japanese combatants largely uncharacterized (New Zealand author Errol Brathwaite's novel was an exception that proved the rule, as we have seen in Chapter 1). As far as it went, this omission answered the writers' needs, as it reinforced the sense that an exchange of words between Allied and Japanese antagonists was almost unknown. But this recourse was hard to sustain in a tale of life behind barbed wire or jungle growth, entailing as it did a social world in which vocal captor-captive exchanges were inescapably necessary.

Some noteworthy portrayals of the FEPOW experience followed the example of the combat novel and kept captor-captive exchanges to a minimum. Other fiction writers, however, showed no such reluctance and embraced the staple propaganda stereotypes, casting Japanese captors as childish, vindictive, and insectiform. The recirculation of these stereotypes sought to close the book on the FEPOW experience, as if to say that a set of essentialist characteristics for Japanese servicemen would suffice to explain their behavior and the suffering of their prisoners. Yet these were old wares with a rich pedigree, and while they may have proved suitable for purposes of denigration they could hardly be said to have emerged from the FEPOW experience itself.[5] Close examination, furthermore, reveals that, far from facilitating historical accuracy and creative sensitivity, bedding down the FEPOW narrative in this manner tended to result in bland characterization and in sham, sentimental plot lines. Among the most influential of such novels, Pierre Boulle's *The Bridge over the River Kwai* (1954; *Le Pont de la rivière Kwaï*, 1952) also stands as the most remiss in these respects. The role reversals central to Boulle's story (the British as competent foremen, the Japanese as bumbling nincompoops) overstates whatever advantage the British may have had in negotiating with their captors, but conceals this deception behind an upstaged Japanese colonel who, comically incompetent, takes the text almost to the point of burlesque—a style reprised three years later in David Lean's film adaptation.[6] Masao Miyoshi draws attention to the power relations implicit in this scenario:

> Power is at the heart of the two colonels' conflict, but even this struggle is soon so internalized as to render the British-Japanese rivalry forgotten. Colonel Nicolson's strife-ridden interior (as acted by Alec Guinness) gradually replaces the external battlefield: he must assert his, Britain's, and the West's supremacy, and to accomplish that mission all other concerns and persons must be overpowered.[7]

Whether as novel or film, the story says far less about conditions on the Burma-Siam railway than about the need for mid-twentieth century ideologues to reimagine the past after the fashion of long-standing cultural stereotypes.[8] As literature scholar Roger Bourke writes, "There is a deep and sad historical irony here: that the best-known, most popular and notable account of the prisoner-of-war experience under the Japanese should happen to be the least authentic."⁹

Subsequent works would seek to complicate Boulle's and Lean's arrangement, backing away from a captor-captive binary to explore the multiple oppositions functioning within groups as well as between them. Nor was there any shortage of case studies on which to build. Extant stories of captivity reveal instances in which prisoner conduct left much to be desired, although accounts do not always agree on particulars. Among the most intriguing debacles was one that took place in Fukuoka Camp #17, where the black market, a mainstay of almost every camp, and a crucial way in which to supplement meagre food rations, slipped into racketeering. The situation in Camp #17, variously reported, became notorious, although it was distinct only in degree, never in kind, from other such camps in Japan. Some survivors who remembered the feuding and its effect on camp society would take pains, by writing memoirs, to set the record straight, but fiction writers knew that the 'who did what' details were murky and, in any case, far less interesting than the drama of a camp population policing, purging, and exploiting itself.¹⁰ Diving head first into the maelstrom was the British writer James Clavell, who used a clash of wills between two prisoners as a structure for *King Rat* (1962) and, in the process, managed to avoid characterizing any Japanese guards or commandants at all (they figure only to check for radios and announce the end of the war). The stick figure woodenness of Clavell's Japanese is akin to that of Boulle's portrayals: these are background entities at the margins of the text, leaving the central conflict to the prisoners' own devising. Indeed, the hatred that prisoners nurture for one another is made all the more shocking by the irrelevance of the guards.¹¹

If the possibility of a bad, or morally ambiguous, prisoner was required to undermine the easy opposition structuring Boulle's narrative, so too was the possibility of a Japanese captor who either showed compassion to the prisoners or supplied them with a cogent justification for his actions. The choice between depicting kindly Japanese guards or depicting tormentors was not, however, one to which fiction writers usually gave much attention. In the worlds they constructed, there was always room for the occasional good egg, but public preference and historical record were united in paying more attention to atrocity than to charity. Most of these novels have tended to dwell on brutal moments; thus, Colonel Nicholson endures solitary confinement under the heat of the tropical sun; Joe Harman undergoes crucifixion in *A Town Like Alice* (1950); Jack Celliers is buried alive in van der Post's *The Seed and the Sower* (1963); civilian prisoners starve to death in J. G. Ballard's *Empire of the Sun* (1984); Digger Keen's friend is killed before his very eyes in David Malouf's *The Great World* (1990); and Tiny Middleton is reduced to a sobbing skeleton in Richard Flanagan's *The Narrow Road to the Deep North* (2013). Of these, van der Post's novel merits singling out on two grounds: first, for his curious decision to bisect the narrative with a protracted public school reminiscence (the most overt reinstatement of the analogy so far); and second, for his adamant opinion that one did not have to fall back on—or at any rate rely on—a legacy of cultural stereotypes, as Boulle had done, in order to illustrate Japanese behavior at its cruelest. Van der Post's opinion of Japanese servicemen, particularly striking in his sympathetic rendition of an imprisoned war criminal, forced readers to approach cultural values relatively rather than through objectification. In a literary genre that has avoided probing Japanese intentions and mentalities, van der Post's novel acted as a corrective and indicated to other writers how further corrections of the kind could be made (Flanagan's portrayal of a Korean guard took a similar course).[12]

Sympathetic renditions of Japanese soldiers, guards, and interrogators remain an obvious avenue of exploration for contemporary authors of FEPOW novels, the purpose and deployment of which were only partially anticipated in van der Post's work. The arrival of these, as yet unwritten, characters would signal a reshaping of the genre and, as a not incidental aftereffect, might overturn its banishment from multicultural curricula and courses on post/colonialism.[13] On the other hand, contemporary writers must not feel obliged to emulate van der Post's cultural relativism, given that ungentle treatment at the hands of Japanese servicemen was by no means exceptional in POW experience.[14] By the same token, fiction writers must not feel hemmed in by survivor testimonies and oral histories if the genre is not to ossify. It is therefore understandable that some literary ventures have ignored or defied the assumption that captivity is an inseparable fixture of the FEPOW novel, while others have redefined 'captivity' to include types of limitation, constraint, or enchainment in the postwar years. A prominent example is J. G. Ballard's novel *The Kindness of Women* (1991), which omits narration of Jim's imprisonment in China (recounted in *Empire of the Sun*) in favor of narrating the automotive thrills and numbed debauchery to which Jim's adulthood is chained. More recently, Malaysian writer Tan Twan Eng's 2012 novel *The Garden of Evening Mists* adopts a comparative approach, offsetting the enraged feelings of a Chinese Malaysian survivor of imprisonment against the transnational story of a Boer War commando whose own history of survival in a British concentration camp in South Africa, although grievous, has not shackled him to an all-consuming anger against his former captors.[15]

Autobiography likewise offers alternatives to the standard captivity narrative. In particular, Eric Lomax's *The Railway Man* (1995) is remarkable in its matter-of-fact depictions of captivity and torture but all the more remarkable in its account of Lomax and his former interrogator coming together later in life. The latter begins with Lomax reflecting on what he remembers of the man in question, Takashi Nagase, and comparing this knowledge with the abridged version of Nagase's life story that he finds in the *Japan Times*:

> I had been haunted by what he [the newspaper reporter] described for half a century, but so, it now seemed, had one of my tormentors—the only one with a face and a voice, the only one I had ever been able to endow with a personality across the years. He too had nightmares, flash-backs, terrible feelings of loss. The article talked about Nagase atoning for guilt, about visiting Kanchanaburi many times since 1963, when the Japanese government deregulated foreign travel, laying wreaths at the Allied cemetery, and setting up a charitable foundation for the survivors of the Asian labourers who died in such vast numbers.[16]

Subsequently, Lomax strikes up a correspondence with Nagase, meets him in Japan, and, after offering his forgiveness in one of the most affecting passages of the work, moves toward a sincere personal reconciliation.[17] Thus depictions of 'good' and 'bad' Japanese captors may shift away from atrocity reconstructions toward alternative or matching tales of contrition in surviving war veterans. The then/now temporal structure upon which this maneuver depends makes no unfamiliar demands on fiction writers and so, one assumes, can be deployed readily in novelizations of the FEPOW experience. One must acknowledge, though, that a then/now structure does not, of necessity, involve depictions of Japanese confessions or remorse.

While Lomax's autobiography offers a real-life example of these outcomes in the emblematic figure of Nagase, the acclaimed biographer Laura Hillenbrand provides a recalcitrant foil in *Unbroken: A World War II Story of Survival, Resilience, and Redemption* (2010). As Hillenbrand relates it, the former US Army pilot Louis Zamperini faced the same question that most former FEPOWs did in the postwar years, namely, how or whether he could unshackle himself from the memories of imprisonment that afflicted him every day. Especially toward one sadistic jailer, Mutsuhiro 'the Bird'

Watanabe, Zamperini entertains vengeance fantasies that are hard to repress. Once again, a newspaper account offers an especially potent stimulus, alerting readers to the gulf between Zamperini's mental state and the position of forgiveness that Lomax eventually reached:

> One day he opened a newspaper and saw a story that riveted his attention. A former Pacific POW had walked into a store and seen one of his wartime captors. The POW had called the police, who'd arrested the alleged war criminal. As Louie read the story, all of the fury within him converged. He saw himself finding the Bird, overpowering him, his fists bloodying the face, and then his hands locking around the Bird's neck. In his fantasy, he killed the Bird slowly, savoring the suffering he caused, making his tormentor feel all of the pain and terror and helplessness that he'd felt. His veins beat with an electric urgency.[18]

Remarkably, in light of this passage, Zamperini was actually prepared to meet Watanabe and participate in—possibly even initiate—a process of reconciliation, as long as Watanabe could find it in himself to reciprocate. But Watanabe's feelings were not those of Nagase. Having been approached with the suggestion, his response was edgy and contained a stipulation: "Told that Zamperini was coming to Japan and wanted to meet him to offer his forgiveness, Watanabe replied that he would see him and apologize, on the understanding that it was only a personal apology, not one offered on behalf of the Japanese military."[19]

Taken at face value, this statement is neither objectionable nor, at the level of raw technicality, refutable (as a demobilized soldier, Watanabe had no authority to represent the Japanese military). His stipulation, however, stands as a point of distinction: whereas Nagase might have qualified his position in similar or identical terms and would have been just as correct had he done so, conditionality was not built into his correspondence with Lomax. Neither Lomax nor Hillenbrand purports to represent Japanese subjectivities, so it is entirely possible that, unbeknownst to Lomax, Nagase may have considered covering himself in this same manner but then dismissed the option as redundant. More pertinent is the question of why Watanabe should have felt the need to embroider his reply with pedantry. Was he unaware of the redundancy, or is it more probable that 'tactical redundancies' may serve a double purpose in such situations, redirecting attention away from the self toward points of distinction, so finely drawn that the real matter at hand slips quietly between them? Watanabe had only to recollect a few details of his war record and the reputation he had built upon it to find reasons for evasiveness. Taking this possibility into account, one hesitates to say it was unfortunate that the proposed meeting between him and Zamperini failed to transpire. After all, the assenting mode of address adopted by Lomax and Nagase—and sought by van der Post and Buruma—offers only one model of private communication between an injured party and the causal agent of the injury: a sobering realization with ramifications that may be best imagined through—and perhaps should only be imagined in—works of fiction.

Lucky Bastard

If literary writers have disclosed the limits of as well as the potential for reconciliation taking place between former POWs and their erstwhile captors, others have made similar advances in revealing the challenges besetting surviving POWs or their offspring when it comes to narrating their stories to an uninterested or avowedly relativistic general public. Such has been the task of Peter Wells, a New Zealand blogger, dramatist, and filmmaker widely acknowledged as the country's foremost gay novelist before his death from cancer in 2019. For Wells, the literary history of the FEPOW novel, with its signature features of captivity narratives and steadfast intercultural oppositions, is something he acknowledges in his novel *Lucky Bastard* but shrugs off as a structural straitjacket (similarly, the politics of sexuality are not a paramount focal point). Instead, the narrative examines how children may unwittingly shoulder the burden of their father's memories (or their memories of his memories) and how, as adults looking back on their childhood, they confront the daunting task of untangling and retracing the historical moments that have gone into their making. The protagonists in this project, siblings Ross and Alison, traverse the field of memory through museums, oral histories, and guest appearances on television. In narrative terms, these different media enable them to reach a tentative, if incomplete, understanding of their father Eric's FEPOW experience, even as a wholly reconstructed depiction of imprisonment remains out of reach.[20] Offering only backward glances toward imprisonments and deliberately eschewing any notion of a reliably 'original' standpoint, in this relativistic knowledge landscape only the fact of wartime atrocities remains sacrosanct. Wells treats this topic with corresponding delicacy and perhaps a little uncertainty, an inevitable, indeed wholly necessary attribute to the writing of atrocities. The few clues we receive that atrocities did occur, are shrouded in a mixture of stylistic hesitancy and narrative mystery, as when Ross recalls a childhood conversation he had with his father's mistress. As the son of a veteran, Ross is full of youthful inquisitiveness, particularly around the matter of what lies within a box of documents:

"Is it something to do with eating humans?"

She looked at me sharply. Then her face creased into amusement. She ashed the sagging end of her cigarette, brought it to her mouth, sucked in with a thorough sense of enjoyment. As she breathed out a warm fog of smoke, she said, half laughingly, "You've been reading too many war comics, love!"[21]

This passage reflects the tenor of the novel as a whole in its tendency to withhold information, even (perhaps especially) when nothing would be (apparently) lost by learning of it sooner. Later, readers learn that Eric did in fact encounter stories of wartime cannibalism in his capacity as a war crimes investigator, but the narrative shies away from disclosing this fact immediately and thereby complicates one's sense of who or what is being protected: is it the child from the story or the story from the reader? Wells assumes in each case that the recipient has an overfull stock of images and source material ready-to-hand, such that the testimonial risks what Jenny Edkins terms the 'gentrification' of trauma.[22] To prevent the FEPOW experience from seeming pedestrian, Wells edges around or otherwise 'encircles' it, imparting a sense of significance through this act of hesitancy.[23]

This narrative strategy intersects with ongoing scholarly discussions over the need to maintain and/or recover value in stories of traumatic experience that are likely to disseminate among the general public. Arguing that this project necessitates 'empathic unsettlement,' trauma theorist Dominick LeCapra has noted that the "post-traumatic response of unsettlement becomes questionable when it is routinized in a methodology or style that enacts compulsive repetition, including the compulsively repetitive turn to the aporia, paradox, or impasse."[24] Historians and novelists must take care, in this respect, that admissions to the inadequacy of language, apropos the traumatic experience and the traumatized condition, do not become part of a reflexive dismissal or trope of the unspeakable. Given that *Lucky Bastard* takes on a position of silence regarding Eric's experiences, this tendency is a present danger. Yet Wells never says that Eric's trauma is unspeakable, nor does he let the matter rest in silence. At its heart, the novel contains a lacuna, for what happened to Eric remains largely closed off except for what his children glean from their sometimes delicate, sometimes blunt-edged rummaging. In short, it is through the investigatory mode, rather than a captivity narrative, that readers acquire a sense, if not an understanding, of what Eric's experiences have meant for him and his family. The investigations take the narrative away from 'comic book' pastiche, in which 'what actually happened' unfolds as smoothly as the classic filmic depictions of FEPOW captivity. What readers glean instead is trauma's capacity to cross generational boundaries, its location within sites of official memory, and a sense, though never a full disclosure, of the nature of that trauma.

The bulk of the story, then, is preoccupied with the siblings' reconsideration of what Eric means and has meant to them. Sites of public memory facilitate this reexamination, albeit frequently through antithetical provocations against which the characters' own feelings become alternately reinforced and weakened. As Ross and Alison negotiate these sites, the novel reaches for a resounding sense of trauma's influence upon the family unit even as it disturbs any possibility of 'truth' in an absolute sense. These two projects are not wholly complementary and the challenge of achieving a balanced attention between trauma recovery and historical discovery remains central throughout. It is essential to realize here that the recovery *of* trauma, in the sense of a recovered topic of interest, becomes bound to the recovery *from* trauma, in the psychiatric sense of a subject who suffers the debilitating symptoms associated with the condition. As Ross and Alison navigate the sites in which remembrance takes place, they unveil the meaningfulness of the FEPOW experience not just to the reader but also to themselves. In the process, they come to realize that trauma is a condition they carry as well as investigate.

In itself, such a realization is quite enough to be going on with. But Wells adds a combative dimension to their journey, born of the unpleasant knowledge that memory institutions, although stimulating and, in fact, indispensable to their purpose, may inadvertently complicate and even detract from the value that is placed on private memories. The private memories 'in question' are, by their nature, dear to Ross and Alison, remaining, in a sense, sacrosanct to the individual and decidedly not open to criticism. But sites of public memory, to the contrary, are, by their profusion, inherently pluralistic in their approach to specific events, which may include particular perspectives akin to the visitor's, but only as part of a larger collective that decentralizes any one point of view. In short, the act of historical discovery promoted through such places comes to both inform (via prompts) and disrupt (via counter narrative) the meaning attached to individual memory. Thus, even as the novel reaches for a realization of trauma's meaningfulness, that same meaning becomes destabilized within a social and critical milieu unreceptive to any master narrative.

Before examining this tension more closely, one must acknowledge the narrative scenarios in which memories return seamlessly and without any sense of contestation. Wells is clearly intrigued by such moments, among the most arresting of which takes places when Alison, nominally a London business executive, visits the War Memorial Museum in Auckland and experiences the power of recorded testimony:

Inward she went, disappearing like a spot of light on a computer shutting down. Only the old bloke's voice existed. And she was surprised to find her face damp. She was betrayed. She was crying silently.

It was the modesty of the man's voice. He was talking about the most devastating pain and fright a human was capable of sustaining while staying alive. But with an asthmatic draw-in of breath, the old codger would only allow such modest phrases as, "Yes, well, it got a bit rough around there" (his mates killed) and, for what sounded like a life ruined by post-traumatic stress syndrome, "I don't know. I couldn't get it out of my head, you see. Silly what you think of. What you can't stop thinking about." Long pause. "But that's life, isn't it?"[25]

The disembodied voice comes through the headphones and into the novel as if from nowhere, striking a chord in Alison whose responsiveness entails a 'shutdown' of mental resistance, in large part because the man is fundamentally unassertive.[26] In more typical situations, Alison prefers hearing statements that set her up for cutting ripostes, but here all she gets is the bashfulness of an 'old codger' holding forth in his own way. A partly self-administered *coup de grâce* of this sort is an unwelcome, perhaps even shameful, moment of human weakness for a corporate jetsetter who is used to seamless movement from one situation to another. In the traumatized war veteran, she encounters her opposite: a figure who, as oral historian Alison Parr has observed, was expected by wider New Zealand society to 'move on' even though he had grown used to 'staying put' in captivity.[27] (Postwar accounts of British POWs who escaped captivity in Nazi Europe may have fed into popular, but mistaken, notions of captives as men who sought and found escape at every opportunity).[28] So marked is the old man's restraint that he barely registers the enormity of what he has gone through, and almost appears to be speaking of another person's life.[29] Holocaust trauma psychiatrist Dori Laub makes clear how survivors reach this state, and the implications for the listener:

> Massive trauma precludes its registration; the observing and recording mechanisms of the human mind are temporarily knocked out, malfunction. The victim's narrative—the very process of bearing witness to massive trauma—does indeed begin with someone who testifies to an absence, to an event that has not yet come into existence, in spite of the overwhelming and compelling nature of the reality of its occurrence. [. . .]
>
> By extension, the listener to trauma comes to be a participant and co-owner of the traumatic event: through his very listening, he comes to partially

experience trauma in himself. The relation of the victim to the event of the trauma, therefore, impacts on the relation of the listener to it, and the latter comes to feel the bewilderment, injury, confusion, dread and conflicts that the trauma victim feels. He has to address all these, if he is to carry out his function as listener [. . .][30]

As the listener in this case, Alison bears witness to events *reflected in* but not *known to* the testifier, and her tears manifest symptoms that, by all rights, ought to be the old man's but, because of his emotional disconnection, become hers to cry on his behalf. Hereafter, she herself bears witness to what others cannot, although she remains unable to articulate or express the meaning of her own childhood trauma. To get a sense of what that involved, her character becomes part of a still larger project that invites the reader to do as she did in the museum—for just as the recorded testimony touches off emotions within her, so Alison begins to recall memories that she has never fully registered. Thus, some of the novel's most disturbing scenes leave it to the reader to perform an act of witnessing that the characters cannot.

This dynamic comes into play most obviously when Alison hazily recalls a childhood game she played with her brother after they ransacked Eric's box of war crimes documents. As attentive readers, we know that they have subjected themselves to information about the massacre of Australians at Six Mile Road, but their awareness is at the level of play and therefore incomplete. Just as the old man's audio recording feels peculiarly detached from the core of his experience, so Alison's memory is deadpan in its recollection of the reenactment that she and Ross undertook:

> I poured the petrol on (cold water from our hose). He screamed like a girl. I grinned as I watered him all over. He was meant to be dead, anyway, but being Ross he managed to stay alive, to enjoy the pain more deeply. He groaned and moaned, his lids half open, begging me to finish him off. But it was my delight to imagine striking a match.
>
> "BOOM!" I yelled as the flames flickered all over his body. I watched, between half-closed lids, as his flesh fell off, in flakes, straight from the bone. And it was me who ate him. He was tasty, that kid.[31]

Providing a refracted glimpse of atrocity, the sensory imagery encourages speculation as to what it is the children imitate. Certainly, readers are unlikely to pass off their behavior as the product of childhood imagination. More is at work here, traceable to Eric's box, the contents of which remain undisclosed in the narrative, although its effect upon the inquisitive young explorers imparts certain suspicions. Textually speaking, the box is no longer simply a box, but symbolic of the traumatized mind—locked away, hidden, carefully approached, destructive once opened, and shattering in the long term. Naturally, the children open the box, as children must always do if they wish to go through the wardrobe, down the rabbit hole, or on the yellow brick road, but instead of a fantasyland, what lies in wait is an unnameable 'something' that impresses them with the image of atrocity. Afterwards, like an organ grinder's monkey, they follow a routine that has all the appearance of recreation, but is, in fact, a literal 're-creation.' As witnesses to this spectacle, readers perceive the impossibility of disentangling a present-day adult subjectivity from a childhood experience, the traumatic nature of which defies challenge or containment.[32] To 'think outside the box' is impossible, even retrospectively, and the temptation is to grant ourselves a position of lofty detachment, having surmised Alison's condition based on nothing more complex than a 'cause-effect' conjunction. However, readers only ever observe her memories through speculative, fragmentary guesswork. More importantly still, memories of trauma never proceed in the linear fashion of an unsolved equation. On the contrary, the bearer often remains in a state of suspension, and to reduce that condition to 'cause' is to dissociate ourselves from that ongoing disconnection. If readers wish to participate fully in the meaning-generating process, they need to take account of that disconnection, as well as its abstract origins, a process that allows one to perceive the past events—receive them, in fact—on behalf of the testifier. The shared nature of this enterprise is what Dori Laub identifies when he states that, "It is the encounter and the coming together between the survivor and the listener, which makes possible something like a repossession of the act of witnessing. This joint responsibility is the source of the re-emerging truth."[33]

Were *Lucky Bastard* solely about witnessing, Wells would have depicted a society gradually coming to terms with veterans, the forms of imprisonment they endured, and those family members who endure on their behalf. These facets are readily discernible, provided that characters and readers listen carefully to what is said. However, Peter Wells is just as interested in the conflicts that emerge when testimony and listening take place under less favorable, even hostile conditions. A seminal example of the damage this does to the testifier comes across when Ross agrees to a televised interview, knowing that the show addresses his father's role as a Tokyo war crimes investigator, but not knowing that the show's host is decidedly interrogatory. As the interview progresses, this woman uses background information to 'set the scene' before asking whether Eric ever talked about his past. Ross' answer is terse and defensive:

"No, he didn't. And he's not in a fit state any more to answer questions. I don't see your point."

"My point, Ross, is this: an innocent man may have been sent to his death by your father as an act of revenge. Your father won a medal and has been praised as a hero. War is messy, we know that, but we have to fight through the murk of the past—to find the truth." She left an eloquent silence for a moment, then turned straight to the camera. "Never forget this, folks. *If there's a story, we'll find it!*"

"I understand that,' I said, furious. 'But maybe you –"

The cameraman took his head away from the camera.

"—maybe you should think of doing a programme on the psychological and physical after-effects of imprisonment by the Japanese on prisoners of war."

"Oh we did that ages ago. Didn't we, Anne?"[34]

Rather than facilitating testimony, the entertainment community manufactures it through a process that is tantamount to non-listening or outright silencing. Crushingly determined to get to the bottom of Eric's past behavior, the show's host increasingly marginalizes Ross' testimony in pursuit of this objective. This 'truth,' as she terms it, is different from the 're-emerging truth' that Dori Laub considered so essential to the process of hearing testimony, and that he had in mind when noting that it can be more useful, on occasion, not to know too much when receiving the message of the trauma victim.[35] Facts can prove harmful to trauma testimonies, which demand that they be heard on their own terms, and Wells' portrayal of the predatory interviewer dismissing her subject for want of confirmatory information is a case in point. Sometimes history is forged by wringing out and casting off the very people who have struggled to survive it.

The Special Prisoner

A full account of Eric's captivity is forever out of reach to the protagonists of Wells' novel and, compounding this issue, the memory institutions and public figures whom they encounter contest the values that they had thought inherent to the POW experience. In Jim Lehrer's novel *The Special Prisoner*, on the other hand, this structure is reversed—that is, the captivity narrative is established from the outset and undergoes contestation, not from internal discrepancies or alternative versions, so much as parallel histories that originate in contemporary Japanese society. Turning to these, Lehrer is concerned with how and why certain Japanese—the political Right, historical apologists, or just guardedly indifferent citizenry—turn a blind eye to war crimes, even when (or because) the events in question took place over half a century ago. Against this larger agenda, the captivity narrative becomes a backdrop, useful, up to a point, but no longer an end in itself. The author's primary concern is not trauma, as such, but polemics and their place within individual memory, a topic structure that allows his narration to take on features of the profession most Americans associate with him. Concision and abbreviation are good ways of keeping viewers tuned in (electronically, if not intellectually), and so readers cannot expect that Lehrer, best known at the time of publication for his career as a PBS newscaster, will offer a convincing portrayal of war-traumatized minds; he will instead take the condition for granted.[36] What readers of Lehrer can expect, as partial compensation, is a novel that both taps and feeds into public debates, current in 2000 when the novel was published, concerning official apologies for historical wrongs. In 1993, for example, President Clinton apologized to native Hawaiians for actions that had brought about the overthrow of the kingdom of Hawai'i in 1893, while in 1995 Queen Elizabeth II apologized to a Māori tribe for land confiscations that took place under British colonial rule. Although Lehrer does not seem to have had these or other specific instances in mind when he wrote *The Special Prisoner*, his novel has a mid-1990s orientation, in that this was a time when historical reflection and anniversary commemorations featured frequently in the media.[37] Timeliness had been a factor in prompting the American president to issue his apology—1993 marked one hundred years since the end of Hawai'ian independence—and expectations ran high in liberal circles that the fiftieth anniversary of the end of the Second World War would allow states and private individuals to 'redress' past grievances in like fashion.

What did take place across the Asia-Pacific region, however, taught a salutary lesson against invoking abstractions (dates on a calendar) as an adequate counterweight to the interests of politically active communities. Anniversaries can lead to the incorporation of official apologies in commemorative ceremonies, but, in the absence of thorough preparation and consultation across a broad social spectrum, apologies can, just as easily, provoke an equal and opposite reaction. On both sides of the Pacific, scholars of Japan-US relations might have tried harder to temper public expectations and certainly knew well enough to temper their own, particularly when recalling the political climate of the 1980s and the phenomenon, previously discussed in Chapter 2, of 'Japan panic' or 'Japan-bashing.' Japan had achieved a trade surplus over its partners during this period, and journalistic commentary, particularly in the United States, pressed the war metaphors of everyday economic parlance a good deal farther than they ordinarily venture. Among the cultural offshoots was a body of fiction that played on people's fears in the crassest terms, and such fearmongering invariably takes longer to settle down than it does to arise. Japan's asset price 'bubble' had burst by 1991, but, for instance, the Australian playwright Jill Shearer's *Shimada* opened on Broadway in 1992 (the plot concerns a Japanese businessman, who may or may not have been a POW camp guard, taking over a Queensland bicycle factory) and biker communities in the US continued to see brands such as Harley-Davidson as 'classic' or 'original' while brands such as Kawasaki or Suzuki could only ever be imitations.[38]

Whether 'Japan bashing' retained its hold over anglophone public discourse and cultural productions long enough to exert an influence over the contexts of the mid-1990s is hard to estimate. Even if one allows that it may not have done so, there remain sadly numerous examples of lost opportunities for historical revisions and for reconciliation between Japan and the United States, each of which would be, on its own, a worthwhile topic for historical inquiry. The rudimentary summary that I have space for here does no justice to interpenetrating contexts, but it may at least impart a sense of how a work of fiction could emerge from, and be partly structured around, the wreckage of political arguments that broke against unfulfilled expectations. In Japan, the decade was ushered in by the death of Emperor Hirohito in 1989, following a protracted struggle with duodenal cancer, the closing stages of which occasioned a televised commentary almost worshipful in cadence. Public opinion, on the other hand, was more varied than the news channels might have led one to believe, as an especially telling incident revealed in December 1988, when a Communist Party representative asked Hitoshi Motoshima, the mayor of Nagasaki, to issue a statement on the question of the emperor's war guilt. Motoshima was a veteran of the Second World War and municipal representative of the Rising Sun Society, but he was also a Christian, an educator, and an unyielding advocate of free speech. Measuring his words carefully, Motoshima replied that the emperor did bear responsibility for the war but that he had been symbolically exculpated during the US Occupation and should therefore be treated as if blameless.

To this compromise, the center-Right and far-Right responded in unison, if not in the same tone and language. The moment has been described eloquently by Norma Field:

> One conservative organization after another demanded that the mayor withdraw his statement, otherwise threatening noncooperation so long as he remained in office. When the city representatives to the prefectural legislature called on him, the mayor told them that retracting his words would be tantamount to death for him. Japanese publications quoting the mayor always

add "political" in brackets before "death." No doubt that is accurate enough, but I prefer to leave it plain. After all, this was the response of a man who unexpectedly found himself faced with daily threats of *physical* death.[39]

These threats were not idle: roughly a year later, when the police relaxed their protection, a member of the right-wing group *Seikijuku* shot Motoshima in the back.[40] He survived the assassination attempt, but examples of right-wing Japanese groups influencing or silencing their opponents would not be limited, in that decade, to his case. A less violent but more successful instance of right-wing intervention occurred in 1993, when Prime Minister Morihiro Hosokawa's planned attendance at war-memorial services was to have involved a description of the Second World War as an "aggressive war and a mistake." In the event, however, fellow Liberal Democrats and members of the Japan Bereaved Families Association (*Nihon Izokukai*), a group with conservative politics, forced Hosokawa to scale back his rhetoric and instead refer only to "aggressive acts."[41] (Emphasizing "acts" placed blame on individual units of the military, whereas "war" would have placed blame on the state). The language used set the trend for the fiftieth anniversary, and by then hitherto marginal stories relating to article 9 of the Japanese constitution, history textbook content, and official visits to the Yasukuni Shrine were appearing in Western media with relative frequency.

The anniversary year of 1995 was embarrassing for some institutions in the United States as well. Curators at the Smithsonian National Air and Space Museum had planned an exhibition commemorating the end of the Asia-Pacific war (and the start of the Cold War) by featuring the *Enola Gay* as an exhibit. Having learned of these preparations, representatives of the American Legion and the Air Force Association successfully lobbied to de-emphasize the suffering wrought on Japanese civilians by the atomic bombings. Matters were not helped by the gang rape, in that same year, of a twelve-year-old Okinawan schoolgirl by three US Marines. Outraged protests made it clear that the presence of US military bases was no longer unquestionably accepted by the Okinawan public. As the fiftieth anniversary approached, political watchdogs on both sides of the Pacific were at least as aggressive toward attempts at historical revisionism within their own countries as they were hostile to antithetical positions abroad.[42] In *Japanese by Spring* (1993), African American satirist Ishmael Reed anticipated the sort of rhetoric that was to shape this and other such occasions. Dr. Yamato, the acting president of *Tojo no Daigaku*, which had been Jack London College before a Japanese buyout, explains the role that the college will play under its new leadership:

"On December 8, Tojo no Daigaku will celebrate the fiftieth anniversary of the attack on Pearl Harbor. Many of the businessmen and leading citizens of Oakland will join. They will apologize for the invasion of the Pacific by American forces. The Soviets apologized to the people of Afghanistan for invading their country. The Japanese recently apologized to the Koreans. And now it's time for the United States to apologize. We're bringing the USS *Missouri* to the Port of Oakland for the occasion." He pointed to the scale model, and with a pointer identified some of the figures standing on the *Missouri*. Instead of Japanese diplomats dressed in formal clothes, it showed Dr. Yamato receiving an 'apology' document from the mayor of the city of Oakland, who represented the United States. To add to the humiliation, at the end of the signing, the flag of Commodore Perry, whose black ships were the scourge of the Japanese, would be burned. Perry's flag had flown on the *Missouri* during the Japanese signing of the ignominious surrender document. The supposed signing ceremony was scheduled to take place during a three-day 'apology' festival.[43]

Pushed to the outrageous extreme that satire always inhabits, Dr. Yamato's language is nonetheless only a few steps beyond the heated rhetoric of the mid-1990s.[44]

The Special Prisoner derives from these public discourses and to some extent plays upon them or, rather, upon the prejudices that Lehrer depicts his characters as having (and imagines his anglophone readers as sharing) with respect to them. It is only as the narrative progresses that an interrogation of prejudice, rather than its mere depiction or purveyance, becomes apparent in the text. The opening sequences of the novel offer no forewarning that these twists and turns lie ahead. On the contrary, the acting assumption is that each and every Japanese person—civilian, military, and veteran alike—remains, to this day, skilled at obfuscation and denial and that there should be a proper accounting, if necessary, at the hands of a strong-willed 'accountant.' This mandate supplies one meaning of the novel's title, the referent of which is its main character, John Watson, a Methodist minister and former FEPOW who traps a Japanese man in a hotel room and subjects him to initially gentle, then rigorous, and ultimately fatal questioning as to his military background. Watson suspects Tashimoto, his victim, of being an interrogator at Camp Sengei 4 in Japan, to which he was taken as a young US Army pilot, after parachuting from his stricken B-29. His past suffices as a motive, if not a justification, for Watson's actions, and Lehrer devotes the first half of the novel to the role reversal that finds Watson the master of his former tormentor, while the second half leads up to Watson's murder trial. The first half merits more of our attention here, for in it a then/now temporal sequence is followed, not so much as a way to encapsulate the past in the present, as to shed light on the contexts in which remembrance is forged.

As a literary scenario, the chance encounter between two unreconciled enemies in changed circumstances, a common fantasy of survivors such as Zamperini, offers immediate advantages to an author. Most obviously, it facilitates contemplation of past events using the ready-made structure of two interlocutors, whose dialogue may be Socratic (truth seeking, in an abstract sense), eristic (persistently and aggressively polarized), or pacifying (reaching for agreement, even in the midst of conflict). In all probability, such discussions will shift between the different modes at different times, with correspondingly different investments in mood, affect, and socio-political agenda. Consistent in every stage, however, will be a juridical motif that, whether fully confronted or entirely dormant in the mind and language of either party, will necessarily hang over the conversation like the sword of Damocles, because it is the swift justice of the executioner, rather than the deliberative justice sought by lawyers before a judge and jury, that is impending.

But Watson's postwar profession of Methodist minister and bishop complicates, rather than furthers, this process, mainly by introducing the possibility of moral absolution for Tashimoto, even as the latter insists upon his innocence. The result of these conflicting positions—forgiveness offered where guilt is dis-claimed—is a stilted, telegraphed series of declamations:

> "I forgave you long ago," said Watson.
> "I have never done anything to you." The Japanese man remained standing rigidly, defiantly.
> "You were a terrible man, possibly one of the worst God ever put on the face of this earth."
> "I am a wonderful man."[45]

What saves their dialogue from the pitfall of didacticism is the collapsing of difference, at least to some extent, between the two positions. Tashimoto's passive aggression sends Watson into a pique of active aggression or, in Bakhtinian terms, 'carnival justice.'[46] Acting thus reveals to Watson the possibility of his own equivalent guilt, in historical terms, and demands that readers ask the same question that he later asks of himself: what could drive him, an ordained bishop to whom mercy and pardon are supposedly second nature, to commit an act of murder? In answer to this question, two possibilities beckon, both of which recollect Watson's long struggle to forgive his Japanese captors in the aftermath of liberation. As readers later learn, this process was grueling indeed and led eventually toward a career in the clergy—to the profession of forgiveness, one might say.[47] Of course, Tashimoto's murder renders this forgiveness of questionable value and authenticity, unless one grants that forgiveness may be undone by a referent's incapacity or unwillingness to pursue a course of self-examination and repentance.

Such a qualification might be termed 'contingent forgiveness' and requires mutual engagement for its sustenance. Had Tashimoto cooperated and admitted his guilt, then the amnesty that Watson offered would have been full and unreserved—if, that is, the reader buys into this neat, clear-cut division of responsibility. Less neat is the hypothesis that Watson never genuinely forgave the Japanese to begin with, largely because doing so would presuppose a feeling of guiltlessness on his own part, and Watson, as a bomber pilot, might well have questioned his entitlement (as some surviving airmen did in the postwar years, if only in private).[48] The careful, almost excruciating, balance that one must strike even when exploring this issue dispassionately is illustrated in an argument by the philosopher Anthony Grayling:

> If the Allied bombing campaigns did in fact involve the commission of wrongs, then even if these wrongs do not compare in scale with the wrongs committed by the Axis powers, they do not thereby cease to be wrongs. The figure of 800,000 civilians killed by Allied bombing, almost all of them in the course of deliberately indiscriminate attacks on urban areas, is staggeringly high in its own right, and even so says nothing about the injured, traumatised and homeless, who in many respects suffered worse. The debate about the question has often been clouded by comparing what the Allies did with what the Axis did in the way of immoral actions, always (and rightly) to the credit of the Allies—only to leave matters there, as if drawing the comparison by itself resolves matters. It does not; which is the reason for revisiting the question and trying to settle it.[49]

The novel's flashback sequences reveal that Watson had himself been troubled by the dropping of incendiary bombs on Japanese population centers, and as already mentioned, he turned to a career in the church partly as a way to assuage his guilt. Seen in this way, Watson's capacity to forgive is not undone by Tashimoto's shamelessness as much as by the concurrent evocation of complex, perhaps even psychopathological feelings that threaten Watson's sense of selfhood. This newly destabilized subjectivity sweeps aside the matter of Watson's theological or philosophical disposition.[50]

As events unfold, instances of Tashimoto's shamelessness and the return of Watson's combined feelings of guilt and hatred increasingly manifest themselves in the text. In a later sermon, Watson admits to having carried vestigial hatreds, and certainly Tashimoto, who owns up to nothing, is resistant on every count.[51] But the possibility of moral equivalence between these two men remains more a speculative than a fully realized thesis. Lehrer would have his readers understand that forgiveness at the individual level is every bit as challenging as apology, although it is seldom perceived as such.[52] Granting that the challenge of forgiveness brings with it a psychological dimension as fraught with pitfalls as the moral ambiguity Watson carries from his record of wartime bombing runs, Lehrer does not permit either to distract too much from Tashimoto, whose obduracy remains the real bone of contention. Tashimoto's language is worth appraising:

> I am a Japanese man named Tashimoto but not the one you had your unfortunate encounter with in World War II. But let me speak for him, if I must. Let me speak for him and all of us who survived that terrible experience. Let me say that I regret any harm and suffering that was inflicted on you unnecessarily by anyone connected with the Imperial Army of Japan. But I do not offer you an apology. I served in that army, and I make no apologies to you or to anyone else for that service.[53]

While not modeled on any one speech, Tashimoto's diction conforms to perceived precedents in Japanese official statements of the late twentieth century, meaning that he stops short of apology while alluding to wrongdoing in the same breath.[54] Rhetorical horse trading of this sort may make his speech seem like a casual, throwaway affair, but it also maintains equilibrium between remorse and apologetics in a way that, if delivered in a delicate fashion, might answer the needs of the aggrieved party and preserve Tashimoto's dignity as well. Referring to the "terrible experience" of the war is a deliberately vague, yet crucial, means of sustaining the arrangement, for it implies a shared suffering that was not wholly of Japan's making (Allied troops entering Nazi Germany in 1944 would encounter a similar argument from civilians who felt that the carpet bombing, dehousing, and starvation that they had endured neutralized the issue of Nazi war guilt).[55]

Nor do readers need to be told what Tashimoto's statement means. The atomic bombings and the firebombing missions that preceded them have at various times taken on the discursive function of shielding Japanese officials from unwelcome historical interrogation or otherwise have provoked arguments that political scientist Elizabeth S. Dahl has aptly termed 'duelling victimhoods.'[56] This image does as well for understanding what takes place between Tashimoto and Watson, each of whom remains intensely aware of his own particular grievance and disdainful of the other's.[57] The difficulties that beset Prime Minister Hosokawa and the American curators of the Smithsonian Museum echo here in the up-to-date reader's mind, and when one notes that the novel's chronology locates the events in 1995 (five years prior to the time of publication), the characters' representative quality becomes especially clear.[58] Naturally, Tashimoto's murder tests the limits of this arrangement, and Lehrer devotes the second half of his novel to picking over the details of historical arguments, with the added imperative of reexamining Watson's subjectivity once it becomes clear that he did indeed mistake Tashimoto for his former captor. Getting the wrong man does not invalidate Watson's grievances, which have a life of their own in the world of politics and international relations, but it does suggest an obtuse, unreasoning confusion. Effectively, his mistake puts Watson on the defensive for the rest of the novel and, more to the point, encourages readers to approach Japanese interpretations of history through a less partisan lens. Although Tashimoto's murder is a tabloid-style crime of passion, it serves another purpose, which is to arrest the sense of righteousness associated with Watson's position. Lehrer banishes high-toned posturing from the rest of the novel, in favor of a humbled, consolidated Watson who, having been the de facto champion of FEPOW grievances, now refuses to defend himself.

The closing sequences of the narrative suggest that Lehrer's intention was to craft a novel that would curtail historical apologetics and monocultural biases—and the novel would indeed be such, were it not for a final twist that sees Watson, now serving a jail term, receive a letter from Singapore informing him that the Tashimoto whom he killed had been every bit as brutal there as his counterpart had been in Japan.[59] The letter has a redemptive quality that could turn everything around, reverse all the valences, yet one more time. But Watson discards the letter and the possibility, giving no reasons, and quietly passes away in his sleep, leaving readers to take what they will from his decision. Is it resignation to the unrecoverability of the past, martyrdom of the unjustly vanquished—or is it perhaps a rewriting of the "lest we forget" dictum into "lest we forget *to remind others*"?[60]

Reversing Roles

"Always forgive your enemies. Seldom does anything annoy them more": this piece of gnomic wisdom, commonly attributed to Mark Twain or, with variations, to Oscar Wilde, encapsulates the dilemmas and contradictions that Lehrer undertakes to portray. Forgiveness is of such value, these writers would have us know, that even if one cannot summon loving or noble feelings in support of it, baser emotions may suffice. But the idealism of the humorist has its cynical flip side, cautioning us to remember that vanity and spite can underpin the motives of the forgiver, with serious implications for the manner in which forgiveness is to be received. In its most extreme formulation, forgiveness may even be advanced—and taken—as a form of revenge.[61] One may read Lehrer's novel as illustrative of these truisms but also as illustrating, inadvertently, the unlikelihood of crafting a novel that supplies models of successful apology and reconciliation between formerly antagonistic peoples while grounding the narrative in recent polemics.[62] Although Lehrer and Wells successfully break free from the captivity narrative that had long dominated the FEPOW novel, the tone of both works, and Lehrer's especially, remains divisive even as they question and complicate how people become invested in the politics of memory. Unassailably present in the narrative background is the realization that a full reckoning with the ethical and cultural legacy of the atomic bombings of Hiroshima and Nagasaki has yet to take place.[63]

Narrative discomfort of this sort, centered as it is around changing 'locations' of victimhood (geographical and ideological), remains a relatively new aspect of the genre, as does the shifting moral landscape that underpins it. That said, it would be a mistake to assume that a cultural production which juxtaposes the FEPOW narrative with the atomic bombings—and, in turn, the Manhattan Project that made them possible—is, by that fact alone, wholly unknown to the anglophone world. On the contrary, such conjunctions are as old as the FEPOW narrative itself. In September 1945, RKO Radio Pictures released *First Yank into Tokyo*, a film that was originally scripted around an American hero trying to acquire a new type of gun. In due course, real-life news of the atomic bombings necessitated quick changes to the plot, the result of which was the wholly imaginary scenario of an American FEPOW whose knowledge of nuclear physics, were he liberated and in Allied hands, might serve the war effort. Accordingly, a heroic rescue mission takes place and the newly-freed physicist is spirited back to the United States where he becomes part of the Manhattan Project and, by contributing to that collective research effort, exacts vengeance upon his former captors.[64] These twists in the production history of *First Yank into Tokyo* reveal that the FEPOW narrative served an obscurantist function in the United States that would distract attention from Hiroshima and Nagasaki (the bombing of Pearl Harbor would also draw attention away from the atomic bombings). In like turn, the story of the Manhattan Project, retold in American fiction writing throughout the rest of the twentieth century, would carefully airbrush the atomic bombings out of the narrative.

5 Scientists and Hibakusha: Project Novels

I cannot forgive the cruel behavior of the United States, which caused the atomic destruction and which even now menaces the rights of such insignificant people as my family and me. I am forced to worry excessively about the health of my two children because I am a bomb victim. I am filled with sorrow and indignation over what has happened.
—Fumiko Harada, "A Second-Generation Victim"

NASO recognises that a nuclear conflagration is conceivable and that such could originate within the Northern Hemisphere. This being the case, it regards New Zealand as being likely to escape the most severe consequences of both a nuclear holocaust and the aftermath of a nuclear winter. It follows that this country could, therefore, be one of the last refuges of civilisation left in the world capable of accepting responsibility for the administration of enlightened global reconstruction.
—Draft Principles of Assembly, Nuclear Aftermath Strategy Organisation, Taupo, New Zealand, 1985

The perceived or actual recalcitrance of Japanese public figures when it comes to owning up to the misdeeds of the war years is matched, in equal turn, by the perceived or actual recalcitrance of American public figures and commemorations that take the atomic bombings of Hiroshima and Nagasaki as their putative topic. The unwillingness of either side to engage the Other's perspective has resulted in the shoring up of apparently 'discrete' historical narratives that favor the perception of one's own side as victimized. In their examination of the discourses surrounding this arrangement, historians Laura Hein and Mark Selden characterize the *status quo* as a form of etiquette: "American commemorations of the bombings leave out Japanese victims, whereas Japanese ones leave out victims of Japanese aggression. The Americans falsified the arithmetic of suffering and loss by silencing the voices of *hibakusha* (atomic bomb victims), while the Japanese silence on the larger issues of war preserved the image of a virtuous nation of innocent victims."[1] As we have seen in the previous chapter, in the anglophone world FEPOW narratives bear the traces of this phenomenon and a fiction writer such as Jim Lehrer, taking the pivotal moment of the 1995 fiftieth anniversary commemoration as his departure point, experienced both difficulty and inspiration in portraying imagined conversations between a surviving FEPOW and a veteran of the Imperial Japanese Army. Ineluctably, these two characters move from studied disregard to mutual antagonism and, finally, violence, the denouement spurred on by Watson's inability to engage the bombing of Hiroshima as a topic.

If American fiction writers have tended to shy away from the events of August 6th and 9th, 1945, the same cannot be said of the initial newspaper coverage, which struck a balance between the wartime use of the Bomb and the story of its development (the latter serving to continue a series of rumors that had sprung up concerning Los Alamos).[2] Likewise, the meanings that American cultural productions have ascribed to the atomic bombings (particularly of Hiroshima, given its status as the first of the two) have inspired a process of scholarly consideration that is ongoing across of range of humanities and social science disciplines. Within these research publications, three communities invariably occasion interest: *hibakusha*, both in the immediate aftermath of the Bomb and in the years following; interlocutors such as the oral historian, psychotherapist, or documentarian; and Allied veterans of the Pacific War.[3] How these figures are seen to understand themselves, each other, and contemporary society is a question that intrigues researchers, and yet, across the disciplines, a fourth actor—or rather the cultural productions that he has come to inhabit—remains notably disengaged from the conversation. Literary portrayals of those scientists who worked on the Manhattan Project (hereafter 'Project novels') have steadily increased in number since the mid-twentieth century, but scholarly attempts to connect these portrayals with research into how Hiroshima has been depicted have yet to emerge. This demurral is matched—and, one assumes, probably encouraged—by the structure of Project novels themselves, which tend to either reduce the bombings of Hiroshima and Nagasaki to condensed retrospectives or to omit any mention of the bombings once the Project reaches completion.

As in the previous chapter, part of my purpose in what follows is to illustrate how difficult it has become for literary writers to maintain this historical and canonical exclusivity into the twenty-first century. Yet Project novels differ significantly from FEPOW narratives insofar as the latter, from their inception, involved authors from throughout the anglophone world and beyond, whereas the former, until quite recently, has been almost wholly the province of American authors. Why this should be so is impossible to say with any certainty and the lack of any British literature on the topic is especially curious, given that the Manhattan Project would not have reached completion as soon as it did without the inclusion of British scientific research (the transatlantic race for the Bomb involved rivalry between allies as well as a sense that the Bomb had to be acquired before Nazi Germany completed its project to acquire the same).[4] However, the fact that the Manhattan Project took place within the territorial boundaries of the United States is surely a contributing factor (POW camps, by contrast, were scattered throughout the Asia-Pacific). Then, too, there were the multifarious meanings associated with the Bomb in the immediate postwar years, meanings that differed greatly depending on one's ideology, but which tended, on balance, to inspire future-oriented speculations rather than retrospectives on the war years. As cultural historian Robert Jacobs has noted, an alchemical narrative developed around the Bomb, one which viewed the nuclear age as "an age of transformation. To people around the world, nuclear weapons announced that the past was gone and the future had arrived."[5] In the minds of many, this was a terrifying future in which another war was just round the corner—a war in which the United States would itself fall victim to a nuclear strike[6]—and so science fiction writers made it their paramount concern to portray World War III as vividly as possible, in the hope that bold depictions would lessen the likelihood of a real-life conflagration.[7] These prognostications manifested far beyond the realm of fiction writing, with public intellectuals urgently discussing whether atomic energy would usher in an era of world peace or reduce humanity to 'troglodytes.'[8] As we shall see in due course, the doomsday scenario dreamed up in NASO's draft principles, excerpted in the second epigraph to this chapter, was anticipated in a number of literary works. Whether in fiction or nonfiction writings, the New Zealand imaginary was oriented toward its 'place' as a bastion of anti-nuclearism rather than a culture from which retrospectives on the atomic bombings and the Manhattan Project could emerge.

In the course of the last twenty years or so, the canon of Project novels has diversified beyond its American roots to encompass New Zealand writing, in the form of James George's novel *Ocean Roads* (2006), and Canadian writing, represented by Dennis Bock's *The Ash Garden* (2001). To appreciate the narrative contours from which these two authors diverge, I shall first disclose the cultural background informing Project novels; and then, in a subsequent section, map the literary history of Project novels, paying particular attention to the writings of Upton Sinclair, Michael Amrine, Haakon Chevalier, George E. Simpson & Neal R. Burger, Joseph Kanon, and Nora Gallagher. Unlike the many biographies of J. Robert Oppenheimer that occasion scholarly interest, these works have inspired hardly any critical commentary, perhaps because they comprise a series that remained, throughout the twentieth century, remarkably resistant to reinvention.[9] Observing that this is likely the case, I avoid dwelling upon any one particular work in favor of probing the boundaries behind which authors shelter and upon which their writing, in large part, depends. These are narrative boundaries, born of the temptation to comfortably and convincingly settle the Manhattan Project in its New Mexican environs and then make of it an American story that exists in isolation from historical junctures on the other side of the Pacific. Having bought into this thinking, authors then go on to resist, however implicitly, a transpacific or comparative framing of 'their' story (or the 'atomization' of the narrative into divergent ethnic or national subjectivities) that might otherwise diversify the meanings that Americans attach to the figure of the Project scientist and perhaps to nuclear physicists generally.[10] In the absence of any such efforts on the author's part, to read Project novels is to enter into a world of social, intellectual, and scientific endeavor that obscures, quite effectively, the larger confinement of the narrative itself.

Trending Nuclear

Even before the Project novel began to take on the features that it retains to this day, boundaries of discourse were in operation that separated images of institutional cooperation and scientific achievement from images of urban devastation and the erasure of human life. The specifics of these discourses, as they are reflected in and shaped by Project novels, warrant consideration. For now though, a rhetorical question: If a writer of historical novels pens a work that recollects the production of a weapon hitherto alien to human societies, should that writer feel bound to disclose, at least to some degree, the use, if any, to which that weapon was eventually put? One would hardly expect it of a story of the first Walther pistol, Nambu machine gun, or Kalashnikov rifle, weapons whose namesakes could not have imagined the future battlefields on which their wares would feature. But what if such weapons had only been used on a single occasion? What if a single pull of the trigger could—did—destroy entire cities? Would these factors make a difference to what we, as readers, ought to expect from a retrospective account? The subtext to these questions is whether the writing of apocalypse can or should change the narrative direction, and while I admit to skepticism regarding the assertion that 'Los Alamos was one story, Hiroshima another,' the purpose of this chapter is neither to defend nor oppose the writer who upholds such a stance. Instead, I draw attention to the salient features of the Project novel and argue that these betray unease on the writer's part, an unease that suggests a dormant—not yet dawning—awareness that the aforementioned questions remain pressing.

That Project novels have shied away from modes of comparative cultural and historical enquiry makes them of a piece with nuclear-themed cultural productions of the United States. Addressing these, historian Paul Boyer succinctly observes that public commentary on the atomic bombings has tended to splinter off and diverge from the topic at hand, veering away from Hiroshima towards distinctly related but nonetheless discrete topic areas, especially those associated with the early Cold War era.[11] This impulse towards digression has transcended the boundaries of medium and genre, outlasted the Cold War, and shaped the output of successive generations of writers and artists. Thus, it would be accurate to say that what many studies document in American film, literature, comic books, journalism, museum exhibitions, and other source material is not so much the quest to ascribe meaning to the mass destruction of Hiroshima, but rather this selfsame reflex towards evasion. As these studies continue to expand, the thoroughness of the research enterprise is affirmed and, if the search for, and inclusion of, new media stands as an objective and achievement in itself, then by those standards—which are the standards of the archivist and the antiquarian in the first instance—the field of study has undergone a healthy regeneration several times over. But additions cannot substitute for revisions at the critical and theoretical levels, and these latter facets are, in turn, intimately bound up with—if not necessarily dependent upon—the willingness of writers and artists to enter into a dialogue with—act alongside, anticipate, understudy—the scholar-critic. Absent that, the ideal of creative exchange and critical reformulation between new research publications and the cultural productions they examine, becomes a one-sided conversation. Such a scenario, of course, does not foreclose the possibility of writers breaking new ground without assistance from the scholarly community. But if writers, in the words of Howard Zinn, are at their best when they make it their business "to transcend conventional wisdom, to transcend the word of the establishment, to transcend the orthodoxy, to go beyond and escape what is handed down by the government or what is said in the media," then much of the literary writing that touches on Hiroshima betrays a need for critical intervention.[12]

Most humanities scholars would readily enter into a dialogue with literary and other artistic communities, a case in point being the 'Nuke York, New

York' exhibition at Cornell University in 2011, which illustrated the ways in which tropes of victimhood have been displaced from Hiroshima and projected onto the urban landscape of New York across a range of American media.[13] However, when one seeks out literary productions that have engaged scholarship pertaining to Hiroshima, then one is liable to conclude that such efforts are unreciprocated. One finds, as science-fiction scholar Paul Brians found in the 1980s, that most endeavors seek neither to portray the 'death immersion' that followed the bombings nor push back the boundaries of long-standing—some would say 'mythic'—notions, such as that of bombing Japan in order to receive an unconditional surrender.[14] Having written approvingly of the works of John Hersey, Edita Morris, and Masuji Ibuse, Brians cast a reproachful eye on the mediocrity that permeates science-fiction writing ('SF') in respect to Hiroshima:

> Compared to these works, the vast bulk of SF's early treatments of the theme pale into something worse than insignificance: into a shameful inadequacy which is the result of a failure to look steadily and feelingly on the face of atomic destruction. It is difficult to avoid the conclusion that what has occurred is a massive failure of nerve compounded by the aversion to realism endemic to the SF of the period.[15]

To Brians' trinity of well-regarded authors one may now add the likes of Martin Booth, Joy Kogawa, Kamila Shamsie, James George, and Dennis Bock, non-American authors who have written with sensitivity of those Japanese and/or foreign nationals who survived the atomic bombings or otherwise reminded readers that the Manhattan Project was never an exclusively American undertaking.[16] Their works are indeed 'transcendent,' but if one casts about for contemporary American authors then one struggles to find anyone of comparable caliber, although Lydia Millet's daring depiction of a 'resurrected' J. Robert Oppenheimer visiting Hiroshima's Peace Memorial Park in *Oh Pure and Radiant Heart* (2005) deserves honorable mention, as does the outrageous satire of James Morrow's *Shambling towards Hiroshima* (2009). Consequently, those humanities scholars who interrogate the ways in which Hiroshima features in American writing often find themselves transitioning from a descriptive mode of criticism to one which is, if not exactly prescriptive, then at least advisory, aimed, for the most part, at a creative writing community that still prefers to look above the mushroom cloud rather than beneath it.

The frustrations that follow this state of affairs are hardly confined to the US, nor are they only ever observed by the scholarly community. Literary writers have stepped forward to venture opinions on the matter, as Joy Kogawa did when she tasked her fellow Canadians to take up a more emotive response to war and the atomic bombings:

> We need to acknowledge the appetite for war, the fears that feed it, the hunger for vengeance, the blood lust. It is fresh blood that the dogs of war always demand. And so I believe we need to be graphic in our remembering, visceral in our imagining. We need to understand how the past is demonstrably present, so that the salivating beasts with their mad thirst may drink and feel and realize the close, close connection between ourselves and the ones we devour. We need to taste the blood and know it to be our own.[17]

The humanism imbued in Kogawa's appeal is at its most effective when considered as the universal heritage—and bequest—of all the formerly belligerent peoples involved in the war. But if her message bears the stamp of a universalist mandate, it is especially pertinent to those most reluctant to hear it and, on that score, Americans have a record of response that demands attention, oscillating as it does between ambiguity and indifference.[18] These trends are reflected in and reinforced by the Project novel, which offered its readers a story that made turning away from Hiroshima unnecessary because the narrative of the text fulfilled that function on their behalf. Most readers, admittedly, might never have picked up on this process, for the Manhattan Project's undisputed success at facilitating scientific breakthroughs was itself a story worth telling and the characters of the scientists who worked on the project, whether real or imagined, were compelling. But by embedding the literary imagination in scientific contexts and the 'political climate' of the war era, writers could 'contain' their consideration of the aerial deployment, military-civilian (mostly civilian) targets, and longer-term effects of the weapons that resulted from the Project, not the least of which was the 'atomic bomb disease' alluded to in the first epigraph to this chapter.

Once the American public learned of the Project, literary novels almost immediately sprang up that attempted to describe it in realistic, linear terms. Typically, these narratives invested heavily in the characterization of a select few scientists and military personnel whose integration into the Project's administrative apparatus invariably entails a sacrifice of individualism. Employing pseudonyms for the well-known public figures of J. Robert Oppenheimer, Leó Szilárd, Enrico Fermi, et al., or writing their genius onto a type of virtuosic 'everyman,' the narrative goes on to describe the scientist's dissatisfaction with the institutionalization to which he is subjected and uses the tension as a means to engage in a socio-political critique and/or manifesto for the US. Structurally speaking, the potential for a retrospective meditation on the decisions that led to Hiroshima has therefore always existed within these novels, although in practice such potential is hardly ever realized. The location of the didactic component in a type of attenuated appendix, after the fact of the Project's completion and following on from the end of the Pacific War, explains why meditations on Hiroshima conclude rather abruptly, for when V-J Day arrives, the time to discuss Hiroshima passes swiftly and the void is filled by more 'current' affairs. Within this format, those who venture anything more substantial about Hiroshima—or rather the possibility that the Bomb might be dropped on a Japanese target rather than on Nazi Germany, as was the initial thinking in the scientific community—must find room for their thoughts alongside or within the narrative of the Project's development, or, failing that, depart from the linear mode and break up the narrative into different time periods. Scientists, in short, must be made to seem morally contemplative as well as productive.

As an exercise in characterization, the figure of the ethical scientist presented no great challenge to science fiction writers of the mid-twentieth century, who were used to portraying scientists in a heroic light.[19] But to a writer of historical fiction, certain questions followed as a matter of course. For a start, there was the old and thorny issue of narrative 'voice' intruding into or misrepresenting individual characters, which, in turn, raised the problem of whether such writing could be construed as defamation by those (still living) characters who might, upon picking up a copy of the published book, take issue with how they were supposed to have behaved. One early precedent that provoked the ire of prominent scientists was the 1947 Hollywood film *The Beginning or the End?*, a production that had involved consultations with prominent Manhattan Project figures but which lost the support of many scientists once the overt fictionalization became apparent.[20] Even if a writer was prepared to risk libel action, a model of ethics for war-related research had not then (nor has it since) been formalized in respect to real-life scientific communities. Hence the issue of what historical characters could or should be made to say on the subject appeared then—and remains now—altogether uncertain. Returning the dilemma to its historical context, Jeffrey Kovac reminds us: "In 1905, no one could have imagined that Albert Einstein's work on special relativity and the equivalence of matter and energy would have led to the production of a fission bomb 40 years later."[21] This element of uncertainty was definitive, both to the scientists who worked on the Manhattan Project, and to those authors who recreated the events on the written page. Each community readily understood that the efforts required to create the Bomb were so taxing that most scientists would not have pondered the outcome except in a preconceived and largely material sense. One retrospective piece by a former member of the Manhattan Project was explicit on the point:

> Before Hiroshima, we scientists worked frantically. First, to build an atomic bomb before the Germans did. And second, to bring to an end the awful carnage of that terrible war. Under that kind of pressure, there was little or no time to think about sociological problems, and, since we did not even know whether a bomb could be built at all, it was hard to take any such philosophical thoughts seriously.[22]

Needless to say, such thoughts became a good deal easier once the project reached completion. Indeed, public debates surrounding research on the hydrogen bomb, a hypothetical weapon that some project scientists considered genocidal, may have redirected attention away from the bombings of the Second World War.[23] In any case, literary writers showed no inclination to complicate the 'straightforward' thinking of the war years and, if offered an alternative, would probably not have had it any other way, for the Project scientists' studied disinterest towards the ramifications of the Bomb did nothing to retard the creative imagination. On the contrary, the picture of a scientific community laboring towards an end whose power was unknown to them except on the level of physics enabled writers to sustain the attention of their readers with relative ease. Furthermore, a narrative that reinvested in a shoulder-shrugging trend of compliance on the part of Project scientists had the effect of rendering any meditation on Hiroshima unnecessary, both for characters within the novel and the novel's readers. Thus, a key reason for the recurrence of the Project novel throughout the twentieth century lies not so much in the questions that it asks, as its capacity to avoid the more awkward ones. As for the theme of victimization, when this occurs, which it does not always, it has little if anything to do with the many and varied injuries endured by *hibakusha*, instead focusing upon the less corporeal sacrifices (career ambitions, family harmony, and political integrity) of the project scientists.

Aside from the schematic that I have provided, a couple of other qualities are consistent enough within Project novels to merit mention. First, there is a fixation upon the mind of the scientist as an anomalous object, prone to fantastic feats of ingenuity but just as capable of exhibiting the more egregious social neuroses of the day. The man in question could be a cool, level-headed visionary tirelessly working for the betterment of humanity— or, in a Dr. Strangelove incarnation, an obsessive-compulsive. Throughout the Cold War, nuclear-themed fiction and films, such as Eugene Burdick and Harvey Wheeler's novel *Fail-Safe* (1962), continued to hold the scientist accountable, not only for the creation of the Bomb, but also for the prevalence of nuclear anxiety that readers encountered in daily life, and Project novels certainly toyed with scapegoating of this sort.[24] Keeping recriminations in check, however, was a heavy investment in the mythologization of the Project as one of the greatest scientific feats ever undertaken, as well as a parallel mythologization of the principal figures associated with it.[25] Nothing about these latter trends was inconsistent, for the earliest publicly-reported celebrations of the scientists' success employed procreational language (the Bomb as child; Los Alamos as parent) which implied a clear link between the Manhattan Project and the dawn of the nuclear age.[26] To speak of this 'birthing' process in laudatory terms was entirely acceptable, perhaps even one's bounden duty if one felt, as several newspaper cartoonists did, that the Bomb was akin to a scepter signifying international authority.[27] Less acceptable was the notion that the scientists were not all of a piece in their political allegiances, a revisionist position which Margot Norris has put forward, reminding us that there were, in fact, two Projects, one in Los Alamos and the other in Chicago, the latter playing host to *émigré* scientists whose political activity and moral outspokenness ran contrary to the wishes of the military apparatus.[28] As one might have expected, their story is downplayed or otherwise omitted from early Project novels, as well as filmic portrayals, both of which stress the Los Alamos component above all.[29] Only towards the end of the twentieth and beginning of the twenty-first century would publications begin to allow for more pluralistic political stances, although this development coincides with—and perhaps stimulates—an increased emphasis on love and romance, themes that do not counter, but nonetheless distract, from the diversity of politics on display.

Project Novels

By anyone's standards, the first Project novel to come off the press must be taken as a peculiarity. Perhaps the most charitable way in which to approach Upton Sinclair's *O Shepherd, Speak!* (1949) is as a botched attempt to reinstate the epic notion of divine intervention on the human plane. Sinclair's would-be demigod, Lanny Budd, is certainly as unbending and multifarious as any archaic deity, appearing at various times to be steering the entire war, although it is truer to say that he just happens to be present at almost every juncture. Variously employed as an art expert, presidential agent, military interrogator, trauma therapist-cum-hypnotist, acting colonel, father, husband, and associate of Roosevelt, Hitler, Stalin, Paton, and Einstein, to name just a few, Budd is the personification of what every rank and file soldier must have wished himself to be: at the scene and on the case. (One longs to see him metamorphose into an American cousin of George MacDonald Fraser's Flashman, but it appears that Sinclair expected readers to take his creation seriously). Mercifully, Budd's omnipresence does not encompass Hiroshima, although it manages to take in the Battle of the Bulge, the last moments of Roosevelt's life, the liberation of Dachau, and a *tête-à-tête* with Hermann Göring. For a writer of socialist realism, this was a significant, even brazen, departure from the world of labor movements. Just as surprising is Sinclair's disregard for the main character bequeathed him by Great War literature: the common foot soldier, a man whose plight was sufficiently evocative on its own terms without slipping into omnipresent 'heroism.' It is worth noting, however, that the bold newspaper headlines of 1945 were still vivid in public memory at the time of publication. Seen this way, Sinclair's work functions as a stock check, wherein a lot of things are itemized but not stared at fully. As Paul Boyer reminds us, in the immediate aftermath of the war, Hiroshima "was not yet accessible to the creative core of consciousness."[30] For all its considerable length, Sinclair's novel remains a breezy voyage into the truly unknown, which makes it valuable as an illustration of scattered public notions jostling one another without apology. One of these notions was of Los Alamos as "a secret society, a consecrated utopia," a glamorous rendition of what was, after all, a heavily guarded compound, although Sinclair does give much attention to the Los Alamos security procedures and a run-through of the Trinity test—safe, practical topics that set the tone for what would follow.[31] Hiroshima and Nagasaki hardly figure at all in the text, largely because Sinclair cannot restrain his eagerness to launch into a socialist critique of post-war American society, but also because the humanization of the enemy is a privilege reserved for the Germans. Throughout Europe, Budd encounters military leaders on every side, but the same courtesy is not granted the Japanese who remain essentially 'faceless,' true to the manner of their depiction in the better-known combat novels previously discussed in Chapter 1. 'Effacing' the enemy allows Hiroshima to function as an event without a human visage and explains why Edita Morris wrote *The Flowers of Hiroshima* (1959) and Kurt Vonnegut wrote *Cat's Cradle* (1963), partly as a countercommentary on the blindness of the American public. Their works paint a picture (more accurately, the blindness of those who are barely aware that a picture exists) on a canvas that authors such as Sinclair preferred to leave blank.

More sophisticated than Sinclair's work is Michael Amrine's *Secret* (1950), which contains one of the first fully realized portraits of the Project scientist and also illustrates the beginnings of a structural avoidance of Hiroshima through displaced victimization. The picture that Amrine initially draws of the Project might be seen as a distant reflection of the Edenic mode of writing that was becoming familiar through journalistic depictions of post-war atomic tests in the South Pacific, of which the 1946 Bikini Atoll test was the first:[32]

> It was a city of young people, scientists and war workers, a city overfed, glutted with money for workers and knowledge for scientists, and the nights were long. The city was hidden from the world and the families hid from each other. The birthrate was the highest in America, and it became a city of tiny children, it was a place of atoms and woods and children. Their laughter was everywhere in the Happy Valley.[33]

If there is a snake in this garden it cannot represent knowledge, for that is already present in abundance. Rather, it comprises interference in the day-to-day running of the operation by those administrators and military personnel who have nothing to do with the research effort. Confronting this avaricious behavior is Halverson, an Oppenheimer stand-in who comes across as a sensitive, grounded, altogether reluctant Project participant. Halverson despises the military, first on a basis of administrative inefficiency, but also on moral grounds. While listening to a pontificating colonel, he realizes: "The trouble with the Army mind was that it was an extreme extension of the philosophical concept that no man can envision his own death."[34] Diagnoses of this sort lead to the scientist exculpating or, more properly, martyring himself by shouldering the moral burden of the Bomb's development—to such an extent that, in narrative terms, it is the scientist rather than the victims of his creation who becomes the object of pity. Evasiveness is built into this arrangement, part of which involves emphasizing the conflicts of interest between the Army and those Project scientists more inclined towards civilian administrative procedures. This style of writing, although turgid and weighty, is made easier by the infamously bureaucratic nature of the Project, and also by the familiarity of the 1950s readership with the military euphemisms of the war years. It was more universally familiar to talk of how people could become lost in paperwork than to acknowledge a more literal entombment. Bureaus, offices, departments, committees, and functionaries draw the reader's attention at every turn. Overreliant on this wall of words, the novel skims over the destruction of Hiroshima, dwelling only upon a series of human curiosities, such as one survivor who had been partially protected by a garden fence, leaving his skin 'leonine.'[35] The story concludes with a feature common to depictions of the Manhattan Project in the literatures of other countries: the scientist's moral crusade against nuclear weapons, impelled by fear, distantly aware of Hiroshima, but having more to do with vague and muddled suspicions that the US military cannot be trusted to exercise restraint.[36]

As in Sinclair's case, the wife figure in Amrine's novel remains in the background, not yet transformed into the redeeming agent she would become. This changes in Haakon Chevalier's *The Man Who Would Be God* (1960), a novel that charts the scientist's fall from charismatic polymath to monomaniacal automaton and observes his decline through the eyes of those closest to him. Although Chevalier is distracted by updating the Project narrative to reflect the fears that pervaded the Communist witch hunts of the 1950s (during which Oppenheimer's political sympathies fell under suspicion, although he denied Party membership at a security hearing in 1954), the main thrust of the novel comes from portraying the scientist as suffering from a Faustian or Frankenstein-style obsession that eventually consumes him. Acting the part of a tragic chorus, the scientist's wife goes from being the submissive alter ego envisaged by Sinclair and Amrine, to a worrisome, morally astute (but not too articulate) dissenter. Not yet a chief actor, she voluntarily absents herself or is otherwise secluded from the bulk of the narrative, where she remains in mute opprobrium, a sure sign that something is rotten in the state of New Mexico. Representative of the chauvinism is this extraordinary passage:

> Tanya was waiting up for him when he got home—though he had at last made her understand that he had resolved to forgo all sexual indulgence during this difficult period when the embryo of the Monster was coming to maturity. She had contrived to seduce him several times in the last year and a half, and as he found her, not less, but rather more, desirable than ever, he had had to harden himself against her.[37]

As a typical piece of Cold War discourse, feminine sexuality is here both an aberrant site of danger and a force for redemption. To remain resistant is to let go of a final lifeline and plunge headlong into an abyss of dehumanization, and yet capitulating involves an emasculation that threatens the future of the Project. Such is the impossible choice that confronts the scientist, and, by the end of the novel, he has made it, metamorphosing into a *dominus factotum* at the beck and call of the military.

Twenty years later, the subject of atomic research, past or present, was proving almost impossible to create without the specter of Soviet espionage, and authors freely indulged their imagination in this respect, even as pointed questions regarding the necessity of Hiroshima gathered momentum. In their novel *Fair Warning* (1980), George E. Simpson and Neal R. Burger offer a scene of President Truman being told by admirals and generals that the Bomb is inexpedient, and remaining convinced that, if not militarily justifiable, its value lies in political leverage.[38] These moments of budding revisionism are intriguing but also frustrating to encounter, in that they reveal an increased awareness of the controversies surrounding the decision to drop the Bomb, but just at the very moment when these controversies emerge in the text they are swept aside by the pace of the narrative. This pace was given impetus by the marriage of the Project novel with the Cold War espionage thriller, the culmination of which is Joseph Kanon's hard-boiled novel, *Los Alamos* (1997). Published two years after the fiftieth anniversary of the end of the Second World War, Kanon manages to retain some revisionist material, most obviously disseminated through the character of the *émigré* scientist Eisler, who comes closest to criticizing the Bomb's manufacture and whose suicide is framed as atonement. But there is a twist. When it emerges that Eisler has been passing documents to the Soviets, the motive behind his suicide gets called into question. The reader may choose, apparently, between atonement for the Bomb that led to Hiroshima or for an act of espionage that will feed into the nuclear rivalry of the Cold War. Kanon leaves Eisler's martyrdom unexplained, illustrating at a stroke his intention to encourage the reader to imagine what they will but also his sense that, at the time of publication, American readers were not yet ready for a lengthy critique of the events of August 1945 (although Eisler's character does speak suggestively of the parallels between Nazism and the 'Germanisation' of an American culture possessed of the Bomb).[39]

Up until the present day, Project novels have steadily enlarged the space given over to issues pertaining to Hiroshima, but even as this trend becomes more evident, a variety of literary 'countermeasures' have become evident as well. That is to say, whereas novelists have opened up their narratives to a limited discussion of the atomic bombings, their hesitancy is present at every turn and these discussions do not proceed far. What is perhaps surprising is that the novels show no indications of collapsing under the weight of this arrangement. On the contrary, one of the latest Project novels, Nora Gallagher's *Changing Light* (2007), goes further than any other in its insistence on the moral ambiguity of Hiroshima (and unwittingly continues a tradition of women's writing, traceable to wartime missives, that express doubt as to the justification for the bombing while falling short of condemning it outright).[40] Most of the story takes place in New Mexico, which is romanticized as a land of past civilizations, unique architecture, and animistic pueblos, all of which fall into an established literary and aesthetic tradition of contradistinction with the Manhattan Project.[41] Unaware of the polarity is Eleanor Garrigue, a New York artist who seeks refuge there from her domineering husband and ends up sheltering Leo, a young scientist who is sick with radiation poisoning. In due course, a Harlequin-style romance takes hold of both characters, successfully diverting the narrative from an otherwise strong move towards contemplating the nature of the Bomb and, optimistically, a critique of the male-oriented culture of Los Alamos (a feature that has led to the silencing of women's accounts).[42] Much of this nascent contemplation derives from Leo's story, which takes him towards a point of moral doubt, fed, in large part, by his witnessing a friend's overexposure to and subsequent death from radiation. Prior to this moment, Leo had imagined the moment of the Bomb's detonation as the sole source of its destructive power, but his friend's fatal exposure in the laboratory brings home its unique and lingering power. No longer abstract, the damage it unleashes becomes a personal notion and the Army's unwillingness to register the event suggests to Leo that what the scientists unwittingly ignore, the Army knowingly conceals. Unable to reconcile himself to this moral apathy, Leo makes a deduction: "He saw, even as the scientists had thought they were the smart ones, who had been in charge all along. What came to his mind was simple. Los Alamos was not a lab; it was a factory. The people who owned the bomb will own the world."[43] Taking the theme of the disgruntled scientist to its logical conclusion, Gallagher has Leo turn escape artist, and the first image we have of him is of someone who creeps under fences while recalling the plight of his sister, a concentration camp prisoner in Europe.[44] The equivalence of these two people, one in a death camp, the other manufacturing death on a mass scale, opens up a line of comparative enquiry. Why, one might ask, should American writers have so little trouble embracing the idea of Los Alamos as a death-producing 'camp' and then turn away from contemplating the destruction wrought upon two cities as a direct consequence? But as with other Project novels, the answer to that question is readily apparent. If Los Alamos belongs to the US, so too do its victims—namely the self-abnegating scientist—because, in identifying victims, it is easier and preferable to imagine one's own countrymen in that position rather than those of a land on the other side of the Pacific.

Lifeboat New Zealand

In New Zealand, as elsewhere in the anglophone world, it was possible to imagine one's national culture through the prism of victimhood. In particular, the plight of Allied FEPOWs remained a paramount memory in the war's aftermath, one that could, and sometimes did, function in dialectical opposition to the atomic bombings. Yet the sense of the Pacific War's geographical proximity and the prospect of a new East-West split, this time organized around a Communist-Capitalist divide, combined to give the Cold War a sense of spatial and temporal immediacy sufficient to occlude most other considerations. In his 1947 memoir of captivity under the Japanese, for example, journalist James Bertram struck a resoundingly philosophical tone when he recalled a speech given by a Japanese Colonel to the prisoners assembled before him at the war's end. Measuring his words carefully, the Colonel had warned the FEPOWs against treating Japan too harshly during the Allied Occupation of his country and, in a corollary point, reminded them that Japan had stood as a bulwark against Communism. The speech was well-received.[45]

Much as Japan was reconceived in these terms, literary writers in the immediate postwar years would reimagine New Zealand through the prism of the Cold War, again as something of a bulwark—but in the still larger prospect of the island nation serving as a holdout for humanity in the aftermath of thermonuclear war. So, if the reality of the atomic bombings was something to which Japanese culture had to adjust, the near-future imagination of New Zealand as a final refuge required a good deal of consideration too. Among other things, this meant that the Manhattan Project as a topic for New Zealand fiction writers was effectively shelved for the rest of the century, as was any extensive consideration of Hiroshima and Nagasaki and the survivors of those 'small-scale' bombings (unprecedented by the standards of the Second World War, they were frighteningly antiquated compared to the hydrogen devices that superseded them in the early 1950s). One should note, in all fairness, that the literary progenitors of the 'lifeboat New Zealand' scenario had their origins in the British imagination in the first instance and, more generally, in a pervasive anglophone culture that saw the prospect of nuclear apocalypse as always already present.[46] Aldous Huxley's *Ape and Essence* (1948) was the first novel to indulge the premise, imagining a post-apocalyptic world in which New Zealand has somehow maintained a working infrastructure, a faith in science and reason, and a willingness to explore irradiated zones beyond its borders. Rather than beginning with Australia or Papua New Guinea, a New Zealand 'Rediscovery Expedition' alights in California in the year 2108, where they encounter a mass of devil-worshipping, baby-sacrificing, corpse-exhuming locals whose practices, while barbaric, are all traceable to 'the Thing.' Alternately overdone and understated, Huxley's narrative is at its strongest during an epitaph to the blunders of Western civilization rendered by an 'Arch Vicar' who, alone among the Californians, has read enough history to wax ironical when a presumptuous New Zealander upholds the virtues of science and humanism.[47]

Huxley's didacticism anticipated John Wyndham's *The Chrysalids* (1955), another British novel that imagines a post-lapsarian religion, this time based in Newfoundland. Although not devil-worshipping, the denizens of this novel embrace infanticide, following a religious mandate intertwined with a eugenicist directive to guard against deformities (termed 'offences'). The rule and its practice suits everyone except for a small group of outwardly unblemished children who are driven to despair in concealing their congenital telepathy. Choosing to go on the run, they establish contact with New Zealand, a land where telepathy is the rule rather than the exception. Huxley's dour criticism of the arrogance upholding science and reason gives way here to the heady optimism of a diaspora converging on New Zealand as a promised land of somewhat arrogant pundits who state their position in the following terms: "We are the New People—your kind of people. The people who can think-together. We're the people who are going to build a new kind of world—different from the Old People's world, and from the savages.'"[48] Entrenched in this imperative is a distant reflection on the much-trumpeted success of New Zealand's welfare state of the 1950s, although once New Zealanders themselves began to imagine a post-apocalyptic future they were less given to idealizations.

Nor were they alone in their skepticism. Across the Tasman, some began to reconsider whether human survival in the aftermath of an atomic war was at all likely, or, granting the premise, desirable. Among the most frequently cited nuclear fictions, Nevil Shute's *On the Beach* (1957) gained widespread attention partly because it mercilessly pulled the plug on the notion of an Oceanic 'safe zone' beyond the reach (or consideration) of antagonists in the northern hemisphere.[49] Just as cynical, New Zealand author Janet Frame likewise chose to see disaster as inescapable, although more in terms of its socio-cultural origins than its geopolitics. Her novel *Intensive Care* (1970) antedates the state-endorsed normalization of global catastrophe to the Great War, which instills an unending willingness to mass homicide in its participants. Home from the war, one of the New Zealand veterans, Tom Livingstone, makes a quick adjustment back to civilian life and takes up work in a cement factory. The transition is deceptive, however, for Tom remains fascinated by images whose symbolic value attests to the war's continual hold over his mind. Foremost among these is the factory's flame, responsible for controlling furnace pressure and also emblematic of the 'eternal flame' of (frequently military) memory found at memorials and epitaphs all over the world. Tom's gaze is dedicated, but not restive, and certainly not reflective, except in the ironic sense common to Frame's writing. Through him, readers gradually come to see the human mind as a series of pistons, pulleys, flares, and levers, hardly as distinct from the world of the mechanical as one would assume. This in itself is a disturbing hypothesis, but Frame goes further still, suggesting that the *en masse* militarization of modern man has created a demonstrable interface between mechanical warfare and the mechanics of the human mind, such that the notion of death on a vast scale no longer occasions resistance, or even surprise. Within this apparently nondescript 'bloke,' the well-practiced urge to kill rests imperfectly disarmed, ever ready for reactivation. As Frame puts it, "Died and died and died in the War. Because the War never ended, they forgot the trick of ending it, because they didn't know it was still going on and on and on, and if they saw it was there they kept looking away and pretending it wasn't there, like with the mental people."[50] Less a comment on demobilization in the practical sense, in this passage Frame is suggesting an ongoing recirculation of wartime prerogatives in national cultures such that, with every passing conflict, their use grows steadily more tolerable until societies become conditioned to war without their knowing it. When a third world war wipes out much of the global population in a subsequent section of the novel, the hypothesis appears vindicated and New Zealand, intact to a degree, responds to the disaster with a series of well-managed purges.

Frame's work drew from, and fed into, resurgent fears of all things nuclear that were common throughout the anglophone world during the 1980s, an era when British Prime Minister Margaret Thatcher and US President Ronald Reagan brought a hard-line vision of geopolitics to international relations, leading to a shift in strategic discourse away from the idea of Mutually Assured Destruction toward the possibility of a 'winnable' nuclear war.[51] During this era, nonfiction publications in Australia and New Zealand took a leaf out of Huxley and Shute's works and began to entertain the possibility that the antipodes would become a refuge for the world's population or, in a reverse scenario, that a post-nuclear world might one day be repopulated therefrom.[52] Acting to preempt these doomsday scenarios, or at least to ensure that New Zealand would in no way contribute to their eventuality, a home-grown peace movement grew steadily in prominence from its beginnings in the 1960s. Its purpose was to disengage New Zealand from superpower rivalry in the Pacific region. During the mid-1970s, this movement exhibited itself most obviously through a 'Peace Squadron' of small boats that protested against the docking of nuclear-capable vessels in

New Zealand ports, most famously in January 1979 when one protester managed to climb on board the submarine *USS Haddo* as it entered port.[53] The peace movement gathered pace throughout the 1980s, gaining international attention in 1985 when Prime Minister David Lange participated in an Oxford Union debate. Recalling the moment in his memoir, Lange defended his country's position: "We were being told by the United States that we could not decide for ourselves how to defend ourselves, but had to let others decide that for us. That, I said, was exactly the totalitarianism we were fighting against. The audience roared."[54] Predictably, official responses in the United States tended to be terse. The US Permanent Representative to NATO, David Abshire, described New Zealand as being "like an ostrich with its head in the sand" and one of the consequences to New Zealand's official nuclear-free identity, declared in 1987, was the ending of any Prime Ministerial visits to the White House (a period lasting eleven years).[55] If political relations soured during this period, creative writers took a different view. On both sides of the Pacific, they found the New Zealand position interesting, even inspiring. Science fiction author Poul Anderson's short story collection, *Maurai & Kith* (1982), tapped into the rising tide of antinuclear sentiment in New Zealand to imagine the US-New Zealand standoff in futuristic terms, as taking place between an ecologically-minded Māori technocracy and the 'sky people,' descendants of those Americans who have survived the worst of a nuclear war. Anderson even goes the same route as Walter M. Miller Jr.'s iconic novel *A Canticle for Leibowitz* (1960), suggesting that a recovered world civilization would eventually rediscover nuclear weapons and use them again. This cyclical doomsday scenario is preempted by the Māori, who act the part of the world's scientific conscience and global police force all-in-one. Only a culture such as theirs, combining mana and scientific know-how, is able to balance the odds.[56]

Hibakusha Projects

Ten weeks after the end of the war, a series of pyrotechnic 're-enactments' of the *Enola Gay*'s journey, accompanied by a pseudo-detonation of the Bomb itself, drew large crowds in Texas and California, thereby contributing to a culture that literature scholar Peter Schwenger has dubbed the 'Disneyfication' of Hiroshima.[57] Such events are explicable partly because news of the catastrophic death tolls in the Pacific War, and during the war between Nazi Germany and the Soviet Union, had inured Allied civilians to a world in which such happenings were apparently usual.[58] Furthermore, the innumerable war dead, Japanese, to be sure, but especially those of one's own side, underscored the righteousness of the prevailing power in ways that were powerful, implicit, and not wholly rational. As Elaine Scarry puts it, "the legitimacy of the outcome [of war] outlives the end of the contest because so many of its participants are frozen in a permanent act of participation: that is, the winning issue or ideology achieves for a time the force and status of material 'fact' by the sheer weight of the multitudes of damaged and opened human bodies."[59] If this psychological undercurrent ran through every Allied anglophone country, it was nowhere more apparent than in the United States, where breaking news of the Manhattan Project's existence added luster to the realization that the war was over. The revelation that the US Army had secluded an entire community away from prying eyes made it well-nigh inevitable that the 'atomic city' of Los Alamos would occasion more interest than the bombed cities of Hiroshima and Nagasaki. Borrowing an analogy from linguistics, historian Jon Hunner summarizes the process succinctly:

> Searching for the atomic bomb and prevented from seeing it because of the shield of secrecy, US citizens saw the residential community instead. In the development of an atomic culture, the ultimate code switch inserted the suburban utopia of postwar Los Alamos for the terrifying image of a bomb capable of annihilating Japanese communities.[60]

The increased salience of nuclear issues during the 1980s and the accompanying visibility of world peace movements, on the other hand, emerged during a different socio-political climate and might have resulted in greater attention to *hibakusha* as well. In point of fact, several English-language books on the topic were indeed issued by Japanese publishers, each of which included translated testimonies from *hibakusha* as well as photographs of burned limbs and torsos, keloid scars, and bombed-out landscapes.[61] The latter two of these publications went through several print runs, and yet the range and extent of their readership was more limited than it would otherwise have been had they appeared under a nominally anglophone imprint. Furthermore, the phenomenon of 'Japan-bashing' or 'Japan Panic,' previously explored in Chapter 2, reached its zenith during the 1980s and preempted any groundswell of sympathy from arising in anglophone cultures.[62] Add to this the overarching fixation upon near-future nuclear apocalypses, which tended, on balance, to obscure contemporaneous and Second World War nuclearism from public view, and the occlusion of *hibakusha* as a topic of interest appears all but inevitable during the period in question.[63]

It had not always been thus, nor was the obfuscation absolute. In 1964, Alan Swallow published *Friends of the Hibakusha*, edited by the peace activist

Virginia Naeve, and three years later Random House published *Death in Life*, Robert Jay Lifton's pioneering study of the psychological effects of the bombings. Naeve's work included a section on the Hiroshima Maidens, a group of schoolgirls who, having endured various conditions of disability and deformity in the aftermath of the bombing, journeyed as adults to New York City for plastic surgery at Mount Sinai Hospital. Their much-publicized sojourn received its fullest narration thirty years later when Viking Penguin published journalist Rodney Barker's *The Hiroshima Maidens* (1985), a searing account that brought home to readers the challenges facing survivors. The story of the Hiroshima Maidens and its recollection in Barker's work centralized the *hibakusha* story for public consideration in the United States and, to be sure, the episode afforded a number of instances where improved intercultural understanding was realized. However, it was also an inherently gendered episode insofar as male *hibakusha* were never considered for medical treatment, and the gender of those who were more fortunate remained a constituent feature of the journalism that surrounded them. In this dynamic, the United States was implicitly figured as masculine and benevolent, Japan as feminine and grateful.[64] As Robert Jacobs has observed:

> [The American press] used [the women's] journey to obfuscate the nation's sense of guilt about the bombing of Hiroshima and Nagasaki, by turning the whole event into a triumphant narrative of science and compassion. In this narrative the Japanese are allowed to be present but only in a childlike, dependent and ultimately grateful position. The heroes are the US doctors and philanthropists, who make the decisions, bear the costs and perform the miraculous surgeries, thus restoring life, happiness, and beauty to the Japanese women.[65]

Ironically, this discursive situation had been anticipated and all but allegorized in American author Edwin Lanham's 1970 novel *The Clock at 8:16* (the title is in reference to the minute after which the Bomb detonated over Hiroshima). In Lanham's story, an American soldier on leave in Japan seeks out a Japanese man with whom he has been corresponding, even as he remains wholly unaware that his pen friend is a scarred survivor of Hiroshima. When the latter's sister Kumiko asks her brother why he never revealed his condition, he replies: "There are no photographs of *my* face. We were having a good correspondence and why shouldn't I continue to be what he thought I was?"[66] Later in the narrative, the American finally learns of his host family's status as *hibakusha*, a revelation that follows the moment in which he succeeds in taking Kumiko's virginity. In this way, the knowledge that she provides him is counterbalanced and diminished, in narrative terms, by his power to bring new sexual experience to her.[67]

With hardly any exceptions, anglophone literary depictions of *hibakusha* remain overwhelmingly gendered and often sexualized, facets that hold true even in the most recent Project novels.[68] James George and Dennis Bock's works, to which I now turn, are truly groundbreaking in the literary history of the genre, because both grant roughly equal narrative attention to the Project scientist and the *hibakusha* as characters, something that hitherto no other writers had ever attempted. That said, it remains a curious and troubling fact that in neither instance does a male *hibakusha* emerge fully characterized. In taking the measure of their respective novels, therefore, one must simultaneously bear in mind the narrow narrative confines that have previously held Project novels *in situ* and from which George and Bock significantly diverge, while likewise granting that the normative model of *hibakusha* as female takes the development only so far. Of the two texts, *Ocean Roads* comes across as the more hesitant insofar as the *hibakusha*, Akiko, and the Project scientist, Isaac, become peripherally aware of one another and yet never meet, nor exchange any form of dialogue. The narrative oscillates back and forth between 1945 and 1989, focusing on 'signature' episodes in the lives of both characters as well as those of Isaac's son Caleb, a physics student, and his half-brother Troy, a soldier. Every one of these characters experiences debilitation, Isaac by mental illness, Caleb by leukemia, Troy by a form of PTSD; and there is also a purposeful irony in that Akiko, scarred by the bombing of Nagasaki, is nonetheless an accomplished dancer who has adjusted, to the extent that she is able, to her identity as *hibakusha*. In total contrast is Isaac, whose history of working on the Manhattan Project leads to a mental breakdown, the precise nature of which remains undisclosed until the narrative's closing sections.

In a throwback to Janet Frame's oeuvre, George has Caleb query the medical policy of the hospital in which his father resides: "How sane do you have to be before they let you out of here?" Isaac's response is laconic: "Perhaps you're approaching it from the wrong direction."[69] As in much of the rest of the narrative, the meaning is left dangling, although attentive readers are unlikely to find themselves casting about for possible inferences. Relocating madness to 'the world outside' is something of a prerequisite trope to fictions of insane asylums, but in a New Zealand novel about nuclear weapons its meaning is more specific. Of a certainty, the gesture is to nuclear proliferation and, more simply still, the continued existence of nuclear weaponry of any type. Seen this way, Isaac's incarceration almost takes on the quality of a personal decision, born of the realization that governments, military institutions, and national populations exist in a state of willful nonchalance toward the nuclear holocausts that have already happened and those that may still happen (although his mental breakdown, disclosed later in the narrative, suggests that rational argumentation developed only after the fact). An important corollary here is that New Zealand, not nuclear-free at the time of this exchange but emphatically so in 1989 as well as at the time of the novel's publication, is not exempt from criticism and may require a more concerted critique on the grounds that the success of the anti-nuclear movement has served to camouflage a history of militarism or otherwise brought about a sense of moral detachment to match the disengagement of a nuclear-free identity. At certain points, the narrative appears to nudge readers toward self-criticism, as when Caleb decides to shock New Zealanders into a heightened state of politicization through acts of terrorism, such as positioning an oil drum filled with napalm in Auckland's Victoria Park with a timed detonator set to go off at 8:15.[70] Provocatively, George does not disclose the referentiality of this number, as though to say that the legitimacy of Isaac and Caleb's position is demonstrable within any reader whose ignorance requires a (non-existent) intervention on the author's part.

Isaac's breakdown happens in Antarctica, a site that literature scholar Elizabeth DeLoughrey locates along a literary continuum stretching back at least as far as Victor Frankenstein, whose journey there likewise involved examining the ethics of scientific endeavor.[71] Prior to this moment, however, Isaac comes close to recuperation in New Zealand. In an evocative passage, his Māori lover Etta photographs him at the shoreside and imagines him as "A man of waves and troughs."[72] The description is double-edged, suggesting as it does a mechanized form of observation such as that provided in the 'waves' of an electrocardiogram or Geiger counter, while 'troughs' hints at the lows to which his psychology will plummet. That New Zealand could serve as a counteractant to a technocentric worldview taps into the literary and cultural idea of the land as a refuge from nuclearism and segues easily into the trope of redemptive romance after the fashion of Nora Gallagher. (The high tide of Japan's 'bubble economy' had also inspired Ian Middleton's 1990 novella *Reiko* and Peter Wells' 1991 short story "Of Memory and Desire," both of which figured New Zealand as an antidote to/for Japan's workaholic culture). Isaac's guilt, however, is too great for a New Zealand 'solution,' aware as he is that he had begun work on the Manhattan Project in the full knowledge that a moral reckoning would be inevitable.[73] To this, one must also add that New Zealand's status as a redemptive land free of militaristic cultures becomes heavily problematized as the narrative proceeds, although these sections concern other characters than Isaac.[74]

Paul Boyer has observed that the sixtieth anniversary of the end of the Second World War occasioned some anxiety in the US, for it was accompanied by the realization that nuclear weapons remained in place even after the end of the Cold War.[75] Published a year after the anniversary, George's novel taps into similar concerns, although the author is also attentive to the 2003 American-led invasion of Iraq, which led him to imagine parallels between that war, including the subsequent insurgency, and the Vietnam War. While the Iraq-Vietnam comparison does not find its way into *Ocean Roads*, the Vietnam War and the atomic bombings of the Pacific War are consciously interlinked in the romance that grows between Akiko and Troy.[76] The relationship between these two displaces the one between Akiko and Caleb, which is gentler and involves heavily aestheticized perspectives on the impermanence of things:

> She is always leaving pieces of herself everywhere, he thinks. Not in the house itself, but out on tree branches, on the old river stones that fringe the driveway. Even down in the dunes. Scarves, earrings, once a bangle so thin he had to lift it to the light to see the whole of its circle. At first he had picked the pieces up, returned them to the bedside table in her room, but something else would appear. Her carelessness had puzzled him, she the most careful of people, until one day he found one of her scarves tied to a tree branch at the edge of the dunes. The knot showed deliberation and effort. *Intention*. He ran his fingers through it, the wool soft. After that he'd stop now and then on his way past. In September's chill westerlies the scarf's strands separated one by one. The rain strafed it, a hailstorm dissolved it, until October found it gone, each fibre a single migrating bird.[77]

The object lesson here transcends any single explanation. Akiko herself is the most obvious point of reference, the scarf's strands providing a hint at the potential of her *hibakusha* body to unravel at any moment; similarly, it anticipates Caleb's declining health following the onset of leukemia and the terminal prognosis his doctor delivers; while later on it contrasts disturbingly with Isaac's placid indifference to a fellow patient's failure to commit suicide by making a noose out of tied socks. As Isaac musingly puts it, "I've always been curious about knots."[78] On a more abstract level, the disappearing scarf also hints at the fragility of human relationships, a lesson that Akiko personally teaches Caleb when she embarks upon a clandestine affair.

Taken together, this multilayered reading of the human condition grants her behavior a sense of inexorability that distracts from the erotic complicity inherent to its development. Shorn of the philosophic dimension, the susceptibility that Akiko shows to Troy's clumsy advances, and her identity as a young woman from a formerly belligerent power, makes her something close to the 'spoils of war' that Asian American filmmaker Renee Tajima sees as the commonest role for East/Southeast Asian women in American cultural productions (likewise identifiable in the characters of Keiko and Alan in Wendy Catran's 2004 novel *The Swap*, previously discussed in Chapter 3).[79]

That George's *hibakusha* character should so easily follow this well-trodden paradigm detracts somewhat from the sections of the narrative that offer incisive perspectives on the moral cost of the Pacific War and subsequent conflicts. For example, Akiko's avoidance of the circle around which her dancing class performs, remains a mysterious behavioral tic, explicable by the psychological link it forms to the 'ground zero' of an atomic explosion (the term itself contains a circle). In one episode, the narrative breaks from describing her dance to a retrospective scene in which Troy recalls shooting an enemy sniper in Vietnam.[80] In this fashion, the two circles of the dance and his telescopic sight are juxtaposed and an analogy between the American bombing of Nagasaki and New Zealand's involvement in the Vietnam War becomes apparent. While the shooting to death of a Viet Cong sniper and the atomic bombing of Nagasaki are hardly equivalent in scale, the mutual allusion destabilizes New Zealand's identity as a land at peace with itself and the world. As literature scholar Anthony Carrigan confirms, in George's novel New Zealand cannot serve as a restorative counterweight to sites of nuclear violence.[81] The same method of double-allusion is used later on, when Akiko chops vegetables while watching television and, coming upon a news item about Vietnam War protesters, looks down momentarily to see tomato juice on her wrist and palm.[82] Once again, a link is established between two 'Asian wars,' both of which were 'total' in the sense that bomb runs resulted in a high death toll among the civilian populace below. In her magisterial study of how bodily injury is elided from war texts, Elaine Scarry notes that campaign and battle narratives seldom grant much attention to the dead.[83] By objectifying the televised image of war through the eyes of a *hibakusha*, George directs the reader's attention to the missing component and, by extension, a collusiveness in New Zealand media and society.

At a conference in 1995, Robert Jay Lifton characterized the bombing of Hiroshima as a raw nerve in American society: "That is, every time Hiroshima is mentioned or raised, it hurts. And of course, with a raw nerve you try to protect it, but it never works completely because the only way to overcome a raw nerve is to get to its cause. And that means to confront what really happened at Hiroshima."[84] If George's purpose is to touch a few raw nerves in New Zealand society, Dennis Bock, writing after the all-too-important fiftieth anniversary commemorations of the end of the war, has little to say about Hiroshima and postwar nuclearism as they occur in Canadian history and memory. In actuality, the Canadian settings are altogether secondary in this narrative and, arguably, an odd choice. As literature scholar Sherrill Grace dryly opines, staging a confrontation between a *hibakusha* and a Project scientist in a Southern Ontario garden is rather unlikely.[85] Be that as it may, the confidence with which the narrative draws the two characters together is of a piece with other post-1995 writings, notably Jim Lehrer's *The Special Prisoner* (2000), a novel which, as the previous chapter explored, was structured around a discussion between a surviving FEPOW and his might-have-been wartime interrogator. For Bock, as with Lehrer, the narrative retains its forward momentum by focusing on the prospect of dialogue between two parties whose personal histories intersect, but whose preconceived notions regarding the categories of victim and perpetrator are at odds with one another. Another commonality is that both authors take 1995 as the nominal present moment to which their respective narratives return after retrospective pieces, Bock's story opening with the Project scientist Anton Böll delivering a commemorative speech at Columbia University. There he meets Emiko, one of the Hiroshima Maidens and now a documentarian intent on interviewing Manhattan Project participants.[86] Although initially hesitant, Böll invites her to his Ontario home where he shows her film footage that he took while visiting Hiroshima in the immediate aftermath. These unique materials, combined with Böll's unrepentant opinion on the Project's necessity, sustain Emiko's interest through the denouement of the story when Böll reveals that he intervened on her behalf to ensure that she was one of the patients taken to the US for reconstructive surgery in 1955.[87]

Unlike other literary exemplars, the *hibakusha* woman in this story is in no way sexualized. The narrative dwells upon Emiko's time in a Hiroshima hospital and her body is a focus of attention, but as a site of injury rather than erotic pleasure (the explosion leaves half her face disfigured). Within these moments, Emiko's hospitalization is significant, primarily, for the way in which her physical injuries are compounded by successive instances of othering, in which her condition feeds into scientific knowledge without her consent: "We seemed to them interesting experiments, as you might find the extended and exceptional life of a gnat or beetle interesting."[88] After she journeys to the United States, the process is repeated more publicly when Emiko joins Reverend Tanabe Yasaka on an episode of the TV show *This Life in Focus*, which profiles famous individuals by narrating their life stories with the aid of guests who have known them at one time or another.[89] Even though the bombing is not Disneyfied, it is sensationalized and Bock delicately alerts readers to the ordeal this involves for Rev. Yasaka especially (Yasaka, himself a *hibakusha*, is responsible for organizing the Maidens' time in the United States). On this show, Emiko's 'appearance' is closed off to the audience behind a screen, where she formally thanks them for their kindness, a symbolic moment that encapsulates the half-present 'place' of *hibakusha* in American culture.[90] Asian Studies scholar Theodore Goossen perceptively notes that Emiko's face is metaphorical of postwar Japan, rebuilt with American help, and of the victimhood of Hiroshima.[91] Less obviously, her reconstructed face is illustrative of the covering over of the 'raw nerve' of Hiroshima in American cultural memory.[92]

The process of covering-over presages a reverse process of dis-covering by which Böll, as the Project scientist, will better realize what his atomic research has wrought and express remorse. This possibility is hinted at when Böll tells Emiko: "You are that magic person [my wife's] been waiting for me to meet."[93] However, Bock's narrative generates further complexity by acknowledging that if the Hiroshima Maidens became part of the preferred narrative of American goodwill in ways that elided Hiroshima itself from consideration, the Project scientist could, in turn, find himself inserted into a prefabricated narrative of nefarious motivations wholly out of step with how he thought of himself at Los Alamos.[94] Thus, if an expression of remorse is to take place, both parties must refrain from imposing their judgment upon the Other, dispense with their preconceptions as much as possible, and show themselves willing to hear what the Other has to say. The challenge that this poses to Emiko is apparent from the moment she arrives in his house: "I was glad he hadn't offered to pick me up. This way I wasn't beholden. I could leave whenever I wanted to, which I planned to do the following day. The fewer niceties, the better."[95] From the outset, Emiko's demeanor is unreceptive to expressions of guilt or remorse and, as a consequence, her inability to offer forgiveness is readily apparent. As for Böll, the justifications he offers for participating in atomic research are wholly intellectual: "I was living in my head then. I had shut myself off. Anywhere, under any conditions. I am not proud of this. But it is the nature of concentration, of discipline."[96] If atomic research demanded a level of personal commitment that was different only in degree from those of other wartime endeavors, rather than being in a category of its own, this possibility undercuts the basis of a critique that focuses on that profession exclusively. Böll forcefully advances this argument, thereby disturbing the hitherto clear-cut moral boundaries between his world and, as he points out, civilian Japanese during the war years, a line of reasoning that places Emiko on the defensive and reverses the position of interviewer/forgiver, and interviewee/guilty party. In his study of how forgiveness takes place, Stephen Cherry notes that, for the prospective forgiver, a danger is always present insofar as empathy "draws them into the chaotic, broken, and possibly cruel world of the perpetrator. This is to venture into the most uninviting and unattractive territory."[97] Böll never asks Emiko to forgive him and, at first, his defensiveness works only to force her into a position of unwilling identification with his position.

In due course, Böll's defenses relax somewhat and Emiko even allows him to touch the scars on her face (the mistreatment her appearance occasioned in prior years means that Böll's unflinching acquaintance is significant).[98] As in George's novel, there are shades of Mary Shelley's *Frankenstein* here, namely the figure of the scientist coming to terms with his creation in a moment that combines horror and sympathy. Yet, whereas Victor Frankenstein intentionally stitched together 'the Monster' out of cadavers, here, Emiko's bodily condition is not the original intention of the Project scientist but rather a by-product of the atomic bomb. At this point, Böll comes as close as he ever does to offering an apology, but instead reveals that he was the one who arranged for her to come to the United States:

> "This was my opportunity to give something back. So much had been taken from you. I needed to help any way I could. Only a small gesture, a moment of grace. You would deny me that? You would have been left back there, don't you see? Your life would be different. You would be horribly scarred. Still that little girl. Forever that little girl."
> "You kidnapped my life," she said.
> "This was your freedom. You don't understand what I did for you."
> "But it wasn't for me. You did this for yourself."[99]

This is the moment in which Victor Frankenstein could be said to have redeemed himself by recuperating the physical injuries inflicted on his creation. However, although Böll is correct in assuming that the putting together of injured bodies is an act of inherent goodness in itself, this truth is by no means larger than the self-serving motivation it supposedly invalidates (his decision to work on the Manhattan Project purely to satisfy his desire for research is in no way different from helping a Hiroshima 'Maiden,' a 'project' that likewise serves his own purposes). Finding herself immobilized within this heavily structured landscape of self-authorized redemption, Emiko cannot offer forgiveness. As the victim, her story must be hers to tell if she is to enter into the role of forgiver, but its appropriation by Böll, along with the distasteful insinuation that she might be obliged to him, makes this impossible, and so the narrative closes with a finely crafted moral impasse.

Hostile Islands

In his 1995 book *The End of Victory Culture*, cultural commentator Tom Engelhardt stated that "The atomic bomb that levelled Hiroshima also blasted openings into a netherworld of consciousness where victory and defeat, enemy and self, threatened to merge."[100] Simply put, the totality of the Bomb, and the decision to use it, could never be considered in any sense 'conventional' and so the righteousness of the victory it supposedly brought about was open to question. The immediate response was a form of intellectual and creative partitioning, whereby the Manhattan Project occupied one (dominant) historical and literary narrative, while the atomic bombings occupied a (secondary) narrative of their own. An entire literary history gradually took form to shore up this arrangement, one that allowed little room for Hiroshima and Nagasaki. Over time, American reading habits, and the cultural productions that formed them, would become mutually reinforcing to the extent that hardly anyone noticed what had happened. As a case in point, historian Laura Hein, a relative of Oppenheimer, reflected upon her students at Northwestern University and their preference for Oppenheimer as a topic of interest: "They leap to explore his personal dilemma while determinedly avoiding the hundreds of thousands of other sad stories that began in Hiroshima and Nagasaki fifty years ago."[101]

In the decades since the explosions themselves, Project novels have sometimes veered off into different emphases, lured by the immediacy of Red Scare or civil rights themes, but the tenor remains strikingly monotonous, tied to a self-aggrandizement that allows little in the way of criticism. In Foucauldian terms, this outcome might be said to bear the imprint of a top-down 'regime of truth' in which certain topics become sanctioned as worthwhile (or 'sense') while others are excluded (as 'non-sense'). The dominant 'voice' overseeing these divisions remains statist, emphasizing technological achievements rather than human consequences.[102] Given the fixity of the narrative boundaries out of which Project novels emerged during the twentieth century, the most recent innovations have necessarily had to break the mold, embracing a transpacific interfusion of stories and not confining themselves to moral questions that derive from the politics of the United States. Indeed, James George's novel is so concerned with upending the idea of New Zealand's peaceful self-image that he simply takes the guilt of the Project scientist as assumed, while for Dennis Bock the steadfastness of opposing, but inseparable, narratives is itself the topic.

Coda: Oceanic Sympathies

There was a rustle outside Louie's cell, and a face appeared. The man greeted Louie cheerfully, in English, by name. Louie stared up at him.

The man was a Kwajalein native, and he explained that the American castaways were the talk of the island. A sports fanatic, he had recognized Louie's name, which Louie had given to his captors. Prattling about track, football, and the Olympics, he paused only rarely to ask Louie questions. Once Louie got one or two words off, the native bounded back into his narrative.

After a few minutes, the native glanced at his watch and said he had to leave. Louie asked him what had happened to the marines whose names were carved into the wall. In the same chipper tone, the native replied that the marines were dead. All of the POWs held on that island, he said, were executed.

—Laura Hillenbrand, *Unbroken*

In an impassioned article that decries the intellectual marginality visited upon Pacific Studies within the fields of postcolonial, transnational, and global literary studies, Alice Te Punga Somerville put the matter bluntly: "To write about the Pacific is to constantly feel unacknowledged."[1] While this observation may appear a little terse, those humanities scholars who research Pacific Island communities and territories are unlikely to dispute the truth of it. Moreover, any scholar of the Second World War whose vantage point stretches further east than the 'Eastern Front' will likewise adopt a defensive mode at some point, a trend that began with those servicemen who returned from the Pacific Theater of Operations and found that their military campaigns were no longer part of the general conversation. Among them, veteran and historian William Manchester ran up against this heedlessness almost immediately: "It was rather diminishing to return in 1945 and discover that your own parents couldn't even pronounce the names of the islands you had conquered."[2] New Zealand journalist James Bertram waxed similarly: "How much, one may wonder, of this curious flood-lit quality that war gives to remote and unhistoric places will survive the war generations? Who now really remembers Mafeking, or Cocos Island?"[3] Over the course of the present study, fiction writers across all pertinent genres reinscribe this sense of a part remaining forever auxiliary to a main.[4] From tones that are sometimes mournful, occasionally affronted, most often resigned, the end result comes through as a quietism that contrasts with the profundity of a given story's narrative.

Selecting among the methods available to probe this state of affairs, my preference has been to investigate the history of genres—their beginnings, politically-inflected contours, and present-day exemplars—while asking why it should be that authors might remain committed to a given genre's ideological inheritance even if doing so should come at the expense of originality. This question and its derivatives has so preoccupied me that, in my pursuit of an answer, I have sometimes felt that I risked downplaying the creative maturity otherwise evident in my primary source material, of which Vivienne Plumb's tongue-in-cheek utilization of the gothic, David Guterson's imagery of maritime and wintertime worlds, and Peter Wells' portrayal of intergenerational trauma are but a few examples.

Still and all, the question of ideological boundedness cannot be wished away with panegyrics to an author's stylistic or narrative craftsmanship. As a contributory factor to the marginalization of war literature that takes the Pacific as a setting, the inner workings of ideology are a paramount area of concern. Yet, here too, there is a potential pitfall for the researcher, insofar as one's own political predilections can skew what might otherwise be an evenhanded appraisal of other people's. As a moral framework, I have found it tempting, for instance, to embrace the dictum that Americans tend to cast their eyes 'above the mushroom cloud' while Japanese prefer to see what happened 'below the cloud.'[5] While this saying does contain a kernel of truth, any formulation that reduces a war to a single binary and a single event is fit only for discussions concerning those same components. Most wars have typically involved more than one signature event that former antagonists mutually acknowledge, all but guaranteeing the splintering of conversations in other directions. Yet even if one abstracts a single event and summarizes it with such succinctness, this in itself may be a form of 'overlooking' insofar as it neglects—as I have been at pains to stress in my study—that there is more than one way of refusing sympathy to an actual or onetime enemy nation. Take, for instance, the sentiments of British soldiers serving in Burma, as contained in George MacDonald Fraser's biography:

> We had no slightest thought of what it [the two atomic bombings] would mean for the future, or even what it meant at the time; we did not know what the immediate effect of those bombs had been on their targets, and we didn't much care. We were of a generation to whom Coventry and the London Blitz and Clydebank and Liverpool and Plymouth were more than just names; our country had been hammered mercilessly from the sky, and so had Germany; we had seen the pictures of Belsen and of the frozen horror of the Russian front; part of our higher education had been devoted to techniques of killing and destruction; we were not going to lose sleep because the Japanese homeland had taken its turn.[6]

At no point does Fraser suggest that a single wartime event stands in moral equivalence to another. Rather, his language comes close to an admission that what matters most, as an inexorable endpoint to human psychology rather than a prescribed rule, is whatever happens to be most consequential to one's home society. This point of view may be a distasteful one, but it is by no means peculiar to Fraser. In 2011, the meltdowns and explosions at the Fukushima Nuclear Power Plant stirred recollections in Japan about the *Lucky Dragon* incident of 1954, when the crew of a Japanese fishing boat had been exposed to radiation carried from a US thermonuclear weapon test at Bikini Atoll.[7] The subsequent media discussions, however, made little or no mention of how fallout from that same blast had irradiated the inhabitants of the Marshall Islands, an omission that brings me to this coda's epigraph.[8]

The biographer Laura Hillenbrand recounts an episode of Olympian Louis Zamperini's time as a FEPOW, during which he was kept on Kwajalein Atoll (the largest in the Marshall Islands), before being taken to Japan to work at hard labor. What comes through, at first glance, is a sense of absurdity and cruelty in Zamperini's encounter with a non-ethnic Japanese who, far from being sympathetic to his plight, wishes only to pump him for information about his athletic career. To be sure, the desensitization that total war brought to subject peoples, including indigenes, is one way in which to read the piece (which might call to mind Elaine Scarry's point that if pain is effortlessly grasped by a person who experiences it, for a person outside the sufferer's body what is effortless is *not* grasping it).[9] A second and altogether different reading of this passage, on the other hand, might concentrate on points of historical detail, the significance of which are somewhat lost in the passage's—that is, Zamperini's—sense of socio-cultural disorientation. To state the obvious, the Marshallese man who visits Zamperini is comfortably multilingual, well-informed about international sports, and permitted a certain freedom of movement as a colonial subject of the Empire of Japan.[10] These attributes throw down a challenge, of sorts, not only to Zamperini but to present-day scholarship on the Second World War that neglects the histories and subjectivities of Indigenous communities. To borrow a simile from historian Greg Dvorak, indifference of this sort is akin to concrete, in that it forges a monolithic whole by discounting or marginalizing island histories—'coralline' histories, in Dvorak's lexicon—that fall outside this linear approach.[11] In this coda, I would like to close my study by offering some thoughts as to how and why a consideration of Pacific Island writings on the Pacific War and its aftermath should be important, for the suffering endured by Indigenous communities is arguably more 'overlooked' than any other phenomenon.[12]

Whereas history writing may betray a concretizing agenda, literary writing must grapple with a legacy less methodological and more content-based, namely an assortment of colonialist tropes, myths, and sentimental narratives. As the Samoan writer and poet Albert Wendt has noted, "If we [Pacific Islanders] appeared at all in colonial poetry and fiction we were seen as exotic, as peripheral, as 'extras' in the epic, as stereotypes or as noble and heroic forms of escape."[13] Colonialist modes of representation have undoubtedly gained purchase upon war writing and film adaptation, requiring of scholars a sensitivity as to where—or whether at all—the one leaves off and the other begins.[14] Put another way, can war as a historical context constitute a caveat to a nominally postcolonial, scholarly, and creative mandate (or vice-versa)? As far as literary writing on the Pacific War by *papālangi* (White) writers is concerned, it seems to me that there are at least three classificatory subcategories that matter here, the first being James Michener's and, in New Zealand, Errol Brathwaite's reinstatement of the South Seas genre. These two authors embraced most, if not all, of the aspects Wendt subsequently identified, their portrayal of Indigenous subjects being, in point of fact, a matter of authorial (self)indulgence more than anything else (Michener was all too aware of the tendency, disparaging the most flagrant examples in literary history even as he settled his work within them).[15] To the untrained eye, the second category might look no different from the first. One finds it in work such as Hillenbrand's where, once again, the Indigenous subject is peripheral to the narrative plotline. In this instance, however, peripherality is less resultant from a particular aesthetic and more a matter of recognition that, at the time of the Pacific War, atolls could be labor camps, prisons, or execution grounds even as they remained Indigenous homelands (on Kwajalein Atoll, the Japanese used Zamperini as a test subject for chemical and/or biological weapon experiments, a topic that would demand attention in its own right even if Hillenbrand had not been writing a biography). As a third category, one encounters *papālangi* authors for whom the project of centralizing Indigenous characters and their histories is of paramount importance, albeit one that carries with it a danger of literary authors presuming that they possess a truth-telling power bordering on the hegemonic (an accusation that Epeli Hauʻofa leveled against his own discipline of anthropology).[16]

Needless to say, Indigenous authors possess no inherent immunity against the internalization of colonialist tropes or other ideological blind spots. In the words of literature scholar Dorothy Lane, "All postcolonial people ... are, in a sense, islanders when they continue to accept the codes of colonial discourse—the books—that define them from abroad. The flip side of that recognition, however, is that the island can also be usefully employed by postcolonial writers to interrogate many of the assumptions of insularity."[17] The point is well made, although one must also keep in mind that on some islands—Kwajalein and its satellite camp island of Ebeye, most notably—the neo-colonial relationship has drastically reduced the vocational prospects and traditional migration routes of Indigenous people.[18] The narrowing of work and cultural horizons along lines prescribed by the US military led Epeli Hauʻofa to worry that some islanders might find themselves "confined to mental reservations if not physical ones."[19] Furthermore, Indigenous writing on the Pacific War has, to date, been less concerned with repudiating notions of insularity than with 'setting the record straight' as to specific points of wartime conduct. Thus Vincent Eri's novel *The Crocodile* (1970) made it clear that, given a choice between Americans and Australians, Papuans preferred the former in their attitudes to Indigenous people; while Sam Alasia's *Fataʻabu* (2003) noted the anticolonial resistance movement that sprang up in the Solomon Islands once the war had formally ended, as well as the lack of recognition granted the islanders for their own wartime service (Guadalcanal being an overwhelmingly 'American' victory).[20] Niuean author John Pule's magical realist novel *The Shark That Ate the Sun* (1992) is more a story of Pasifika on the streets of Auckland, but also contains the following passage:

> I want you to always look upon me, to cast shadows of islanders a few miles off the American site. Maybe just to beautify the image in tourist magazines, put a little colour in the mothers' yellow eyes. Paint a hotdog in the child's

hand and, if the original has Kwajalein in the background, instead have them posing in front of a travel agent. Show the reef at night when the sea is sparkling and hide the missiles that fly from California.[21]

Pule assumes that his reference to Kwajalein requires little explanation. Similarly, in Māori author Cathie Dunsford's novel *Manawa Toa: Heart Warrior* (2000), there are a couple of instances in which miscarried fetuses born of Marshallese Islander women stand out from the narrative with shocking vividness (although the work is primarily concerned with French nuclear testing on Moruroa atoll).[22] The pan-Oceanic political solidarity underpinning these passages is shot through with outrage, for the nuclearization of the Pacific has resulted, not in the retirement of the imagery Wendt itemized but, on the contrary, depends upon it as part of a discourse that permits the continued testing of nuclear weapons and/or their delivery systems (Hawaiian artist Solomon Enos has produced a series of hand-painted panels as a reminder of the human cost of these tests).[23] A thoroughgoing critique of this discourse, along with its self-serving conceit that the Pacific is free of population centers and therefore 'remote' from areas that 'matter,' is best served by an examination of work that is set in or around Kwajalein.[24] Robert Barclay's novel *Meḷaḷ* (2002) remains the most compelling narrative to make good on this objective, while also reminding readers that Kwajalein's position in an American Pacific is traceable at least as far back as the Pacific War. At this point, it may be objected that Barclay is a non-Indigenous writer, and yet Wendt held back from the idea that *papālangi* ought not to write about Pacific Islanders; and, in another context, one might recall the defense of Anglo-Indian or Raj fiction by B. J. Moore-Gilbert, who argued that the myth of the 'gorgeous east,' common in metropolitan Britain at the time of the British Empire, had been disparaged or corrected in Anglo-Indian fiction, a point that greatly complicates the notion of an ideology so total that White writers cannot see outside it.[25] More immediately pertinent, perhaps, have been the widespread endorsements of Barclay's novel, among others by Teresia Teaiwa and Patricia Grace, as well as the novel's accession to a finalist position for the 2002 Kiriyama Prize for fiction.[26]

In an investigation of how masculinities are socially constructed on and around Kwajalein, Greg Dvorak recalled how, as part of his childhood education on that island, Marshallese were reduced to "happy bystanders, singing and cheering elatedly as these [American] victors arrived, hands outstretched to receive chocolate bars and cans of SPAM—on the sidelines, watching the real world pass them by."[27] Such images contained both a blatant untruth (Pacific Islanders fought on the side of the Japanese, just as they did on the Allied side) and a painful irony (the postwar relationship would reduce a substantial number of Marshallese to destitution and servitude).[28] Barclay's narrative may be described as the antithesis to this form of textual and historical erasure, although it does not list each and every way in which the Marshallese people have been oppressed or misrepresented. Its starting point is, in a literal sense, the forced starting point for those Marshallese who make a living by working at—and, as Dvorak noted, sometimes achieving a sense of masculinity through—the US Navy base on Kwajalein, to which they journey on a daily basis from the insalubrious island of Ebeye. In her reading of *Meḷaḷ*, literature scholar Simone Oettle-Van Delden describes Ebeye as a rubbish dump and its relationship with Kwajalein as apartheid, the difference being that island geography makes it easy for the Americans to maintain the system.[29] Whether or not the analogy holds, Barclay swiftly disposes of the idea of the atoll as an untouched 'paradise.' Ebeye is a land of rusting industrial machinery, polluted water, discolored sand, and slum dwellers whose only real chance of self-advancement lies in securing a permanent job on the base (although the majority are either family relatives or relocated Marshallese from other islands).[30] Such is the ambition that Rujen nurtures for his son, Jebro, although it has brought no sense of contentment into his own life beyond what a salary provides. In fact, the narrative opens with Rujen sleeplessly walking through a concrete blockhouse, pellet gun in hand, a sequence that recalls the soldiering of the Pacific War, while also serving as a leitmotif for a late-twentieth-century Marshallese sensibility that cannot fully—or is, by default, not allowed to—move beyond that 'original' wartime period. In an image that signals the author's flirtation with magical realism, Rujen attempts to flush away the sewage clogging his toilet, only to find more sewage rising up in his kitchen sink a few moments later.[31] To attentive readers, this man's predicament raises the issue of whether Marshallese people possess any resources by which they might cope with, and comprehend, the past's continual intrusion into the present.

At times, Barclay's narrative appears to defy the foundation of any such question, so multi-layered are the historical traumas visited upon the bodies of the Marshallese. We learn that Rujen's wife had been exposed to fallout from the 1954 Bikini Atoll test and that, in common with other female survivors, she had endured multiple miscarriages, including, by implication, severely deformed fetuses: "He [Rujen] sat on a bucket, his back against a broken Japanese washing machine, looking from his wife's shoulders hunched over and working to the rainbow tornado being swallowed by the rain."[32] As before, the narrative takes an image of malfunctioning or defunct domestic technology and charges it with implications, suggesting, in this case, an inerasable defilement along with the failure of consumer culture—as material products or as ideology—to deliver meaningful compensation. The littering of the landscape with articles of a non-Indigenous provenance is a narrative feature worth commenting upon in itself, as it conveys the impression of a chaotic cartography in which the 'contributions' of one colonial regime abut those of the next. The effect is to reinforce a sense of psychic numbing, consequent to characters whose lives have been pockmarked by violent ruptures, another notable example being Rujen's deceased father, Ataji, who suffered permanent eye damage after a beating at the hands of American police and, before that, two bullet wounds from Japanese soldiers when he refused their demands to work on military infrastructure projects.[33] Significantly, this layering of colonial histories comes across as a collective whole rather than a tottering hierarchy of traumatizing agents. A catalogic chant by the ancient dwarf Ṇoniep instantiates the point:

> Ṇoniep chanted of the Spanish who claimed the islands and promised life through Christ and gave death by syphilis; he chanted of the Germans who became rich by forcing the Marshallese to work at making copra for them, the Germans, bringing mumps and measles and TB, who punished and tortured those not working as ordered; he chanted of the blackbirders, slavers like Bully Hayes who often snatched an entire island's population; he chanted of Christian missionaries from Boston and Hawai'i who forbade the people from chanting the chants and practicing the magic that taught the ways of navigation and healing and proper living; he chanted of the Japanese who came and pushed out the Germans and worked the people even harder and brought so many settlers that at one time there were more Japanese living in the islands than Marshallese; he chanted of the Americans who brought the bomb and jellyfish babies and *Happy Days* on TV. Ṇoniep chanted into the tree the names of plants good for making balms to put on burns, of medicines that heal.[34]

Literature scholar Elizabeth DeLoughrey's concept of tidalectics advances the idea of indigeneity and sovereignty in the Pacific as being tied not only to land but to maritime origins, whereby "regional aquatic routes often sustain local roots."[35] In *Meḷaḷ* this mentality is acted upon by Jebro, who defies Rujen by journeying with his younger brother to their birth island of Tar-Wōj, significant both as the land where Ataji is buried and as Ṇoniep's present abode. The latter two characters have an anticolonial sensibility in common, Ṇoniep's being the more important because he symbolizes in himself—and creates further symbols through his magical chanting—a historically aware and culturally revitalized world view that the newest generation of Marshallese could inhabit also. Jebro's journey to Tar-Wōj is thus a coming of age in more than one sense, for by his defiant actions, and the significance he grants them, the reader perceives an attitudinal shift, one that takes him away from Rujen's more institutionalized and compliant relationship with the Americans toward an Indigenous cultural assertiveness (or what some scholars might describe as political willfulness from the 'fractal fringe').[36] In practical terms, this means giving up Rujen's proposal of a lifetime job at the Kwajalein sewage plant and instead becoming a fisherman. But it also means accepting a degree of accommodation with the Americans, not so much as a colonial subject, but as someone whose regard for the sea offers a 'route' that, similarly plied by at least some Americans, is the starting point for a friendship of benefit to both.[37]

While *Meḷaḷ* stops short of a politically radical mandate and cannot, on its own, correct the widespread indifference to Pacific Studies deplored by Alice Te Punga Somerville, the focus on shared Oceanic sympathies at the end of the narrative usefully anticipated Greg Dvorak's call for the United States to conceive of itself in less continental and more Oceanic terms: "Oceanizing America here can mean cultivating an awareness of being an Oceanian citizen: infusing a sense of accountability, humility, gratitude, and a real, equal sense of community with Pacific Islander communities throughout the shared ocean, not just its outer rim."[38] This ocean-centric belongingness need not be—should not be—'the sole province' of the United States, New Zealand, or the other large, English-speaking nations of the Pacific, nor will it disestablish the hard questions that former colonial powers can ask of themselves (in Japan's case, for example, why it should be that Micronesians are still imagined to prefer the Japanese as 'patrons' over other colonial powers).[39] There will still be commemorations, publications, and other forms of representation that recollect the war years and their long atomic shadows in preferential ways, but by encouraging within oneself an Oceanic sensitivity, one may find Ṇoniep's balms and medicines beginning to work.

Acknowledgments

The circumstances that occasioned this project's initial version were unpropitious. In September 2010, an earthquake hit Christchurch, New Zealand, resulting in the temporary—but still months-long—closure of public buildings. Inspectors were on hand to do the necessary checks, and in February 2011, most buildings had reopened, just in time for a shallower earthquake that did more damage than the previous year's. Writing up one's doctoral thesis can be an enjoyable, if rather sequestered, undertaking but to have one's solitude imposed tectonically as well as administratively will take some of the luster off. Then and since, Cantabrians have shouldered far more serious costs and so it does not behoove me to dwell on those days, except to note that I was fortunate in not having financial worries compound the situation. Thus, my first debt of gratitude is to those scholarship committee members, respectively of Education New Zealand and the University of Canterbury, who saw something in a wide-eyed British student with plenty of ideas and little actual knowledge, at least at that point, of New Zealand literature.

In the years that followed, I proceeded on the supposition that the different genres and historical episodes to which I had given my attention were best suited to journal articles rather than a monograph. Accordingly, sections of what would become *Beyond Hostile Islands* appeared as standalone publications elsewhere: Chapter 1's in *arcadia* 49.2 (2014); Chapter 2's in *Journal of Commonwealth Literature*, 49.1 (2014) and *Journal of American Studies*, 51.3 (2017); Chapter 3's in *Comparative Literature Studies*, 40.4 (2013); Chapter 4's in *War, Literature & the Arts,* 23 (2011) and *Common Knowledge*, 21.3 (2015); and Chapter 5's in *Comparative American Studies*, 12.3 (2014). Meeting the standards of these journals took my research quite a ways beyond what it had been at the doctoral level, and, in more than a few instances, the incorporation of fresh primary source material meant a complete rewrite. Although those onetime articles appear in a heavily reworked form (including, where applicable, substantial changes from British to US English spellings to follow FUP guidelines), I am grateful to the various publishing houses for permission to republish them.

The monograph stage could have arrived by any number of routes, but an obviously preferable one came in the form of research funding while I was a contractual associate professor at Doshisha University, Kyoto. That funding was courtesy of a Grant-in-Aid for Scientific Research, awarded by Kakenhi/the Japan Society for the Promotion of Science (JSPS). To my delight, I also had library borrowing privileges at Doshisha's Graduate School of Global Studies, internal successor to one of the finest American Studies book collections in Japan. Wandering through the stacks, I reflected back on the days of forced library closures in post-earthquake Christchurch and saw that there would never be a better time for knitting the parts of what I had presumed (erroneously) to be already a book into an improved whole. Nor did I fail to put those funds to proper use. Biennial conferences organized by the Australian and New Zealand American Studies Association (ANZASA) are invariably worth attending and, by these means, I received valuable feedback at Australian Catholic University in 2017, and at University of Auckland in 2019. Turning eastward rather than south, I had the unique experience of presenting a paper in 2018 at Royal Military College, Canada, while in 2019 I became acquainted with another learned society, the American Association of Australasian Literary Studies (AAALS), which accepted my paper for inclusion in their 2019 conference at University of Alaska, Fairbanks. If I have not yet expressed gratitude to these societies and institutions, I do so here and fulsomely.

Maureen Montgomery, Paul Millar, and Adam Lam did sterling work in their supervisory roles while I was a student. Just round the corner, so to speak, I also found much-needed guidance from Patrick Evans, Ken Henshall, and Mark Williams; and in Wellington, historian Alison Parr was kind enough to grant access to her taped interviews in the Oral History Centre of the National Library of New Zealand. Though I did not know it at the time, the next step toward taking my project further came through the pointers I received from my doctoral thesis examiners, Lawrence Jones of Otago University and Naoko Shibusawa of Brown University. An all-too-brief stint as a researcher at University of Turku provided the crucial opportunity to throw some of my ideas at Prof. Joel Kuortti, who caught some, discarded others, and returned one or two of his own. At Doshisha University, I fondly recall having brown bag discussions with Prof. Gavin J. Campbell, who subjected chapters of my manuscript to his impressive knowledge of Japanese history and transnationalism. Dr. Antony Goedhals, University of

Pretoria, primed and loaded me for the grand rewrite, offering amiable, step-by-step, sometimes daunting tales of his own journey to a similar end.

From the word go, Fred Nachbaur, Director of Fordham University Press, struck a careful balance between encouraging this project and apprising me of the hurdles it would have to surmount, while book series editor G. Kurt Piehler suggested some important tweaks to manuscript content. More extended commentary came from John Casey (University of Illinois Chicago) and Erin Mercer (Massey University), whose formal reviews were most insightful. Patrick Porter agreed to venture beyond more familiar International Security and Strategy disciplinary territory to write a Foreword. Beyond questions of content, others have assisted in technical capacities: M. J. Devaney through her skills as a bibliographer, Lis Pearson through her copyediting, and Michael Goldstein through creating the index. To all the aforementioned persons, I express sincere thanks and, of course, any remaining defects and infelicities are mine alone.

Notes

Introduction

1. David Livingstone Smith, *The Most Dangerous Animal: Human Nature and the Origins of War* (New York: St. Martin's Griffin, 2007), 192–195.
2. See Joanna Bourke, *An Intimate History of Killing: Face-to-Face Killing in Twentieth-Century Warfare* (New York: Basic Books, 1999), 220.
3. Keith Lowe, *The Fear and the Freedom: How the Second World War Changed Us* (London: Penguin, 2017), 37–38.
4. Christopher Thorne, "Racial Aspects of the Far Eastern War of 1941–1945," *Proceedings of the British Academy* 66 (1980): passim; John Dower, *War without Mercy: Race and Power in the Pacific War* (New York: Pantheon, 1987); Michael Renov, "Warring Images: Stereotype and American Representations of the Japanese, 1941–1991," in *The Japan/America Film Wars: WWII Propaganda and its Cultural Contexts*, eds. Abé Mark Nornes and Yukio Fukushima (Langhorne: Harwood Academic Publishers, 1994), 104–105; James Weingartner, "War against Subhumans: Comparisons between the German War against the Soviet Union and the American War against Japan, 1941–1945," *Historian* 58 (3) (1996): 563; Gerald F. Linderman, *The World within War: America's Combat Experience in World War II* (New York: Free Press, 1997); and Peter Schrijvers, *The GI War against Japan: American Soldiers in Asia and the Pacific during World War II* (Basingstoke, UK: Palgrave Macmillan, 2002).
5. Peter Darman, *Posters of World War II* (London: Brown Reference Group, 2008), 174, 188, 223; Zbynek Zeman, *Selling the War: Art and Propaganda in World War II* (London: Orbis, 1978), 52.
6. Oliver Stone and Peter Kuznick, *The Untold History of the United States* (London: Ebury Publishing, 2012), 149.
7. Stevan Eldred-Grigg and Hugh Eldred-Grigg, *Phoney Wars: New Zealand Society in the Second World War* (Dunedin, New Zealand: Otago University Press, 2017), 102–103.
8. Gordon Slatter, *A Gun in My Hand* (Christchurch, New Zealand: Pegasus Press, 1959), 135.
9. John A. Lynn, *Battle: A History of Combat and Culture*, second edition (New York: Basic Books, 2008), 229.

10. Larry McMurtry, *Horseman, Pass By* (1961; repr. New York: Simon & Schuster, 2004), 111.

11. Jennifer Haytock, *The Routledge Introduction to American War Literature* (New York: Routledge, 2018), 6.

12. George MacDonald Fraser, *Quartered Safe Out Here: A Recollection of the War in Burma* (1993; repr. London: HarperCollins, 2000), 37–38.

13. Jeffrey Walsh, *American War Literature, 1914 to Vietnam* (London: Macmillan, 1982), 115.

14. Paul Lyons, *American Pacificism: Oceania in the U.S. Imagination* (London: Routledge, 2006), 4.

15. Alice Te Punga Somerville, *Once Were Pacific: Māori Connections to Oceania* (Minneapolis: University of Minnesota Press, 2012), xvii.

16. Epeli Hau'ofa, "Anthropology and Pacific Islanders," in *We Are the Ocean: Selected Works* (Honolulu: University of Hawai'i Press, 2008), 9.

17. Erin Mercer, *Telling the Real Story: Genre and New Zealand Literature* (Wellington: Victoria University Press, 2017), 14.

18. Elizabeth McMahon, *Islands, Identity and the Literary Imagination* (London: Anthem Press, 2016), 5.

19. Gavin Francis, *Island Dreams: Mapping an Obsession* (Edinburgh: Canongate, 2020), 3.

20. Doreen D'Cruz and John C. Ross, *The Lonely and the Alone: The Poetics of Isolation in New Zealand Fiction* (Amsterdam: Rodopi, 2011), xvi.

21. Miles Fairburn, "Is There a Good Case for New Zealand Exceptionalism?" in *Disputed Histories: Imagining New Zealand's Pasts*, eds. Tony Ballantyne and Brian Moloughney (Dunedin, New Zealand: Otago University Press, 2006), 150.

22. Geoff Lealand, *A Foreign Egg in Our Nest: American Popular Culture in New Zealand* (Wellington: Victoria University Press, 1988), 28.

23. Elaine Stratford, "Disciplinary Formations, Creative Tensions, and Certain Logics," in *Contemporary Archipelagic Thinking: Toward New Comparative Methodologies and Disciplinary Formations*, eds. Michelle Stephens and Yolanda Martínez-San Miguel (Lanham: Rowman & Littlefield, 2020), 62–63.

24. Paul Fussell, *Wartime: Understanding and Behavior in the Second World War*, revised edition (New York: Oxford University Press, 1990), 119.

25. Ronald Takaki, *Double Victory: A Multicultural History of America in World War II* (Boston: Little, Brown, 2000), 173–174.

26. Elaine Scarry, *The Body in Pain: The Making and Unmaking of the World* (New York: Oxford University Press, 1985), 12.

27. Robert A. Newman, *Enola Gay and the Court of History* (New York: Peter Lang, 2014), 134–135.

28. Alfred Kern, "Hang the Enola Gay," in *When War Becomes Personal: Soldiers' Accounts from the Civil War to Iraq*, ed. Donald Anderson (Iowa City: University of Iowa Press, 2008), 91.

29. Bernard Lewis, "The Question of Orientalism," in *Orientalism: A Reader*, ed. A. L. Macfie (Edinburgh: Edinburgh University Press, 2000), 264.

30. Laura Doyle, "Inter-Imperiality and Literary Studies in the Longer *Durée*," *PMLA* 130 (2) (2015): 337.

31. John W. Dower, "Triumphal and Tragic Narratives of the War in Asia," in *Living with the Bomb: American and Japanese Cultural Conflicts in the Nuclear Age*, eds. Laura Hein and Mark Selden (New York: M. E. Sharpe, 1997), 44–45.

32. Mako Yoshikawa, "The Veterans Project Number 2," *Missouri Review* 37 (3) (2014): 78–79.

33. Akihiko Tanaka and Masayuki Tadokoro, "The 1980s: The Decade of Neoliberalism," in *The History of US-Japan Relations*, ed. Makoto Iokibe, trans. Tosh Minohara (Singapore: Palgrave Macmillan, 2017), 210–211.

34. Lowe, *The Fear and the Freedom*, 41–42.

35. David Mura, *Turning Japanese: Memoirs of a Sansei* (New York: Anchor Books, 1991), 236.

36. J. D. F. Jones, *Storyteller: The Many Lives of Laurens van der Post* (London: John Murray, 2001), 51.

37. Daniel Martin Varisco, *Reading Orientalism: Said and the Unsaid* (Seattle: University of Washington Press, 2007), 33–43.

38. Stuart Hall, "The Spectacle of the 'Other,'" in *Representation: Cultural Practices and Signifying Practices*, ed. Stuart Hall (London: Sage, 1997), 228.

39. W. H. Auden and Christopher Isherwood, *Journey to a War* (1939; repr. New York: Octagon, 1972), 36.

40. Lisa Lowe, *Critical Terrains: French and British Orientalisms* (Ithaca: Cornell University Press, 1991), 5.

41. Writers and artists from imperial countries did not necessarily wholeheartedly embrace the idea of their home culture's supposed superiority to "the East." As John M. MacKenzie notes, "imperial texts can display considerable heterogeneity, revealing doubts and contradictions, both hegemonic and counter-hegemonic thought." John M. MacKenzie, *Orientalism: History, Theory and the Arts* (Manchester, UK: Manchester University Press, 1995), 13.

42. Recent scholarship that revises Edward Said's original thesis has argued that imperial subjects of the Austro-Hungarian Empire looked to "the East" (within their own domains or beyond) to underpin self-criticism, a project made somewhat easier by the fact that this particular imperial formation possessed no overseas territories and was concerned only with the domestic situation. However, some Americans who went to Southeast Asia during the Vietnam War experienced a change in outlook similar to Auden and Isherwood's. See Robert Lemon, *Imperial Messages: Orientalism as Self-Critique in the Habsburg Fin de Siècle* (New York: Camden House, 2011), 2; and Judy Tzu-Chun Wu, *Radicals on the Road: Internationalism, Orientalism, and Feminism during the Vietnam Era* (Ithaca: Cornell University Press, 2013), 3.

43. Varisco, *Reading Orientalism*, 48–49.

44. American propagandists had used ape imagery to depict World War I Germans and would use it again to depict World War II Japanese. See Benjamin L. Alpers, *Dictators, Democracy, and American Public Culture: Envisioning the Totalitarian Enemy, 1920s–1950s* (Chapel Hill: University of North Carolina Press, 2003), 190.

45. Brigitte N. Fielder, "Animal Humanism: Race, Species, and Affective Kinship in Nineteenth-Century Abolitionism," *American Quarterly* 65 (3) (2013): 488.

46. Susan Brocker, *Dreams of Warriors* (Auckland: HarperCollins, 2010), 124.

47. For an extended reading of Brocker's novel, see Daniel McKay, "Other Ways to Treat an Animal: Natural Horsemanship and the Ethnic Other," *Journal of Postcolonial Writing* 55 (5) (2019): passim.

48. Michael Richardson, "Enough Said," in *Orientalism: A Reader*, 211–12; Robert Irwin, *Dangerous Knowledge: Orientalism and Its Discontents* (New York: Overlook Press, 2006), 289–290.

49. Jonathan Wisenthal, "Inventing the Orient," in *A Vision of the Orient: Texts, Intertexts, and Contexts of Madame Butterfly*, eds. Jonathan Wisenthal, Sherrill Grace, Melinda Boyd, Brian McIlroy, and Vera Micznik (Toronto: University of Toronto Press, 2006), 5.

50. John Updike, *Couples* (1968; repr. New York: Knopf, 1987), 32.

51. Philip Kan Gotanda, *Yankee Dawg You Die* (New York: Dramatists Play Service, 1991), 6, 48.

52. Mary Louise Pratt, *Imperial Eyes: Travel Writing and Transculturation* (New York: Routledge, 1992), 7.

53. Viet Thanh Nguyen, *The Sympathizer* (New York: Grove, 2015), 129.

54. Marilyn Lake and Henry Reynolds, *Drawing the Global Colour Line: White Men's Countries and the International Challenge of Racial Equality* (Cambridge: Cambridge University Press, 2008), 190–194; and David C. Atkinson, *The Burden of White Supremacy: Containing Asian Migration in the British Empire and the United States* (Chapel Hill: University of North Carolina Press, 2016), 192–195.

55. James A. Michener, *Tales of the South Pacific* (1947; repr. New York: Ballantine, 1984), 24–25.

56. James A. Michener, "Until They Sail," in *Return to Paradise* (1951; repr. Harmondsworth, UK: Penguin, 1982), 229.

57. Daniel McKay, "All Aboard the U.S.S. *New Zealand*? Voyaging through the Literary Responses to the American 'Occupation,' 1942–1944," *Neohelicon* 39 (2012): 325–326.

58. Gilly Carr and Keir Reeves, "Islands of War, Islands of Memory," in *Heritage and Memory of War: Responses from Small Islands*, eds. Gilly Carr and Keir Reeves (New York: Routledge, 2015), 8.

59. John Carlos Rowe, "Transpacific Studies and the Cultures of US Imperialism," in *American Studies as Transnational Practice: Turning toward the*

Transpacific, eds. Yuan Shu and Donald Pease (Hanover: Dartmouth College Press, 2015), 260.

60. William J. Schafer, *Mapping the Godzone: A Primer on New Zealand Literature and Culture* (Honolulu: University of Hawai'i Press, 1998), xiv–xv.

61. Rajeev S. Patke, *Poetry and Islands: Materiality and the Creative Imagination* (London: Rowman & Littlefield International, 2018), 115.

62. Ian McGibbon, "New Zealand's Strategic Approach," in *Kia Kaha: New Zealand in the Second World War*, ed. John Crawford (Auckland: Oxford University Press, 2000), 16.

63. David Horner, "The ANZAC Contribution: Australia and New Zealand in the Pacific War," in *The Pacific War: From Pearl Harbor to Hiroshima*, ed. Daniel Marston (Oxford: Osprey Publishing, 2005), 156; and Bruce M. Petty, Introduction to *New Zealand in the Pacific War: Personal Accounts of World War II*, ed. Bruce M. Petty (Jefferson: McFarland, 2008), 7.

64. John Crawford, "A Campaign on Two Fronts," in *Kia Kaha: New Zealand in the Second World War*, ed. John Crawford (Auckland: Oxford University Press, 2000), 149–153.

65. On the topic of Australia's plan to resist Japanese occupation after an anticipated military defeat, see Sue Rosen, *Scorched Earth: Australia's Secret Plan for Total War under Japanese Invasion in World War II* (Crows Nest, Australia: Allen and Unwin, 2017).

66. Jo Smith, "Aotearoa/New Zealand: An Unsettled State in a Sea of Islands," *Settler Colonial Studies* 1 (1) (2011): 112–113.

67. Elizabeth McMahon and Bénédicte André, "Literature and the Literary Gaze," in *The Routledge International Handbook of Island Studies*, ed. Godfrey Baldacchino (Abingdon, UK: Routledge, 2018), 302.

68. Godfrey Baldacchino, "Islands as Novelty Sites," *Geographical Review* 97 (2) (2007): 166.

69. Te Punga Somerville, *Once Were Pacific*, 82.

70. George McMillan, *The Old Breed: A History of the First Marine Division in World War II* (Washington, DC: Infantry Journal Press, 1949), 4.

71. Marc Shell, *Islandology: Geography, Rhetoric, Politics* (Stanford: Stanford University Press, 2014), 96–97.

72. *A Gathering of Men*, dir. Wayne Ewing (Arlington: PBS, 1990).

73. Karl Hack and Kevin Blackburn, "*The Bridge on the River Kwai* and *King Rat*: Protest and Ex-Prisoner of War Memory in Britain and Australia," in *Forgotten Captives in Japanese-Occupied Asia*, eds. Karl Hack and Kevin Blackburn (Abingdon, UK: Routledge, 2008), 152.

74. Petra Rau, "Long Shadows and Blind Spots," in *Long Shadows: The Second World War in British Fiction and Film*, ed. Petra Rau (Evanston: Northwestern University Press, 2016), 10.

75. Daniel McKay, "Not My River Kwai: Novels of Imprisonment under the Japanese," *Rondo* 2 (2018): passim.

76. Laura Fenrich, "Mass Death in Miniature: How Americans Became Victims of the Bomb," in *Living with the Bomb: American and Japanese Cultural Conflicts in the Nuclear Age*, eds. Laura Hein and Mark Selden (New York: M. E. Sharpe, 1997), 125–126.

77. Kai Erikson, *A New Species of Trouble: The Human Experience of Modern Disasters* (New York: Norton, 1994), 189–190.

1. Revelations and Comedy: The Combat Novel

1. William Broyles Jr., "Why Men Love War," in *The Vietnam Reader*, ed. Walter Capps (New York: Routledge, 1991), 69.

2. Sam Childers, *Another Man's War: The True Story of One Man's Battle to Save Children in the Sudan* (Nashville: Thomas Nelson, 2009), 205.

3. Sebastian Junger, *War* (New York: Twelve, 2010), 144–145.

4. Roger Luckhurst, "In War Times: Fictionalizing Iraq," *Contemporary Literature* 53 (4) (2012): 719.

5. Joseph Heller, "Conversations with Joseph Heller," edited by Kathi Vosevich, in *Understanding the Literature of World War II: A Student Casebook to Issues, Sources, and Historical Documents*, ed. James H. Meredith (Westport: Greenwood, 1999), 57.

6. Ron Kovic, *Born on the Fourth of July* (1976; repr. New York: Akashic, 2016), 160.

7. Marianna Torgovnick, *The War Complex: World War II in Our Time* (Chicago: University of Chicago Press, 2005), 2–3.

8. Samuel Hynes, *The Soldiers' Tale: Bearing Witness to Modern War* (New York: Viking, 1997), 27–28.

9. Jock Phillips, "The Quiet Western Front: The First World War and New Zealand Memory," in *Race, Empire and First World War Writing*, ed. Santanu Das (Cambridge: Cambridge University Press, 2011), 235–244.

10. Ichiro Takayoshi, *American Writers and the Approach of World War II, 1935–1941: A Literary History* (New York: Cambridge University Press, 2015), 14–16.

11. Keith Gandal, *The Gun and the Pen: Hemingway, Fitzgerald, Faulkner, and the Fiction of Mobilization* (New York: Oxford University Press, 2008), 36.

12. Hynes, *The Soldiers' Tale*, 96.

13. Erin Mercer, *Repression and Realism in Post-War American Literature* (New York: Palgrave Macmillan, 2011), 43–47.

14. Peter Bowman, *Beach Red* (London: Michael Joseph, 1946), 60.

15. John W. Aldridge, "The War Writers Ten Years Later," in *Contemporary American Novelists*, ed. Harry T. Moore (Carbondale: Southern Illinois University Press, 1964), 33–34.

16. Pearl K. Bell, "The Wars of James Jones," *Commentary* 65 (4) (1978): 90.

17. John Limon, "The Second World War in American Fiction," in *The Edinburgh Companion to Twentieth-Century British and American War Literature*,

eds. Adam Piette and Mark Rawlinson (Edinburgh: Edinburgh University Press, 2012), 110.

18. Alex Vernon, *Soldiers Once and Still: Ernest Hemingway, James Salter, and Tim O'Brien* (Iowa City: University of Iowa Press, 2004), 47–48.

19. Sean Brawley and Chris Dixon, *Hollywood's South Seas and the Pacific War: Searching for Dorothy Lamour* (New York: Palgrave Macmillan, 2012), 158–159.

20. Daqing Yang, "The Malleable and the Contested: The Nanjing Massacre in Postwar China and Japan," in *Perilous Memories: The Asia-Pacific War(s)*, eds. T. Fujitani, Geoffrey M. White, and Lisa Yoneyama (Durham: Duke University Press, 2001), 51.

21. Clark Lee, *They Call It Pacific: An Eye-Witness Story of Our War against Japan from Bataan to the Solomons* (New York: Viking Press, 1943), 280.

22. Rana Mitter, *China's War with Japan, 1937–1945: The Struggle for Survival* (London: Penguin, 2013), 11.

23. Vernon McKenzie, "Treatment of War Themes in Magazine Fiction," *Public Opinion Quarterly* 5, (2) (1941): 228; Michaela Hoenicke Moore, *Know Your Enemy: The American Debate on Nazism, 1933–1945* (New York: Cambridge University Press, 2010), xv. New Zealanders likewise acknowledged the distinction between Germans and Nazis. See Stevan Eldred-Grigg and Hugh Eldred-Grigg, *Phoney Wars: New Zealand Society in the Second World War* (Dunedin, New Zealand: Otago University Press, 2017), 101–103.

24. Geoffrey M. White, "Disney's *Pearl Harbor*: National Memory at the Movies," *Public Historian* 24 (4) (2002): 110.

25. Leo Braudy, "Flags of Our Fathers/Letters from Iwo Jima," *Film Quarterly* 60 (4) (2007): 17.

26. Jeffrey Walsh, *American War Literature: 1914 to Vietnam* (London: Macmillan, 1982), 113–114.

27. Michaela Hönicke, "'Know Your Enemy': American Wartime Images of Germany, 1942–1943," in *Enemy Images in America History*, eds. Ragnhild Fiebig-von Hase and Ursula Lehmkuhl (New York: Berghahn Books, 1997), 231–235.

28. Rami Mähkä, "A Killer Joke? World War II in Post-War British Television and Film Comedy," in *Historical Comedy on Screen: Subverting History with Humour*, ed. Hannu Salmi (Bristol, UK: Intellect, 2011), 138.

29. Daniel McKay, "Not Quite the End of the Line: The Prisoner of War Film from David Lean to the Present," *Dalhousie Review* 97 (1) (2017): 114–16.

30. Valerie Holman and Debra Kelly, "War in the Twentieth Century: The Functioning of Humour in Cultural Representation," *Journal of European Studies* 31 (3–4) (2001): 249.

31. Christie Davis, "Humour Is Not a Strategy in War," *Journal of European Studies* 31 (3–4) (2001): 400–403.

32. Hal Erikson, *Military Combat Films: A Critical Survey and Filmography of Hollywood Releases since 1918* (Jefferson: McFarland, 2012), 12.

33. James Jones, *WWII: A Chronicle of Soldiering* (1975; repr. Chicago: University of Chicago Press, 2014), 20–21.

34. Paul Fussell, *The Great War and Modern Memory* (New York: Oxford University Press, 1975), 28; Hynes, *The Soldiers' Tale*, 145–147. From the 1950s onward, Japanese filmmakers also produced comedies set during the war years, the popularity of which depended in large part on depicting private soldiers as victims of Japanese militarism. See Michael Baskett, "Dying for a Laugh: Post-1945 Japanese Service Comedies," *Historical Journal of Film, Radio and Television* 23 (4) (2003).

35. Craig M. Cameron, *American Samurai: Myth, Imagination, and the Conduct of Battle in the First Marine Division, 1941–1951* (New York: Cambridge University Press, 1994), 89.

36. Joanna Bourke, *An Intimate History of Killing: Face-to-Face Killing in Twentieth-Century Warfare* (New York: Basic Books, 1999), 193.

37. Gene Santoro, "A Marine Reflects on Fighting Horror with Humor in the Pacific," *World War II* 25 (5) (2011): 17.

38. Matthew Samuel Ross, "James Jones's Codes of Conduct," PhD dissertation (Las Vegas: University of Nevada, 2012), 104.

39. Leon Uris, *Battle Cry* (1953; repr. New York: Avon, 2005), 2.

40. Aaron B. O'Connell, *Underdogs: The Making of the Modern Marine Corps* (Cambridge: Harvard University Press, 2012), 32.

41. Peter Aichinger, *The American Soldier in Fiction, 1880–1963: A History of Attitudes toward Warfare and the Military Establishment* (Ames: Iowa State University Press, 1975), 87.

42. James Jones, *The Thin Red Line* (1962; repr. London: Penguin Classics, 2014), 117.

43. Andrew Jonathan Huebner, "The Embattled Americans: A Cultural History of Soldiers and Veterans, 1941–1982," PhD dissertation (Providence: Brown University, 2004), 237.

44. Peter G. Jones, *War and the Novelist: Appraising the American War Novel* (Columbia: University of Missouri Press, 1976), 172.

45. Jones, *The Thin Red Line*, 11.

46. Norman Mailer, *Cannibals and Christians* (New York: Dial, 1966), 112.

47. Joseph J. Waldmeir, *American Novels of the Second World War* (The Hague: Mouton, 1969), 19; and Robert F. Kiernan, *American Writing since 1945: A Critical Survey* (New York: Frederick Ungar, 1983), 12.

48. M. Paul Holsinger, "The 'Western' Fiction of World War II," in *World War II in Asia and the Pacific and the War's Aftermath, with General Themes*, ed. Loyd E. Lee (Westport: Greenwood, 1998), 283.

49. R. Barton Palmer, "Filming the Spiritual Landscape of James Jones's *The Thin Red Line*," in *Twentieth-Century American Fiction on Screen*, ed. R. Barton Palmer (New York: Cambridge University Press, 2007), passim; Jon Robert

Adams, *Male Armor: The Soldier-Hero in Contemporary Culture* (Charlottesville: University of Virginia Press, 2008), 42–50; and David Boulting, "Lethal Enclosure: Masculinity under Fire in James Jones's *The Thin Red Line*," in *Performing Masculinity*, eds. Rainer Emig and Antony Rowland (Basingstoke, UK: Palgrave Macmillan, 2010), passim.

50. Paul Fussell, *Wartime: Understanding and Behavior in the Second World War* (New York: Oxford University Press, 1989), 8–9.

51. Cameron, *American Samurai*, 98.

52. Tregaskis notes that US Marines contemplated participating in trophy hunting even before they set foot on Guadalcanal. Richard Tregaskis, *Guadalcanal Diary* (1943; repr. New York: Modern Library, 2000), 14.

53. John Limon, *Writing After War: American War Fiction from Realism to Postmodernism* (New York: Oxford University Press, 1994), 138.

54. Jones, *The Thin Red Line*, 61.

55. Jones, *The Thin Red Line*, 70.

56. Alberto Casadei, "The Dead Hero, the Dead Body: Anti-Epic and Research of Meaning in the Fictional Representation of World War II," in *Memories and Representations of War: The Case of World War I and World War II*, eds. Elena Lamberti and Vita Fortunati (Amsterdam: Rodopi, 2009), 288.

57. Jones, *The Thin Red Line*, 76–77.

58. Jones, *The Thin Red Line*, 143.

59. Gerald F. Linderman, *Embattled Courage: The Experience of Combat in the American Civil War* (New York: Free Press, 1987), 113–115.

60. Huebner, "The Embattled Americans," 242.

61. Jones, *The Thin Red Line*, 192.

62. Yuval Hoah Harari, *The Ultimate Experience: Battlefield Revelations and the Making of Modern War Culture, 1450–2000* (Basingstoke, UK: Palgrave Macmillan, 2008), 10.

63. Harari, *The Ultimate Experience*, 15–16.

64. Harari, *The Ultimate Experience*, 20.

65. Jones, *The Thin Red Line*, 179.

66. Jones, *The Thin Red Line*, 181–182.

67. Steven Ray Carter, "James Jones, an American Master: A Study of His Mystical, Philosophical, Social, and Artistic Views," PhD dissertation (Columbus: Ohio State University, 1975), 128. For an examination of how Jones' own combat experiences inspired his writing, see Robert Blaskiewicz, "James Jones on Guadalcanal," *War, Literature, and the Arts* 20 (1–2) (2008).

68. Harari, *The Ultimate Experience*, 2.

69. Jones, *The Thin Red Line*, 194.

70. Jones, *The Thin Red Line*, 204–205, 284–286, 329–330.

71. Morris Dickstein, *Leopards in the Temple: The Transformation of American Fiction 1945–1970* (Cambridge: Harvard University Press, 2002), 30.

72. Edmond L. Volpe, "James Jones—Norman Mailer," in *Contemporary American Novelists*, ed. Harry T. Moore (Carbondale: Southern Illinois University Press, 1964), 106–107.

73. As one study puts it, "[Jones] was in a world of outcasts, sons of unemployed miners and factory workers who had little education and no prospects for a job during the depths of the depression. The army was a refuge, a relatively safe haven for the young renegades and castaways of American society. James Jones, a self-designated outcast since high school days, found a refuge in this stratified society of the old army." See George Hendrick, Helen How, and Don Sackrider, *James Jones and the Handy Writers' Colony* (Carbondale: Southern Illinois University Press, 2001), 22–23.

74. John Bodnar, *The "Good War" in American Memory* (Baltimore: Johns Hopkins University Press, 2010), 36.

75. Jones, *The Thin Red Line*, 487.

76. Arne Axelsson, "Fun as Hell: War and Humor in Some Post–World War II American Novels," *Studia Neophilologica* 54 (2) (1982): 263.

77. Stewart Lone, "Between Bushido and Black Humour," *History Today* (September 2005): 21; and Nathan Vernon, *Anti-Foreign Imagery in American Pulps and Comic Books, 1920–1960* (Jefferson: McFarland, 2012), 127.

78. Errol Braithwaite, *An Affair of Men* (London: Collins, 1961), 78.

79. Braithwaite, *An Affair of Men*, 51.

80. Braithwaite, *An Affair of Men*, 128.

81. Braithwaite, *An Affair of Men*, 131.

82. Debbie Barnard, "Serving the Master: Cannibalism and Transoceanic Representations of Cultural Identity," *International Journal of Francophone Studies* 8 (3) (2005): 323–325; and Jan Nederveen Pieterse, *White on Black: Images of Africa and Blacks in Western Popular Culture* (New Haven: Yale University Press, 1998), 115.

83. Robin R. Coleman, *Horror Noire: Blacks in American Horror Films from the 1890s to Present* (New York: Routledge, 2011), 36–45; and Kevin Dunn, "Lights . . . Camera . . . Africa: Images of Africa and Africans in Western Popular Films of the 1930s," *African Studies Review* 39 (1) (1996): 149–151.

84. Brathwaite, *An Affair of Men*, 155.

85. John Parkin, "Humouring a Lost Cause," *Journal of War and Culture Studies* 2 (3) (2009): 275.

86. Denis Cosgrove, *Geography and Vision: Seeing, Imagining and Representing the World* (London: I. B. Tauris, 2008), 196.

87. Sean Brawley and Chris Dixon, "Searching for Dorothy Lamour: War and Sex in the South Pacific, 1941–45," *Australasian Journal of American Studies* 18 (1) (1999).

88. Judith A. Bennett, *Natives and Exotics: World War II and Environment in the Southern Pacific* (Honolulu: University of Hawai'i Press, 2009), 11.

89. Of the three, Ruhen's novel is perhaps the least remembered. Its plot focuses on a solitary coast watcher in the Solomon Islands who becomes the

guardian of a White female refugee fleeing southward. As with the other two works and as with all combat novels of the era, the Japanese hardly feature in it, except at a distance. The main tension of the novel is sexual, as the following passage reveals: "The earth beneath the groundsheet seemed inimical to sleep, the atmosphere too moistly heavy; but in all honesty he knew that the enemy was the presence of the woman in the hut across the dark clearing. She was so flamboyantly female; and remembered glimpses of her disturbed the quiescent male in him, that alter ego, not quite understood, not quite accepted, not ever to be rejected, that usurped his veins and his muscles and shuttered his reasoned vision at times that were seldom so inconvenient as this." Olaf Ruhen, *Scan the Dark Coast* (London: Hodder and Stoughton, 1969), 122.

90. Philip D. Beidler, "*South Pacific* and American Remembering; or, 'Josh, We're Going to Buy This Son of a Bitch!'" *Journal of American Studies* 27 (2) (1993): 209. To this day, Michener's depiction of war in the South Pacific remains influential, and not just in the United States. In a survey of writers and artists for whom the Pacific serves as their topic or locale, for example, Auckland-based writer Graeme Lay gives pride of place to Michener (alongside a couple of official New Zealand war paintings) in his chapter "War in the South Pacific," in *In Search of Paradise: Artists and Writers in the Colonial South Pacific* (Auckland: Godwit, 2008), 240–247.

91. Rhona J. Berenstein, "White Heroines and Hearts of Darkness: Race, Gender and Disguise in 1930s Jungle Films," *Film History* 6 (3) (1994).

92. James A. Michener, *The World Is My Home: A Memoir* (London: Secker and Warburg, 1992), 107.

93. Jolisa Margaret Gracewood, "All at Sea: Literature of the Pacific War," PhD dissertation (Ithaca: Cornell University, 2005), 140.

94. Brathwaite, *An Affair of Men*, 30. On the matter of enemy profiling, see Patrick Porter, *Military Orientalism: Eastern War through Western Eyes* (London: Hurst, 2009).

95. Brathwaite, *An Affair of Men*, 112.

96. Shades of the same sort of unprovoked violence endured by Bougainville Islanders, this time during their civil war, have been described by New Zealand author Lloyd Jones. Jones portrays villagers as victimized by Papuan and rebel forces alike, the latter using refurbished weapons left behind by the Japanese. Lloyd Jones, *Mister Pip* (Auckland: Penguin, 2006), 100.

97. As Peter Bishop puts it, "In a sense, Tibet's peripheral place gave permission for many Europeans and Americans to use it as an imaginative escape, as a sort of time out, a relaxation from rigid rational censorship. Time and again Tibet was endowed with all the qualities of a dream, a collective hallucination." Peter Bishop, *The Myth of Shangri-La: Tibet, Travel-Writing and the Western Creation of Sacred Landscape* (Berkeley: University of California Press, 1989), 7.

98. Brathwaite, *An Affair of Men*, 255.

99. Brathwaite, *An Affair of Men*, 249.

100. Sue Townsend, *The Queen and I* (1992; repr. London: Penguin, 2002), 266.

101. Marie Thorsten, *Superhuman Japan: Knowledge, Nation, and Culture in US-Japan Relations* (Abingdon, UK: Routledge, 2012), 23.

102. John Honey, "Japan-bashing: A New Literary Genre?" *OIU Journal of International Studies* 8 (2) (1995): 92.

2. Camera Men: Postwar Japan-Bashing

1. Ruth Benedict, *The Chrysanthemum and the Sword: Patterns of Japanese Culture* (1946; repr. Boston: Mariner Books, 1989), 314.

2. John Foster Dulles was willing to concede in 1954 that Japan might export products to Southeast Asia, but he did not foresee entry into the American market. The occupation of Japan, however, had brought with it such an array of consumer products that many Japanese had no trouble envisaging reversed transpacific trade flows as a general principle. See Kenkichiro Koizumi, "In Search of Wakon: The Cultural Dynamics of Manufacturing Technology in Postwar Japan," *Technology and Culture* 43 (1) (2002): 30–31, 41–48; and George R. Packard, "The Coming U.S.-Japan Crisis," *Foreign Affairs* 66 (2) (1987): 351.

3. For retrospectives on this era, see the radio documentaries "Misunderstanding Japan," *Archive on 4*, directed by Keith Moore, aired August 8, 2015, on the BBC, and "NUMMI," *This American Life*, directed by Ira Glass, aired July 17, 2015, on PRX.

4. Paul Ingrassia, *Engines of Change: A History of the American Dream in Fifteen Cars* (New York: Simon & Schuster, 2012), 191–192.

5. Daniel McKay, "Ghosts in the Shell: On South Africa, the USA and Japan," *Safundi* 14 (4) (2013): 427–428.

6. Ian Littlewood, *The Idea of Japan: Western Images, Western Myths* (Chicago: Ivan R. Dee, 1996); Ian Buruma, "Wake up, America," in *The Missionary and the Libertine: Love and War in East and West* (New York: Vintage, 2001), passim; and Andrew C. McKevitt, "Consuming Japan: Cultural Relations and the Globalizing of America, 1973–1993," PhD dissertation (Philadelphia: Temple University, 2009), 89–135.

7. James A. Michener, *The World Is My Home* (London: Secker and Warburg, 1992), 306–307.

8. See Frederick L. Schodt, *America and the Four Japans: Friend, Foe, Model, Mirror* (Berkeley: Stone Bridge Press, 1994), 59.

9. Although many among the war generation were taken aback at Japan's rise, not everyone condemned it. US Navy veteran Martin Bronfenbrenner consciously dissociated himself from critics of Japan's trade policies and offered a counterperspective in "Japan-Bashing: A View from 'Over There,'" *Challenge* 28 (6) (1986): passim; while another navy man, David W. Plath, profiled Japanese society "on the road," suggesting that Americans and Japanese had autofixation in common. David W. Plath, "My-Car-isma: Motorizing the Showa Self," *Daedalus* 119 (3) (1990): passim.

10. Although New Zealand had no domestic auto industry of its own, in the 1960s and 1970s, it did produce the Trekka, a vehicle similar to the Land Rover but that was built with imported Škoda engines. Drivers noticed the difference, and production tailed off in 1973. See Michael Stevenson, *This is the Trekka* (Wellington: Creative New Zealand, 2003), 11–39.

11. Prior to when Japanese began to visit New Zealand regularly for both business and pleasure, about forty Japanese women had gone to New Zealand as brides of Korean War servicemen.

12. Greta Aiyu Niu, "Techno-Orientalism, Nanotechnology, Posthumans, and Post-Posthumans in Neal Stephenson's and Linda Nagata's Science Fiction," *MELUS* 33 (4) (2008): 84.

13. David Mura, *Turning Japanese: Memoirs of a Sansei* (New York: Anchor Books, 1992), 8.

14. This genre drew on themes of invasion that had emerged in the "future war" novels of the late nineteenth century and thus possessed a certain lineage or "pedigree," although these precursors were never acknowledged by the authors. See Madison J. Davis, "Interpreting the East to the West," *World Literature Today* 80 (6) (2006): 14; Takayuki Tatsumi, *Full Metal Apache: Transactions between Cyberpunk Japan and Avant-Pop America* (Durham: Duke University Press, 2006), 63–70; and David Walker, "Godless Heathen: China in the American Bestseller," in *East by South: China in the Australasian Imagination*, eds. Charles Ferrall, Paul Millar, and Keren Smith (Wellington: Victoria University Press, 2005), passim.

15. Masao Miyoshi, *Off Center: Power and Culture Relations between Japan and the United States* (Cambridge: Harvard University Press, 1991), 63.

16. Studies from the 1980s tend to itemize political disputes between Japan and the US with little attention to ideologies. A precursor to Morley and Robins' study that goes further than these is Roland Robertson, "Japan and the USA: The Interpenetration of National Identities and the Debate about Orientalism," in *Dominant Ideologies*, eds. Nicholas Abercrombie, Stephen Hill, and Bryan S. Turner (London: Routledge, 1990), passim.

17. Edward W. Said, *Orientalism* (1978; repr. London: Penguin, 2003), 38.

18. David A. Boxwell, "Orientalism," in *American History through Literature: 1870–1920*, volume 2, eds. Tom Quirk and Gary Scharnhorst (Farmington Hills: Thomson Gale, 2006), 799.

19. For a critical reading of Hollywood films of the era, see Christine Cornea, "Techno-Orientalism and the Postmodern Subject," in *Screen Methods: Comparative Readings in Film Studies*, eds. Jacqueline Furby and Karen Randell (London: Wallflower Press, 2005), passim. For a nonscholarly discussion of techno-Orientalism as it features in mainstream films, see Umapagan Ampikaipakan and Johanan Sen, "Techno-Orientalism," *What The Flick*, podcast audio, March 18, 2012, http://www.bfm.my/wtf-technoorientalism-1703.html.

20. Bruce Sterling, "Shinkansen," *Whole Earth Review* 69 (Winter 1990): 76.

21. Toshiya Ueno, "Techno-Orientalism and Media-Tribalism: On Japanese Animation and Rave Culture," *Third Text* 13 (47) (1999): 95.

22. David S. Roh, Betsy Huang, and Greta A. Niu, Introduction to *Techno-Orientalism: Imagining Asia in Speculative Fiction, History, and Media*, eds. David S. Roh, Betsy Huang, and Greta A. Niu (New Brunswick: Rutgers University Press, 2015), 3, 7.

23. Ingrassia, *Engines of Change*, 196.

24. Akio Morita, "The Trouble with the American Economy," in *Rediscovering America: Japanese Perspectives on the American Century*, eds. Peter Duus and Kenji Hasegawa (Berkeley: University of California Press, 2011), 331.

25. That the trade disputes were analogous to war became a commonplace assumption. As the automobile executive Lee Iacocca put it, "Right now, we're in the midst of another major war with Japan. This time it's not a shooting war, and I guess we should be thankful for that. The current conflict is a trade war. But because our government refuses to see this war for what it really is, we're well on the road to defeat." Lee Iacocca, *Lee Iacocca: An Autobiography* (New York: Bantam Books, 1984), 315.

26. Mitsuko Shimomura, "Glorious America, Where Are You?" in *Rediscovering America: Japanese Perspectives on the American Century*, eds. Peter Duus and Kenji Hasegawa (1981; repr. Berkeley: University of California Press, 2011), 315–316.

27. William Manchester, *Goodbye Darkness: A Memoir of the Pacific War* (London: Michael Joseph, 1981), 282; and Edward Tabor Linenthal, *Sacred Ground: Americans and Their Battlefields* (Urbana: University of Illinois Press, 1993), 192–196.

28. Weber's narrative dwells on the effect of Japanese tourism upon Pacific Islanders, as in the case of a Samoan taxi driver: "The Japs have taken over the real-estate market again, like they did back in the mid-to-late eighties. They come in, buy millions of dollars of property in a few weeks, real estate people jack up the prices, they buy more, and so on. The locals, we ain't got a chance, man." Joe Weber, *Honorable Enemies* (New York: Putnam's, 1994), 84.

29. David Farber and Beth Bailey, "The Fighting Man as Tourist: The Politics of Tourist Culture in Hawaii during World War II," *Pacific Historical Review* 65 (4) (1996): passim.

30. Louis Turner and John Ash, *The Golden Hordes: International Tourism and the Pleasure Periphery* (London: Constable, 1975), 19.

31. Mike Crang, "Travel/Tourism," in *Cultural Geography: A Critical Dictionary of Key Concepts*, eds. David Atkinson Peter Jackson and David Sibley (London: I. B. Tauris, 2005), 39.

32. Megumi Kato, *Narrating the Other: Australian Literary Perceptions of Japan* (Clayton: Monash University Press, 2008), 177–184.

33. Dong-Hoo Lee, "East Asian Images in Selected American Popular Films from 1930 to 1993," PhD dissertation (New York: New York University, 1996), 218–219.

34. Susan D. Moeller, "Pictures of the Enemy: Fifty Years of Images of Japan in the American Press, 1941–1992," *Journal of American Culture* 19 (1) (1996): 36.

35. Emily S. Rosenberg, *A Date Which Will Live: Pearl Harbor in American Memory* (Durham: Duke University Press, 2003), 54.

36. Kato, *Narrating the Other*, 169.

37. Patrick Evans, *The Long Forgetting: Post-Colonial Literary Culture in New Zealand* (Christchurch: Canterbury University Press, 2007), 16.

38. Keri Hulme, "Kaibutsu-San," *Landfall* 39 (4) (1985): 460.

39. Hulme, "Kaibutsu-San": 463–464.

40. Hulme's deployment of the Japanese tourist's camera as an object of menace was part of the discourse of the era. Commenting on the images associated with Japan, Scott L. Montgomery observes that "the stereotype for Japanese malehood," the "worn macho of the samurai," has been "traded in for the insidious technical prowess of a (otherwise ridiculous) camera-clicking Sony drone." Scott L. Montgomery, "Objects of Uncommon Interest: Reflections on Japan and 'the Japanese,'" *Massachusetts Review* 33 (2) (1992): 266.

41. By the early 1970s, Japanese photographers had already garnered a certain amount of attention from foreign admirers, including a young Ian Buruma, although these photographers were professional rather than touristic and focused on domestic scenes. See Ian Buruma, *A Tokyo Romance: A Memoir* (London: Atlantic Books, 2018), 53–53.

42. John Urry, *The Tourist Gaze*, second edition (London: Sage, 2001), 2.

43. As a literary creation, Mr. Moto predated the United States' involvement in the Second World War by some six years, but even his earliest appearance contained a sinister foreboding that anticipated the coming conflict. As Laurence Goldstein observes in *Your Turn, Mr. Moto* (1935), the political instinct of "the sophisticated hero of Marquand's novel—and his sophistication is clearly on view in his elegant phrasing and sinuous syntax—is to retreat into the kind of tribal solidarity that constitutes pre-combat behavior. From this moment of the first novel in the series, Mr. Moto becomes a villain, not just a diplomat from a rival nation, and the violent (if necessary) destruction of his imperial power becomes the chief goal of an enlightened American foreign policy." So powerful was this predictive quality that in 1941, American servicemen routinely referred to the Japanese as "Mr. Moto," although this practice was short lived, and in the postwar years the Mr. Moto series came to an end (Little, Brown republished the novels in the mid-1980s). See Laurence Goldstein, "'The Imagination Problem': Winfield Townley Scott and the American wars," *War, Literature, and the Arts* 14 (1–2) (2002): 64; and William White, "Mr. Marquand's 'Mr. Moto,'" *American Speech* 23 (2) (1948): passim.

44. In 1985, Keri Hulme was awarded the Booker Prize for her 1984 novel *The Bone People*, which was published just two months before "Kaibutsu-San," a circumstance that, in combination with the quiet rumblings of Japanophobic sentiment in larger New Zealand society, may have fostered an indulgent attitude to the author's politics.

45. Misha Kavka, "Out of the Kitchen Sink," in *Gothic NZ: The Darker Side of Kiwi Culture*, eds. Misha Kavka, Jennifer Lawn, and Mary Paul (Dunedin, New Zealand: Otago University Press, 2006), 57.

46. Vivienne Plumb, "The Wife Who Spoke Japanese in Her Sleep," in *The Wife Who Spoke Japanese in Her Sleep* (Dunedin, New Zealand: Otago University Press, 1993), 32–33.

47. Ron Tanner, "Toy Robots in America, 1955–75: How Japan Really Won the War," *Journal of Popular Culture* 28 (3) (1994): 125.

48. Truman Capote, *Breakfast at Tiffany's and Three Stories* (1958; repr. New York: Vintage, 1993), 7.

49. Michael Crichton, *Rising Sun* (New York: Arrow Books, 1992), 121.

50. Crichton, *Rising Sun*, 107.

51. Crichton, *Rising Sun*, 79.

52. David Lawrence Abney, "Japan Bashing: A History of America's Anti-Japanese Acts, Attitudes, and Laws," PhD dissertation (Tempe: Arizona State University, 1995), 317.

53. Crichton, *Rising Sun*, 168–169.

54. Crichton, *Rising Sun*, 166–167.

55. Crichton, *Rising Sun*, 121.

56. Floyd D. Cheung, "Imagining Danger, Imagining Nation: Postcolonial Discourse in *Rising Sun* and *Stargate*," *Jouvert: A Journal of Postcolonial Studies* 2 (2) (1998): paragraph 15, https://legacy.chass.ncsu.edu/jouvert/v2i2/CHEUNG.HTM.

57. Robyn Rodriguez and Vernadette Gonzalez observe that the rise of Japan's export industry also enabled young Asian American males to express their masculinity through association, particularly in the subculture of "rice rocket" car imports. Robyn Rodriguez and Vernadette Gonzalez, "Asian American Auto/Biographies: The Gendered Limits of Consumer Citizenship in Import Subcultures," in *Alien Encounters: Popular Culture in Asian America*, eds. Mimi Thi Nguyen and Thuy Linh Nguyen Tu (Durham: Duke University Press, 2007), 255.

58. Crichton, *Rising Sun*, 392.

59. Crichton, *Rising Sun*, 32–33, 71.

60. Robin W. Winks, "The Sinister Oriental: Thriller Fiction and the Asian Scene," *Journal of Popular Culture* 19 (2) (1985): 51.

61. This fear recurs in thriller novels of the era. Reviewing Tom Clancy's *Debt of Honor* (1994), the critic Christopher Buckley summarizes it as follows: "It all plays into the crudest of cultural paranoia, namely, that what these beastly yellow inscrutables are really after is—*our women*." Christopher Buckley, "Megabashing Japan: World War II Wasn't Half Enough for Tom Clancy," *The New York Times Book Review*, October 28, 1994, 28.

62. Heather J. Hicks, *The Culture of Soft Work: Labor, Gender, and Race in Postmodern American Narrative* (New York: Palgrave Macmillan, 2009), 149; and Gary Y. Okihiro, *Margins and Mainstreams: Asians in American History and Culture* (Seattle: University of Washington Press, 2014), 138.

63. Carroll W. Pursell, *The Machine in America: A Social History of Technology* (Baltimore: Johns Hopkins University Press, 2007), 330.

64. In Gibson's own words, "The Sony Walkman has done more to change human perception than any virtual reality gadget. I can't remember any technological experience since that was quite so wonderful as being able to take music and move it through landscapes and architecture." Interview with William Gibson, *Time Out*, October 6, 1993, 49.

65. Crichton, *Rising Sun*, 15.

66. Carl Eugene Loeffler, "Video in Japan," *Whole Earth Review* 69 (Winter 1990): 84.

67. Ken Provencher, "Japan in Transnational Hollywood: Industry and Identity, 1985–1995," PhD dissertation (Los Angeles: University of Southern California, 2013), 2.

68. Crichton, *Rising Sun*, 72–74.

69. Crichton, *Rising Sun*, 150–156.

70. Crichton, *Rising Sun*, 288–289. The narrative is broken up into a series of episodes in which Smith is the pupil and Connor the learned "Japanologist," with the latter discoursing on Japanese culture from the vantage point of the perpetual outsider. See Jacob Raz and Aviad E. Raz, "'America' Meets 'Japan': A Journey for Real between Two Imaginaries," *Theory, Culture, and Society* 13 (3) (1996): 156.

71. Crichton, *Rising Sun*, 297.

72. Alexander Moore, "Rosanzerusu is Los Angeles: An Anthropological Inquiry of Japanese Tourists," *Annals of Tourism Research* 12 (4) (1985): 632.

73. Lon Kurashige, *Japanese American Celebration and Conflict: A History of Ethnic Identity and Festival, 1934–1990* (Berkeley: University of California Press, 2002), 191–201.

74. Crichton, *Rising Sun*, 136–140.

75. Crichton may have been aware that the distinction between Japanese nationals and Asian Americans had been violently blurred on several occasions in the decade preceding the publication of his novel. See Moon H. Jo and Daniel D. Mast, "Changing Images of Asian Americans," *International Journal of Politics, Culture and Society* 6 (3) (1993): 432–435.

76. The Japanese American Citizens' League, for example, listed Crichton's novel in its collection of "Japan-bashing" material. See Narrelle Morris, *Japan-Bashing: Anti-Japanism since the 1980s* (Abingdon, UK: Routledge, 2011), 103–107.

77. Frank Chin and Jeffrey Paul Chan, "Racist Love," in *Seeing through Shuck*, ed. Richard Kostelanetz (New York: Ballantine Books, 1972), passim.

78. Sheng-mei Ma, *The Deathly Embrace: Orientalism and Asian American Identity* (Minneapolis: University of Minnesota Press, 2000), xi–xiii; and Jane Chi Hyun Park, *Yellow Future: Oriental Style in Hollywood Cinema* (Minneapolis: University of Minnesota Press, 2010), xi.

79. Jodi Kim, *Ends of Empire: Asian American Critique and the Cold War* (Minneapolis: University of Minnesota Press, 2010), 132–33; and Emily Cheng,

"Meat and the Millennium: Transnational Politics of Race and Gender in Ruth Ozeki's *My Year of Meats*," *Journal of Asian American Studies* 12 (2) (2009): 191–192.

80. Michael J. Blouin, *Japan and the Cosmopolitan Gothic: Specters of Modernity* (New York: Palgrave Macmillan, 2013), 111.

81. Ruth L. Ozeki, *My Year of Meats* (New York: Viking, 1998), 29–30.

82. Ozeki, *My Year of Meats*, 33.

83. Ozeki, *My Year of Meats*, 43–44. On the underdevelopment of expatriated Japanese males as characters in Ozeki's writing, see Cheryl J. Fish, "The Toxic Body Politic: Ethnicity, Gender, and Corrective Eco-Justice in Ruth Ozeki's *My Year of Meats* and Judith Helfand and Daniel Gold's *Blue Vinyl*," *MELUS* 34 (2) (2009): 54.

84. Andrew H. Wallis, "Toward a Global Eco-Consciousness in Ruth Ozeki's *My Year of Meats*," *Interdisciplinary Studies in Literature and Environment* 20 (4) (2013): 843.

85. Monica Chiu, "Postnational Globalization and (En)gendered Meat Production in Ruth L. Ozeki's *My Year of Meats*," *LIT: Literature Interpretation Theory* 12 (1) (2001): 113.

86. Chiu, "Postnational Globalization and (En)gendered Meat Production in Ruth L. Ozeki's *My Year of Meats*": 101.

87. Ruth L. Ozeki, "From Meat to Potatoes: An Interview with Ruth Ozeki," *Foreign Literature Studies* 31 (6) (2009): 6.

88. Ozeki, *My Year of Meats*, 132–133.

89. Ozeki, *My Year of Meats*, 138.

90. Mari Suvanto, "Images of Japan and the Japanese: The Representations of the Japanese Culture in the Popular Literature Targeted at the Western World in the 1980s–1990s," PhD dissertation (Jyväskylä: University of Jyväskylä, 2002), 48–49.

91. Crichton, *Rising Sun*, 142. Critiques of Japan bashing also mentioned the sexual undertones associated with samurai references, as in one review of Crichton's novel which suggested that a suitable cover for the paperback version "might be a caricature of World War II-era Prime Minister Tojo skulking off into Rockefeller Center with Doris Day over one shoulder and an eighteen-inch dildo sheathed where his samurai sword would have been." See Karl Taro Greenfeld, "Return of the Yellow Peril," *Nation* (May 1992): 636.

92. Ozeki, *My Year of Meats*, 139.

93. Ozeki, *My Year of Meats*, 34, 190.

94. Ozeki, *My Year of Meats*, 265.

95. Ozeki, *My Year of Meats*, 267.

96. Laura Anh Williams, "Gender, Race, and an Epistemology of the Abattoir in *My Year of Meats*," *Feminist Studies* 40 (2) (2014): 249.

97. Ozeki, *My Year of Meats*, 276.

98. Nina Cornyetz, "The Meat Manifesto: Ruth Ozeki's Performative Poetics," *Women and Performance* 12 (1) (2001): 218.

99. Crichton, *Rising Sun*, 398.

100. Emily Russell, *Reading Embodied Citizenship: Disability, Narrative, and the Body Politic* (New Brunswick: Rutgers University Press, 2011), 131. An important stylistic difference between Crichton and Ozeki is that the former began with a self-conscious political agenda, whereas the latter came to her political position in the course of writing. See Ruth L. Ozeki, "'A Universe of Many Worlds': An Interview with Ruth Ozeki," *MELUS* 38 (3) (2013): 161.

101. Ozeki, *My Year of Meats*, 299.

102. Leigh Johnson, "Conceiving the Body: Sandra Cisneros and Ruth L. Ozeki's Representations of Women's Reproduction in Transnational Space," *Transformations: The Journal of Inclusive Scholarship and Pedagogy* 19 (2) (2008–9): 36.

103. Ozeki, *My Year of Meats*, 302.

104. McKenzie Wark, "From Fordism to Sonyism: Perverse Readings of the New World Order," *New Formations* 15 (1991): 45.

105. Robert F. Arnold, "Termination or Transformation? The 'Terminator' Films and Recent Changes in the U.S. Auto Industry," *Film Quarterly* 52 (1) (1998): 22–23.

106. Betsy Huang, "Premodern Orientalist Science Fictions," *MELUS* 33 (4) (2008): 23–24.

107. Mimi Thi Nguyen and Thuy Linh Nguyen Tu make this observation in connection with the character Data in Steven Spielberg's 1985 film *The Goonies* in the Introduction to *Alien Encounters: Popular Culture in Asian America*, eds. Mimi Thi Nguyen and Thuy Linh Nguyen Tu (Durham: Duke University Press, 2007), 1–4.

108. Stephen Hong Sohn, "Minor Character, Minority Orientalisms, and the Borderlands of Asian America," *Cultural Critique* 82 (Fall 2012): 155.

3. Captive Memories: Internment North and South

1. The play takes the shooting of Japanese POWs in February 1943 as its subject matter, an incident sparked by the prisoners' resisting their guards. This event and Australia's 1944 Cowra breakout are frequently cited in Australasian scholarship as pivotal instances in which the differences between Japanese and Allied cultures, or between the military codes of the same, became insurmountable. See Mike Nicolaidi and Eric Thompson, *The Featherston Chronicles: A Legacy of War* (Auckland: HarperCollins, 1999).

2. Much of the background detail provided here is indebted to a television documentary that chronicled the 1995 production. See *Shuriken: Prisoners of Culture*, directed by Steve La Hood (Wellington: Ninox Films, 1996).

3. Transnational Australasian scholarship over the last fifty years has taken significant steps toward breaking up this dyad. A noteworthy recent publication is Marilyn Lake and Henry Reynolds' *Drawing the Global Colour Line: White Men's Countries and the International Challenge of Racial Equality* (Cambridge: Cambridge University Press, 2008); an older one is Charles A. Price's *The Great*

White Walls are Built: Restrictive Immigration to North America and Australasia, 1836–1888 (Canberra: Australian Institute of International Affairs in association with Australian National University Press, 1974). Thus far, such works have tended to emphasize the interconnectedness of transpacific migration and anti-immigration political trends without addressing the internment of Japanese civilians/minorities.

4. Fu-jen Chen and Su-lin Yu, "Reclaiming the Southwest: A Traumatic Space in the Japanese American Internment Narrative," *Journal of the Southwest* 47 (4) (2005): 555.

5. The work of historian Takashi Fujitani anticipates this chapter to an extent and makes a convincing case for the need to revisit government and military policies during the war years from a comparative perspective, one that discourages seeing American and Japanese policies (especially those that pertain to colonized/ethnic minority subjects) as mutually disinterested. As Fujitani puts it, "The model of each total war regime throughout the world strengthening itself by mobilizing colonial subjects and racialized minorities stimulated the others to follow, resulting in a global system of mutual and multidirectional agitation and emulation." Takashi Fujitani, "Ethnic and Colonial Soldiers and the Politics of Disavowal," in *Race for Empire: Koreans as Japanese and Japanese as Americans During World War II*, ed. Takashi Fujitani (Berkeley: University of California Press, 2011), 10. While the present chapter is similarly concerned in part with outlining a particular wartime phenomenon—the intimate connections between Japanese and Australasian camp systems—it is especially interested in the emergence of literary writers, such as Wendy Catran, who exhibit a new awareness of transpacific histories, a trend that parallels trends in historical research spearheaded by Fujitani.

6. For a cursory overview of Wendy Catran's young adult writing, see Doreen Darnell, "Wendy Catran," *Talespinner* 19 (May 2005): 16–17.

7. In her study of Asian American writing, Patti Duncan has noted that some writers do attempt a "gap-filling" project that addresses the omissions within mainstream histories, whereas others prefer to leave pointed silences that serve political agendas. Patti Duncan, *Tell This Silence: Asian American Women Writers and the Politics of Speech* (Iowa City: University of Iowa Press, 2004), viii.

8. Anne Whitehead, *Trauma Fiction* (Edinburgh: Edinburgh University Press, 2004), 81–82.

9. King-Kok Cheung, *Articulate Silences: Hisaye Yamamoto, Maxine Hong Kingston, Joy Kogawa* (Ithaca: Cornell University Press, 1993), 3–4.

10. Trevor Dodman, "'Going All to Pieces': *A Farewell to Arms* as Trauma Narrative," *Twentieth Century Literature* 52 (3) (2006): 250.

11. Dodman, "Going All to Pieces," 251.

12. Nan Taylor, "Human Rights in World War II in New Zealand," *New Zealand Journal of History* 23 (2) (1989): 109.

13. Ron Crocombe, *Asia in the Pacific Islands: Replacing the West* (Suva, Fiji: IPS Publications, 2007), 48.

14. Robert Lowry, *Fortress Fiji: Holding the Line in the Pacific War, 1939–45* (Sutton, Australia: R. W. Lowry, 2006), 27.

15. Elizabeth Wood-Ellem, "Behind the Battle Lines: Tonga in World War II," paper presented at the seventh Tongan History Conference, Canberra, January 1997, 8.

16. The only book-length attempt to imagine what this social milieu must have entailed is Maurice Gee's novel *Live Bodies* (1998), although Gee makes no mention of the Japanese. In a short interview on the Te ara website, a former internee recalls the living conditions on Somes Island (teara.govt.nz/en/speech/13033/prisoners-of-war-on-somes-island).

17. On the matter of negotiated exchanges of internees in the United States for American POWs in Japanese hands, see Bruce Elleman, *Japanese-American Civilian Prisoner Exchanges and Detention Camps, 1941–45* (New York: Routledge, 2006).

18. Ken McNeil, "A Brief History of the Japanese in New Zealand," *Nyujirando Kenkyu* 3 (June 1997): 69–72.

19. The novel has been taught in American high schools, although its graphic descriptions of battle and sexual awakening have occasioned controversy. For details of the controversy, see Jenny Brantley, "Clorox the Dishes and Hide the Books: A Defense of *Snow Falling on Cedars*," in *Censored Books*, volume 2, *Critical Viewpoints, 1985–2000*, ed. Nicholas J. Karolides (Lanham: Scarecrow Press, 2002).

20. Guterson's decision to take *Moby-Dick*, and Ahab more particularly, as a literary progenitor for a novel of the Pacific War was anticipated by Norman Mailer some four decades prior. See Bernard Horn, "Ahab and Ishmael at War: The Presence of *Moby-Dick* in *The Naked and the Dead*," *American Quarterly* 34 (4) (1982).

21. David Guterson, *Snow Falling on Cedars* (New York: Vintage, 1995), 31.

22. Whitehead, *Trauma Fiction*, 85.

23. David Guterson, *Snow Falling on Cedars*, 39.

24. Since at least as far back as the Vietnam War, disabled veterans have been figured in American culture as "disruptive others." See Martin F. Norden, "Bitterness, Rage, and Redemption: Hollywood Constructs the Disabled Vietnam Veteran," in *Disabled Veterans in History*, ed. David A. Gerber (Ann Arbor: University of Michigan Press, 2015), 96–97.

25. Guterson, *Snow Falling on Cedars*, 54.

26. Guterson, *Snow Falling on Cedars*, 111.

27. Guterson, *Snow Falling on Cedars*, 84.

28. Guterson, *Snow Falling on Cedars*, 97.

29. Werner Sollors, *Beyond Ethnicity: Consent and Descent in American Culture* (New York: Oxford University Press, 1986), 6.

30. Guterson, *Snow Falling on Cedars*, 202.
31. Guterson, *Snow Falling on Cedars*, 85.
32. Guterson, *Snow Falling on Cedars*, 199.
33. Cheung, *Articulate Silences*, 4–5.
34. Guterson, *Snow Falling on Cedars*, 8.
35. Emily Roxworthy, *The Spectacle of Japanese American Trauma: Racial Performativity and World War II* (Honolulu: University of Hawai'i Press, 2008), 4.
36. Guterson, *Snow Falling on Cedars*, 250–251.
37. Guterson, *Snow Falling on Cedars*, 424.
38. Guterson, *Snow Falling on Cedars*, 86.
39. Heike Paul, "Old, New and 'Neo' Immigrant Fictions in American Literature: The Immigrant Presence in David Guterson's *Snow Falling on Cedars* and T. C. Boyle's *The Tortilla Curtain*," *Amerikastudien* 46 (2) (2001): 257.
40. Guterson, *Snow Falling on Cedars*, 458.
41. Gurleen Grewal, "Memory and the Matrix of History: The Poetics of Loss and Recovery in Joy Kogawa's *Obasan* and Toni Morrison's *Beloved*," in *Memory and Cultural Politics: New Approaches to American Ethnic Literatures*, eds. Amritjit Singh, Joseph T. Skerrett Jr., and Robert E. Hogan (Boston: Northeastern University Press, 1996), 141.
42. Although antiwar sentiments peaked in New Zealand during the Vietnam War, a subdued sense of disquiet was discernable during the Korean War as well. On this matter, one observer notes that "in the fifth form one boy dismissed the Army speaker who, he said, 'treated war as a game.' We mocked him and, when he persisted, ostracised him. Thirteen years later when I was teaching in a secondary school, a Navy officer fresh from the war in Korea addressed the assembly. A group of sixth formers protested saying, 'This is obscene—he's pretending war is a game.' This time many of the staff and senior boys agreed." See Jack Shallcrass, "Tidal Changes," in *One of the Boys? Changing Views of Masculinity in New Zealand*, ed. Michael King (Auckland: Heinemann, 1988), 23–24.
43. Michael King recalls the social pressures to participate in or otherwise venerate military service as being entrenched. Michael King, *Being Pakeha Now: Reflections and Recollections of a White Native* (Auckland: Penguin, 1999), 24–26.
44. Wendy Catran, *The Swap* (South Melbourne, Australia: Lothian Books, 2004), 12. This theme of New Zealand soldiers defending foreign civilian women against the unwelcome advances of American servicemen appears elsewhere in New Zealand literature. A noteworthy example is M. K. Joseph's *A Soldier's Tale* (1976) and its film version (1988).
45. On the term "dueling victimhoods," see Elizabeth S. Dahl, "Is Japan Facing Its Past? The Case of Japan and Its Neighbors," in *The Age of Apology: Facing up to the Past*, eds. Mark Gibney, Rhoda E. Howard-Hassmann, Lean-Marc Coicaud, and Niklaus Steiner (Philadelphia: University of Pennsylvania Press, 2008), 250.

46. The deleterious effects of coercive mothers in the New Zealand family are a running theme throughout New Zealand literature, and the disappointment of Alan's mother on learning of his spousal choice exacerbates the difficulties associated with recovery from war trauma. For a study of the confluence of puritanism and maternal dictates in New Zealand literature, see Alistair Fox, *The Ship of Dreams: Masculinity in Contemporary New Zealand Fiction* (Dunedin, New Zealand: Otago University Press, 2008).

47. During the Second World War, women had to abandon this gender role and fill job vacancies left by soldiers who went overseas. But when the soldiers returned, most women gave up their jobs because they shared—or were convinced that they shared—the "ideal" of domestic family life. See Deborah Montgomerie, "Sweethearts, Soldiers, Happy Families: Gender and the Second World War," in *The Gendered Kiwi*, eds. Caroline Daley and Deborah Montgomerie (Auckland: Auckland University Press, 1999), 165–166.

48. Wendy Catran, *The Swap*, 139.

49. I have in mind here the enforced practice in concentration camps of referring to corpses as "figures." Primo Levi also recalls how some Jews, designated "prominents," took up quasi-official positions that gave them a measure of authority over their fellow captives. These "prominents," unable to express any anguish toward their guards, became especially vindictive toward the people they were meant to minister. See Primo Levi, *Survival in Auschwitz*, trans. Stuart Woolf (1958; repr. New York: Touchstone, 1996), 90–91.

50. Wendy Catran, *The Swap*, 188.

51. Kalí Tal, *Worlds of Hurt: Reading the Literature of Trauma* (New York: Cambridge University Press, 1996), 7.

52. The difficulties Catran faced have led at least one reviewer to criticize the novel's ending as being "rather rushed." See Fran Knight, "*The Swap*," *Magpies* 19 (4) (2004): 40–41. The judgment may be valid in part, but one must take into account the encumbrances that authors encounter when adopting a "multimodal" approach.

53. Brian Russell Roberts and Michelle Ann Stephens, "Archipelagic American Studies: Decontinentalizing the Study of American Culture," in *Archipelagic American Studies*, eds. Brian Russell Roberts and Michelle Ann Stephens (Durham: Duke University Press, 2017), 9–10.

54. P. Scott Corbett, "In the Eye of the Hurricane: Americans in Japanese Custody during World War II," in *Forgotten Captives in Japanese Occupied Asia*, eds. Kevin Blackburn and Karl Hack (Abingdon, UK: Routledge: 2008), 120.

55. Jamie Ford, *Hotel on the Corner of Bitter and Sweet* (London: Allison and Busby, 2009), 281.

56. Lizzie Oliver, *Prisoners of the Sumatra Railway: Narratives of History and Memory* (London: Bloomsbury, 2018), 97–98; and Sean Brawley, Chris Dixon, and Beatrice Trefalt, *Competing Voices from the Pacific War: Fighting Words* (Santa Barbara: Greenwood Press, 2009), 196.

4. The Poetics of Apology: FEPOW Narratives

1. Throughout the rest of the twenty-first century, Lean's film provided the 'generalised subject' that framed anglophone discussions of Japanese-run camps. Its ubiquitous discursive presence irritated memoirists but also acted as a spur to correctives. See Frances Haughton, "'To the Kwai and Back': Myth, Memory and Memoirs of the 'Death Railway,' 1942–1943," *Journal of War and Culture Studies* 7 (3) (2014): 225.

2. Public school analogies gained currency because the majority of extant nonfiction writings on captivity were authored by members of the officer class, who typically had attended public school. See Joan Beaumont, "Rank, Privilege, and Prisoners of War," *War and Society* 1 (1) (1983): passim.

3. Christopher Hitchens, "P. G. Wodehouse: The Honorable Schoolboy," in *Arguably: Essays* (London: Atlantic Books, 2011), 268.

4. This supposition was literalized in the portrayal of a football match between Germans and Allied POWs in the 1981 film *Escape to Victory*. For a study of the ways in which the British public school paradigm shaped POW films, see Nicholas J. Cull, "'Great Escapes': 'Englishness' and the Prisoner of War Genre," *Film History* 14. (3–4) (2002): passim.

5. The challenges of depicting atrocity in a field of cultural representation already encumbered by preconceptions of the Other are also evident in the fact that once British authors and journalists became aware of the Armenian genocide during the Great War, they took the opportunity to re-inscribe stereotypes of Turkish barbarity. See Jo Laycock, *Imagining Armenia: Orientalism, Ambiguity and Intervention* (Manchester: Manchester University Press, 2016), 107–112.

6. Ian Watt, literary scholar and former prisoner on the Burma-Siam railway, treats the quasi-burlesque as an intentional feature of Boulle's novel. He is critical of the film version and, more significantly, of the credence given to both versions by readers and viewers: "The actual circumstances of our experience on the Kwai were not, of course, reflected in the novel or the movie; there is no reason why they should have been. But it is surely the deep blindness of our culture and media, both to the obdurate stubbornness of reality and to the stubborn continuities of history, which allowed the public to accept the plausibility of Nicholson's triumphs over his Japanese captors." Ian Watt, "The Humanities on the River Kwai," *Stanford Humanities Review* 8 (1) (2000): 31.

7. Masao Miyoshi, *Off Center: Power and Culture Relations between Japan and the United States* (Cambridge: Harvard University Press, 1991), 178.

8. Daniel McKay, "Not Quite the End of the Line: The Prisoner-of-War Film from David Lean to the Present," *Dalhousie Review* 97 (1) (2017): 113–115.

9. Roger Bourke, *Prisoners of the Japanese: Literary Imagination and the Prisoner-of-War Experience* (St. Lucia: University of Queensland Press, 2006), 88.

10. For accounts of what took place in Fukuoka Camp #17, see Charles Balaza, *Life as an American Prisoner of War of the Japanese* (Fairfield: 1st Books, 2002), 169–170; and Gene S. Jacobsen, *We Refused to Die: My Time as a Prisoner*

of War in Bataan and Japan, 1942–1945 (Salt Lake City: University of Utah Press, 2004), 189.

11. Clavell knew how to stoke old rivalries, deliberately suggesting that under conditions of captivity, nationalities would always revert to their base components: pedantic class consciousness where the British were concerned, thievery in the case of the Australians, and gangsterism for the money-grubbing Americans. Whether one finds these reductions provocative or amusing, the novel lures one into investing in the divisions and thereby undermines the notion of prisoners as socially intact, politically homogeneous, and united in support of "civilized" values.

12. Daniel McKay, "Guarded Truths: Korean Characters in POW Narratives, and POW Narratives in Korean History," *Studia Neophilologica* 90 (1) (2018): 53–54.

13. Even if the canon of FEPOW writing were to develop in this manner, these latter outcomes are far from guaranteed. In the nineteenth century, the Indian Mutiny of 1857–59 gave rise to a body of British literature that drew attention to acts of violence perpetrated against White soldiers and civilians by sepoy troops. As humanities scholar Christopher Herbert argues, Victorian writing on this incident is a good deal more self-critical and politically multivalent than twentieth-century scholars have supposed. Christopher Herbert, *War of No Pity: The Indian Mutiny and Victorian Trauma* (Princeton: Princeton University Press, 2008), 5. The political vectors of postcolonial critiques, however, seldom allow that nineteenth-century British authors might successfully adopt self-critical, antipatriotic positions in respect to empire.

14. Taking the opposite view, the social historian Ken Worpole has advocated revisionism as a policy for republished FEPOW writings, arguing that the genre is hampered by the unreconstructed prejudices of some surviving FEPOWs. Ken Worpole, *Dockers and Detectives*, second edition (Nottingham, UK: Five Leaves Publications, 2008), 92.

15. Daniel McKay, "Don't Hate the British: Old Boer Wisdom in Tan Twan Eng's *The Garden of Evening Mists*," *Wasafiri* 30 (3) (2015): 53.

16. Eric Lomax, *The Railway Man* (Bath, UK: Chivers, 1995), 253.

17. Lomax, *The Railway Man*, 288–290. Lomax and Nagase's story of reconciliation has its parallel in the equally remarkable tale of Nabou Fujita, the only Japanese aviator of World War II to bomb the continental United States. In 1995, Fujita journeyed to Brookings, Oregon, to participate in commemorative events, after strenuous advocacy on the part of local boosters, coupled with his own sincere contrition, laid the necessary groundwork. See Derek Hoff, "Igniting Memory: Commemoration of the 1942 Japanese Bombing of Southern Oregon, 1962–1998," *Public Historian* 21 (2) (1999): 77–80.

18. Laura Hillenbrand, *Unbroken: A World War II Story of Survival, Resilience, and Redemption* (London: Fourth Estate, 2011), 352.

19. Hillenbrand, *Unbroken*, 396.

20. As part of his prewriting, Peter Wells examined book-length studies of the FEPOW experience as well as official records and photographs and also

visited former camp sites in Borneo ("Unravelling the Atrocities of War," *Sunday Star Times* [Auckland], October 28, 2007).

21. Peter Wells, *Lucky Bastard* (Auckland: Vintage, 2007), 168.

22. Jenny Edkins, *Trauma and the Memory of Politics* (Cambridge: Cambridge University Press, 2003), 15.

23. Overdependence on the theme of trauma in stories of war veterans has the unfortunate side effect of making such stories appear "stereotypical," as American writers of Iraq War literature have increasingly discovered. See Roger Luckhurst, "In War Times: Fictionalizing Iraq," *Contemporary Literature* 53 (4) (2012): 719.

24. Dominick LaCapra, *Writing History, Writing Trauma* (Baltimore: Johns Hopkins University Press, 2001), 47.

25. Wells, *Lucky Bastard*, 230.

26. Wells had similar epiphanies as he did the research for his novel, although he makes his ambivalence clear in an interview: "Now one appreciates [the war generation's] stoicism and modesty and civility. But actually growing up with them—with someone who doesn't talk, finds difficulty in expressing emotions—isn't necessarily an easy experience." Philip Matthews, "A Visitor from Hawke's Bay," *New Zealand Listener*, October 5, 2007, 36.

27. Alison Parr has suggested that war fiction may perform a public service by anticipating the issues and concerns of war veterans before veterans themselves do. By implication, writers of war fiction ought to avail themselves of the testimonies of those veterans whose experiences they purport to represent. Alison Parr, *Silent Casualties: New Zealand's Unspoken Legacy of the Second World War* (North Shore City, New Zealand: Tandem Press, 1995), 21.

28. Juliette Pattinson, Lucy Noakes, and Wendy Ugolini, "Incarcerated Masculinities: Male POWs and the Second World War," *Journal of War and Culture Studies* 7 (3) (2014): 182.

29. Just as Peter Wells is indebted to Alison Parr's work, so she benefits, in turn, from Jock Phillips' study of masculinity in New Zealand society, in which he cites war as a celebrated test of a (culturally constructed) manhood that exacts a price by narrowing the scope of permissible forms of public bereavement. Where returned servicemen are concerned, both researchers see a mutually reinforcing confluence between the inexpressible (in psychological terms with respect to individual veterans) and the impermissible (in sociocultural terms as regards public attitudes toward the expression of private injury). The upshot of this unfortunate arrangement is that veterans' families have at times had to share in and accommodate a form of suffering that has no sanctioned outlet elsewhere. See Jock Phillips, *A Man's Country? The Image of the Pakeha Male, a History* (Auckland: Penguin Books, 1987), 192–198.

30. Dori Laub, "Bearing Witness or the Vicissitudes of Listening," in *Testimony: Crises of Witnessing in Literature, Psychoanalysis, and History*, eds. Shoshana Felman and Dori Laub (New York: Routledge, 1992), 57.

31. Wells, *Lucky Bastard*, 373–374.

32. As trauma theorist Cathy Caruth puts it, "The flashback or traumatic re-enactment conveys, that is, both *the truth of an event*, and *the truth of its incomprehensibility*." Introduction to *Trauma: Explorations in Memory*, ed. Cathy Caruth (Baltimore: Johns Hopkins University Press, 1995), 153.

33. Dori Laub, "Truth and Testimony: The Process and the Struggle," *Trauma* 69.

34. Wells, *Lucky Bastard*, 319–320.

35. Laub, "Bearing Witness or the Vicissitudes of Listening," 61.

36. Lehrer could touch on trauma as a theme without delving into its meaning, partly because, at the time of publication, American readers had grown used to trauma as a topic or trope in cultural productions and news features. See Kirby Farrell, *Post-Traumatic Culture: Injury and Interpretation in the Nineties* (Baltimore: Johns Hopkins University Press, 1998), 2.

37. The 1990s were important for Australia too and culminated in the opening of a museum at Hell Fire Pass on what had been the Burma-Siam Railway by Prime Minister John Howard in 1998. See Jean Beaumont, "Prisoners of War in Australian National Memory," in *Prisoners of War, Prisoners of Peace: Captivity, Homecoming and Memory in World War II*, ed. Barbara Hately-Broad (London: Berg, 2005), 193.

38. Narrelle Morris, "Destructive Discourse: 'Japan Bashing' in the United States, Australia, and Japan in the 1980s and 1990s," PhD dissertation (Perth, Australia: Murdoch University, 2006), 245–246; and Esperanza Miyake, "Politicizing Motorcycles: Racialized Capital of Technology, Techno-Orientalism, and Japanese Temporality," *East Asian Journal of Popular Culture* 2 (2) (2016): 212.

39. Norma Field, *In the Realm of a Dying Emperor: Japan at Century's End* (New York: Pantheon, 1991), 180.

40. For another account of what prompted Mayor Motoshima to speak out, see Erna Paris, *Long Shadows: Truth, Lies, and History* (London: Bloomsbury, 2000), 149–152.

41. Norma Field, "War and Apology: Japan, Asia, the Fiftieth, and After," *positions: East Asia Cultures Critique* 5 (1) (1997): 3–5.

42. Laura Hein and Mark Selden, "Commemoration and Silence: Fifty Years of Remembering the Bomb in America and Japan," in *Living with the Bomb: American and Japanese Cultural Conflicts in the Nuclear Age*, eds. Laura Hein and Mark Selden (New York: M. E. Sharpe, 1997), 22.

43. Ishmael Reed, *Japanese by Spring* (New York: Atheneum, 1993), 149.

44. It is worth remarking that the caricature of Japan and the United States as pugilists in a sparring contest was inaptly reductive given that rivalry between institutions, lobbyists, and private individuals on both sides of the Pacific meant that neither nation was in any sense unified against the other. As the oral historian Philip Seaton writes with respect to the individual Japanese he interviewed, "The Japanese are frequently accused of 'failing to address the past' or of 'denial,'

'ignorance' and 'amnesia' concerning the war . . . The reality, however, is that debate over how to address war responsibility issues has ensured that war history remains highly contested in Japan and Japanese people have been unable to settle on a dominant narrative of the conflict." Philip Seaton, "'Do You Really Want to Know What Your Uncle Did?': Coming to Terms with Relatives' War Actions in Japan," *Oral History* 34 (1) (2006): 59. There were voices in the scholarly and publishing world in both Japan and the United States that engaged in informed self-criticism during this period. See, in particular, two semiautobiographical essays: Richard H. Minear, "Atomic Holocaust, Nazi Holocaust: Some Reflections," in *Learning to Glow: A Nuclear Reader*, ed. John Bradley (Tucson: University of Arizona Press, 2000); and Ota Masakuni, "The Position of Japan in an Awareness on the Matter of 'Inter-Asia'," trans. Aisa Kiyosue, *Inter-Asia Cultural Studies* 2 (3) (2001).

45. Jim Lehrer, *The Special Prisoner* (New York: Random House, 2000), 22.

46. On the topic of "carnival justice," see Katherine Maynard, Jarod Kearney, and James Guimond, *Revenge versus Legality: Wild Justice from Balzac to Clint Eastwood and Abu Ghraib* (Abingdon, UK: Birkbeck Law Press, 2010), 8–15.

47. Lehrer, *The Special Prisoner*, 111–116.

48. Elizabeth Rosner, *Survivor Café: The Legacy of Trauma and the Labyrinth of Memory* (Berkeley: Counterpoint, 2017), 100–101.

49. A. C. Grayling, *Among the Dead Cities: The History and Moral Legacy of the WWII Bombing of Civilians in Germany and Japan* (London: Bloomsbury, 2006), 5–6.

50. In his study of forgiveness, Solomon Schimmel cautions against viewing the practice in binary terms: "Each of the dimensions of forgiveness or non-forgiveness, the emotional, the cognitive, and the behavioral, can vary in intensity and range. Anger, hatred, compassion, and love, though difficult to measure, are not all-or-nothing emotions." Solomon Schimmel, *Wounds Not Healed by Time: The Power of Repentance and Forgiveness* (Oxford: Oxford University Press, 2002), 46. The possibility that forgiveness may be psychologically undone by the forgiver's own burden of guilt is, however, a topic that awaits fuller exploration.

51. Lehrer, *The Special Prisoner*, 158–159.

52. Aaron Lazare makes this same point in his study of apologies in society and culture. Aaron Lazare, *On Apology* (Oxford: Oxford University Press, 2004), 228–229.

53. Lehrer, *The Special Prisoner*, 88.

54. Gi-Wook Shin, "Historical Reconciliation in Northeast Asia: Past Efforts, Future Steps, and the U.S. Role," in *Confronting Memories of World War II: European and Asian Legacies*, eds. Daniel Chirot, Gi-Wook Shin, and Daniel Sneider (Seattle: University of Washington Press, 2014), 161–162; and Janet S. K. Watson, "'A Sideshow to the War in Europe': Nation, Empire, and the British Commemoration of the Pacific War," in *The Pacific War: Aftermaths, Remembrance, and Culture*, eds. Christina Twomey and Ernest Koh (Abingdon, UK: Routledge, 2015), 43.

55. Petra Rau, "Reflections on the Enemy: From Evil Nazis to Good Germans," in *The Edinburgh Companion to Twentieth-Century British and American War Literature*, eds. Adam Piette and Mark Rawlinson (Edinburgh: Edinburgh University Press, 2012), 342.

56. Elizabeth S. Dahl, "Is Japan Facing Its Past? The Case of Japan and Its Neighbors," in *The Age of Apology: Facing Up to the Past*, eds. Mark Gibney, Rhoda E. Howard-Hassmann, Jean-Marc Coicaud, and Niklaus Steiner (Philadelphia: University of Pennsylvania Press, 2008), 250; John Dower, "Triumphal and Tragic Narratives of the War in Asia," in *Living with the Bomb: American and Japanese Cultural Conflicts in the Nuclear Age*, eds. Laura Hein and Mark Selden (New York: M. E. Sharpe, 1997), 44; and Kamila Szczepanska, "Addressing the Allied POW Issue in Japan: The Case of POW Research Network Japan," *Japan Forum* 26 (1) (2014): 94.

57. The attitudes expressed by the Japanese and American characters in Lehrer's narrative are extreme, but one hears visitors' making similar remarks at war memorials and museums; even if they find themselves questioning their prior notions of who was the victim and who the aggressor, they may also invoke a "balancing" example from their own national history, one that they still believe serves to qualify the messages they are receiving. In his study of Japanese visitors to the Arizona memorial, for example, Yujin Yaguchi has noted that a segment of the visitors, while appreciating the educational value of the memorial, state the need for Americans to learn more about Hiroshima and Nagasaki. Yujin Yaguchi, "War Memories across the Pacific: Japanese Visitors at the Arizona Memorial," in *The Unpredictability of the Past: Memories of the Asia-Pacific War in US- East Asian Relations*, ed. Marc Gallicchio (Durham: Duke University Press, 2007), 241–242.

58. Lehrer, *The Special Prisoner*, 19.

59. Lehrer, *The Special Prisoner*, 220–221.

60. The trope of the final letter that comes to an incarcerated man as a form of vindication is by no means confined to American literature. In Momo Iida's story about the American pilot of the plane that undertook weather observation in advance of the *Enola Gay*'s mission, for example, the pilot is committed to a mental hospital where he receives a letter from a philosopher praising his repentance. The plotline mirrors almost perfectly that concerning Watson's "vindication" in *The Special Prisoner*. See Naomi Matsuoka, "The Wrong Stuff: The Hiroshima Pilot in Japanese Fiction," *Comparative Literature Studies* 24 (3) (1987): 268–269.

61. James Dawes, *Evil Men* (Cambridge: Harvard University Press, 2013), 142–143.

62. The novel might also be seen as anticipating a more skeptical turn in public discussions of official apology, an example of which is Gorman Beauchamp, "Apologies All Around: Today's Tendency to Make Amends for the Crimes of History Raises the Question: Where Do We Stop?," *American Scholar* 76 (4) (2007): passim.

63. This observation recurs in scholarly writing as much as it does fiction. As American literary scholar James Dawes found out personally when he interviewed veterans of Japan's war in China, even those who have admitted to the misdeeds of their youth find it irksome to recapitulate these events in front of one whose own national history is decidedly checkered: "It mattered to the veterans that I was a U.S. writer. Americans, they believed, must not be allowed to continue averting their gaze from the filthy details of their wars." Dawes, *Evil Men*, 13.

64. Jerome F. Shapiro, *Atomic Bomb Cinema: The Apocalyptic Imagination on Film* (New York: Routledge, 2011), 55.

5. Scientists and Hibakusha: Project Novels

1. Laura Hein and Mark Selden, "Commemoration and Silence: Fifty Years of Remembering the Bomb in America and Japan," in *Living with the Bomb: American and Japanese Cultural Conflicts in the Nuclear Age*, eds. Laura Hein and Mark Selden (New York: M. E. Sharpe, 1997), 7.

2. George E. Webb, "The Manhattan Project Revealed: Local Press Response to the Atomic Bomb Announcements, August–September 1945," in *The Atomic Bomb and American Society: New Perspectives*, eds. Rosemary B. Mariner and G. Kurt Piehler (Knoxville: University of Tennessee Press, 2009), 45–47.

3. For a study that interlinks all three, see Adam Piette, "The Fictions of Nuclear War, from Hiroshima to Vietnam," in *The Edinburgh Companion to Twentieth-Century British and American War Literature*, eds. Adam Piette and Mark Rawlinson (Edinburgh: Edinburgh University Press, 2012), passim.

4. Guy Hartcup, *The Effects of Science on the Second World War* (Basingstoke, UK: Palgrave Macmillan, 2000), 173–174; and Peter K. Parides, "To Run with the Swift: Vannevar Bush, James Conant, and the Race to the Bomb—How American Science Was Drafted into Wartime Service," in *The Atomic Bomb and American Society: New Perspectives*, eds. Rosemary B. Mariner and G. Kurt Piehler (Knoxville: University of Tennessee Press, 2009), 33.

5. Robert Jacobs, *The Dragon's Tail: Americans Face the Atomic Age* (Amherst: University of Massachusetts Press, 2010), 3.

6. Martha A. Bartter, *The Way to Ground Zero: The Atomic Bomb in American Science Fiction* (Westport: Greenwood Press, 1988), 129.

7. David Seed, *Under the Shadow: The Atomic Bomb and Cold War Narratives* (Kent: Kent State University Press, 2013), 2.

8. Robert Wuthnow, *Be Very Afraid: The Cultural Response to Terror, Pandemics, Environmental Devastation, Nuclear Annihilation, and Other Threats* (New York: Oxford University Press, 2010), 29.

9. For a survey of Oppenheimer biographies, see Lindsey Michael Banco, "The Biographies of J. Robert Oppenheimer: Desert Saint or Destroyer of Worlds," *Biography* 35 (3) (2012): passim.

10. See Daniel Dotson, "Portrayal of Physicists in Literary Works," *CLCWeb: Comparative Literature and Culture* 11 (2) (2009): http://docs.lib.purdue.edu/clcweb/vol11/iss2/5.

11. Paul Boyer, "Exotic Resonances: Hiroshima in American Memory," in *Hiroshima in History and Memory*, ed. Michael J. Hogan (Cambridge: Cambridge University Press, 1996), 182–85.

12. Howard Zinn, "Artists in Times of War," *CLCWeb: Comparative Literature and Culture* 9 (1) (2007): https://docs.lib.purdue.edu/clcweb/vol9/iss1/21/.

13. Robert Jacobs and Mick Broderick, "Nuke York, New York: Nuclear Holocaust in the American Imagination from Hiroshima to 9/11," *Asia-Pacific Journal* 10 (6) (2012): http://apjjf.org/2012/10/11/Robert-Jacobs/3726/article.html.

14. The term "death immersion" originates with Robert Jay Lifton. "Is Hiroshima Our Text?" in *The Future of Immortality and Other Essays for a Nuclear Age*, (New York: Basic Books, 1987), 32.

15. Paul Brians, "Nuclear War in Science Fiction, 1945–59 ('La guerre nucléaire en science-fiction, 1945–59')," *Science Fiction Studies* 11 (3) (1984): 258–259.

16. In the immediate postwar years, some presidential advisors came to the conclusion that the success of the Manhattan Project was the result of qualities of character that were quintessentially American, qualities that were absent elsewhere in the world. See Shane J. Maddock, "Defending the American Way and Containing the Atom," in *The Atomic Bomb in American Society: New Perspectives*, eds. Rosemary B. Mariner and G. Kurt Piehler (Knoxville: University of Tennessee Press, 2009), 123.

17. Joy Kogawa, "Three Deities," in *Literary Environments: Canada and the Old World*, ed. Britta Olinder (Brussels: Peter Lang, 2006), 16.

18. Sheila Johnson, *The Japanese through American Eyes* (Stanford: Stanford University Press, 1988), 39.

19. Walter Hirsch, "The Image of the Scientist in Science Fiction: A Content Analysis," *American Journal of Sociology* 63 (5) (1958): 507–508.

20. Joyce A. Evans, *Celluloid Mushroom Clouds: Hollywood and the Atomic Bomb* (Boulder: Westview Press, 1998), 27–29.

21. Jeffrey Kovac, "Science, Ethics and War: A Pacifist's Perspective," *Science and Engineering Ethics* 19 (2) (2013): 2.

22. R. R. Wilson, "Hiroshima: The Scientists' Social and Political Reaction," *Proceedings of the American Philosophical Society* 140 (3) (1996): 350.

23. Michael A. Day, "Oppenheimer and Rabi: American Cold War Physicists as Public Intellectuals," in *The Atomic Bomb in American Society: New Perspectives*, eds. Rosemary B. Mariner and G. Kurt Piehler (Knoxville: University of Tennessee Press, 2009), 310–311.

24. John T. Dorsey, "The Responsibility of the Scientist in Atomic Bomb Literature," *Comparative Literature Studies* 24 (3) (1987): 277.

25. David K. Hecht, "The Atomic Hero: Robert Oppenheimer and the Making of Scientific Icons in the Early Cold War," *Technology and Culture* 49 (4) (2008): 951.

26. Peggy Rosenthal, "The Nuclear Mushroom Cloud as Cultural Image," *American Literary History* 3 (1) (1991): 66.

27. Martin J. Sherwin, *A World Destroyed: Hiroshima and Its Legacies*, third edition (Stanford: Stanford University Press, 2003), xxiv; and Robert Jacobs, "Dodging Dystopia: The Role of Nuclear Narratives in Averting Global Thermonuclear Warfare," in *Nonkilling History: Shaping Policy with Lessons from the Past*, ed. Antony Adolf (Honolulu: The Center for Global Nonviolence, 2010).

28. Margot Norris, "Dividing the Indivisible: The Fissured Story of the Manhattan Project," *Cultural Critique* 35 (1996): 8.

29. See Christoph Laucht, "An Extraordinary Achievement of the 'American Way': Hollywood and the Americanization of the Making of the Atom Bomb in *Fat Man & Little Boy*," *European Journal of American Culture* 28 (1) (2009): passim.

30. Paul Boyer, *By the Bomb's Early Light: American Thought and Culture at the Dawn of the Atomic Age* (Chapel Hill: University of North Carolina Press, 1994), 250.

31. Upton Sinclair, *O Shepherd, Speak!* (London: T. Werner Laurie, 1949), 334.

32. Peter B. Hales, "The Atomic Sublime," *American Studies* 32 (1) (1991): 16–20.

33. Michael Amrine, *Secret* (Cambridge: Riverside Press, 1950), 46–47.

34. Amrine, *Secret*, 60.

35. Amrine, *Secret*, 96.

36. John T. Dorsey, "Atomic Bomb Literature in Japan and the West," *Neohelicon* 14 (2) (1987): 331.

37. Haakon Chevalier, *The Man Who Would Be God* (London: Jonathan Cape, 1960), 306.

38. George E. Simpson and Neal R. Burger, *Fair Warning* (New York: Delacorte Press, 1980), 170.

39. See Paul Williams, *Race, Ethnicity and Nuclear War: Representations of Nuclear Weapons and Post-Apocalyptic Worlds* (Liverpool, UK: Liverpool University Press, 2011), 196.

40. Judy Barrett Litoff, "'Over the Radio Yesterday I Heard the Starting of Another War': Women's Wartime Correspondence, Hiroshima, Nagasaki, and the End of World War II," in *The Atomic Bomb and American Society: New Perspectives*, eds. Rosemary B. Mariner and G. Kurt Piehler (Knoxville: University of Tennessee Press, 2009), 93–94.

41. Cyndy Hendershot, "Mythical and Modern: Representations of Los Alamos," *Journal of the Southwest* 41 (4) (1999): 478; and Mark Fiege, "The Atomic Scientists, the Sense of Wonder, and the Bomb," *Environmental History* 12 (3) (2007): passim.

42. Mary Anne Schofield, "Lost Almost and Caught between the Fences: The Women of Los Alamos, 1943–1945 and Later," in *The Atomic Bomb in American Society: New Perspectives*, eds. Rosemary B. Mariner and G. Kurt Piehler (Knoxville: University of Tennessee Press, 2009), 65–67.

43. Nora Gallagher, *Changing Light* (New York: Vintage, 2007), 110.

44. Gallagher, *Changing Light*, 5.

45. James Bertram, *The Shadow of a War: A New Zealander in the Far East 1939–1946* (London: Victor Gollancz, 1947), 275–276.

46. Literary scholar Lawrence Jones experienced a recurrent nightmare of nuclear war prior to his move from Oregon to New Zealand in the 1960s, although he makes clear that emigration was as much informed by his disenchantment with the American political climate as the prospect of a nuclear showdown. See Lawrence Jones, "The Mushroom Cloud, the Long White Cloud and the Cloud of Unknowing," *Landfall* 203 (2002): passim.

47. Aldous Huxley, *Ape and Essence* (1948; repr. London: Vintage, 2005), 87–99.

48. John Wyndham, *The Chrysalids* (London: Michael Joseph, 1955), 222.

49. In a retrospective article, Philip Beidler draws attention to the setting of Shute's novel: "A nice geographic touch for the times, in both book and movie, is its setting in Australia, a vivid, interesting place of great appeal to post-World War II Americans. A vigorous young democracy of the land down under, something of a Pacific counterpart or national alter-ego, quaintly British and brawlingly American, it had figured highly in the Pacific War against the Japanese." Philip Beidler, "Remembering *On the Beach*," *War, Literature, and the Arts: An International Journal of the Humanities* 21 (1–2) (2009): 374.

50. Janet Frame, *Intensive Care* (1970; repr. Auckland: Century Hutchinson, 1987), 86.

51. Daniel Cordle, *Late Cold War Literature and Culture: The Nuclear 1980s* (London: Palgrave Macmillan, 2017), 3–4.

52. A. Barrie Pittock, *Beyond Darkness: Nuclear Winter in Australia and New Zealand* (Melbourne: Sun Books, 1987), 132; and Wren Green, Tony Cairns, and Judith Wright, *New Zealand after Nuclear War* (Wellington: New Zealand Planning Council, 1987), 129–132.

53. Kevin Clements, *Back from the Brink: The Creation of a Nuclear-Free New Zealand* (Wellington: Allen and Unwin/Port Nicholson Press, 1988), 108–116.

54. David Lange, *Nuclear Free: The New Zealand Way* (Auckland: Penguin Books, 1990), 115.

55. David M. Abshire, *Preventing World War III: A Realistic Grand Strategy* (New York: Harper & Row, 1988), 121; and James M. McCormick, "The New Zealand–United States Relationship in the Era of Globalization," in *Sovereignty Under Siege? Globalisation And New Zealand*, eds. Robert Patman and Christ Rudd (Aldershot, UK: Ashgate Publishing, 2005), 216.

56. Poul Anderson, "Progress," in *Maurai & Kith* (New York: Tor, 1982), 132–133.

57. Peter Schwenger and John Whittier Treat, "America's Hiroshima, Hiroshima's America," *boundary 2* 21 (1) (1991): 235.

58. Wuthnow, *Be Very Afraid*, 26; Abé Mark Nornes, "Cherry Trees and Corpses: Representations of Violence from WWII," in *The Japan/America Film Wars: WWII Propaganda and its Cultural Contexts*, eds. Abé Mark Nornes and Fukushima Yukio (Chur, Switzerland: Harwood Academic Publishers, 1994), 152.

59. Elaine Scarry, *The Body in Pain: The Making and Unmaking of the World* (Oxford: Oxford University Press, 1985), 62.

60. Jon Hunner, "Reinventing Los Alamos: Code Switching and Suburbia at America's Atomic City," in *Atomic Culture: How We Learned to Stop Worrying and Love the Bomb*, eds. Scott C. Zeman and Michael A. Amundson (Boulder: University Press of Colorado, 2004), 37.

61. Committee for the Compilation of Materials on Damage Caused by the Atomic Bombs in Hiroshima and Nagasaki, *The Impact of the A-Bomb: Hiroshima and Nagasaki, 1945–85*, trans. Eisei Ishikawa, MD and David L. Swain (Tokyo: Iwanami Shoten, 1985); *Hibakusha: Survivors of Hiroshima and Nagasaki*, trans. Gaynor Sekimori (Tokyo: Kōsei Publishing, 1986); and Naomi Shohno, *The Legacy of Hiroshima: Its Past, Our Future*, trans. Tomoko Nakamura (Tokyo: Kōsei Publishing, 1986).

62. In 1989, for example, two films with the title *Black Rain* premiered. The first, released in May, was a Japanese adaptation of Masuji Ibuse's novel of the atomic bombing of Hiroshima; the second, released in September, was an American thriller about a New York City policeman who journeys to Osaka in order to combat a crime syndicate run by a *hibakusha*.

63. Joseph Masco, *The Nuclear Borderlands: The Manhattan Project in Post-Cold War New Mexico* (Princeton: Princeton University Press, 2006), 4.

64. Yuki Miyamoto, "In the Light of Hiroshima: Banalizing Violence and Normalizing Experiences of the Atomic Bombing," in *Reimagining Hiroshima and Nagasaki: Nuclear Humanities in the Post-Cold War*, eds. N. A. J. Taylor and Robert Jacobs (Abingdon, UK: Routledge, 2018), 127.

65. Robert Jacobs, "Reconstructing the Perpetrator's Soul by Reconstructing the Victim's Body: The Portrayal of the 'Hiroshima Maidens' by the Mainstream American Media," *Intersections: Gender and Sexuality in Asia and the Pacific* 24 (2010): http://intersections.anu.edu.au/issue24/jacobs.htm.

66. Edwin Lanham, *The Clock at 8:16* (New York: Doubleday, 1970), 17.

67. Lanham, *The Clock at 8:16*, 259–68.

68. Among the reasons for this gendering is the legacy of World War II-era cultural stereotypes that come to bear on Japanese men and women. As we saw in Chapter 1, combat narratives remain the principal genre for the depiction of Japanese men, and these narratives, in turn, seldom permit any departure from the stereotype of the fanatical militarist. Locked within this genre, Japanese men are hardly ever acknowledged as victims of the atomic bombings. Then there is the gendering of the bomb itself, always an explicitly male device in the language used to describe it. On learning of the successful detonation of the world's first hydrogen bomb in 1952, for example, the physicist Edward Teller declared: "It's a boy." That the "birthing" of the ultimate manifestation of technocultural maleness should inspire creative writers to write the evidence of its arrival onto/within the bodies of female characters suggests, at minimum, that a sexualized world view

has obscured the indiscriminate destruction wrought by the original bombing. Edward Teller, "The Consequences of the Atomic Bomb: The End of the Soviet Union and the Beginning of Environmental Hysteria," in *The Writing on the Cloud: American Culture Confronts the Atomic Bomb*, eds. Alison M. Scott and Christopher D. Geist (Lanham: University Press of America, 1997), 3.

69. James George, *Ocean Roads* (Wellington: Huia, 2006), 79.

70. George, *Ocean Roads*, 42.

71. Elizabeth DeLoughrey, "Satellite Planetarity and the Ends of the Earth," *Public Culture* 26 (2) (2014): 267.

72. George, *Ocean Roads*, 164.

73. George, *Ocean Roads*, 342.

74. One reviewer has pointed out similarities in imagery between George's descriptions of New Mexico and Auckland's sand dunes, arguing that by drawing this parallel, George suggests a shared history between the two places. See Louise O'Brien, "Only Connect," *Dominion Post*, September 30, 2006.

75. Paul Boyer, "Sixty Years and Counting: Nuclear Themes in American Culture, 1945 to the Present," in *The Atomic Bomb in American Society: New Perspectives*, eds. Rosemary B. Mariner and G. Kurt Piehler (Knoxville: University of Tennessee Press, 2009), 3-4.

76. Siobhan Harvey, "The Ghosts of My Life," *NZ Listener*, October 14, 2006, 41.

77. George, *Ocean Roads*, 38.

78. George, *Ocean Roads*, 243.

79. Renee E. Tajima, "Lotus Blossoms Don't Bleed: Images of Asian Women," in *Making Waves: An Anthology of Writings by and About Asian American Women*, ed. Asian Women United (Boston: Beacon Press, 1989), 308.

80. George, *Ocean Roads*, 128-131.

81. Anthony Carrigan, "Postcolonial Disaster, Pacific Nuclearization, and Disabling Environments," *Journal of Literary and Cultural Disability Studies* 4 (3) (2010): 266-268.

82. George, *Ocean Roads*, 202.

83. Scarry, *The Body in Pain*, 64.

84. Robert Jay Lifton, "Hiroshima in America: Fifty Years of Denial," in *The Writing on the Cloud: American Culture Confronts the Atomic Bomb*, eds. Alison M. Scott and Christopher D. Geist (Lanham: University Press of America, 1997), 205.

85. Sherrill Grace, *Landscapes of War and Memory: The Two World Wars in Canadian Literature and the Arts, 1977-2007* (Edmonton: University of Alberta Press, 2014), 321.

86. The character Emiko is wholly fictional. Of the original Hiroshima Maidens, all returned to Japan and only one subsequently made the United States her home.

87. Böll's apologetics might recall the real-life position of project scientist Edward Teller, sometimes called "the father of the hydrogen bomb," who

participated in the same conference in 1995 as Robert Jay Lifton and delivered a robust defense of his life's work that contrasted markedly with Lifton's stance.

88. Dennis Bock, *The Ash Garden* (New York: Vintage International, 2003), 29.

89. This section of Bock's novel is a thinly veiled account of an episode from the TV show *This Is Your Life*, in which Rev. Kiyoshi Tanimoto met a number of guests including Robert A. Lewis, copilot of the *Enola Gay*. The episode aroused a number of reactions from public commentators, recalled in the opening of Rodney Barker's *The Hiroshima Maidens* (1985) and in Chapter 8 of British journalist Anne Chisholm's *Faces of Hiroshima* (1985). See Peter J. Kuznick, "Defending the Indefensible: The Tragic Life of Hiroshima Pilot Paul Tibbets, Jr.," in *The Unfinished Atomic Bomb: Shadows and Reflections*, eds. David Lowe, Cassandra Atherton, and Alyson Miller (Lanham: Lexington Books, 2018), 23–24.

90. Bock, *The Ash Garden*, 220.

91. Theodore Goossen, "Writing the Pacific War in the Twenty-First Century: Dennis Bock, Rui Umezawa, and Kerri Sakamoto," *Canadian Literature* 179 (2003): 57.

92. Literature scholar Marianna Torgovnick echoed Lifton's observation fifteen years later, stating that "U.S. cultural memory has exercised extraordinary means to evade a shared memory of Hiroshima and Nagasaki almost like an animate being building up a plethora of mutually reinforcing defensive psychological formations." Marianna Torgovnick, "Gone Nuclear: Representing Hiroshima and Nagasaki in the United States," *Nanzan Review of American Studies* 32 (2010): 36.

93. Bock, *The Ash Garden*, 227.

94. The disparity between the project scientist's self-image and his public representation was experienced by J. Robert Oppenheimer who, by the mid-1960s, had lost control of his story and found that the ethics and motivation he had at Los Alamos had been overlooked in the work of literary writers. See David K. Hecht, *Storytelling and Science: Rewriting Oppenheimer in the Nuclear Age* (Amherst: University of Massachusetts Press, 2015), 109.

95. Bock, *The Ash Garden*, 190.

96. Bock, *The Ash Garden*, 207.

97. Stephen Cherry, *Healing Agony: Re-Imagining Forgiveness* (London: Bloomsbury Continuum, 2012), 159.

98. Bock, *The Ash Garden*, 251.

99. Bock, *The Ash Garden*, 262.

100. Tom Engelhardt, *The End of Victory Culture: Cold War America and the Disillusioning of a Generation* (New York: Basic Books, 1995), 6.

101. Laura Hein, "Learning about Patriotism, Decency, and the Bomb," in *Living with the Bomb: American and Japanese Cultural Conflicts in the Nuclear Age*, eds. Laura Hein and Mark Selden (New York: M. E. Sharpe, 1997), 285.

102. James J. Farrell, "Making (Common) Sense of the Bomb in the First Nuclear War," *American Studies* 36 (2) (1995): 7.

Coda

1. Alice Te Punga Somerville, "Where Oceans Come From," *Comparative Literature* 69, (1) (2017): 27.
2. William Manchester, "Okinawa: The Bloodiest Battle of All," in *The Best American Essays of the Century*, eds. Joyce Carol Oates and Robert Atwan (New York: Houghton Mifflin, 2000), 500.
3. James Bertram, *The Shadow of a War: A New Zealander in the Far East, 1939–1946* (London: Victor Gollancz, 1947), 70.
4. My study has focused on literary sources, but the same observation holds true when it comes to documentation pertaining to the fiftieth anniversary commemorations. See, for example, Janet S. K. Watson, "'A Sideshow to the War in Europe': Nation, Empire, and the British Commemoration of the Pacific War," in *The Pacific War: Aftermaths, Remembrance, and Culture*, eds. Christina Twomey and Ernest Koh (Abingdon, UK: Routledge, 2015), 33–34.
5. Sigeru Huzinaga and Kiyomi Kutsuzawa, "Nazi Holocaust and Atomic Holocaust: Transforming Spiritual Crisis into an Ideology of Humanity," *Review of Japanese Culture and Society* 11, (12) (1999): 43–44.
6. George MacDonald Fraser, *Quartered Safe Out Here: A Recollection of the War in Burma* (1993; repr. London: HarperCollins, 2000), 323.
7. Jon Mitchell, *Poisoning the Pacific: The US Military's Secret Dumping of Plutonium, Chemical Weapons, and Agent Orange* (Lanham: Rowman & Littlefield, 2020), 46–47.
8. Greg Dvorak, "Who Closed the Sea? Archipelagoes of Amnesia between the United States and Japan," *Pacific Historical Review* 83, (2) (2012): 351; and Yu-Fang Cho, "Nuclear Diffusion: Notes toward Reimagining Reproductive Justice in a Militarized Asia Pacific," *Amerasia Journal* 41, (3) (2015): 9.
9. Elaine Scarry, *The Body in Pain: The Making and Unmaking of the World* (New York: Oxford University Press, 1985), 4.
10. Micronesians experienced racial prejudice under the Japanese but also had work, consumer, and travel opportunities that integrated them more fully into a Japanese-run Pacific economy than would be the case under an American (non)equivalent. See Lina Poyer, Suzanne Falgout, and Laurence M. Carucci, "The Impact of the Pacific War on Modern Micronesian Identity," in *Globalization and Culture Change in the Pacific Islands*, ed. Victoria S. Lockwood (Upper Saddle River: Pearson Education, 2004), 308–309.
11. Greg Dvorak, *Coral and Concrete: Remembering Kwajalein Atoll between Japan, America, and the Marshall Islands* (Honolulu: University of Hawai'i Press, 2018), 25.
12. The multiple layers of colonial mistreatment endured by Pacific Islanders is matched by the disregard for island communities shown by colonialist powers in the Indian Ocean, a case in point being the US-British removal of the Chagossians from Diego Garcia to Mauritius. For an impassioned statement on their behalf, see David Vine, *Island of Shame: The Secret History of*

the U.S. Military Base on Diego Garcia (Princeton: Princeton University Press, 2009), 18.

13. Albert Wendt, Introduction to *Nuanua: Pacific Writing in English since 1980*, ed. Albert Wendt (Honolulu: University of Hawai'i Press, 1995), 2.

14. Geographer James E. Randall notes that almost all of the most compelling works of island fiction have been turned into feature films at some point, which is likewise the case for works set during the Pacific War. James E. Randall, *An Introduction to Island Studies* (Lanham: Rowman & Littlefield, 2021), 69. See also Greg Jericho, "War in the Tropics," *etropic* 4 (2005): passim.

15. Stephen J. May, *Michener's South Pacific* (Gainesville: University Press of Florida, 2011), 117.

16. Epeli Hau'ofa, "Pasts to Remember," in *We Are the Ocean: Selected Works* (Honolulu: University of Hawai'i Press, 2008), 61.

17. Dorothy F. Lane, *The Island as Site of Resistance: An Examination of Caribbean and New Zealand Texts* (New York: Peter Lang, 1995), 4.

18. Micronesians routinely confront perspectives that refer to their lands as 'unsinkable aircraft carriers.' See Elizabeth DeLoughrey, "Island Studies and the US Militarism of the Pacific," in *The Challenges of Island Studies*, ed. Ayano Ginoza (Singapore: Springer Nature, 2020), 33.

19. Epeli Hau'ofa, "Our Sea of Islands," in *We Are the Ocean: Selected Works* (Honolulu: University of Hawai'i Press, 2008), 31.

20. Michelle Keown, *Pacific Islands Writing: The Postcolonial Literatures of Aotearoa/New Zealand and Oceania* (Oxford: Oxford University Press, 2007), 86–87; and Paul Sharrad, "South Pacific," in *The Novel in Australia, Canada, New Zealand, and the South Pacific Since 1950*, eds. Coral A. Howells, Paul Sharrad, and Gerry Turcotte (New York: Oxford University Press, 2017), 134.

21. John Pule, "The Shark That Ate the Sun," in *Nuanua: Pacific Writing in English since 1980*, ed. Albert Wendt (Honolulu: University of Hawai'i Press, 1995), 166.

22. Cathie Dunsford, *Manawa Toa: Heart Warrior* (North Melbourne, Australia: Spinifex, 2000), 33, 49.

23. Michelle Keown, "Waves of Destruction: Nuclear Imperialism and Anti-Nuclear Protest in the Indigenous Literatures of the Pacific," *Journal of Postcolonial Writing* 54, (5) (2018): 595–597.

24. Paul Sharrad, "Imagining the Pacific," *Meanjin* 49, (4) (1990): 599.

25. Albert Wendt, "Towards a New Oceania," *Mana Review* 1, (1) (1976): 58; and B. J. Moore-Gilbert, "'Gorgeous East' versus 'Land of Regrets,'" in *Orientalism: A Reader*, ed. A. L. Macfie (Edinburgh: Edinburgh University Press, 2000), 275–276.

26. Robert C. Kiste, review of *Meḷaḷ: A Novel of the Pacific*, by Robert Barclay, *Contemporary Pacific* 16, (1) (2004): 208.

27. Greg Dvorak, "'The Martial Islands': Making Marshallese Masculinities between American and Japanese Militarism," *Contemporary Pacific* 20, (1) (2008): 58–59.

28. The relationship of Native Americans to lands used by the Manhattan Project was similarly complex. The location of the Hanford plant interfered with traditional fishing areas, while at Los Alamos at least one project scientist, William Ogle, was of Native American descent. See George E. Webb, "The Manhattan Project Revealed: Local Press Response to the Atomic Bomb Announcements, August–September 1945," in *The Atomic Bomb and American Society: New Perspectives*, eds. Rosemary B. Mariner and G. Kurt Piehler (Knoxville: University of Tennessee Press, 2009), 55; and Todd A. Hanson, "Exploding the Strangelove Myth: Cold War Nuclear Weapons Work and the Testing Times of William Ogle," in *The Atomic Bomb and American Society: New Perspectives*, eds. Rosemary B. Mariner and G. Kurt Piehler (Knoxville: University of Tennessee Press, 2009), 276.

29. Simone Oettli-Van Delden, "Problematizing the Postcolonial: Deterritorialization and Cultural Identity in Robert Barclay's *Melal*," *World Literature Written in English* 39, (2) (2002): 40–41.

30. Robert Barclay, *Meḷaḷ: A Novel of the Pacific* (Honolulu: University of Hawai'i Press, 2002), 8–9.

31. Barclay, *Meḷaḷ*, 5.

32. Barclay, *Meḷaḷ*, 21.

33. Barclay, *Meḷaḷ*, 23–24.

34. Barclay, *Meḷaḷ*, 86.

35. Elizabeth DeLoughrey, *Routes and Roots: Navigating Caribbean and Pacific Island Literatures* (Honolulu: University of Hawai'i Press, 2007), 96.

36. Mimi Sheller, "Archipelagoes as the Fractal Fringe of Coloniality: Demilitarizing Caribbean and Pacific Islands," in *Contemporary Archipelagic Thinking: Toward New Comparative Methodologies and Disciplinary Formations*, eds. Michelle Stephens and Yolanda Martínez-San Miguel (Lanham: Rowman & Littlefield, 2020), 288.

37. David Gugin, "Beyond the Tenth Horizon: Robert Barclay's *Melal*," *Pacific Asia Inquiry* 8, (1) (2017): 17.

38. Greg Dvorak, "Oceanizing American Studies," *American Quarterly* 67, (3) (2015): 612–613.

39. Naoto Sudo, *Nanyo-Orientalism: Japanese Representations of the Pacific* (Amherst: Cambria Press, 2010), 183.

Bibliography

Abney, David Lawrence. "Japan Bashing: A History of America's Anti-Japanese Acts, Attitudes, and Laws." PhD dissertation. Arizona State University, 1995.
Abshire, David M. *Preventing World War III: A Realistic Grand Strategy*. New York: Harper and Row, 1988.
Adams, Jon Robert. *Male Armor: The Soldier-Hero in Contemporary Culture*. Charlottesville: University of Virginia Press, 2008.
Aichinger, Peter. *The American Soldier in Fiction, 1880–1963: A History of Attitudes toward Warfare and the Military Establishment*. Ames: Iowa State University Press, 1975.
Aldridge, John W. "The War Writers Ten Years Later." In *Contemporary American Novelists*. Edited by Harry T. Moore. Carbondale: Southern Illinois University Press, 1964.
Alpers, Benjamin L. *Dictators, Democracy, and American Public Culture: Envisioning the Totalitarian Enemy, 1920s 1950s*. Chapel Hill: University of North Carolina Press, 2003.
Ampikaipakan, Umapagan, and Johanan Sen. "Techno-Orientalism." *What The Flick*, podcast audio, March 18, 2012. http://www.bfm.my/wtf-techno orientalism-1703.html.
Amrine, Michael. *Secret*. Cambridge: Riverside Press, 1950.
Anderson, Poul. "Progress." In *Maurai & Kith*. New York: Tor, 1982.
Arnold, Robert F. "Termination or Transformation? The 'Terminator' Films and Recent Changes in the U.S. Auto Industry." *Film Quarterly*, Vol. 52 (1) (1998): 20–30.
Atkinson, David C. *The Burden of White Supremacy: Containing Asian Migration in the British Empire and the United States*. Chapel Hill: University of North Carolina Press, 2016.
Auden, W. H., and Christopher Isherwood. *Journey to a War* [1939]. Reprint, New York: Octagon, 1972.
Axelsson, Arne. "Fun as Hell: War and Humor in Some Post–World War II American Novels." *Studia Neophilologica*, Vol. 54 (2) (1982): 263–286.
Balaza, Charles. *Life as an American Prisoner of War of the Japanese*. Fairfield: 1st Books, 2002.

Baldacchino, Godfrey. "Islands as Novelty Sites." *Geographical Review*, Vol. 97 (2) (2007): 165–174.
Banco, Lindsey Michael. "The Biographies of J. Robert Oppenheimer: Desert Saint or Destroyer of Worlds." *Biography*, Vol. 35 (3) (2012): 492–515.
Barclay, Robert. *Meḷaḷ: A Novel of the Pacific*. Honolulu: University of Hawai'i Press, 2002.
Barnard, Debbie. "Serving the Master: Cannibalism and Transoceanic Representations of Cultural Identity." *International Journal of Francophone Studies*, Vol. 8 (3) (2005): 321–339.
Bartter, Martha A. *The Way to Ground Zero: The Atomic Bomb in American Science Fiction*. Westport: Greenwood Press, 1988.
Baskett, Michael. "Dying for a Laugh: Post-1945 Japanese Service Comedies." *Historical Journal of Film, Radio and Television*, Vol. 23 (4) (2003): 291–310.
Beauchamp, Gorman. "Apologies All Around: Today's Tendency to Make Amends for the Crimes of History Raises the Question: Where Do We Stop?" *American Scholar*, Vol. 76 (4) (2007): 83–93.
Beaumont, Joan. "Prisoners of War in Australian National Memory." In *Prisoners of War, Prisoners of Peace: Captivity, Homecoming and Memory in World War II*. Edited by Barbara Hately-Broad. London: Berg, 2005.
———. "Rank, Privilege, and Prisoners of War." *War and Society*, Vol. 1 (1) (1983): 67–94.
Beidler, Philip. "Remembering *On the Beach*." *War, Literature, and the Arts: An International Journal of the Humanities*, Vol. 21 (1–2) (2009): 370–382.
Beidler, Philip D. "*South Pacific* and American Remembering; or, 'Josh, We're Going to Buy This Son of a Bitch!'" *Journal of American Studies*, Vol. 27 (2) (1993): 207–222.
Bell, Pearl K. "The Wars of James Jones." *Commentary*, Vol. 65 (4) (1978): 90–92.
Benedict, Ruth. *The Chrysanthemum and the Sword: Patterns of Japanese Culture* [1946]. Reprint, Boston: Mariner Books, 1989.
Bennett, Judith A. *Natives and Exotics: World War II and Environment in the Southern Pacific*. Honolulu: University of Hawai'i Press, 2009.
Berenstein, Rhona J. "White Heroines and Hearts of Darkness: Race, Gender and Disguise in 1930s Jungle Films." *Film History*, Vol. 6 (3) (1994): 314–339.
Bertram, James. *The Shadow of a War: A New Zealander in the Far East, 1939–1946*. London: Victor Gollancz, 1947.
Bishop, Peter. *The Myth of Shangri-La: Tibet, Travel-Writing and the Western Creation of Sacred Landscape*. Berkeley: University of California Press, 1989.
Blaskiewicz, Robert. "James Jones on Guadalcanal." *War, Literature, and the Arts*, Vol. 20 (1–2) (2008): 275–292.
Blouin, Michael J. *Japan and the Cosmopolitan Gothic: Specters of Modernity*. New York: Palgrave Macmillan, 2013.
Bock, Dennis. *The Ash Garden*. New York: Vintage International, 2003.

Bodnar, John. *The "Good War" in American Memory*. Baltimore: Johns Hopkins University Press, 2010.

Boulting, David. "Lethal Enclosure: Masculinity under Fire in James Jones's *The Thin Red Line*." In *Performing Masculinity*. Edited by Rainer Emig and Antony Rowland. Basingstoke, UK: Palgrave Macmillan, 2010.

Bourke, Joanna. *An Intimate History of Killing: Face-to-Face Killing in Twentieth-Century Warfare*. New York: Basic Books, 1999.

Bourke, Roger. *Prisoners of the Japanese: Literary Imagination and the Prisoner-of-War Experience*. St. Lucia: University of Queensland Press, 2006.

Bowman, Peter. *Beach Red*. London: Michael Joseph, 1946.

Boxwell, David A. "Orientalism." In *American History through Literature: 1870–1920*, Volume 2. Edited by Tom Quirk and Gary Scharnhorst. Farmington Hills: Thomson Gale, 2006.

Boyer, Paul. *By the Bomb's Early Light: American Thought and Culture at the Dawn of the Atomic Age*. Chapel Hill: University of North Carolina Press, 1994.

———. "Exotic Resonances: Hiroshima in American Memory." In *Hiroshima in History and Memory*. Edited by Michael J. Hogan. Cambridge: Cambridge University Press, 1996.

———. "Sixty Years and Counting: Nuclear Themes in American Culture, 1945 to the Present." In *The Atomic Bomb in American Society: New Perspectives*. Edited by Rosemary B. Mariner and G. Kurt Piehler. Knoxville: University of Tennessee Press, 2009.

Braithwaite, Errol. *An Affair of Men*. London: Collins, 1961.

Brantley, Jenny. "Clorox the Dishes and Hide the Books: A Defense of *Snow Falling on Cedars*." In *Censored Books*, Volume 2, *Critical Viewpoints, 1985–2000*. Edited by Nicholas J. Karolides. Lanham: Scarecrow Press, 2002.

Braudy, Leo. "Flags of Our Fathers/Letters from Iwo Jima." *Film Quarterly*, Vol. 60 (4) (2007): 16–23.

Brawley, Sean, and Chris Dixon. *Hollywood's South Seas and the Pacific War: Searching for Dorothy Lamour*. New York: Palgrave Macmillan, 2012.

———. "Searching for Dorothy Lamour: War and Sex in the South Pacific, 1941–45." *Australasian Journal of American Studies*, Vol. 18 (1) (1999): 3–18.

Brawley, Sean, Chris Dixon, and Beatrice Trefalt. *Competing Voices from the Pacific War: Fighting Words*. Santa Barbara: Greenwood Press, 2009.

Brians, Paul. "Nuclear War in Science Fiction, 1945–59 ('La guerre nucléaire en science-fiction, 1945–59')." *Science Fiction Studies*, Vol. 11 (3) (1984): 253–263.

Brocker, Susan. *Dreams of Warriors*. Auckland: HarperCollins, 2010.

Bronfenbrenner, Martin. "Japan-Bashing: A View from 'Over There.'" *Challenge*, Vol. 28 (6) (1986): 58–61.

Broyles, William Jr. "Why Men Love War." In *The Vietnam Reader*. Edited by Walter Capps. New York: Routledge, 1991. Article originally published in 1984.

Buckley, Christopher. "Megabashing Japan: World War II Wasn't Half Enough for Tom Clancy." *The New York Times Book Review*, October 28, 1994.
Buruma, Ian. *A Tokyo Romance: A Memoir*. London: Atlantic Books, 2018.
———. "Wake Up, America." In *The Missionary and the Libertine: Love and War in East and West*. New York: Vintage, 2001.
Cameron, Craig M. *American Samurai: Myth, Imagination, and the Conduct of Battle in the First Marine Division, 1941–1951*. New York: Cambridge University Press, 1994.
Capote, Truman. *Breakfast at Tiffany's and Three Stories* [1958]. Reprint, New York: Vintage, 1993.
Carr, Gilly, and Keir Reeves. "Islands of War, Islands of Memory." In *Heritage and Memory of War: Responses from Small Islands*. Edited by Gilly Carr and Keir Reeves. New York: Routledge, 2015.
Carrigan, Anthony. "Postcolonial Disaster, Pacific Nuclearization, and Disabling Environments." *Journal of Literary and Cultural Disability Studies*, Vol. 4 (3) (2010): 266–268.
Carter, Steven Ray. "James Jones, an American Master: A Study of His Mystical, Philosophical, Social, and Artistic Views." PhD dissertation. Ohio State University, 1975.
Caruth, Cathy. Introduction to *Trauma: Explorations in Memory*. Edited by Cathy Caruth. Baltimore: Johns Hopkins University Press, 1995.
Casadei, Alberto. "The Dead Hero, the Dead Body: Anti-Epic and Research of Meaning in the Fictional Representation of World War II." In *Memories and Representations of War: The Case of World War I and World War II*. Edited by Elena Lamberti and Vita Fortunati. Amsterdam: Rodopi, 2009.
Catran, Wendy. *The Swap*. South Melbourne, Australia: Lothian Books, 2004.
Chen, Fu-jen, and Su-lin Yu. "Reclaiming the Southwest: A Traumatic Space in the Japanese American Internment Narrative." *Journal of the Southwest*, Vol. 47 (4) (2005): 551–570.
Cheng, Emily. "Meat and the Millennium: Transnational Politics of Race and Gender in Ruth Ozeki's *My Year of Meats*." *Journal of Asian American Studies*, Vol. 12 (2) (June 2009): 191–220.
Cherry, Stephen. *Healing Agony: Re-Imagining Forgiveness*. London: Bloomsbury Continuum, 2012.
Cheung, Floyd D. "Imagining Danger, Imagining Nation: Postcolonial Discourse in *Rising Sun* and *Stargate*." *Jouvert: A Journal of Postcolonial Studies*, Vol. 2 (2) (1998). https://legacy.chass.ncsu.edu/jouvert/v2i2/CHEUNG.HTM.
Cheung, King-Kok. *Articulate Silences: Hisaye Yamamoto, Maxine Hong Kingston, Joy Kogawa*. Ithaca: Cornell University Press, 1993.
Chevalier, Haakon. *The Man Who Would Be God*. London: Jonathan Cape, 1960.
Childers, Sam. *Another Man's War: The True Story of One Man's Battle to Save Children in the Sudan*. Nashville: Thomas Nelson, 2009.

Chin, Frank, and Jeffrey Paul Chan, "Racist Love." In *Seeing Through Shuck*. Edited by Richard Kostelanetz. New York: Ballantine Books, 1972.

Chiu, Monica. "Postnational Globalization and (En)gendered Meat Production in Ruth L. Ozeki's *My Year of Meats*." *LIT: Literature Interpretation Theory*, Vol. 12 (1) (2001): 99–128.

Cho, Yu-Fang. "Nuclear Diffusion: Notes toward Reimagining Reproductive Justice in a Militarized Asia Pacific." *Amerasia Journal*, Vol. 41 (3) (2015): 1–24.

Clements, Kevin. *Back from the Brink: The Creation of a Nuclear-Free New Zealand*. Wellington: Allen and Unwin/Port Nicholson Press, 1988.

Coleman, Robin R. *Horror Noire: Blacks in American Horror Films from the 1890s to Present*. New York: Routledge, 2011.

Committee for the Compilation of Materials on Damage Caused by the Atomic Bombs in Hiroshima and Nagasaki. *The Impact of the A-Bomb: Hiroshima and Nagasaki, 1945–85*. Translated by Eisei Ishikawa, MD and David L. Swain. Tokyo: Iwanami Shoten, 1985.

Corbett, P. Scott. "In the Eye of the Hurricane: Americans in Japanese Custody during World War II." In *Forgotten Captives in Japanese Occupied Asia*. Edited by Kevin Blackburn and Karl Hack. Abingdon, UK: Routledge: 2008.

Cordle, Daniel. *Late Cold War Literature and Culture: The Nuclear 1980s*. London: Palgrave Macmillan, 2017.

Cornea, Christine. "Techno-Orientalism and the Postmodern Subject." In *Screen Methods: Comparative Readings in Film Studies*. Edited by Jacqueline Furby and Karen Randell. London: Wallflower Press, 2005.

Cornyetz, Nina. "The Meat Manifesto: Ruth Ozeki's Performative Poetics." *Women and Performance*, Vol. 12 (1) (2001): 207–224.

Cosgrove, Denis. *Geography and Vision: Seeing, Imagining and Representing the World*. London: I. B. Tauris, 2008.

Crang, Mike. "Travel/Tourism." In *Cultural Geography: A Critical Dictionary of Key Concepts*. Edited by David Atkinson, Peter Jackson, and David Sibley. London: I. B. Tauris, 2005.

Crawford, John. "A Campaign on Two Fronts." In *Kia Kaha: New Zealand in the Second World War*. Edited by John Crawford. Auckland: Oxford University Press, 2000.

Crichton, Michael. *Rising Sun*. New York: Arrow Books, 1992.

Crocombe, Ron. *Asia in the Pacific Islands: Replacing the West*. Suva, Fiji: IPS Publications, 2007.

Cull, Nicholas J. "'Great Escapes': 'Englishness' and the Prisoner of War Genre." *Film History*, Vol. 14 (3–4) (2002): 282–295.

Dahl, Elizabeth S. "Is Japan Facing Its Past? The Case of Japan and Its Neighbors." In *The Age of Apology: Facing up to the Past*. Edited by Mark Gibney, Rhoda E. Howard-Hassmann, Lean-Marc Coicaud, and Niklaus Steiner. Philadelphia: University of Pennsylvania Press, 2008.

Darman, Peter. *Posters of World War II*. London: Brown Reference Group, 2008.
Darnell, Doreen. "Wendy Catran." *Talespinner*, Vol. 19 (May 2005): 16–17.
Davis, Christie. "Humour Is Not a Strategy in War." *Journal of European Studies*, Vol. 31 (3–4) (2001): 395–412.
Davis, Madison J. "Interpreting the East to the West." *World Literature Today*, Vol. 80 (6) (2006): 13–15.
Dawes, James. *Evil Men*. Cambridge: Harvard University Press, 2013.
Day, Michael A. "Oppenheimer and Rabi: American Cold War Physicists as Public Intellectuals." In *The Atomic Bomb in American Society: New Perspectives*. Edited by Rosemary B. Mariner and G. Kurt Piehler. Knoxville: University of Tennessee Press, 2009.
D'Cruz, Doreen, and John C. Ross. *The Lonely and the Alone: The Poetics of Isolation in New Zealand Fiction*. Amsterdam: Rodopi, 2011.
DeLoughrey, Elizabeth. "Island Studies and the US Militarism of the Pacific." In *The Challenges of Island Studies*. Edited by Ayano Ginoza. Singapore: Springer Nature, 2020.
———. *Routes and Roots: Navigating Caribbean and Pacific Island Literatures*. Honolulu: University of Hawai'i Press, 2007.
———. "Satellite Planetarity and the Ends of the Earth." *Public Culture*, Vol. 26 (2) (2014): 257–280.
Dickstein, Morris. *Leopards in the Temple: The Transformation of American Fiction 1945–1970*. Cambridge: Harvard University Press, 2002.
Dodman, Trevor. "'Going All to Pieces': *A Farewell to Arms* as Trauma Narrative." *Twentieth Century Literature*, Vol. 52 (3) (2006): 249–274.
Dorsey, John T. "Atomic Bomb Literature in Japan and the West." *Neohelicon*, Vol. 14 (2) (1987): 325–334.
———. "The Responsibility of the Scientist in Atomic Bomb Literature." *Comparative Literature Studies*, Vol. 24 (3) (1987): 277–290.
Dotson, Daniel. "Portrayal of Physicists in Literary Works." *CLCWeb: Comparative Literature and Culture*, Vol. 11 (2) (2009). http://docs.lib.purdue.edu/clcweb/vol11/iss2/5.
Dower, John. "Triumphal and Tragic Narratives of the War in Asia." In *Living with the Bomb: American and Japanese Cultural Conflicts in the Nuclear Age*. Edited by Laura Hein and Mark Selden. New York: M. E. Sharpe, 1997.
———. *War without Mercy: Race and Power in the Pacific War*. New York: Pantheon, 1987.
Doyle, Laura. "Inter-Imperiality and Literary Studies in the Longer *Durée*." *PMLA*, Vol. 130 (2) (2015): 336–347.
Duncan, Patti. *Tell This Silence: Asian American Women Writers and the Politics of Speech*. Iowa City: University of Iowa Press, 2004.
Dunn, Kevin. "Lights . . . Camera . . . Africa: Images of Africa and Africans in Western Popular Films of the 1930s." *African Studies Review*, Vol. 39 (1) (1996): 149–175.

Dunsford, Cathie. *Manawa Toa: Heart Warrior*. North Melbourne, Australia: Spinifex, 2000.

Dvorak, Greg. *Coral and Concrete: Remembering Kwajalein Atoll between Japan, America, and the Marshall Islands*. Honolulu: University of Hawai'i Press, 2018.

———. "'The Martial Islands': Making Marshallese Masculinities between American and Japanese Militarism." *Contemporary Pacific*, Vol. 20 (1) (2008): 55–86.

———. "Oceanizing American Studies." *American Quarterly*, Vol. 67 (3) (2015): 609–617.

———. "Who Closed the Sea? Archipelagoes of Amnesia between the United States and Japan." *Pacific Historical Review*, Vol. 83 (2) (2012): 350–372.

Edkins, Jenny. *Trauma and the Memory of Politics*. Cambridge: Cambridge University Press, 2003.

Eldred-Grigg, Stevan, and Hugh Eldred-Grigg. *Phoney Wars: New Zealand Society in the Second World War*. Dunedin, New Zealand: Otago University Press, 2017.

Elleman, Bruce. *Japanese-American Civilian Prisoner Exchanges and Detention Camps, 1941–45*. New York: Routledge, 2006.

Engelhardt, Tom. *The End of Victory Culture: Cold War America and the Disillusioning of a Generation*. New York: Basic Books, 1995.

Erikson, Hal. *Military Combat Films: A Critical Survey and Filmography of Hollywood Releases since 1918*. Jefferson: McFarland, 2012.

Erikson, Kai. *A New Species of Trouble: The Human Experience of Modern Disasters*. New York: Norton, 1994.

Evans, Joyce A. *Celluloid Mushroom Clouds: Hollywood and the Atomic Bomb*. Boulder: Westview Press, 1998.

Evans, Patrick. *The Long Forgetting: Post-Colonial Literary Culture in New Zealand*. Christchurch: Canterbury University Press, 2007.

Ewing, Wayne, dir. *A Gathering of Men*. Arlington: PBS, 1990.

Fairburn, Miles. "Is There a Good Case for New Zealand Exceptionalism?" In *Disputed Histories: Imagining New Zealand's Pasts*. Edited by Tony Ballantyne and Brian Moloughney. Dunedin, New Zealand: Otago University Press, 2006.

Farber, David, and Beth Bailey. "The Fighting Man as Tourist: The Politics of Tourist Culture in Hawaii during World War II." *Pacific Historical Review*, Vol. 65 (4) (1996): 641–660.

Farrell, James J. "Making (Common) Sense of the Bomb in the First Nuclear War." *American Studies*, Vol. 36 (2) (1995): 5–41.

Farrell, Kirby. *Post-Traumatic Culture: Injury and Interpretation in the Nineties*. Baltimore: Johns Hopkins University Press, 1998.

Fenrich, Laura. "Mass Death in Miniature: How Americans Became Victims of the Bomb." In *Living with the Bomb: American and Japanese Cultural Conflicts in the Nuclear Age*. Edited by Laura Hein and Mark Selden. New York: M. E. Sharpe, 1997.

Fiege, Mark. "The Atomic Scientists, the Sense of Wonder, and the Bomb." *Environmental History*, Vol. 12 (3) (2007): 578–613.
Field, Norma. *In the Realm of a Dying Emperor: Japan at Century's End*. New York: Pantheon, 1991.
———. "War and Apology: Japan, Asia, the Fiftieth, and After." *positions: East Asia Cultures Critique*, Vol. 5 (1) (1997): 1–51.
Fielder, Brigitte N. "Animal Humanism: Race, Species, and Affective Kinship in Nineteenth-Century Abolitionism." *American Quarterly*, Vol. 65 (3) (2013): 487–514.
Fish, Cheryl J. "The Toxic Body Politic: Ethnicity, Gender, and Corrective Eco-Justice in Ruth Ozeki's *My Year of Meats* and Judith Helfand and Daniel Gold's *Blue Vinyl*." *MELUS*, Vol. 34 (2) (2009): 43–62.
Ford, Jamie. *Hotel on the Corner of Bitter and Sweet*. London: Allison and Busby, 2009.
Fox, Alistair. *The Ship of Dreams: Masculinity in Contemporary New Zealand Fiction*. Dunedin, New Zealand: Otago University Press, 2008.
Frame, Janet. *Intensive Care* [1970]. Reprint, Auckland: Century Hutchinson, 1987.
Francis, Gavin. *Island Dreams: Mapping an Obsession*. Edinburgh: Canongate, 2020.
Fraser, George MacDonald. *Quartered Safe Out Here: A Recollection of the War in Burma* [1993]. Reprint, London: HarperCollins, 2000.
Fujitani, Takashi. "Ethnic and Colonial Soldiers and the Politics of Disavowal." In *Race for Empire: Koreans as Japanese and Japanese as Americans during World War II*. Edited by Takashi Fujitani. Berkeley: University of California Press, 2011.
Fussell, Paul. *The Great War and Modern Memory*. New York: Oxford University Press, 1975.
———. *Wartime: Understanding and Behavior in the Second World War*, revised edition. New York: Oxford University Press, 1990.
Gallagher, Nora. *Changing Light*. New York: Vintage, 2007.
Gandal, Keith. *The Gun and the Pen: Hemingway, Fitzgerald, Faulkner, and the Fiction of Mobilization*. New York: Oxford University Press, 2008.
George, James. *Ocean Roads*. Wellington: Huia, 2006.
Gibson, William. Interview. *Time Out*, October 6, 1993.
Glass, Ira, dir. "Nummi." *This American Life*. Aired July 7, 2015, on PRX.
Goldstein, Laurence. "'The Imagination Problem': Winfield Townley Scott and the American Wars." *War, Literature, and the Arts*, Vol. 14 (1–2) (2002): 59–77.
Goossen, Theodore. "Writing the Pacific War in the Twenty-First Century: Dennis Bock, Rui Umezawa, and Kerri Sakamoto." *Canadian Literature*, Vol. 179 (2003): 56–69.
Gotanda, Philip Kan. *Yankee Dawg You Die*. New York: Dramatists Play Service, 1991.

Grace, Sherrill. *Landscapes of War and Memory: The Two World Wars in Canadian Literature and the Arts, 1977–2007*. Edmonton: University of Alberta Press, 2014.

Gracewood, Jolisa Margaret. "All at Sea: Literature of the Pacific War." PhD dissertation. Cornell University, 2005.

Grayling, A. C. *Among the Dead Cities: The History and Moral Legacy of the WWII Bombing of Civilians in Germany and Japan*. London: Bloomsbury, 2006.

Green, Wren, Tony Cairns, and Judith Wright. *New Zealand after Nuclear War*. Wellington: New Zealand Planning Council, 1987.

Greenfeld, Karl Taro. "Return of the Yellow Peril," *Nation* (May 11), 1992: 636.

Grewal, Gurleen. "Memory and the Matrix of History: The Poetics of Loss and Recovery in Joy Kogawa's *Obasan* and Toni Morrison's *Beloved*." In *Memory and Cultural Politics: New Approaches to American Ethnic Literatures*. Edited by Amritjit Singh, Joseph T. Skerrett Jr., and Robert E. Hogan. Boston: Northeastern University Press, 1996.

Gugin, David. "Beyond the Tenth Horizon: Robert Barclay's *Melal*." *Pacific Asia Inquiry*, Vol. 8 (1) (2017): 7–19.

Guterson, David. *Snow Falling on Cedars*. New York: Vintage, 1995.

Hack, Karl, and Kevin Blackburn, "*The Bridge on the River Kwai* and *King Rat*: Protest and Ex-Prisoner of War Memory in Britain and Australia." In *Forgotten Captives in Japanese-Occupied Asia*. Edited by Karl Hack and Kevin Blackburn. Abingdon, UK: Routledge, 2008.

Hales, Peter B. "The Atomic Sublime." *American Studies*, Vol. 32 (1) (1991): 5–31.

Hall, Stuart. "The Spectacle of the 'Other.'" In *Representation: Cultural Practices and Signifying Practices*. Edited by Stuart Hall. London: Sage, 1997.

Hanson, Todd A. "Exploding the Strangelove Myth: Cold War Nuclear Weapons Work and the Testing Times of William Ogle." In *The Atomic Bomb and American Society: New Perspectives*. Edited by Rosemary B. Mariner and G. Kurt Piehler. Knoxville: University of Tennessee Press, 2009.

Harari, Yuval Noah. *The Ultimate Experience: Battlefield Revelations and the Making of Modern War Culture, 1450–2000*. Basingstoke, UK: Palgrave Macmillan, 2008.

Hartcup, Guy. *The Effects of Science on the Second World War*. Basingstoke, UK: Palgrave Macmillan, 2000.

Harvey, Siobhan. "The Ghosts of My Life." *NZ Listener* (October 14, 2006): 40–41.

Haughton, Frances. "'To the Kwai and Back': Myth, Memory and Memoirs of the 'Death Railway,' 1942–1943." *Journal of War and Culture Studies*, Vol. 7 (3) (2014): 223–235.

Hauʻofa, Epeli. "Anthropology and Pacific Islanders." In *We Are the Ocean: Selected Works*. Honolulu: University of Hawaiʻi Press, 2008. Article originally published in 1975.

———. "Our Sea of Islands." In *We Are the Ocean: Selected Works*. Honolulu: University of Hawai'i Press, 2008. Article originally published in 1993.

———. "Pasts to Remember." In *We Are the Ocean: Selected Works*. Honolulu: University of Hawai'i Press, 2008. Article originally published in 2000.

Haytock, Jennifer. *The Routledge Introduction to American War Literature*. New York: Routledge, 2018.

Hecht, David K. "The Atomic Hero: Robert Oppenheimer and the Making of Scientific Icons in the Early Cold War." *Technology and Culture*, Vol. 49 (4) (2008): 943–966.

———. *Storytelling and Science: Rewriting Oppenheimer in the Nuclear Age*. Amherst: University of Massachusetts Press, 2015.

Hein, Laura. "Learning about Patriotism, Decency, and the Bomb." In *Living with the Bomb: American and Japanese Cultural Conflicts in the Nuclear Age*. Edited by Laura Hein and Mark Selden. New York: M. E. Sharpe, 1997.

Hein, Laura, and Mark Selden. "Commemoration and Silence: Fifty Years of Remembering the Bomb in America and Japan." In *Living with the Bomb: American and Japanese Cultural Conflicts in the Nuclear Age*. Edited by Laura Hein and Mark Selden. New York: M. E. Sharpe, 1997.

Heller, Joseph. "Conversations with Joseph Heller." Edited by Kathi Vosevich. In *Understanding the Literature of World War II: A Student Casebook to Issues, Sources, and Historical Documents*. Edited by James H. Meredith. Westport: Greenwood, 1999.

Hendershot, Cyndy. "Mythical and Modern: Representations of Los Alamos." *Journal of the Southwest*, Vol. 41 (4) (1999): 477–485.

Hendrick, George, Helen How, and Don Sackrider. *James Jones and the Handy Writers' Colony*. Carbondale: Southern Illinois University Press, 2001.

Herbert, Christopher. *War of No Pity: The Indian Mutiny and Victorian Trauma*. Princeton: Princeton University Press, 2008.

Hibakusha: Survivors of Hiroshima and Nagasaki. Translated by Gaynor Sekimori. Tokyo: Kōsei Publishing, 1986.

Hicks, Heather J. *The Culture of Soft Work: Labor, Gender, and Race in Postmodern American Narrative*. New York: Palgrave Macmillan, 2009.

Hillenbrand, Laura. *Unbroken: A World War II Story of Survival, Resilience, and Redemption*. London: Fourth Estate, 2011.

Hirsch, Walter. "The Image of the Scientist in Science Fiction: A Content Analysis." *American Journal of Sociology*, Vol. 63 (5) (1958): 506–512.

Hitchens, Christopher. "P. G. Wodehouse: The Honorable Schoolboy." In *Arguably: Essays*. London: Atlantic Books, 2011. Article originally published in 2004.

Hoff, Derek. "Igniting Memory: Commemoration of the 1942 Japanese Bombing of Southern Oregon, 1962–1998." *Public Historian*, Vol. 21 (2) (1999): 65–82.

Holman, Valerie, and Debra Kelly. "War in the Twentieth Century: The Functioning of Humour in Cultural Representation." *Journal of European Studies*, Vol. 31 (3–4) (2001): 247–263.

Holsinger, M. Paul. "The 'Western' Fiction of World War II." In *World War II in Asia and the Pacific and the War's Aftermath, with General Themes*. Edited by Loyd E. Lee. Westport: Greenwood, 1998.

Honey, John. "Japan-Bashing: A New Literary Genre?" *OIU Journal of International Studies*, Vol, 8 (2) (1995): 89–94.

Hönicke, Michaela. "'Know Your Enemy': American Wartime Images of Germany, 1942–1943." In *Enemy Images in America History*. Edited by Ragnhild Fiebig-von Hase and Ursula Lehmkuhl. New York: Berghahn Books, 1997.

Horn, Bernard. "Ahab and Ishmael at War: The Presence of *Moby-Dick* in *The Naked and the Dead*." *American Quarterly*, Vol. 34 (4) (1982): 379–395.

Horner, David. "The ANZAC Contribution: Australia and New Zealand in the Pacific War." In *The Pacific War: From Pearl Harbor to Hiroshima*. Edited by Daniel Marston. Oxford, UK: Osprey Publishing, 2005.

Huang, Betsy. "Premodern Orientalist Science Fictions." *MELUS*, Vol. 33 (4) (2008): 23–43.

Huebner, Andrew Jonathan. "The Embattled Americans: A Cultural History of Soldiers and Veterans, 1941–1982." PhD dissertation. Brown University, 2004.

Hulme, Keri. "Kaibutsu-San," *Landfall*, Vol. 39 (4) (1985): 458–464.

Hunner, Jon. "Reinventing Los Alamos: Code Switching and Suburbia at America's Atomic City." In *Atomic Culture: How We Learned to Stop Worrying and Love the Bomb*. Edited by Scott C. Zeman and Michael A. Amundson. Boulder: University Press of Colorado, 2004.

Huxley, Aldous. *Ape and Essence* [1948]. Reprint, London: Vintage, 2005.

Huzinaga, Sigeru, and Kiyomi Kutsuzawa. "Nazi Holocaust and Atomic Holocaust: Transforming Spiritual Crisis into an Ideology of Humanity." *Review of Japanese Culture and Society*, Vol. 11 (12) (1999): 43–53.

Hynes, Samuel. *The Soldiers' Tale: Bearing Witness to Modern War*. New York: Viking, 1997.

Iacocca, Lee. *Lee Iacocca: An Autobiography*. New York: Bantam Books, 1984.

Ingrassia, Paul. *Engines of Change: A History of the American Dream in Fifteen Cars*. New York: Simon & Schuster, 2012.

Irwin, Robert. *Dangerous Knowledge: Orientalism and Its Discontents*. New York: Overlook Press, 2006.

Jacobs, Robert. "Dodging Dystopia: The Role of Nuclear Narratives in Averting Global Thermonuclear Warfare." In *Nonkilling History: Shaping Policy with Lessons from the Past*. Edited by Antony Adolf. Honolulu: The Center for Global Nonviolence, 2010.

———. *The Dragon's Tail: Americans Face the Atomic Age*. Amherst: University of Massachusetts Press, 2010.

———. "Reconstructing the Perpetrator's Soul by Reconstructing the Victim's Body: The Portrayal of the 'Hiroshima Maidens' by the Mainstream American Media." *Intersections: Gender and Sexuality in Asia and the Pacific*, Vol. 24 (2010). http://intersections.anu.edu.au/issue24/jacobs.htm.

Jacobs, Robert, and Mick Broderick. "Nuke York, New York: Nuclear Holocaust in the American Imagination from Hiroshima to 9/11." *Asia-Pacific Journal*, Vol. 10 (6) (2012). http://apjjf.org/2012/10/11/Robert-Jacobs/3726/article.html.

Jacobsen, Gene S. *We Refused to Die: My Time as a Prisoner of War in Bataan and Japan, 1942–1945*. Salt Lake City: University of Utah Press, 2004.

Jericho, Greg. "War in the Tropics." *Etropic*, Vol. 4 (2005). https://doi.org/10.25120/etropic.4.0.2005.3439.

Jo, Moon H., and Daniel D. Mast. "Changing Images of Asian Americans." *International Journal of Politics, Culture, and Society*, Vol. 6 (3) (1993): 417–441.

Johnson, Leigh. "Conceiving the Body: Sandra Cisneros and Ruth L. Ozeki's Representations of Women's Reproduction in Transnational Space." *Transformations: The Journal of Inclusive Scholarship and Pedagogy*, Vol. 19 (2) (2008–9): 32–41.

Johnson, Sheila. *The Japanese through American Eyes*. Stanford: Stanford University Press, 1988.

Jones, James. *The Thin Red Line* [1962]. Reprint, London: Penguin, 2014.

———. *WWII: A Chronicle of Soldiering* [1975]. Reprint, Chicago: University of Chicago Press, 2014.

Jones, J. D. F. *Storyteller: The Many Lives of Laurens van der Post*. London: John Murray, 2001.

Jones, Lawrence. "The Mushroom Cloud, the Long White Cloud and the Cloud of Unknowing." *Landfall*, Vol. 203 (2002): 139–149.

Jones, Lloyd. *Mister Pip*. Auckland: Penguin, 2006.

Jones, Peter G. *War and the Novelist: Appraising the American War Novel*. Columbia: University of Missouri Press, 1976.

Junger, Sebastian. *War*. New York: Twelve, 2010.

Kato, Megumi. *Narrating the Other: Australian Literary Perceptions of Japan*. Clayton: Monash University Press, 2008.

Kavka, Misha. "Out of the Kitchen Sink." In *Gothic NZ: The Darker Side of Kiwi Culture*. Edited by Misha Kavka, Jennifer Lawn, and Mary Paul. Dunedin, New Zealand: Otago University Press, 2006.

Keown, Michelle. *Pacific Islands Writing: The Postcolonial Literatures of Aotearoa/New Zealand and Oceania*. Oxford: Oxford University Press, 2007.

———. "Waves of Destruction: Nuclear Imperialism and Anti-Nuclear Protest in the Indigenous Literatures of the Pacific." *Journal of Postcolonial Writing*, Vol. 54 (5) (2018): 585–600.

Kern, Alfred. "Hang the Enola Gay." In *When War Becomes Personal: Soldiers' Accounts from the Civil War to Iraq*. Edited by Donald Anderson. Iowa City: University of Iowa Press, 2008.

Kiernan, Robert F. *American Writing since 1945: A Critical Survey*. New York: Frederick Ungar, 1983.

Kim, Jodi. *Ends of Empire: Asian American Critique and the Cold War*. Minneapolis: University of Minnesota Press, 2010.

King, Michael. *Being Pakeha Now: Reflections and Recollections of a White Native*. Auckland: Penguin, 1999.
Kiste, Robert C. Review of *Meḷaḷ: A Novel of the Pacific*, by Robert Barclay. *Contemporary Pacific*, Vol. 16 (1) (2004): 208–211.
Kogawa, Joy. "Three Deities." In *Literary Environments: Canada and the Old World*. Edited by Britta Olinder. Brussels: Peter Lang, 2006.
Koizumi, Kenkichiro. "In Search of Wakon: The Cultural Dynamics of Manufacturing Technology in Postwar Japan." *Technology and Culture*, Vol. 43 (1) (2002): 29–49.
Kovac, Jeffrey. "Science, Ethics and War: A Pacifist's Perspective." *Science and Engineering Ethics*, Vol. 19 (2) (2013): 449–460.
Kovic, Ron. *Born on the Fourth of July* [1976]. Reprint, New York: Akashic, 2016.
Knight, Fran. "*The Swap.*" *Magpies*, Vol. 19 (4) (2004): 40.
Kurashige, Lon. *Japanese American Celebration and Conflict: A History of Ethnic Identity and Festival, 1934–1990*. Berkeley: University of California Press, 2002.
Kuznick, Peter J. "Defending the Indefensible: The Tragic Life of Hiroshima Pilot Paul Tibbets, Jr." In *The Unfinished Atomic Bomb: Shadows and Reflections*. Edited by David Lowe, Cassandra Atherton, and Alyson Miller. Lanham: Lexington Books, 2018.
LaCapra, Dominick. *Writing History, Writing Trauma*. Baltimore: Johns Hopkins University Press, 2001.
La Hood, Steve, dir. *Shuriken: Prisoners of Culture*. Wellington: Ninox Films, 1996.
Lake, Marilyn, and Henry Reynolds. *Drawing the Global Colour Line: White Men's Countries and the International Challenge of Racial Equality*. Cambridge: Cambridge University Press, 2008.
Lane, Dorothy F. *The Island as Site of Resistance: An Examination of Caribbean and New Zealand Texts*. New York: Peter Lang, 1995.
Lange, David. *Nuclear Free: The New Zealand Way*. Auckland: Penguin Books, 1990.
Lanham, Edwin. *The Clock at 8:16*. New York: Doubleday, 1970.
Laub, Dori. "Bearing Witness or the Vicissitudes of Listening." In *Testimony: Crises of Witnessing in Literature, Psychoanalysis, and History*. Edited by Shoshana Felman and Dori Laub. New York: Routledge, 1992.
———. "Truth and Testimony: The Process and the Struggle." In *Trauma: Explorations in Memory*. Edited by Cathy Caruth. Baltimore: Johns Hopkins University Press, 1995.
Laucht, Christoph. "An Extraordinary Achievement of the 'American Way': Hollywood and the Americanization of the Making of the Atom Bomb in *Fat Man & Little Boy*." *European Journal of American Culture*, Vol. 28 (1) (2009): 41–56.
Lay, Graeme. *In Search of Paradise: Artists and Writers in the Colonial South Pacific*. Auckland: Godwit, 2008.
Laycock, Jo. *Imagining Armenia: Orientalism, Ambiguity, and Intervention*. Manchester, UK: Manchester University Press, 2016.

Lazare, Aaron. *On Apology*. Oxford: Oxford University Press, 2004.
Lealand, Geoff. *A Foreign Egg in Our Nest: American Popular Culture in New Zealand*. Wellington: Victoria University Press, 1988.
Lee, Clark. *They Call It Pacific: An Eye-Witness Story of Our War against Japan from Bataan to the Solomons*. New York: Viking Press, 1943.
Lee, Dong-Hoo. "East Asian Images in Selected American Popular Films from 1930 to 1993." PhD dissertation. New York University, 1996.
Lehrer, Jim. *The Special Prisoner*. New York: Random House, 2000.
Lemon, Robert. *Imperial Messages: Orientalism as Self-Critique in the Habsburg Fin de Siècle*. New York: Camden House, 2011.
Levi, Primo. *Survival in Auschwitz* [1958]. Translated by Stuart Woolf. Reprint, New York: Touchstone, 1996.
Lewis, Bernard. "The Question of Orientalism." In *Orientalism: A Reader*. Edited by A. L. Macfie. Edinburgh: Edinburgh University Press, 2000. Article originally published in 1982.
Lifton, Robert Jay. "Hiroshima in America: Fifty Years of Denial." In *The Writing on the Cloud: American Culture Confronts the Atomic Bomb*. Edited by Alison M. Scott and Christopher D. Geist. Lanham: University Press of America, 1997.
———. "Is Hiroshima Our Text?" In *The Future of Immortality and Other Essays for a Nuclear Age*. New York: Basic Books, 1987.
Limon, John. "The Second World War in American Fiction." In *The Edinburgh Companion to Twentieth-Century British and American War Literature*. Edited by Adam Piette and Mark Rawlinson. Edinburgh: Edinburgh University Press, 2012.
———. *Writing after War: American War Fiction from Realism to Postmodernism*. New York: Oxford University Press, 1994.
Linderman, Gerald F. *Embattled Courage: The Experience of Combat in the American Civil War*. New York: Free Press, 1987.
———. *The World within War: America's Combat Experience in World War II*. New York: Free Press, 1997.
Linenthal, Edward Tabor. *Sacred Ground: Americans and Their Battlefields*. Urbana: University of Illinois Press, 1993.
Litoff, Judy Barrett. "'Over the Radio Yesterday I Heard the Starting of Another War': Women's Wartime Correspondence, Hiroshima, Nagasaki, and the End of World War II." In *The Atomic Bomb and American Society: New Perspectives*. Edited by Rosemary B. Mariner and G. Kurt Piehler. Knoxville: University of Tennessee Press, 2009.
Littlewood, Ian. *The Idea of Japan: Western Images, Western Myths*. Chicago: Ivan R. Dee, 1996.
Loeffler, Carl Eugene. "Video in Japan." *Whole Earth Review*, Vol. 69 (Winter 1990): 84–86.
Lomax, Eric. *The Railway Man*. Bath, UK: Chivers, 1995.
Lone, Stewart. "Between Bushido and Black Humour." *History Today* (September 2005): 20–27.

Lowe, Keith. *The Fear and the Freedom: How the Second World War Changed Us*. London: Penguin, 2017.
Lowe, Lisa. *Critical Terrains: French and British Orientalisms*. Ithaca: Cornell University Press, 1991.
Lowry, Robert. *Fortress Fiji: Holding the Line in the Pacific War, 1939–45*. Sutton, Australia: R. W. Lowry, 2006.
Luckhurst, Roger. "In War Times: Fictionalizing Iraq." *Contemporary Literature*, Vol. 53 (4) (2012): 713–737.
Lynn, John A. *Battle: A History of Combat and Culture*, second edition. New York: Basic Books, 2008.
Lyons, Paul. *American Pacificism: Oceania in the U.S. Imagination*. London: Routledge, 2006.
Ma, Sheng-mei. *The Deathly Embrace: Orientalism and Asian American Identity*. Minneapolis: University of Minnesota Press, 2000.
MacKenzie, John M. *Orientalism: History, Theory and the Arts*. Manchester, UK: Manchester University Press, 1995.
Maddock, Shane J. "Defending the American Way and Containing the Atom." In *The Atomic Bomb in American Society: New Perspectives*. Edited by Rosemary B. Mariner and G. Kurt Piehler. Knoxville: University of Tennessee Press, 2009.
Mähkä, Rami. "A Killer Joke? World War II in Post-War British Television and Film Comedy." In *Historical Comedy on Screen: Subverting History with Humour*. Edited by Hannu Salmi. Bristol, UK: Intellect, 2011.
Mailer, Norman. *Cannibals and Christians*. New York: Dial, 1966.
Manchester, William. *Goodbye Darkness: A Memoir of the Pacific War*. London: Michael Joseph, 1981.
———. "Okinawa: The Bloodiest Battle of All." In *The Best American Essays of the Century*. Edited by Joyce Carol Oates and Robert Atwan. New York: Houghton Mifflin, 2000.
Masakuni, Ota. "The Position of Japan in an Awareness on the Matter of 'Inter-Asia.'" Translated by Aisa Kiyosue. *Inter-Asia Cultural Studies*, Vol. 2 (3) (2001): 473–475.
Masco, Joseph. *The Nuclear Borderlands: The Manhattan Project in Post-Cold War New Mexico*. Princeton: Princeton University Press, 2006.
Matsuoka, Naomi. "The Wrong Stuff: The Hiroshima Pilot in Japanese Fiction." *Comparative Literature Studies*, Vol. 24 (3) (1987): 264–276.
Matthews, Philip. "A Visitor from Hawke's Bay." *New Zealand Listener*, October 5, 2007.
May, Stephen J. *Michener's South Pacific*. Gainesville: University Press of Florida, 2011.
Maynard, Katherine, Jarod Kearney, and James Guimond, *Revenge versus Legality: Wild Justice from Balzac to Clint Eastwood and Abu Ghraib*. Abingdon, UK: Birkbeck Law Press, 2010.
McCormick, James M. "The New Zealand–United States Relationship in the Era of Globalization." In *Sovereignty Under Siege? Globalisation And New Zealand*.

Edited by Robert Patman and Chris Rudd. Aldershot, UK: Ashgate Publishing, 2005.

McGibbon, Ian. "New Zealand's Strategic Approach." In *Kia Kaha: New Zealand in the Second World War.* Edited by John Crawford. Auckland: Oxford University Press, 2000.

McKay, Daniel. "All Aboard the U.S.S. *New Zealand*? Voyaging through the Literary Responses to the American 'Occupation,' 1942–1944," *Neohelicon*, Vol. 39 (2012): 321–335.

———. "Don't Hate the British: Old Boer Wisdom in Tan Twan Eng's *The Garden of Evening Mists*." *Wasafiri*, Vol. 30 (3) (2015): 50–56.

———. "Ghosts in the Shell: On South Africa, the USA and Japan." *Safundi*, Vol. 14 (4) (2013): 425–441.

———. "Guarded Truths: Korean Characters in POW Narratives, and POW Narratives in Korean History." *Studia Neophilologica*, Vol. 90 (1) (2018): 44–55.

———. "Not My River Kwai: Novels of Imprisonment under the Japanese." *Rondo*, Vol. 2 (2018): 115–123.

———. "Not Quite the End of the Line: The Prisoner of War Film from David Lean to the Present." *Dalhousie Review*, Vol. 97 (1) (2017): 248–259.

———. "Other Ways to Treat an Animal: Natural Horsemanship and the Ethnic Other." *Journal of Postcolonial Writing*, Vol. 55 (5) (2019): 656–669.

McKenzie, Vernon. "Treatment of War Themes in Magazine Fiction." *Public Opinion Quarterly*, Vol. 5 (2) (1941): 227–232.

McKevitt, Andrew C. "Consuming Japan: Cultural Relations and the Globalizing of America, 1973–1993." PhD dissertation. Temple University, 2009.

McMahon, Elizabeth. *Islands, Identity and the Literary Imagination*. London: Anthem Press, 2016.

McMahon, Elizabeth, and Bénédicte André. "Literature and the Literary Gaze." In *The Routledge International Handbook of Island Studies*. Edited by Godfrey Baldacchino. Abingdon, UK: Routledge, 2018.

McMillan, George. *The Old Breed: A History of the First Marine Division in World War II*. Washington, DC: Infantry Journal Press, 1949.

McMurtry, Larry. *Horseman, Pass By* [1961]. Reprint, New York: Simon & Schuster, 2004.

McNeil, Ken. "A Brief History of the Japanese in New Zealand." *Nyujirando Kenkyu*, Vol. 3 (June 1997): 60–79.

Mercer, Erin. *Repression and Realism in Post-War American Literature*. New York: Palgrave Macmillan, 2011.

———. *Telling the Real Story: Genre and New Zealand Literature*. Wellington: Victoria University Press, 2017.

Michener, James A. *Tales of the South Pacific* [1947]. Reprint, New York: Ballantine, 1984.

———. *The World Is My Home: A Memoir*. London: Secker and Warburg, 1992.

———. "Until They Sail." In *Return to Paradise* [1951]. Reprint, Harmondsworth, UK: Penguin, 1982.

Minear, Richard H. "Atomic Holocaust, Nazi Holocaust: Some Reflections." In *Learning to Glow: A Nuclear Reader*. Edited by John Bradley. Tucson: University of Arizona Press, 2000. Article originally published in 1995.

Mitchell, Jon. *Poisoning the Pacific: The US Military's Secret Dumping of Plutonium, Chemical Weapons, and Agent Orange*. Lanham: Rowman & Littlefield, 2020.

Mitter, Rana. *China's War with Japan, 1937–1945: The Struggle for Survival*. London: Penguin, 2013.

Miyake, Esperanza. "Politicizing Motorcycles: Racialized Capital of Technology, Techno-Orientalism, and Japanese Temporality." *East Asian Journal of Popular Culture*, Vol. 2 (2) (2016): 209–224.

Miyamoto, Yuki. "In the Light of Hiroshima: Banalizing Violence and Normalizing Experiences of the Atomic Bombing." In *Reimagining Hiroshima and Nagasaki: Nuclear Humanities in the Post-Cold War*. Edited by N. A. J. Taylor and Robert Jacobs. Abingdon, UK: Routledge, 2018.

Miyoshi, Masao. *Off Center: Power and Culture Relations between Japan and the United States*. Cambridge: Harvard University Press, 1991.

Moeller, Susan D. "Pictures of the Enemy: Fifty Years of Images of Japan in the American Press, 1941–1992." *Journal of American Culture*, Vol. 19 (1) (1996): 29–42.

Montgomerie, Deborah. "Sweethearts, Soldiers, Happy Families: Gender and the Second World War." In *The Gendered Kiwi*. Edited by Caroline Daley and Deborah Montgomerie. Auckland: Auckland University Press, 1999.

Montgomery, Scott L. "Objects of Uncommon Interest: Reflections on Japan and 'the Japanese.'" *Massachusetts Review*, Vol. 33 (2) (1992): 261–285.

Moore, Alexander. "Rosanzerusu Is Los Angeles: An Anthropological Inquiry of Japanese Tourists." *Annals of Tourism Research*, Vol. 12 (4) (1985): 619–643.

Moore, Keith, dir. "Misunderstanding Japan." *Archive on 4*. Aired August 8, 2015, on the BBC.

Moore, Michaela Hoenicke. *Know Your Enemy: The American Debate on Nazism, 1933–1945*. New York: Cambridge University Press, 2010.

Moore-Gilbert, B. J. "'Gorgeous East' versus 'Land of Regrets.'" In *Orientalism: A Reader*. Edited by A. L. Macfie. Edinburgh: Edinburgh University Press, 2000. Article originally published in 1986.

Morita, Akio. "The Trouble with the American Economy." In *Rediscovering America: Japanese Perspectives on the American Century*. Edited by Peter Duus and Kenji Hasegawa. Berkeley: University of California Press, 2011. Article originally published in 1989.

Morris, Narrelle. "Destructive Discourse: 'Japan Bashing' in the United States, Australia, and Japan in the 1980s and 1990s." PhD dissertation. Murdoch University, 2006.

———. *Japan-Bashing: Anti-Japanism since the 1980s*. Abingdon, UK: Routledge, 2011.

Mura, David. *Turning Japanese: Memoirs of a Sansei*. New York: Anchor Books, 1991.

Newman, Robert A. *Enola Gay and the Court of History*. New York: Peter Lang, 2014.

Nguyen, Mimi Thi, and Thuy Linh Nguyen Tu. Introduction to *Alien Encounters: Popular Culture in Asian America*. Edited by Mimi Thi Nguyen and Thuy Linh Nguyen Tu. Durham: Duke University Press, 2007.

Nguyen, Viet Thanh. *The Sympathizer*. New York: Grove, 2015.

Nicolaidi, Mike, and Eric Thompson. *The Featherston Chronicles: A Legacy of War*. Auckland: HarperCollins, 1999.

Niu, Greta Aiyu. "Techno-Orientalism, Nanotechnology, Posthumans, and Post-Posthumans in Neal Stephenson's and Linda Nagata's Science Fiction." *MELUS*, Vol. 33 (4) (2008): 73–76.

Norden, Martin F. "Bitterness, Rage, and Redemption: Hollywood Constructs the Disabled Vietnam Veteran." In *Disabled Veterans in History*. Edited by David A. Gerber. Ann Arbor: University of Michigan Press, 2015.

Nornes, Abé Mark. "Cherry Trees and Corpses: Representations of Violence from WWII." In *The Japan/America Film Wars: WWII Propaganda and its Cultural Contexts*. Edited by Abé Mark Nornes and Fukushima Yukio. Chur, Switzerland: Harwood Academic Publishers, 1994.

Norris, Margot. "Dividing the Indivisible: The Fissured Story of the Manhattan Project." *Cultural Critique*, Vol. 35 (1996): 5–38.

O'Brien, Louise. "Only Connect." *Dominion Post* (September 30, 2006): 16.

O'Connell, Aaron B. *Underdogs: The Making of the Modern Marine Corps*. Cambridge: Harvard University Press, 2012.

Oettli-Van Delden, Simone. "Problematizing the Postcolonial: Deterritorialization and Cultural Identity in Robert Barclay's *Melal*." *World Literature Written in English*, Vol. 39 (2) (2002): 38–51.

Okihiro, Gary Y. *Margins and Mainstreams: Asians in American History and Culture*. Seattle: University of Washington Press, 2014.

Oliver, Lizzie. *Prisoners of the Sumatra Railway: Narratives of History and Memory*. London: Bloomsbury, 2018.

Ozeki, Ruth L. "From Meat to Potatoes: An Interview with Ruth Ozeki." *Foreign Literature Studies*, Vol. 31 (6) (2009): 1–14.

———. *My Year of Meats*. New York: Viking, 1998.

———. "'A Universe of Many Worlds': An Interview with Ruth Ozeki." *MELUS*, Vol. 38 (3) (2013): 160–171.

Packard, George R. "The Coming U.S.-Japan Crisis." *Foreign Affairs*, Vol. 66 (2) (1987): 348–367.

Palmer, R. Barton. "Filming the Spiritual Landscape of James Jones's *The Thin Red Line*." In *Twentieth-Century American Fiction on Screen*. Edited by R. Barton Palmer. New York: Cambridge University Press, 2007.

Parides, Peter K. "To Run with the Swift: Vannevar Bush, James Conant, and the Race to the Bomb—How American Science Was Drafted into Wartime Service." In *The Atomic Bomb and American Society: New Perspectives*. Edited by Rosemary B. Mariner and G. Kurt Piehler. Knoxville: University of Tennessee Press, 2009.

Paris, Erna. *Long Shadows: Truth, Lies, and History*. London: Bloomsbury, 2000.

Park, Jane Chi Hyun. *Yellow Future: Oriental Style in Hollywood Cinema*. Minneapolis: University of Minnesota Press, 2010.

Parkin, John. "Humouring a Lost Cause." *Journal of War and Culture Studies*, Vol. 2 (3) (2009): 275–288.

Parr, Alison. *Silent Casualties: New Zealand's Unspoken Legacy of the Second World War*. North Shore City, New Zealand: Tandem Press, 1995.

Patke, Rajeev S. *Poetry and Islands: Materiality and the Creative Imagination*. London: Rowman & Littlefield International, 2018.

Pattinson, Juliette, Lucy Noakes, and Wendy Ugolini. "Incarcerated Masculinities: Male POWs and the Second World War." *Journal of War and Culture Studies*, Vol. 7 (3) (2014): 179–190.

Paul, Heike. "Old, New and 'Neo' Immigrant Fictions in American Literature: The Immigrant Presence in David Guterson's *Snow Falling on Cedars* and T. C. Boyle's *The Tortilla Curtain*." *Amerikastudien*, Vol. 46 (2) (2001): 249–265.

Petty, Bruce M. Introduction to *New Zealand in the Pacific War: Personal Accounts of World War II*. Edited by Bruce M. Petty. Jefferson: McFarland, 2008.

Phillips, Jock. *A Man's Country? The Image of the Pakeha Male, a History*. Auckland: Penguin Books, 1987.

———. "The Quiet Western Front: The First World War and New Zealand Memory." In *Race, Empire and First World War Writing*. Edited by Santanu Das. Cambridge: Cambridge University Press, 2011.

Pieterse, Jan Nederveen. *White on Black: Images of Africa and Blacks in Western Popular Culture*. New Haven: Yale University Press, 1998.

Piette, Adam. "The Fictions of Nuclear War, from Hiroshima to Vietnam." In *The Edinburgh Companion to Twentieth-Century British and American War Literature*. Edited by Adam Piette and Mark Rawlinson. Edinburgh: Edinburgh University Press, 2012.

Pittock, A. Barrie. *Beyond Darkness: Nuclear Winter in Australia and New Zealand*. Melbourne: Sun Books, 1987.

Plath, David W. "My-Car-isma: Motorizing the Showa Self." *Daedalus*, Vol. 119 (3) (1990): 229–244.

Plumb, Vivienne. "The Wife Who Spoke Japanese in Her Sleep." In *The Wife Who Spoke Japanese in Her Sleep*. Dunedin, New Zealand: Otago University Press, 1993.

Porter, Patrick. *Military Orientalism: Eastern War through Western Eyes*. London: Hurst, 2009.

Poyer, Lina, Suzanne Falgout, and Laurence M. Carucci. "The Impact of the Pacific War on Modern Micronesian Identity." In *Globalization and Culture Change in the Pacific Islands.* Edited by Victoria S. Lockwood. Upper Saddle River: Pearson Education, 2003.

Pratt, Mary Louise. *Imperial Eyes: Travel Writing and Transculturation.* New York: Routledge, 1992.

Price, Charles A. *The Great White Walls Are Built: Restrictive Immigration to North America and Australasia, 1836–1888.* Canberra: Australian Institute of International Affairs, in association with Australian National University Press, 1974.

Provencher, Ken. "Japan in Transnational Hollywood: Industry and Identity, 1985–1995." PhD dissertation. University of Southern California, 2013.

Pule, John. "The Shark That Ate the Sun." In *Nuanua: Pacific Writing in English since 1980.* Edited by Albert Wendt. Honolulu: University of Hawai'i Press, 1995.

Pursell, Carroll W. *The Machine in America: A Social History of Technology.* Baltimore: Johns Hopkins University Press, 2007.

Randall, James E. *An Introduction to Island Studies.* Lanham: Rowman & Littlefield, 2021.

Rau, Petra. "Long Shadows and Blind Spots." In *Long Shadows: The Second World War in British Fiction and Film.* Edited by Petra Rau. Evanston: Northwestern University Press, 2016.

———. "Reflections on the Enemy: From Evil Nazis to Good Germans." In *The Edinburgh Companion to Twentieth-Century British and American War Literature.* Edited by Adam Piette and Mark Rawlinson. Edinburgh: Edinburgh University Press, 2012.

Raz, Jacob, and Aviad E. Raz. "'America' Meets 'Japan': A Journey for Real between Two Imaginaries." *Theory, Culture, and Society,* Vol. 13 (3) (1996): 153–178.

Reed, Ishmael. *Japanese by Spring.* New York: Atheneum, 1993.

Renov, Michael. "Warring Images: Stereotype and American Representations of the Japanese, 1941–1991." In *The Japan/America Film Wars: WWII Propaganda and Its Cultural Contexts.* Edited by Abé Mark Nornes and Yukio Fukushima. Langhorne: Harwood Academic Publishers, 1994.

Roberts, Brian Russell, and Michelle Ann Stephens, "Archipelagic American Studies: Decontinentalizing the Study of American Culture." In *Archipelagic American Studies.* Edited by Brian Russell Roberts and Michelle Ann Stephens. Durham: Duke University Press, 2017.

Robertson, Roland. "Japan and the USA: The Interpenetration of National Identities and the Debate about Orientalism." In *Dominant Ideologies.* Edited by Nicholas Abercrombie, Stephen Hill, and Bryan S. Turner. London: Routledge, 1990.

Rodriguez, Robyn Magalit, and Vernadette Vicuña Gonzalez. "Asian American Auto/Biographies: The Gendered Limits of Consumer Citizenship in Import

Subcultures." In *Alien Encounters: Popular Culture in Asian America*. Edited by Mimi Thi Nguyen and Thuy Linh Nguyen Tu. Durham: Duke University Press, 2007.

Roh, David S., Betsy Huang, and Greta A. Niu. Introduction to *Techno-Orientalism: Imagining Asia in Speculative Fiction, History, and Media*. Edited by David S. Roh, Betsy Huang, and Greta A. Niu. New Brunswick: Rutgers University Press, 2015.

Rosen, Sue. *Scorched Earth: Australia's Secret Plan for Total War under Japanese Invasion in World War II*. Crows Nest, Australia: Allen and Unwin, 2017.

Rosenberg, Emily S. *A Date Which Will Live: Pearl Harbor in American Memory*. Durham: Duke University Press, 2003.

Rosenthal, Peggy. "The Nuclear Mushroom Cloud as Cultural Image." *American Literary History*, Vol. 3 (1) (1991): 63–92.

Rosner, Elizabeth. *Survivor Café: The Legacy of Trauma and the Labyrinth of Memory*. Berkeley: Counterpoint, 2017.

Ross, Matthew Samuel. "James Jones's Codes of Conduct." PhD dissertation. University of Nevada, Las Vegas, 2012.

Rowe, John Carlos. "Transpacific Studies and the Cultures of US Imperialism." In *American Studies as Transnational Practice: Turning toward the Transpacific*. Edited by Yuan Shu and Donald Pease. Hanover: Dartmouth College Press, 2015.

Roxworthy, Emily. *The Spectacle of Japanese American Trauma: Racial Performativity and World War II*. Honolulu: University of Hawai'i Press, 2008.

Richardson, Michael. "Enough Said." In *Orientalism: A Reader*. Edited by A. L. Macfie. Edinburgh: Edinburgh University Press, 2000. Article originally published in 1990.

Ruhen, Olaf. *Scan the Dark Coast*. London: Hodder and Stoughton, 1969.

Russell, Emily. *Reading Embodied Citizenship: Disability, Narrative, and the Body Politic*. New Brunswick: Rutgers University Press, 2011.

Said, Edward W. *Orientalism* [1978]. Reprint, London: Penguin, 2003.

Santoro, Gene. "A Marine Reflects on Fighting Horror with Humor in the Pacific." *World War II*, Vol. 25 (5) (2011): 16–17.

Scarry, Elaine. *The Body in Pain: The Making and Unmaking of the World*. New York: Oxford University Press, 1985.

Schafer, William J. *Mapping the Godzone: A Primer on New Zealand Literature and Culture*. Honolulu: University of Hawai'i Press, 1998.

Schimmel, Solomon. *Wounds Not Healed by Time: The Power of Repentance and Forgiveness*. Oxford: Oxford University Press, 2002.

Schodt, Frederick L. *America and the Four Japans: Friend, Foe, Model, Mirror*. Berkeley: Stone Bridge Press, 1994.

Schofield, Mary Anne. "Lost Almost and Caught between the Fences: The Women of Los Alamos, 1943–1945 and Later." In *The Atomic Bomb in American Society:*

New Perspectives. Edited by Rosemary B. Mariner and G. Kurt Piehler. Knoxville: University of Tennessee Press, 2009.

Schrijvers, Peter. *The GI War against Japan: American Soldiers in Asia and the Pacific during World War II*. Basingstoke, UK: Palgrave Macmillan, 2002.

Schwenger, Peter, and John Whittier Treat. "America's Hiroshima, Hiroshima's America." *boundary 2*, Vol. 21 (1) (1991): 233–253.

Seaton, Philip. "'Do You Really Want to Know What Your Uncle Did?': Coming to Terms with Relatives' War Actions in Japan." *Oral History*, Vol. 34 (1) (2006): 53–60.

Seed, David. *Under the Shadow: The Atomic Bomb and Cold War Narratives*. Kent: Kent State University Press, 2013.

Shallcrass, Jack. "Tidal Changes." In *One of the Boys? Changing Views of Masculinity in New Zealand*. Edited by Michael King. Auckland: Heinemann, 1988.

Shapiro, Jerome F. *Atomic Bomb Cinema: The Apocalyptic Imagination on Film*. New York: Routledge, 2011.

Sharrad, Paul. "Imagining the Pacific." *Meanjin*, Vol. 49 (4) (1990): 597–606.

———. "South Pacific." In *The Novel in Australia, Canada, New Zealand, and the South Pacific since 1950*. Edited by Coral A. Howells, Paul Sharrad, and Gerry Turcotte. New York: Oxford University Press, 2017.

Shell, Marc. *Islandology: Geography, Rhetoric, Politics*. Stanford: Stanford University Press, 2014.

Sheller, Mimi. "Archipelagoes as the Fractal Fringe of Coloniality: Demilitarizing Caribbean and Pacific Islands." In *Contemporary Archipelagic Thinking: Toward New Comparative Methodologies and Disciplinary Formations*. Edited by Michelle Stephens and Yolanda Martínez-San Miguel. Lanham: Rowman & Littlefield, 2020.

Sherwin, Martin J. *A World Destroyed: Hiroshima and Its Legacies*, third edition. Stanford: Stanford University Press, 2003.

Shimomura, Mitsuko. "Glorious America, Where Are You?" In *Rediscovering America: Japanese Perspectives on the American Century*. Edited by Peter Duus and Kenji Hasegawa. Berkeley: University of California Press, 2011. Article originally published in 1981.

Shin, Gi-Wook. "Historical Reconciliation in Northeast Asia: Past Efforts, Future Steps, and the U.S. Role." In *Confronting Memories of World War II: European and Asian Legacies*. Edited by Daniel Chirot, Gi-Wook Shin, and Daniel Sneider. Seattle: University of Washington Press, 2014.

Shohno, Naomi. *The Legacy of Hiroshima: Its Past, Our Future*. Translated by Tomoko Nakamura. Tokyo: Kōsei Publishing, 1986.

Simpson, George E., and Neal R. Burger. *Fair Warning*. New York: Delacorte Press, 1980.

Sinclair, Upton. *O Shepherd, Speak!* London: T. Werner Laurie, 1949.

Slatter, Gordon. *A Gun in My Hand*. Christchurch, New Zealand: Pegasus Press, 1959.

Smith, David Livingstone. *The Most Dangerous Animal: Human Nature and the Origins of War*. New York: St. Martin's Griffin, 2007.
Smith, Jo. "Aotearoa/New Zealand: An Unsettled State in a Sea of Islands." *Settler Colonial Studies*, Vol. 1 (1) (2011): 112–113.
Sohn, Stephen Hong. "Minor Character, Minority Orientalisms, and the Borderlands of Asian America." *Cultural Critique*, Vol. 82 (Fall 2012): 151–185.
Sollors, Werner. *Beyond Ethnicity: Consent and Descent in American Culture*. New York: Oxford University Press, 1986.
Somerville, Alice Te Punga. *Once Were Pacific: Māori Connections to Oceania*. Minneapolis: University of Minnesota Press, 2012.
———. "Where Oceans Come From." *Comparative Literature*, Vol. 69 (1) (2017): 25–31.
Sterling, Bruce. "Shinkansen." *Whole Earth Review*, Vol. 69 (Winter 1990): 72–76.
Stevenson, Michael. *This is the Trekka*. Wellington: Creative New Zealand, 2003.
Stone, Oliver, and Peter Kuznick. *The Untold History of the United States*. London: Ebury Publishing, 2012.
Stratford, Elaine. "Disciplinary Formations, Creative Tensions, and Certain Logics." In *Contemporary Archipelagic Thinking: Toward New Comparative Methodologies and Disciplinary Formations*. Edited by Michelle Stephens and Yolanda Martínez-San Miguel. Lanham: Rowman & Littlefield, 2020.
Sudo, Naoto. *Nanyo-Orientalism: Japanese Representations of the Pacific*. Amherst: Cambria Press, 2010.
Suvanto, Mari. "Images of Japan and the Japanese: The Representations of the Japanese Culture in the Popular Literature Targeted at the Western World in the 1980s-1990s." PhD dissertation. University of Jyväskylä, 2002.
Szczepanska, Kamila. "Addressing the Allied POW Issue in Japan: The Case of POW Research Network Japan." *Japan Forum*, Vol. 26 (1) (2014): 88–112.
Tajima, Renee E. "Lotus Blossoms Don't Bleed: Images of Asian Women." In *Making Waves: An Anthology of Writings by and About Asian American Women*. Edited by Asian Women United. Boston: Beacon Press, 1989.
Takaki, Ronald. *Double Victory: A Multicultural History of America in World War II*. Boston: Little, Brown, 2000.
Takayoshi, Ichiro. *American Writers and the Approach of World War II, 1935–1941: A Literary History*. New York: Cambridge University Press, 2015.
Tal, Kalí. *Worlds of Hurt: Reading the Literature of Trauma*. New York: Cambridge University Press, 1996.
Tanaka, Akihiko, and Masayuki Tadokoro. "The 1980s: The Decade of Neo-liberalism." In *The History of US-Japan Relations*. Edited by Makoto Iokibe. Translated by Tosh Minohara. Singapore: Palgrave Macmillan, 2017.
Tanner, Ron. "Toy Robots in America, 1955–75: How Japan Really Won the War." *Journal of Popular Culture*, Vol. 28 (3) (1994): 125–154.
Tatsumi, Takayuki. *Full Metal Apache: Transactions between Cyberpunk Japan and Avant-Pop America*. Durham: Duke University Press, 2006.

Taylor, Nan. "Human Rights in World War II in New Zealand." *New Zealand Journal of History*, Vol. 23 (2) (1989): 109–123.

Teller, Edward. "The Consequences of the Atomic Bomb: The End of the Soviet Union and the Beginning of Environmental Hysteria." In *The Writing on the Cloud: American Culture Confronts the Atomic Bomb*. Edited by Alison M. Scott and Christopher D. Geist. Lanham: University Press of America, 1997.

Thorne, Christopher. "Racial Aspects of the Far Eastern War of 1941–1945." *Proceedings of the British Academy*, Vol. 66 (1980): 329–377.

Thorsten, Marie. *Superhuman Japan: Knowledge, Nation, and Culture in US-Japan Relations*. Abingdon, UK: Routledge, 2012.

Torgovnick, Marianna. "Gone Nuclear: Representing Hiroshima and Nagasaki in the United States." *Nanzan Review of American Studies*, Vol. 32 (2010): 39–442.

———. *The War Complex: World War II in Our Time*. Chicago: University of Chicago Press, 2005.

Townsend, Sue. *The Queen and I* [1992]. Reprint, London: Penguin, 2002.

Tregaskis, Richard. *Guadalcanal Diary* [1943]. Reprint, New York: Modern Library, 2000.

Turner, Louis, and John Ash. *The Golden Hordes: International Tourism and the Pleasure Periphery*. London: Constable, 1975.

Ueno, Toshiya. "Techno-Orientalism and Media-Tribalism: On Japanese Animation and Rave Culture." *Third Text*, Vol. 13 (47) (1999): 95–106.

Updike, John. *Couples* [1968]. Reprint, New York: Knopf, 1987.

Uris, Leon. *Battle Cry* [1953]. Reprint, New York: Avon, 2005.

Urry, John. *The Tourist Gaze*, second edition. London: Sage, 2001.

Varisco, Daniel Martin. *Reading Orientalism: Said and the Unsaid*. Seattle: University of Washington Press, 2007.

Vernon, Alex. *Soldiers Once and Still: Ernest Hemingway, James Salter, and Tim O'Brien*. Iowa City: University of Iowa Press, 2004.

Vernon, Nathan. *Anti-Foreign Imagery in American Pulps and Comic Books, 1920–1960*. Jefferson: McFarland, 2012.

Vine, David. *Island of Shame: The Secret History of the U.S. Military Base on Diego Garcia*. Princeton: Princeton University Press, 2009.

Volpe, Edmond L. "James Jones—Norman Mailer." In *Contemporary American Novelists*. Edited by Harry T. Moore. Carbondale: Southern Illinois University Press, 1964.

Waldmeir, Joseph J. *American Novels of the Second World War*. The Hague: Mouton, 1969.

Walker, David. "Godless Heathen: China in the American Bestseller." In *East by South: China in the Australasian Imagination*. Edited by Charles Ferrall, Paul Millar, and Keren Smith. Wellington: Victoria University Press, 2005.

Wallis, Andrew H. "Toward a Global Eco-Consciousness in Ruth Ozeki's *My Year of Meats*." *Interdisciplinary Studies in Literature and Environment*, Vol. 20 (4) (2013): 837–854.

Walsh, Jeffrey. *American War Literature, 1914 to Vietnam*. London: Macmillan, 1982.
Wark, McKenzie. "From Fordism to Sonyism: Perverse Readings of the New World Order." *New Formations*, Vol. 15 (1991): 43–54.
Watson, Janet S. K. "'A Sideshow to the War in Europe': Nation, Empire, and the British Commemoration of the Pacific War." In *The Pacific War: Aftermaths, Remembrance, and Culture*. Edited by Christina Twomey and Ernest Koh. Abingdon, UK: Routledge, 2015.
Watt, Ian. "The Humanities on the River Kwai." *Stanford Humanities Review*, Vol. 8 (1) (2000):1–32.
Webb, George E. "The Manhattan Project Revealed: Local Press Response to the Atomic Bomb Announcements, August–September 1945." In *The Atomic Bomb and American Society: New Perspectives*. Edited by Rosemary B. Mariner and G. Kurt Piehler. Knoxville: University of Tennessee Press, 2009.
Weber, Joe. *Honorable Enemies*. New York: Putnam, 1994.
Weingartner, James. "War against Subhumans: Comparisons between the German War against the Soviet Union and the American War against Japan, 1941–1945." *Historian*, Vol. 58 (3) (1996): 557–573.
Wells, Peter. *Lucky Bastard*. Auckland: Vintage, 2007.
———. "Unravelling the Atrocities of War." *Sunday Star Times* (Auckland), October 28, 2007.
Wendt, Albert. Introduction to *Nuanua: Pacific Writing in English since 1980*. Edited by Albert Wendt. Honolulu: University of Hawai'i Press, 1995.
———. "Towards a New Oceania." *Mana Review*, Vol. 1 (1) (1976): 49–60.
White, Geoffrey M. "Disney's *Pearl Harbor*: National Memory at the Movies." *Public Historian*, Vol. 24 (4) (2002): 97–115.
White, William. "Mr. Marquand's 'Mr. Moto,'" *American Speech*, Vol. 23 (2) (1948): 157–158.
Whitehead, Anne. *Trauma Fiction*. Edinburgh: Edinburgh University Press, 2004.
Williams, Laura Anh. "Gender, Race, and an Epistemology of the Abattoir in *My Year of Meats*." *Feminist Studies*, Vol. 40 (2) (2014): 244–72.
Williams, Paul. *Race, Ethnicity and Nuclear War: Representations of Nuclear Weapons and Post-Apocalyptic Worlds*. Liverpool, UK: Liverpool University Press, 2011.
Wilson, R. R. "Hiroshima: The Scientists' Social and Political Reaction." *Proceedings of the American Philosophical Society*, Vol. 140 (3) (1996): 350–357.
Winks, Robin W. "The Sinister Oriental: Thriller Fiction and the Asian Scene." *Journal of Popular Culture*, Vol. 19 (2) (1985): 49–61.
Wisenthal, Jonathan. "Inventing the Orient." In *A Vision of the Orient: Texts, Intertexts, and Contexts of Madame Butterfly*. Edited by Jonathan Wisenthal, Sherrill Grace, Melinda Boyd, Brian McIlroy, and Vera Micznik. Toronto: University of Toronto Press, 2006.

Wood-Ellem, Elizabeth. "Behind the Battle Lines: Tonga in World War II." Paper presented at the seventh Tongan History Conference. Canberra, January 1997.

Worpole, Ken. *Dockers and Detectives*, second edition. Nottingham, UK: Five Leaves Publications, 2008.

Wu, Judy Tzu-Chun. *Radicals on the Road: Internationalism, Orientalism, and Feminism during the Vietnam Era*. Ithaca: Cornell University Press, 2013.

Wuthnow, Robert. *Be Very Afraid: The Cultural Response to Terror, Pandemics, Environmental Devastation, Nuclear Annihilation, and Other Threats*. New York: Oxford University Press, 2010.

Wyndham, John. *The Chrysalids*. London: Michael Joseph, 1955.

Yaguchi, Yujin. "War Memories across the Pacific: Japanese Visitors at the Arizona Memorial." In *The Unpredictability of the Past: Memories of the Asia-Pacific War in US- East Asian Relations*. Edited by Marc Gallicchio. Durham: Duke University Press, 2007.

Yang, Daqing. "The Malleable and the Contested: The Nanjing Massacre in Postwar China and Japan." In *Perilous Memories: The Asia-Pacific War(s)*. Edited by T. Fujitani, Geoffrey M. White, and Lisa Yoneyama. Durham: Duke University Press, 2001.

Yoshikawa, Mako. "The Veterans Project Number 2." *Missouri Review*, Vol. 37 (3) (2014): 66–85.

Zeman, Zbynek. *Selling the War: Art and Propaganda in World War II*. London: Orbis, 1978.

Zinn, Howard. "Artists in Times of War." *CLCWeb: Comparative Literature and Culture*, Vol. 9 (1) (2007). https://docs.lib.purdue.edu/clcweb/vol9/iss1/21/.

Index

ABCD encirclement, 9
acceptable incompetence, narrative, 34
Affair of Men, An (Brathwaite), 16, 19–20; (un)balancing act, 44; cannibalism portrayal in, 48–49; comedy in, 45–47; constructing Itoh psychology, 50–52; function of racism, 46–47; German Nazi comparisons, 45–46; irrational fear as character feature, 49–50; isolation portrayed in, 50–52; Japanese characterization in, 43–45; Japanese psychology in, 52–53; plot organization in, 47–48; publication of, 43–44; readers at time of publication, 50–51; Shangri-La scenario, 51–52; signature feature, 50–51; stylistic merit of, 43; warrior stereotype, 44
Against the Rising Sun: New Zealanders Remember the Pacific War (Hutching), 108
Air Force Association, 10, 124
Akiko. See *Ocean Roads* (George)
Alan before/after. See *Swap, The* (Catran)
Alasia, Sam, 167
Allied POWs, 87–89, 99, 100, 102–3, 200n4
Allies, 17, 20, 28, 127, 134
Allison. See *Lucky Bastard* (Wells)
'Allo 'Allo!, 33
America: Asian Americanists, 74, 79; culture, 10, 42, 72, 145, 158, 197n24; help from, 158; imagination, 14; posters, 65; scholars, 56; soldiers, 2, 11, 19, 29, 31, 152; thriller writers, 54; veterans, 10, 14, 28; writers, 4, 73–74, 84, 88, 109, 146, 202n23. *See also* Japanese Americans; United States

American Legion, 10, 81, 124
Amrine, Michael, 135, 142–44
Anderson, Poul, 150
anglophone, 23, 70; authors, 12, 109; culture, 15, 27, 53, 147, 151; depictions of Japanese, 32, 44, 153, 200n1; identity, 9; imagination, 22; novelists, 32; war literature, 2, 5; world, 15, 17, 56, 67, 130, 133–34, 146, 149; writing, 20
"Anthropology and Pacific Islanders," essay, 5
anti-Japanese imagery, 11
Aotearoa-New Zealand, 5. *See also* New Zealand writing
Ape and Essence (Huxley), 147–48
apes, imagery of, 180n44
archipelagic narratives, 9, 16, 104–5, 166
Army Game, The, 33
articulate silence, 84–85
Ash Garden, The (Bock), 134, 157–60
Asia-Pacific, 107, 109, 122, 124, 134
Asian American Movement, 21
Asian American writers, real/fake, 74
Associated Press, 31
Atomic Bomb Panels, series, 10
Atwood, Margaret, 7
Auden, W. H., 12–13
Australia, 5, 8, 15, 18, 22, 147, 201n11; choice between Americans and, 167; combat novels from, 50; Cowra breakout in, 195n1; drawing upon business trends in, 63–64; encapsulating sense of transition, 79; importance of 1990s for, 203n37; Japan-bashing in, 62–64; nonfiction publications in, 149; scarcity of novels from and about, 82; Six Mile Road massacre, 119; War Crimes tribunal, 48

244 | Index

Australian and New Zealand American Studies Association (ANZASA), 174
autobiography, captivity narrative, 113–15

Ballard, J. G., 112
Barclay, Robert, 6, 168–71
Barker, Rodney, 152
Bataan Death March, 10
Battle Cry (Uris), 19, 29; opening to, 35
Battle of Okinawa, 27
Battle of the Bulge, 142
Battlefield Gothic, 39
Baxter, Archibald, 27
Bead. See *Thin Red Line, The* (Jones)
Beginning or the End?, The (film), 139
Beloved (Morrison), 97
Benedict, Ruth, 56, 109
Bertram, James, 147, 164
Betrayal from the East: The Inside Story of Japanese Spies in America (Hynd), 86
Big War, The (Myrer), 29
Bikini Atoll, 143, 165, 169
Bly, Robert, 20
Bock, Dennis, 134, 137, 153, 157–58, 161
Böll, Anton. See *Ash Garden, The* (Bock)
Bomb, dropping, 9–10
Booth, Martin, 137
Born on the Fourth of July (Kovic), 27
Boulle, Pierre, 110
Bowman, Peter, 29, 35
Brathwaite, Errol, 16, 19–20, 43, 55, 109, 166. See also *Affair of Men, An* (Brathwaite)
Breakfast at Tiffany's (Capote): camera-toting Japanese, 67–69, 72
Bridge on the River Kwai, The (film), 33, 106–7
Bridge over the River Kwai, The (Boulle), 110
Britain, 9, 17–18, 28, 53–54, 108, 110; censors in, 33
British Fourteenth Army, 22, 23
Brocker, Susan, 14
bubble economy, 11
Budd, Lanny. See *O Shepherd, Speak!* (Sinclair)

Bukowsky, family. See *My Year of Meats* (Ozeki)
Burdick, Eugene, 141
Burger, Neal R., 135, 145
Burma Campaign, 3–4, 22, 165
Burma-Siam Railway, 10, 110, 200n6, 203n37
Buruma, Ian, 106–7

Caleb. See *Ocean Roads* (George)
camera-toting Japanese, stereotype, 67–72, 75, 191n41
Camp Sengei, 4. See also *Special Prisoner, The* (Lehrer)
Campbell, George, 14
Canada, 5, 7, 15, 23, 59, 82, 85, 97, 134, 138, 157
cannibalism, 48–49, 53
Canticle for Leibowitz, A (Miller Jr.), 150
Capote, Turman, 67–68
captivity narrative. See FEPOW narrative
Caravans (Michener), 32–33
carnival justice. See *Special Prisoner, The* (Lehrer)
Caruth, Cathy, 203n32
Cat's Cradle (Vonnegut), 142
Catch-22 (Heller), 30, 50
Catran, Wendy, 16, 21, 83–84, 89, 199n52. See also *Swap, The* (Catran)
Chambers, Ishmael. See *Snow Falling on Cedars* (Guterson)
Changing Light (Gallagher), 145–46
Cherry, Stephen, 159
Cheung, King-Kok, 21, 84
Chevalier, Haakon, 135
Chicago Daily News, 31
Childers, Sam, 26
Chin, Frank, 74
Chin, Vincent, 59
China, 12–13, 31–32, 106, 112, 206n63
Christianity, 45–47, 123, 125–26, 170
Chrysalids, The (Wyndham), 148
City of Canterbury, The, vessel, 88
Civil War, 3
Clancy, Tom, 57
Clavell, James, 111, 201n11
Clinton, Bill, 122

Clock at 8:16, The (Lanham), 152–53
Cold War, 4, 32, 56, 66, 124, 136, 141, 144–45, 147, 155
Collier's, 32
Columbia Pictures Entertainment, 56
combat novel, 16, 20–21, 25–28; (re)mastering enemy, 53–54; Pacific fighting informing, 28–35; principal genre for depiction of Japanese men, 210n68; reluctant beachcombers, 43–53; responses to war, 25–28; revelations, 35–43. See also *Affair of Men, An* (Brathwaite); *Thin Red Line, The* (Jones)
Communism, 33, 123, 144, 147
compassion, depicting, 111–12
Connor, John. See *Rising Sun* (Crichton)
corporate thriller. See thriller
Couples (Updike), 14
Crichton, Michael, 4, 20, 59, 193n75, 195n100. See also *Rising Sun* (Crichton)
Critical Race Studies, 9–10
Crocodile, The (Eri), 167
Cry for Happy (Campbell), 14
Cussler, Clive, 57

Dad's Army, 33
Death in Life (Lifton), 152
Debt of Honor (Clancy), 192n61
disruptive others, 197n24
Draft Principles of Assembly, Nuclear Aftermath Strategy Organisation, 132, 134
Dreams of Warriors (Brocker), immobility in, 14
dueling victimhoods. See *Swap, The* (Catran)
Dulles, John Foster, 188n2
Dunsford, Cathie, 168
Durante, Jimmy, 34

Eastwood, Clint, 32
Ebeye, Marshall Islands, 168–69
Einstein, Albert, 139
Eisler. See *Los Alamos* (Kanon)
Elizabeth II (queen), 53–54, 122

Emiko. See *Ash Garden, The* (Bock)
Empire of the Sun (Ballard), 112
End of Victory Culture, The (Engelhardt), 160
enemy, (re)mastering, 53–54
Eng, Tan Twan, 112
Engelhardt, Tom, 160
Enola Gay, 10; exhibit, 81–82, 124–25, 150
Enos, Solomon, 168
Eri, Vincent, 167
Eric. See *Lucky Bastard* (Wells)
Evans, Nicholas, 14

Fail-Safe (Burdick), 141
Fair Warning (Simpson), 145
Far East Prisoner of War (FEPOW), 6, 10–12. See also FEPOW narrative
Farewell to Arms, A (Hemingway), 85
Fascist Century, 4
Fata'abu (Alasia), 167
Fear in the Night (Brathwaite), 43
FEPOW narrative, 6, 16, 22, 201n13; autobiography as alternative, 113–15; changing preexisting cultural narrative, 108–9; differing from Project novel, 133–34; following example of combat novel, 110–11; *Lucky Bastard* (Wells) as, 115–21; narrative discomfort as genre aspect, 130–31; overview of, 106–8; public school paradigms and, 109–10; revisiting, 108–15; *Special Prisoner* (Lehrer) as, 121–29; sympathetic renditions, 111–13. See also *Lucky Bastard* (Wells); *Special Prisoner, The* (Lehrer)
Fermi, Enrico, 138
Fiji, 16, 21, 86–87, 97
final letter, trope, 205n60
Final Storm, The (Shaara), 32
Finney, Jack, 66
Fires on the Plain (Ooka), 48
First Marine Division, 19
First Yank into Tokyo (film), 130–31
Flags of Our Fathers (film), 32
Flowers of Hiroshima, The (Morris), 142
follower societies. See Japan-bashing
Ford, Jamie, 105

Frame, Janet, 148–50, 153
Francis, Gavin, 7
Frankenstein (Shelley), 159–60
Fraser, George MacDonald, 3–4, 165
Friends of the Hibakusha (Swallow), 151–52
From Here to Eternity (Jones), 29, 35
Fujita, Nabou, 201n17
Fukuoka Camp #17, 111
Fukushima Nuclear Power Plant, 165
Fussell, Paul, 37
future war novels, 189n14

Gallagher, Nora, 135, 145–46, 154
Garden of Evening Mists, The (Eng), 112
Garrigue, Eleanor. See *Changing Light* (Gallagher)
gaze, 18, 53, 65, 95, 149. *See also* tourism
Gee, Maurice, 197n16
Geisha Boy (film), 33
gender, 13, 70, 74–75, 101, 152–53, 199n47
genre, boundaries of, 7, 12. *See also* combat novel; FEPOW narrative; *hibakusha* projects; Japan-bashing; Project novel
gentrification, 116. *See also Lucky Bastard* (Wells)
George, James, 16, 134, 137, 153, 161
Gibson, William, 70
Good War, The (Terkel), 27, 107
Gotanda, Philip K., 14–15
gothic, 58, 64, 66
Grace, Patricia, 168
Grant, flight lieutenant. See *Tales of the South Pacific* (Michener)
Gravity's Rainbow (Pynchon), 30
Grayling, Anthony, 127
Great Depression, 40, 47
Great War, 27–30, 32, 142, 148, 200n5
Great World, The (Malouf), 112
Guadalcanal Campaign, 19, 35, 81
Guadalcanal Diary (Tregaskis), 37
Guam (Guåhan), 3, 62
Gudmundsson, surname, 95. *See also Snow Falling on Cedars* (Guterson)
Gun in My Hand, A (Slatter), 2
Gung Ho (film), 56

Guterson, David, 4, 21, 83–84, 164, 197n20. *See also Snow Falling on Cedars* (Guterson)
guy talk, 27. *See also* combat novel; remasculinization

hakujin, 93–94. *See also Snow Falling on Cedars* (Guterson)
Hall, Willis, 4
Halsey, William, 9
Harada, Fumiko, 132
Harari, Yuval Noah, 40–41
Hauʻofa, Epeli, 5, 167
Hayakawa, Sessue, 33
Heart of Darkness (Conrad), 52
Heaven Knows, Mr. Allison (Shaw), 50
Heine, Carl. See *Snow Falling on Cedars* (Guterson)
Heller, Joseph, 25, 50
Hemingway, Ernest, 28, 85
Herbert, Christopher, 201n13
Hersey, John, 137
hibakusha (atomic bomb victims): silencing of, 132–33
hibakusha projects: anglophone literary depictions, 153; *Ash Garden* (Bock) as, 157–60; Disneyfication of Hiroshima, 150; gender and, 152–53; Hiroshima as raw nerve in American society, 156–57; Hiroshima Maidens, 152; and Japan-bashing, 151; legitimacy of outcome of war outliving end of war, 150–51; object lesson in, 155–56; *Ocean Roads* (George) as, 153–56; publications on, 151–52. *See also* Project novel
Hillenbrand, Laura, 113, 163, 165
Hilton, James, 8
hipparidako, 69. *See also Rising Sun* (Crichton)
Hiroshima, 6, 10, 23, 81, 106, 130–33, 136–40, 142–47, 150–52, 156–60, 205n57, 210n62, 212n92
Hiroshima Maidens, 152, 157–59, 211n86, 212n89
Hiroshima Maidens, The (Barker), 152
Hiryo, sergeant. See *Affair of Men, An* (Brathwaite)
Hitchens, Christopher, 108

Hogan's Heroes, 33
Holden, William, 107
"Hole that Jack Dug, The" (Sargeson), 18
homo sapiens japonensis, 52
Honda Accord, 56
Honey. See "Wife Who Spoke Japanese in her Sleep, The" (Plumb)
Honolulu, US Cruiser, 9
Honorable Enemies (Weber), 62
Hooks, Alvin. See *Snow Falling on Cedars* (Guterson)
Hope, Bob, 34
Horse Whisperer, The (Evans), 14
Horseman, Pass By (McMurtry), 2
Hosokawa, Morihiro, 124, 129
Hotel on the Corner of Bitter and Sweet (Ford), 105
Howard, John, 203n37
Hulme, Keri, 16, 20, 58, 191n40. See also "Kaibutsu-san" (Hulme)
humor, 45, 61; comedic combat narratives, 53–54; cynical flip side of, 130; disruption informing, 49–50; fighting horror with, 33–35
Hutching, Megan, 108
Huxley, Aldous, 147–49
Hwang, David Henry, 59
Hynd, Alan, 86

Iacocca, Lee, 190
Ibuse, Masuji, 137
idealists, 40–41
ideological coproduction, 8
immigration, 58–59
Imperial Japanese Army, 133
Improvised Explosive Device (IED), 26
index of difference, 8
Inside Stories: New Zealand POW's Remember (Hutching), 108
Intensive Care (Frame), 148–50
internment novel, 16, 21–22; archipelagic narratives, 104–5; New Zealand internment, 85–89; overview of, 81–85; veteran as protector in, 97–104; veteran as savior in, 89–97. See also *Snow Falling on Cedars* (Guterson); *Swap, The* (Catran)

Iraq War, 26, 202n23
Isaac. See *Ocean Roads* (George)
Isherwood, Christopher, 12–13
island combat: fighting in Pacific, 28–35; reluctant beachcombers, 43–53; revelations, 35–43. See also combat novel
islandness, 7
isolation, trend, 7–8
It Ain't Half Hot Mum, 33
Itoh, captain. See *Affair of Men, An* (Brathwaite)
Iwo Jima, 32, 37

Japan: anti-Japanese imagery, 2, 4, 11, 77, 90, 92; bubble economy of, 11, 154; cannibalism, 48; captors, 110, 113, 127; caricature of, 203n44; Co-Prosperity Sphere of, 109; constitution of, 124; corporations, 20, 54, 56, 68, 70–73, 78; gendering of, 74; as giant video garden, 71; identity of, 14; immigrants from, 58, 86, 97; Japanophobia, 15, 53, 59, 65; men of, 20, 62, 70, 87, 100, 210n69; militarism of, 31–32, 95, 114, 184n34; occupation of, 188n2; re-industrialization of, 56–57; women of, 51, 87, 152, 189n11
Japan Bereaved Families Association *(Nihon Izokukai)*, 124
Japan Inc., 68
Japan Times, 113
Japan-bashing: critical examination of, 59–62; critiques of, 194n91; emergence of, 55–59; eschewing corporations, 62–67; expatriated Japanese, 67–72; human-to-human relations, 62–67; Japanese Americans incorporating, 72–79; passage, 79–80; pleasure periphery, 59–62; resmasculinization, 67–72
Japanese American Citizens' League, 193n76
Japanese Americans, 6, 11–14; disclosing interment experience of, 97; internment of, 6, 21, 83, 85, 89; Japan-bashing and, 58–59, 72–75; keeping story continental in nature, 105; novel of Japanese Canadian

248 | Index

Japanese Americans *(continued)*
 and, 82; objectifying, 95; patriots opposite of, 95; in Redress Movement, 105; vilifying, 103
Japanese by Spring (Reed), 71, 124
Japanese psychology, 52–53
Japanese-ness, proving, 94. See also *Snow Falling on Cedars* (Guterson)
Japanophobia, 15, 53, 59, 65. *See also* Japan-bashing
Jarhead (film), 25–26
Jews, 33, 87
Jones, James, 4, 29, 35, 109, 186n73. See also *Thin Red Line, The* (Jones)
Jones, Lawrence, 209n46
Jones, Lloyd, 187n96
Junger, Sebastian, 25, 26, 35

"Kaibutsu-san" (Hulme), 16, 19n44; cash flow serving as digestive aid, 67; concealing innate aggressions, 64–65
Kameda, Kiyo, 88
Kanon, Joseph, 135, 145
Kindness of Women, The (Ballard), 112
King Rat (Clavell), 111
Kogawa, Joy, 82, 97, 137–38
Kokoda Trail, 18
Korean War, 36, 99, 100, 189n11, 198n42
Kovic, Ron, 27
Kunioka, Harold, 88
Kuromaku (Richards), 54
Kwajalein Atoll, 165, 167

Lange, David, 150
Lanham, Edwin, 152
Laub, Dori, 118–20
Lean, David, 110
LeCapra, Dominick, 116
Lee, Clark, 31
Lehrer, Jim, 4, 22, 100, 107, 203n36, 205n57
Letters from Iwo Jima (film), 32
Levi, Primo, 199n49
Lewis, Bernard, 10
lifeboat New Zealand, scenario, 146–50
Lifton, Robert Jay, 152, 156–57
"Little Honda," song, 61
Little Tokyo, Los Angeles, 73

Live Bodies (Gee), 197n16
Lomax, Eric, 113–15
Long and the Short and the Tall, The (Hall), 4
Los Alamos (Kanon), 145
Lost Generation, 28, 30–31
Lost Horizon (Hilton), 8
Lucky Bastard (Wells), 16, 22, 107; acknowledging FEPOW novel history, 115–17; encouraging speculation, 119–20; as FEPOW narrative, 115–21; manufacturing testimony in, 120–21; narrative intersecting with need to maintain value of trauma, 116–17; negotiating with memories in, 117–18; withholding information in, 115–17
Lucky Dragon, incident, 165

M. Butterfly (Hwang), 59
MacKenzie, John M., 179n41
Madame Butterfly, 59
Mailer, Norman, 4, 29, 36, 42, 109
Malaysia, 22
Man Alone (Mulgan), 48
Manawa Toa: Heart Warrior (Dunsford), 168–71
Manchester, William, 62, 163
Manhattan Project, 16, 23, 130–31, 133–41, 144, 146–47, 151, 153–54, 157, 159–60, 215n28
Manhattan Project novel. *See* Project novel
Māori, 5, 8, 12, 16, 19–20, 64, 66, 122, 150, 154
marginalization, war literature. *See* solidarity, Pacific Islands
Marlantes, Karl, 1
Marquand, John P., 65
Maruki, Iri, 10
Maruki, Toshi, 10
masculinities, social construction of, 168–69
materialists, 40
Maurai & Kith (Anderson), 150
McClenaghan, Jack, 48
McGill, David, 107
McMurtry, Larry, 2
Means, Florence Crannell, 83, 86

Meḷaḷ (Barclay), 6, 168–71
Melville, Herman, 81
memory, negotiating with, 117–19
Men's Movement, 20
Michener, James A., 15–16, 32–33, 43, 50, 57, 187n90
Micronesians, 213n10, 214n18
Miller, Walter M., Jr., 150
Millet, Lydia, 137
Miyamoto, Kabuo. See *Snow Falling on Cedars* (Guterson)
Moby-Dick (Melville), 81, 90, 197n20
Modernism, 30
Moran, Art. See *Snow Falling on Cedars* (Guterson)
Morita, Akio, 61
Morris, Edita, 137, 142
Morrison, Toni, 97
Morrow, James, 137
Motoshima, Hitoshi, 123–24
Moved-Outers, The (Means), 83
"Mr. Monster." See "Kaibutsu-San" (Hulme)
Mr. Moto, character, 62–67
Mr. Yunioshi. See *Breakfast at Tiffany's* (Capote)
Mulgan, John, 48
Mura, David, 11–12, 58–59, 73
Mutually Assured Destruction, 149
My American Wife! (MAW!), 74–76
My Year of Meats (Ozeki), 4, 21, 59, 80; challenging *MAW!* concept, 76–77; child figure as politically redolent signifier, 78–79; critique of, 75–76; diminishing Japanese in, 75; double entendre in, 75; examining ethnic stereotypes in, 74–75; main purpose of, 75; narrator of, 75; renegotiating stereotypes in, 77; sexual undertones, 77–78; values of camera-toting Japanese in, 75; visual technology, 75
Myer, Anton, 29, 109

Naeve, Virginia, 152
Nagasaki, 6, 23, 106, 123, 130–33, 142, 147, 151–53, 156, 160, 205n57, 212n92
Nagase, Takashi, 113–15
Nakao, Juhei, 88

Nakayama, Yukio, 61
Naked and the Dead, The (Mailer), 4, 29
Nanjing Massacre, 31
Narrow Road to the Deep North, The (Flanagan), 112
national history, 91, 205n57, 206n63
Nazi Germany, 17, 39, 128, 134, 150; censors in, 33
New Britain campaign, 19
New Mexico, 135, 144–46
New York Times, 31
New Zealand, 2, 20–24; American culture as feature of, 8; combat literature from, 25–54; culture, 7–8, 15; defrost cycle of, 63–64; describing in geographic terms, 15–16; diversifying customer base, 63; FEPOW narratives from, 106–31; fiction writing, 7–8, 16, 58, 147; foregrounding sources, 17; greater remove from military, 18–19; internment in, 85–89, 97, 99; internment literature from, 81–105; Japanese immigration to, 58–59; Japanese tourists in, 20, 58, 61–65; literature, 8, 17, 104; New Zealanders as objects, 64–65; observing formation of Japan-bashing in, 79–80; Project literature from, 132–61; source material, 17–18; thriller literature, 55–80; veterans, 148
New Zealand writing, 173–75; balancing "take on" against "pushback," 8; combat novel, 25–54; FEPOW narrative, 106–31; internment novel, 81–105; Japan-bashing, 55–80; overview of, 1–24; Pacific Island solidarity, 163–71; and Pacific War remove, 18–120; preferred settings for, 17–18; Project novels, 132–61
Nguyen, Viet Thanh, 15
1995, anniversary year, 10, 22, 81, 83, 89, 122, 124–25, 129, 133, 156–57, 201n17
Nisei. *See* Japanese Americans
Nishi, Takeichi, 13
No Time for Sergeants, 33
No-No Boy (Okada), 100
Ṇoniep. See *Meḷaḷ* (Barclay)

250 | Index

North Africa, 17–18, 22, 43
North Island, New Zealand, 19
"Nuke York, New York," exhibition, 136–37

O Shepherd, Speak! (Sinclair), 141–42
O'Sullivan, Vincent, 81, 103
Obasan (Kogawa), 97
Occupation, 67, 74, 123, 147
Ocean Roads (George), 16, 134, 153–56
"Of Memory and Desire" (Wells), 154
Oh Pure and Radiant Heart (Millet), 137
Okada, John, 82, 100
Okinawa, 27, 51, 124
On the Beach (Shute), 148
Ooka, Shohei, 48
Oppenheimer, J. Robert, 138
oral history, 107–8, 174
Oranje, vessel, 88
Orientalism, 12, 59, 80. *See also* techno-Orientalism
Orr. See *Catch-22* (Heller)
Otago Daily Times, 43
Ozeki, Ruth, 4, 21, 59, 73, 195n100. See also *My Year of Meats* (Ozeki)

P.O.W. The Untold Stories of New Zealanders as Prisoners of War (McGill), 107–8
Pacific Century, 79
Pacific Rim, term, 16
Pacific Theater of Operations, 163
Pacific War, 2–6, 139, 166–69; and archipelagic narratives, 104–5; as conflict between imperial systems, 9–11; experiences of Japanese civilians/minorities, 103; geographical proximity of, 147; and *hibakusha* projects, 150–60; impact on public consciousness, 91–92; narratives about, 1–24 (*see also* New Zealand writing); opportunities provided by, 42; publicly endorsed trope of, 65; relics of propaganda, 66; veterans of, 21, 49, 83–84, 133
Pacific, fighting in, 28–35
papālangi (White people), 87, 166–67
Parr, Allison, 118, 202n27

Pasifika. See *Shark That Ate the Sun, The* (Pule)
Pearl Harbor, 1, 3, 31–35, 62–63, 86, 125, 131
Pebble Beach Golf Course, 61
Phil Silvers Show, The, 33
Philips Electronics, 70
pleasure periphery, Japan-bashing, 59–62
Plumb, Vivienne, 21, 58, 65–67, 164
Pokeno, New Zealand, 87–88
POW camps, 33, 105, 134
Pratt, Mary Louise, 15
Project novel, 16, 23, 160–61; boundaries of discourse, 135–41; canon of, 134–35; consistent qualities within, 140–41; differing from FEPOW narrative, 133–34; divine intervention, 141–42; enlarging space for Hiroshima-related issues, 145–46; entering dialogues, 136–37; examples of, 141–46; *hibakusha* projects, 150–60; investing in scientist characterization, 138–40; lifeboat New Zealand scenario, 146–50; newspaper coverage, 133; portrait of scientist, 142–44; reinforcing indifference, 138; shying away from modes of comparative cultural/historical enquiry, 136; Soviet espionage specter, 144–45; unwillingness to engage Other's perspective, 132–33; venturing opinions on sensitivity regarding, 137–39; wife figure in, 144; writing with sensitivity in, 137. See also *Ash Garden, The* (Bock); *Ocean Roads* (George)
propaganda, 1–2, 8–9. 12–15, 55, 66, 79, 95, 109–10
psychology, Japanese, 52–53
public language, 9
public schools, 109, 112, 200n2
Puccini, Giacomo, 14
Pule, John, 167–68
Pulitzer Prize, 51
Pynchon, Thomas, 30

Queen and I, The (Townsend), 53–54

Railway Man, The (Lomax), 113
rape, 2, 11, 124
Reagan, Ronald, 149
Red Scare, 66, 160
Rediscovery Expedition, New Zealand, 147–48
Redress Movement, 105
Reed, Ishmael, 71, 124
remasculinization, 67–72
Returned and Services' Association, 82
Richards, Ian, 54
Rising Sun (Crichton), 4, 20, 59; child figure as politically redolent signifier, 78–79; developments predating publication of, 73; intersection of gender and race in, 70–71; Japanese American reaction to, 72–73; love of cars in, 68–69; media technology changing American perceptions, 71–72; narrative of, 68; remasculinization in, 69–70; "teach yourself" sessions, 70–71
Rising Sun Society, 123
RKO Radio Pictures, 130
Roosevelt, Franklin, 85–86
Ross. See *Lucky Bastard* (Wells)
Ruhen, Olaf, 50, 186n89
Russo-Japanese War, 44

Said, Edward, 5, 12–13, 179n42
Saito, Mitsuichi, 88
Sakamoto, Kerri, 82
Sakamura, Eddie. See *Rising Sun* (Crichton)
Samoa, 166, 190n28
San Piedro. See *Snow Falling on Cedars* (Guterson)
Sans Soleil (film), 71
Sargeson, Frank, 18
Saturday Evening Post, 32
Savage, Michael Joseph, 17
Sayonara (Michener), 14
Schlossstein, Steven, 57
science-fiction writing (SF), 137
scientists, characterizing, 138–40. See also Project novel
second history, discovery of, 102–3
2nd New Zealand Division, 17
Second Sudanese Civil War, 26

Second World War, 1, 3, 8, 27, 28, 30, 44, 68, 70, 79, 107, 134, 140, 145, 147, 163, 199n47; and Other, 13–14
"Second-Generation Victim, A" (Harada), 132
Secret (Amrine), 142–44
Sedu. See *Affair of Men, An* (Brathwaite)
Seed and the Sower, The, 111
selling out. See Japan-bashing: Japanese Americans incorporating
Shaara, Jeff, 32
Shambling towards Hiroshima (Morrow), 137
shamelessness, depicting, 127–29. See also *Special Prisoner, The* (Lehrer)
Shamsie, Kamila, 137
Shangri-La, scenario, 51–52
Shark That Ate the Sun, The (Pule), 167–68
Shaw, Charles, 50
Shaw, Irwin, 32
Shearer, Jill, 123
Shelley, Mary, 159
Shimada (Shearer), 123
Shimomura, Mitsuko, 61
Shuriken (O'Sullivan), 81, 83, 89, 103, 195n1
Shute, Nevil, 148–49, 209n49
Simpson, George E., 135, 145
Sinclair, Upton, 135, 141
Sinophobia, 15
Sipuri, village. See *Affair of Men, An* (Brathwaite)
Slatter, Gordon, 2
Slaughterhouse-Five (Vonnegut), 30
slavery, 14, 78, 170
Smith, Peter. See *Rising Sun* (Crichton)
Smithsonian Institution, 10
Smithsonian National Air and Space Museum, 81, 124
Snow Falling on Cedars (Guterson), 4, 21, 83–85; as archipelagic narrative, 104–5; Catran comparison/contrast, 103–4; circulating prejudicial notions, 89–91; internee silencing, 94–95; Ishmael-Hatsue estrangement, 92–95; looking past social veneers, 95–96; *Moby-Dick* in,

Snow Falling on Cedars (continued)
90–91, 95–96; origins of misreadings, 91–92; receding specter of communal destruction, 96–97; superstructure register, 91; veteran as savior in, 89–97
solidarity, Pacific Islands, 163; colonialist modes of representation, 166–67; ideology inner workings, 164–65; lack of immunity against ideological blind spots, 167–68; multi-layered historical traumas, 169–70; Oceanizing America, 17; probing current state of affairs, 164; recounting Zamperini time as FEPOW, 165–66; social construction of masculinities, 168–69; tidalectics, 170–71
Solomon Islands, 19
Somerville, Alice Te Punga, 19, 163, 171
Somes Island, 87, 100
Sone, Monica, 82
Sony Walkman, 70, 193n64
source material, unequal balance between, 17
South Africa, 112–13
South Pacific, 15, 21, 23, 50, 82, 85–86, 108, 143
Special Prisoner, The (Lehrer), 4, 22, 100, 107, 157; captivity narrative as backdrop in, 121–22; carnival justice in, 126; closing sequence of narrative, 129; contingent forgiveness in, 127; depiction of shamelessness in, 127–29; encounter between two unreconciled enemies, 126–27; as FEPOW narrative, 121–29; flashback sequences in, 127–29; Japan-bashing in, 122–23; playing upon public discourses, 125–26; turning blind eye to war crimes in, 121–25
speculation, encouraging, 119–20
stereotypes. *See* camera-toting Japanese, stereotype; Japan-bashing; tourism
subgenre, term, 6
Swallow, Alan, 151–52
Swap, The (Catran), 16, 21, 83–85; approaching with assumptions, 97–99; as archipelagic narrative, 104–5; challenging established bodies of knowledge, 99–100; discovery of second history, 102–3; dueling victimhoods, 100; forcing readers to recognize patterns/traits, 98–99; Guterson comparison/contrast, 103–4; narrative structure in, 100–102; silencing of Japanese families in, 101–2; veteran as protector in, 97–104
Sympathizer, The (Nguyen), 15
sympathy, depicting, 111–13
Szilárd, Leó, 138

Takagi-Little, Jane. *See My Year of Meats* (Ozeki)
Tale for the Time Being, A (Ozeki), 21
Tales of the South Pacific (Michener), 15, 50
Tanimoto, Kiyoshi, 212n89
Tar-Wōj. *See Mełaļ* (Barclay)
Tashlin, Frank, 33
Teaiwa, Teresia, 168
techno-Orientalism, 59–62
Teller, Edward, 210n68
Tenko, 33
Terkel, Studs, 27, 107
Thatcher, Margaret, 149
Thin Red Line, The (Jones), 4, 19–20; acting as sequel, 35–36; assault beginning, 40–41; behavior of mind under combat conditions in, 38–39; complicating anti-war stance, 42–43; cultural standards, 39; dividing narrative, 40–41; experiential gap in, 37; importance of characters in, 37–38; individual character focus, 41–42; personal armament increasing standing in, 39–40; revelations of combat in, 35–43; setting of, 37; Special Note in, 37; unalterable shortcomings of, 36–37
3rd New Zealand Division, 17, 86
This Is Your Life (show), 212n89
This Life in Focus (show). *See Ash Garden, The* (Bock)
thriller, 16, 20–21. *See also* Japan-bashing

tidalectics, 170–71
Tojo no Daigaku, 124–25
Tokyo Olympics of 1964, 67
Tonga, 16, 21, 86–88, 97, 101, 104
Tora! Tora! Tora! (film), 31
Torasi, local guide. See *Affair of Men, An* (Brathwaite)
tourism, 58–59; camera-toting Japanese, 67–72, 75; effect of, 190n28; emergence of Japan-bashing, 55–59; pleasure periphery and, 59–62; tourist gaze, 64–65
Tourists' Bashing (Nakayama), 61
Town Like Alice, A, 33, 111
Townsend, Sue, 53
trade wars, 58, 61, 190n25
trauma fiction, characterizing, 84
trauma, gentrification of. See *Lucky Bastard* (Wells)
Travelling Man (McClenaghan), 48
Tregaskis, Richard, 37
Trekka, 189n10
Truman, Harry, 145
Tsang, Yan-fu, 12–13
Tupou, Sālote, III, 88

Uchida, Yoshiko, 83
Ueno, Joichi, 78. See also *My Year of Meats* (Ozeki)
Unbroken: A World War II Story of Survival, Resilience, and Redemption (Hillenbrand), 113, 163
Union Steam Ship Company, 87
Unit 731, 10
United States, 1, 4, 6–7, 15, 18, 21, 22, 30, 54, 58, 66, 69, 79; assessment of stories from, 32; British comedic productions in, 33; caricature of, 203n44; cultural double-standard, 62; FEPOW narratives and, 122–25, 130–31; "fixed" notions of Japanese culture, 73; humor in, 33–35; internment literature, 81–82, 85–86, 88–89, 95, 103–8; intersection of gender and race, 70; Japanese products in, 56–57; lack of dominant mode of war in, 27; as latecomer to Great War, 27–28; mischaracterizing, 10; 1980s as apprehensive decade, 56; planning takeover of, 20–21; postwar fiction writing, 50; power disparity between Japan and, 20; preferred narratives of, 23; Project novels and, 132, 134, 136, 150–52, 159, 161, 180; public awareness of internment, 21; race relations in, 16; rollback strategies in, 17
"Until They Sail" (Michener), 16
Updike, John, 14, 55, 57
Uris, Leon, 19, 29, 43, 109
USS Haddo, 150

vampires, portraying Japanese as, 65
Van der Post, Laurens, 12, 106–7, 111–12, 115
veteran: protector portrayal, 97–104; savior portrayal, 89–97. See also internment novel; *Snow Falling on Cedars* (Guterson); *Swap, The* (Catran)
Veterans for Peace, 81
victimhood, prism of, 146–50. See also Project novel
Vidal, Gore, 55, 57
Vietnam War, 15, 25, 27, 155–56, 179n42, 197n24, 198n42
Vonnegut, Kurt, 30, 142

Wahine, vessel, 88
War Memorial Museum (Auckland), 117–18. See also *Lucky Bastard* (Wells)
War Relocation Authority, 86
wartime events, staged commemoration of, 81
Watanabe, Mutsuhiro, 113–15
Watson, John. See *Special Prisoner, The* (Lehrer)
Watt, Ian, 200n6
We Will Not Cease (Baxter), 27
Weber, Joe, 62, 190n28
Wells, Peter, 16, 22, 107, 164, 202nn26,29; *Lucky Bastard* (Wells) as FEPOW narrative, 115–21
Wendt, Albert, 166, 168
Whaley, Horace. See *Snow Falling on Cedars* (Guterson)

What It Is Like to Go to War (Marlantes), 1
Wheeler, Harvey, 141
Whistle (Jones), 43
"Wife Who Spoke Japanese in Her Sleep, The" (Plumb), 21; takeover bid in, 65–67
Wodehouse, P. G., 108–9
World Is My Home, The (Michener), 57
Worpole, Ken, 201n14
Wyndham, John, 148

Yankee Dawg You Die (Gotanda), 14–15
Yasaka, Tanabe. See *Ash Garden, The* (Bock)
Yasukuni Shrine, 124
Yoshikawa, Mako, 11–12
Yoshimura, Tim. See *Rising Sun* (Crichton)
Yossarian. See *Catch-22* (Heller)

Zamperini, Louis, 113–15, 126, 165–66
Zinn, Howard, 136

Daniel McKay is associate professor in the English Department, New Mexico Military Institute. His journal articles have appeared in *MELUS, Mosaic, positions: east asia cultures critique,* and *University of Toronto Quarterly,* among others.

World War II: The Global, Human, and Ethical Dimension
G. Kurt Piehler, *series editor*

Lawrence Cane, David E. Cane, Judy Barrett Litoff, and David C. Smith, eds., *Fighting Fascism in Europe: The World War II Letters of an American Veteran of the Spanish Civil War*
Angelo M. Spinelli and Lewis H. Carlson, *Life behind Barbed Wire: The Secret World War II Photographs of Prisoner of War Angelo M. Spinelli*
Don Whitehead and John B. Romeiser, *"Beachhead Don": Reporting the War from the European Theater, 1942–1945*
Scott H. Bennett, ed., *Army GI, Pacifist CO: The World War II Letters of Frank and Albert Dietrich*
Alexander Jefferson with Lewis H. Carlson, *Red Tail Captured, Red Tail Free: Memoirs of a Tuskegee Airman and POW*
Jonathan G. Utley, *Going to War with Japan, 1937–1941*
Grant K. Goodman, *America's Japan: The First Year, 1945–1946*
Patricia Kollander with John O'Sullivan, *"I Must Be a Part of This War": One Man's Fight against Hitler and Nazism*
Judy Barrett Litoff, *An American Heroine in the French Resistance: The Diary and Memoir of Virginia d'Albert-Lake*
Thomas R. Christofferson and Michael S. Christofferson, *France during World War II: From Defeat to Liberation*
Don Whitehead, *Combat Reporter: Don Whitehead's World War II Diary and Memoirs*, edited by John B. Romeiser
James M. Gavin, *The General and His Daughter: The Wartime Letters of General James M. Gavin to His Daughter Barbara*, edited by Barbara Gavin Fauntleroy et al.
Carol Adele Kelly, ed., *Voices of My Comrades: America's Reserve Officers Remember World War II*, foreword by Senators Ted Stevens and Daniel K. Inouye
John J. Toffey IV, *Jack Toffey's War: A Son's Memoir*
Lt. General James V. Edmundson, *Letters to Lee: From Pearl Harbor to the War's Final Mission*, edited by Dr. Celia Edmundson
John K. Stutterheim, *The Diary of Prisoner 17326: A Boy's Life in a Japanese Labor Camp*, foreword by Mark Parillo
G. Kurt Piehler and Sidney Pash, eds., *The United States and the Second World War: New Perspectives on Diplomacy, War, and the Home Front*
Susan E. Wiant, *Between the Bylines: A Father's Legacy*, Foreword by Walter Cronkite
Deborah S. Cornelius, *Hungary in World War II: Caught in the Cauldron*
Gilya Gerda Schmidt, *Süssen Is Now Free of Jews: World War II, The Holocaust, and Rural Judaism*

Emanuel Rota, *A Pact with Vichy: Angelo Tasca from Italian Socialism to French Collaboration*

Panteleymon Anastasakis, *The Church of Greece under Axis Occupation*

Louise DeSalvo, *Chasing Ghosts: A Memoir of a Father, Gone to War*

Alexander Jefferson with Lewis H. Carlson, *Red Tail Captured, Red Tail Free: Memoirs of a Tuskegee Airman and POW, Revised Edition*

Kent Puckett, *War Pictures: Cinema, Violence, and Style in Britain, 1939–1945*

Marisa Escolar, *Allied Encounters: The Gendered Redemption of World War II Italy*

Courtney A. Short, *The Most Vital Question: Race and Identity in the U.S. Occupation of Okinawa, 1945–1946*

James Cassidy, *NBC Goes to War: The Diary of Radio Correspondent James Cassidy from London to the Bulge*, edited by Michael S. Sweeney

Rebecca Schwartz Greene, *Breaking Point: The Ironic Evolution of Psychiatry in World War II*

Franco Baldasso, *Against Redemption: Democracy, Memory, and Literature in Post-Fascist Italy*

G. Kurt Piehler and Ingo Trauschweizer, eds., *Reporting World War II*

Kevin T Hall, *Forgotten Casualties: Downed American Airmen and Axis Violence in World War II*

Chad R. Diehl, ed., *Shadows of Nagasaki: Trauma, Religion, and Memory after the Atomic Bombing*

Daniel McKay, *Beyond Hostile Islands: The Pacific War in American and New Zealand Fiction Writing*

www.ingramcontent.com/pod-product-compliance
Lightning Source LLC
Chambersburg PA
CBHW020400080526
44584CB00014B/1114